Exploring Contemporary

Pamela Marx
Pamela Olson

GoodYearBooks

An Imprint of ScottForesman
A Division of HarperCollinsPublishers

**To Mark
and to Steve**

P. M.

To Wade

P. O.

Acknowledgments

Many thank yous are in order to teachers and leaders of children's groups who have inspired the many ideas and activities in this book, who have tested these activities and who have made valuable suggestions for fiction and non-fiction resources. These thank yous go to Marlene Culver, Margaret Villarreal, Linda Deacon, Melody Conrad, Susan Sides, Kelly Layton, Gail Coyle, Diane Tso, Barbara Sandler, Martha Gustafson, Linda Riddle, Liz Espinoza, Marci Lawson, Rhonda Heth, Angie Cistulli, Lisa Skylar, Norma Marx, Mojca Rasmussen, Kurt Rasmussen, Nancy Scher, Eileen Hatrick, Eitan Sadeh, Debra Vodhanel, Debra Mansfield, Judy Lynn Pelling, Ann Chambers, Anne Miller-Rillo, Gail Eaton, Steve Hopkinson, Mark Goldstein, and the children's librarians of the Glendale Central Library and the Eagle Rock Branch Library.

A thank you also goes to J.A.M. for suggestions and contributions to the Introduction of this book.

A special thanks goes to Tom Nieman, Bobbie Dempsey, and Eden Sommerville for all their vision, help, and energy on this project and those that came before.

A final note of thanks goes to our children, Megan and Holly, Jarett and Jonathan, for providing some of the writing samples included in this book.

GoodYearBooks are available for most basic curriculum subjects plus many enrichment areas. For more GoodYear Books, contact your local bookseller or educational dealer. For a complete catalog with information about other GoodYearBooks please write:

GoodYearBooks
ScottForesman
1900 East Lake Avenue
Glenview, IL 60025

ISBN 0-673-36010-5

1 2 3 4 5 6 7 8 9 - EQ - 99 98 97 96 95 94

TABLE OF CONTENTS

INTRODUCTION

Theories about how to teach and what to teach seem to change every five to ten years. Budgets and resources keep shrinking. Fewer parents volunteer. Even theories about school management are in flux. In the midst of the resulting constraints and confusion, it can be hard to find ways to involve students, their parents and the community in the educational process.

While this book certainly cannot solve all the problems faced daily by educators, it provides a wide variety of low cost activities in a broad range of curriculum subjects that will stimulate student excitement about school and facilitate parent and community involvement in the classroom learning process.

In the planning and organization of this book, several relatively unchanging principles of good education served as a springboard for the development of the lessons and activities included. A short discussion of these principles may be helpful to understand the nature of the learning activities contained in this book:

Use teaching methods that acknowledge that different children learn in different ways. Some students learn best visually—by seeing diagrams and charts and reading information. Some learn best aurally—by listening to lecture and other aural stimuli. Still others learn best kinesthetically—by literally getting their hands dirty. When a teacher provides educational methods that take into account these differences in learning methods, all students are helped to reach their maximum potential. Children who learn best through a particular method have a chance to exercise their learning skills using that method. Lessons geared toward the child's lesser learning modalities still stretch and exercise the child's abilities in those other areas.

Teach children how to learn and think through problems rather than emphasize rote memorization of facts. As we enter the 21st century, we read more and more about how continuing advances in technology will change the job markets of the future. No longer will a person be able to get a job, do it for a lifetime and retire. In the future, rapid technological changes will force people to learn new skills throughout their lifetimes. They may need to learn new jobs, new processes, new equipment. Facts will be less important than a person's ability to think and learn. Classroom learning activities that foster thinking skills and self-confidence within a student are of the utmost importance. The activities in this book are designed to build a child's abilities to observe, reflect and reach conclusions. As such, they provide students with valuable real world skills.

Use classroom assignments and teaching techniques that encourage cooperation and teamwork. Children need to learn to manage their time. They need to be responsible to themselves in completing their own work. They also need to know how to be responsible to others in completing group projects. Valuable skills in communication, discipline and teamwork are taught through cooperative classroom projects. By providing a variety of assignments that give children both sole and cooperative responsibility for completion, a teacher ensures that students are working continually on skills they will need for success later in life.

Assign and schedule student work so that behavior management time is minimized and learning time is maximized. The way in which classwork is assigned as well as the types of activities scheduled can contribute to a positive learning environment in a classroom in which only limited time must be spent on behavior management. Assigning a balance of individual and groups projects for which students are responsible helps foster a controlled, but educationally exciting classroom environment. When a student has "free time," he or she uses it to complete group or individual projects that are pending. Whatever work is finished in class need not be done at home. Accordingly, students are motivated to use class time efficiently. As a result, students are not left with so many times throughout the school day when they are "all finished" and "have nothing to do." "Nothing to do" time invariably leads to behavior issues.

Involve parents in the classroom learning process. Students whose parents believe education is important, themselves believe that education is important. When parents help in the classroom or with classroom projects, the parents begin to understand the classroom educational process and the goals as well as obstacles experienced by the teacher. When parents support the teacher by helping to provide materials or providing services such as cutting, sorting and the like, they actively demonstrate to their children their belief that what happens in the classroom is important. They show this affirmatively when they choose to spend their time helping with classroom projects. Additionally, the family's participation in occasional "family" homework projects and classroom programs to which parents are invited further reinforces a student's feeling that his classroom experience and performance are high priority family matters.

The lessons and cross-curricular activities suggested in this book take into account these educational principles. Every effort has been made to provide ideas for projects that can be completed with the resources available at even the most cash-strapped schools. Some activities do call for preparation time, but the teacher should not feel it is his or her sole responsibility to do the preparation. Sometimes through frustration and bad experiences, teachers decide not to do more interesting projects because they need help and they haven't gotten it before. Most classes, however, have at least a few parents who are willing to do things for the classroom if they are just asked, especially if some of those things can be done at home.

In creating the educational activities in this book, subjects have been divided into general themes that are part of contemporary curriculum studies in most schools. Within each chapter, the theme is explored by providing a variety of activities. Science experiments are often provided in the context of a traditional social studies theme. Themed art master art projects allow a theme to be a starting place for exploring famous artists and art movements. Food and cooking activities provide opportunities in the context of each theme for math-based learning and development of useful real world skills.

The following information describes the educational framework of each chapter. It describes the types of activities provided for each chapter's theme and includes some suggestions for successful use of the ideas.

Lesson Activities

The lesson activities suggested for each theme attempt to provide either a new twist on traditional activities concerning the theme explored or a comprehensive cross-curricular plan for lessons and learning activities on the particular theme. In some cases such as with the multicultural and Native American themes, the lesson activities are literature based. In other cases there is a strong science focus that involves observation, analysis and language skills.

To facilitate use of this book by teachers, most chapters contain general background information for the theme to be covered. The background information provided relates directly to the information the teacher will most likely want at his or her fingertips to successfully present and facilitate the lesson activities. With a few themes such as mathematics, necessary background information is very limited for successful completion of the lesson activities.

While background information is not formatted as a series of information work sheets for students, teachers should feel free to photocopy for student use any of this background information that they think will be helpful to students. Generally, it is written in a style to be understandable by upper grade elementary students.

Writing Activities

Writing activities are suggested that relate thematically to the lesson subject explored in each chapter. These themed writing exercises include suggestions for researched report writing, creative writing including poetry, and cooperative writing experiences. Some provide opportunities for more lesson-based learning and can be substituted for writing exercise suggestions included with the lesson activities.

The more writing experiences children have, the more comfortable they are expressing themselves in the medium. Some students seem to go from year to year with one big report for each year and little other writing of any kind, let alone research-based writing. When the report project arrives each year, the child is baffled, feeling that he or she has no skills or background for completing the project. If, however, we try to move away from the isolated annual report concept to assigning children small research and reporting projects on a continuing basis, they become comfortable with doing basic research. They learn how to find information. (If a child is assigned something and can find no information on it, the child should know that it is acceptable to identify the sources checked with no results.) Children learn how to organize their thoughts on paper through these repeated experiences.

A five-point report concept is referred to in this book and is a good framework for the small report project. A five-point report is really a "spread out" paragraph. The first point is a topic sentence (i.e., what the report is about). The next three points are items of information about the subject. The last point is a conclusion or summation. Small research and reporting projects are good assignments for children to receive on an ongoing basis, not only because they improve research skills, but they also encourage time management. When a child finishes his or her regular work, he or she can spend time completing small theme based tasks. If the projects are not completed in class, they must be done at home. Of course, it is very helpful if the classroom has a set or two of old encyclopedias and a dictionary or two. Old editions of encyclopedias are often available inexpensively from used book stores.

Included in each writing activities section is a list of possible vocabulary words that you can use with the chapter theme. Ideas for use of these words range from the well-recognized (i.e., dictionary research to define the words and sentence-writing using vocabulary words) to slightly more novel approaches. Some combination of these vocabulary activities probably works best. Accordingly, in addition to using vocabulary words as dictionary-skill and sentence-writing opportunities, consider these additional ideas for using themed vocabulary words.

a. Word Board/Graffiti Wall. While one does not want to encourage graffiti, this activity is essentially an ad hoc use of door or bulletin board space. A blank sheet of butcher paper is placed on an otherwise empty door. During the course of theme activities, as children discover words they were unaware of and as they have free classroom time, they can write a word from the vocabulary list or their theme-related reading on the wall with a marker and their initials or name by it. When they are do this, they will take a moment to look up its meaning and define it in a few words on the paper next to the word.

Children can look at the board during free time to explore words classmates have placed on the board or to add vocabulary words of their own so long as they do so quietly and only two at a time.

b. Vocabulary Journal. Most of the chapter vocabularies have 25 to 35 suggested words. During your themed curriculum activities, choose one word or several each day to discuss for a few moments. Ask students how the word or phrases relate to the curriculum theme, what they know about the word and what they would like to find out. This short discussion activity could be a day opener using it right after attendance taking and flag salute. Then at some point during the day students record the word in their journals and write a sentence or two about it.

c. Picture Dictionary. Assign each child one word out of the theme vocabulary list. That child is responsible during the course of theme studies to write the word neatly on a 3 by 5 inch card, briefly state its definition and pictorially illustrate the word with marker, crayon or colored pencil. With some words, students will have to be very creative to come up with a picture. When all the students have completed their word cards, children take turns or work in groups to alphabetize them and mount them on posterboard as part of a chart picture dictionary to be displayed somewhere in the classroom. Ask children to pick their three favorite words, write them in a journal and define them in writing in their own words.

d. Word Game Show. Using a format somewhat similar to the television game show "Jeopardy," reinforce theme-based words and their definitions, at odd moments during the day. To do this, you call out a definition, children raise their hands and answer with the word by saying "What is [insert word]?" To play the game, the class can simply be divided in half to create teams. Have the same teams for at least a week. As you play the game at odd moments during the week, you should be able to get through most of the vocabulary words, sometimes more than once. Give the winning team a small treat such as candy.

Encourage more than a few children to participate by keeping names of those who have given correct answers. While team members can discuss answers between themselves if they have time, the same person cannot give the answer again and again during the week's play.

Art and Craft Activities

These activities relate most strongly to the traditional classroom art exercises in most elementary school classes but are structured to directly complement the lesson theme of the particular chapter. They are craft or art activities that allow children to be creative in the visual arts, often while adding to the depth of their learning on the lesson subject at hand.

Food Activities

Generally, chapter food activities are recipes for classroom cooking. In Chapter 9, Be-A-Scientist, the food activities are more like science experiments using foods as your chemistry materials. The food activities again are designed to directly complement the theme. Some are more fun or "crafty" such as painting flags of the world on cookies or crackers with frosting while exploring different cultures and making vehicle-shaped snacks while investigating technology and transportation themes. Other chapters provide recipe ideas that are designed to introduce children to the flavors and food stuffs used in different cultures such as dishes with Native American origins. Most recipes can also serve as opportunities to enhance math and measuring skills while following a sequence of directions. Recipes should yield about 30 small servings.

When planning food activities, try to look a week ahead. Write up a short note letting parents know what you will need so they can bring in the recipe ingredients. Many of the classroom cooking activities in this book are "pot" recipes. Therefore, an electric soup or stew pot is an invaluable tool for easy classroom cooking. Pans can also be used with hot plates if an all-in-one appliance is not available.

Teachers should also feel flexible about how they organize classroom food activities. Most cooking or baking activities work best with an adult helper. If you plan to cook regularly, you might have a different group of six children participate in the cooking each week. After four to five sessions each child will have had a turn cooking. The session cooks act as servers of the edible results of their activities. While the cooking group cooks, the remainder of the class can have a physical education activity or song or music time.

Another way to organize classroom cooking is to use a classroom hour and have the entire class participate by coming to the cooking table in small groups. Any recipe that utilizes cutting and dicing can easily be coordinated in this way. Pan-fried bread recipes also work well in this format. In fact, nearly any recipe can be used in this way. While one group cooks, the teacher reads aloud a literature book to the other students or the students copy the recipe which will be kept to create a year end recipe book. If they finish their recipe writing and attendant drawings of the dish, students can work on journals, complete small pending projects related to theme subjects or even discuss and work on cooperative group work quietly with members of their group.

Art Masters—Old and New

Using this section, different famous artists and/or styles of art can be explored in the classroom. Most famous artists have done many different things. They have painted in different styles. They have worked with different subject matter. They have used different media. In some chapters, a certain series of artwork done by an artist is explored because it can be directly related to the chapter theme. An example of this is the inclusion of Paul Klee in Chapter 3, Technology and Our Shrinking World; the specific Klee work studied is his pen and ink series on harbor scenes. In other chapters, the artist master or style explored is an extension of principles covered in the chapter such as cubism being explored in Chapter 2, Math-A-Mania, because of its obvious geometric connections or pointillism being explored in Chapter 9, Be-A-Scientist, because the artist was exploring light and color and a scientific approach to painting as he developed his style. Finally, in still other chapters, the art master lesson is taught by having children explore a style of art while using subject matter that relates to the theme. This is done, for example, with the suggestion in Chapter 8, The Ocean - Our Last Frontier. In this chapter, the children are encouraged to explore the brilliant colors of fauvism while using seascapes and fish still lifes as the subject matter for exploring the artistic style.

In attempting to explore an art master with students, it is highly recommended that the teacher or a volunteer parent make a trip to the local library to locate source books that contain pictures of the actual artwork or art style that the students will be emulating. Without such resources, the students and the teacher are shooting in the dark unless the teacher is very familiar with the style to be taught. Even if he or she is, it is hard to merely describe a style to children. It is much better if children can see actual examples of the art master's artwork. If you have local art museums, you might check to see if they have inexpensive art posters available through teacher education programs or if they will give teachers a discount when purchasing art posters for classroom use.

Sharing Activities

This section of each chapter attempts to give teachers a way to bring a study theme to a close with a culminating event. Sometimes sponsorship of an all-school theme related event is suggested. Sometimes assembly or other performance ideas are provided to give children an opportunity to share what they have learned with other classes and/or their parents. Sometimes demonstrations, art shows or other hosted events are suggested by which the class exploring a theme can share what it has learned with another class or two in the school.

General Suggestions for Use of this Book

The foregoing discussion of chapter activities was designed to familiarize teachers with the overall structure of this book and to give helpful suggestions for how to use the individual chapter sections. The following are additional, but more general, thoughts and ideas about how to enhance student learning using the tools provided in this book.

1. Assign a balance of individual and cooperative learning group projects.

Most of the project suggestions in this book are designed to enhance the student's analytical and thinking skills. While facts are presented and are important, at the elementary school level learning how to learn and learning to enjoy learning are the most important objectives. The lesson and related activities here are designed to facilitate factual learning while emphasizing thinking, research, and time organization skills. Some require individual completion. Others require the teamwork of cooperative learning groups. Assign the projects and activities in this book so that children experience a balance between individual and group learning projects. In this way, children learn personal responsibility both for themselves and in a team context.

2. Use journals as a method for enhancing student accountability.

While regurgitation of facts is not emphasized in this book, it is well recognized that, without methods for student accountability, some children will try to slide along on the coattails of others. For children to be accountable for what they have learned, it is important even with classroom demonstration and discussion exercises for children to know they will have to produce something to be turned in and evaluated. In addition to the specific writing suggestions of the lesson and writing activities section of each chapter, it is strongly suggested that each child keep a personal journal of his or her activities and experiences on each theme covered. Classroom discussion will often generate the thoughts to be written in the journal on a given day. A student's own personal record of lesson activity investigations and results is also an important source of journal writing subject matter. In addition, rather than using chapter activity sheets as "fill-in" exercises, you can use the questions and ideas contained in them to help guide what children write in their journals. Journal entries are excellent ways for children to recapture and report on factual presentations by other students, thoughts about scientific investigations and responses to thought-provoking issues.

On the other hand, you may feel that your particular group of students will not do well with a subject-by-subject journal approach. In these cases, you may want to have students record thoughts and ideas within the structure of the provided activity sheets. If you believe your students will have more to write in response to questions than space provided for by the particular sheet, use the activity sheet as an organizing tool and have children write and record responsive information on a separate sheet of paper. A teacher might choose to use a variety of approaches, journaling some themes and using the activity sheets more extensively with other themes.

3. Have a world wall map on display at all times to help maximize student familiarity with places around the world and map reading skills.

So many times a lesson or theme can be enhanced very easily by reference to a wall map of the world. If one is handy at all times, you will be surprised how many lessons provide an opportunity to find a place on our globe and thus reinforce basic geography lessons. You might choose to have one bulletin board continually devoted to displaying a world map. Several activities in different chapters of this book rely on the students using such maps to create displays related to theme based lesson projects. If the map is always there you will undoubtedly find even more ways to incorporate it in your classwork than those ways suggested in this book.

4. Involve your parents on a continuing basis.

The importance of this suggestion cannot be overstated. Identify a general course plan at the beginning of the year. If you think you want to do projects that require some plywood, seed, soda bottles, fabric or other slightly unusual resources, let your parents know this in a letter at the beginning of the year or on a "wish list" of materials at a back-to-school night. Then families can start saving things they might otherwise recycle or toss. Also try to identify early those parents who could help you by making patterns or cutting out items at home. This will help you provide a continuing program of creative projects, especially when funding is limited.

Perhaps even more important than the actual help you receive, however, is the effect the parents' encouraged involvement has on student produc-

tivity and interest. Never minimize how much more invested parents feel in the educational process when they have actively participated and the bootstrap effect this has on the children's investment in the class curriculum.

5. Even if you do not plan to do frequent class cooking, identify three or four cooking projects that you want to do during the course of the year and find parent helpers to facilitate them.

Classroom cooking is a wonderful adventure for children. Even if you are not able to do it on a weekly or monthly basis, plan to do it at least once a quarter, perhaps in conjunction with the culmination of a theme study. This assures that children who do not get kitchen experience at home, learn some basic cooking and nutrition skills. It also provides an exciting and much anticipated new dimension to other classroom activities.

6. Suggested reading books for children vary in reading level due to vast disparities that can exist in reading ability within any grade level.

Peruse the list of suggested reading resources with a flexible frame of mind. Many of the folk tales which are suggested for intensive investigation in certain chapters are picture books, but they continue to be of interest to upper grade children and are all too often kept from them solely because they do not have enough words on a page or significant page length. The number of pages alone does not determine the age level of a book or the complexity of the vocabulary used. Accordingly, it should not be the sole reason a book is chosen or rejected for a certain age level. Conversely, if some books are above your class's reading level, you may choose to read them aloud to your students.

Another reason to think about reading choices flexibly is that some children absolutely hate reading because they are continually forced to read what adults think is good for them. And as they get older, that automatically seems to mean books without pictures. Providing students with legitimate opportunities to review quality picture book literature in conjunction with another educational theme can restimulate a nonreader's interest in reading.

CHAPTER

1

EARTH DAY, EVERY DAY

The activities described in this chapter offer a framework to explore specific environmental issues. These ideas can be used throughout the year to reinforce earth-safe habits or can be used as part of themed classroom activities during an Earth Day or Earth Week event. Areas of investigation covered include: water pollution (with a focus on the water cycle, groundwater and water treatment) and conservation, air pollution, landfill and recycling issues, endangered species, and plant and habitat loss (including rain forest deforestation issues). These issues are part of elementary school curriculum from the fourth through the sixth grades and on.

CHAPTER AT A GLANCE

Lesson Activities

Lesson Activities in this chapter include ideas for reports, class books, murals, scientific investigations and community action projects.

Writing Activities

The Writing Activities include ideas for report writing, poetry, creative writing projects and informational brochures.

Art and Craft Activities

Art and Craft Activities cover a wide range of ideas for classroom decor, such as recreating a rain forest in your room, making musical instruments with an Earth-based theme, and even an idea for a Hat Day.

Food Activities

Food Activities provide classroom recipes which carry out the environmental theme such as "greens" soup and "good earth" cake and also provide several ideas for cooking using food resources and produce that is grown in rain forest climates to help reinforce the student connection between our everyday activities and the ever shrinking rain forests of the world.

Art Masters—Old and New

The Art Masters—Old and New section focuses on exploring the art of two very famous artists. One is Henri Rousseau, well known for his distinctive exotic jungles, and the other is Georgia O'Keefe. O'Keefe is famous for, among other work, a series on different flowers.

Sharing Activities

The Sharing Events section provides ideas for sharing information that the children have learned with other classes at the school. Ideas include putting together a simple Earth Day assembly, all-school or inter-class contests with an earth theme and all-school art displays.

Lesson Activities

Background information

1. Water Pollution and Conservation

a. The Water Cycle

Understanding the cycle of water on our earth helps children see the importance of taking care of water and keeping it clean and healthy. Through class activities, they can see the processes of evaporation, condensation and precipitation reenacted in a contained environment. Water on earth evaporates, condenses and returns to the earth. Winds blow the moisture from one place to another. In this way, if there is pollution in the water in one location of the water cycle, the pollutants can be redistributed elsewhere as the air currents move the air from place to place. Even remote, unindustrialized islands have become concentrated with toxins. The water cycle in our closed environment on earth facilitates this redistribution.

b. One Water Source—Groundwater

Groundwater is the water that is located beneath the surface of the earth. Unless it becomes contaminated, it can be used by people for drinking. The most basic example of human use of this water is the digging of wells on rural property to meet a family's daily water needs. When people use groundwater in this or other ways, they need to make sure it is not polluted. Unfortunately, in many areas of the country, improper dumping of wastes, pesticide use and leaching from dumps has caused groundwater contamination.

Even ordinary, non-hazardous dumping sites can cause groundwater contamination. Toxins, (that over the years have found their ways into regular household waste dumping sites) such as cleaning fluids, household paint products, and dirty car oils can leach into the soil over time contaminating groundwater. While modern landfill sites have sophisticated linings and leachate collection systems, these systems are subject to leakage and breakage over time which can result in slow leaks from landfills. This is why we must always dispose of our wastes in the right kind of landfill—one designated to handle and contain the given waste. It is also why we should try to use more natural products and less toxic petroleum-derived chemical products for ordinary household tasks such as pest control, household cleaning and laundry. Petroleum-derived chemical products should be avoided for two reasons: 1) they result in chemical by-products in the manufacturing process, and 2) they create toxic waste when they are discarded.

c. Water Treatment

Generally speaking, naturally occurring water must be treated before it is safe for people to drink and use. Even today in parts of the world without water treatment facilities, people die from diseases lurking in natural waters. In more industrialized parts of the world, water is often polluted by the dumping of wastes mentioned above. Purification of contaminated water is done in facilities called water treatment plants.

The six basic steps of water treatment are:
- Intake - The plant equipment draws water in from a river, lake, or other above-ground source. Sometimes the water is transported to the place at which it will be treated by a complex delivery system using aqueducts. California is one state with a massive aqueduct system that transports water from northern parts of the state to southern parts of the state.
- Pretreatment - To destroy unpleasant odors and tastes and to remove impurities, chemicals such as chlorine are added to the water to begin the cleaning process.
- Coagulation - The water proceeds to a large standing basin like a huge pool where pretreatment chemicals do their work. The chemicals attach themselves to the impurities in the water and then settle to the bottom of this huge water basin or tub.
- Filtration - The water is filtered through sand, gravel and hard coal to remove remaining impurities.
- Chlorination - The smallest amount of chlorine possible to do the work of killing off bacteria is

added to the water. This helps keep the water clean and healthy.

- Distribution - Clean water is stored in reservoirs and storage tanks and distributed as needed through water mains (huge pipes) to homes and businesses.

d. Water Conservation

Conservation of all our natural resources is important. Water is one of the resources without which we could not live very long. We use water for many things - drinking, cooking, washing clothes and dishes, bathing, watering yards and crops, fighting fires, swimming, toilets and power (called hydroelectric power). We can help conserve water by many little things we do each day. Some may require that we change our habits, but saving water is worth the effort. Some ways in which we can save water daily are:

- Installing low flow shower heads and faucets
- Taking shorter showers
- Cooling drinking water by keeping it in the refrigerator rather than running water to cool it
- Washing dishes by hand
- Not running water while we brush our teeth
- Planting drought resistant plants
- Watering plants in the early morning or in the evening to limit evaporation loss
- Fixing leaky faucets
- Installing water bags in toilets so that less water is used for each flush
- Flushing toilets less
- Washing only full loads of dishes and laundry
- Washing the car with a bucket of water instead of running water

2. Air Pollution

We need clean air to live healthy lives. Polluted air hurts people, plants and animals. We need to be aware of the sources of air pollution and those things we can do to help. Some basic sources of air pollution are:

- Automobile and other vehicle exhaust
- Oil refineries
- Fireplace fires, backyard barbecues and lighter fluids
- Forest fires
- Leaf and garbage burning
- Gasoline-powered yard maintenance equipment such as lawn mowers and leaf blowers
- Factories and other manufacturing operations
- Household sprays and petroleum-derived chemicals

Laws are one way we have tried to cut down on air pollution. Laws have been enacted to help control factory emissions. These laws vary from place to place but they require business owners to limit the pollutants that their plants and factories spew into the air. There are laws that require vehicles to use unleaded fuels in order to help reduce air pollution, to have special equipment to limit their emissions and to be inspected periodically to make sure their emission-controlling equipment is working properly. Laws are also being adopted to require manufacturers of consumer products such as lighter fluids and hair sprays to make their products differently so that unhealthy chemicals do not get into the air.

We should be aware of what lawmakers are doing to try to help us reduce air pollution, but we also need to think about what we can do every day to reduce the pollutants we put into the air. We can use more natural products for cleaning and personal hygiene. We can buy pump sprays instead of aerosols. We can walk or bike more often and combine errands to lessen the amount of time we drive our cars. We have to remember that every little bit counts.

3. Recycling and the Landfill Problem

Today's burgeoning landfill problem is one environmental issue about which we can do something easily everyday. The Earth is a closed environment. The only resources we have are those which are upon or within the Earth. If we use up the resources we have, we cannot make more. What we consume is gone forever. In the last fifty years our habits have changed dramatically. We have become a throw-away society in many things we do. We eat food on disposable plates. We buy food in disposable containers. We diaper babies with disposable diapers. We manufacture products that break faster and are thrown away sooner. We repair less and replace more.

Everything we throw away has to go somewhere, and that place is often the local landfill. Our nation's landfills and dumps are getting fuller and fuller. At the same time, our nation's and the world's populations are getting bigger and bigger.

As landfills fill up, it is hard to find space for new ones. The spaces we find are often places where animals and wild plants live. When we take the space for a landfill, we take the animals' homes.

We can help solve the landfill problem by looking closely at the trash we create. Is it biodegradable? That is, will it naturally break down quickly in the environment? Biodegradable trash includes food wastes and lawn and yard clippings. This trash can be composted to become fertilizer for our yards. Other trash takes a long time to break down. Do glass, plastic, aluminum and paper break down quickly? If not, can they be recycled?

4. Endangered Species and Habitat Loss

On every continent on Earth species of plants and animals are endangered or threatened. These words mean that the given plant or animal may not survive as a species because of changes that are taking place daily on our Earth. Children can explore these concepts in a variety of ways. First, they can explore what people are doing that endangers life forms on Earth. Second, they can explore perhaps the most important environmental zones threatened today — the rain forests of the world. These areas demonstrate all the difficult problems of pollution, urban sprawl and habitat destruction. Finally, they can explore things they can do to help make a difference for plant and animal life on Earth.

a. How Earth is Harmed

What have people done and what do we continue to do that hurts life forms on Earth? The growth of cities and the building of highways destroys habitats for plants and animals. Manufacturing and agricultural operations pollute areas in which animals live and the waters animals drink. Chemical and oil spills have poisoned entire environments, killing off animals, fish, and plants. Hunting animals for skins, tusks, shells, and feathers diminishes animal populations around the world. Trapping animals for pet sales or zoo sales also reduces animal numbers in the wild and causes unnecessary deaths.

Here is a checklist of human activities that have endangered animals:

- Collection of animals from the wild for personal pets or for sale to pet shops
- Hunting of animals for parts such as tusks from elephants, skins from seals and crocodiles and for "just plain fun"
- Poisoning of animal "pests" which has resulted in the death of animal predators as well as unintended death of birds and other passing animals
- Loss of habitat due to growth of cities, building of highways and use as landfills and waste disposal sites
- Chemical and litter pollution that results in unhealthy habitats
- Inadvertent or ill-advised introduction of new animals or insects into an environment which alters the food chain and endangers native animals

b. The Web of Life

Because the Earth is a closed environment, activities such as those listed above that take place in one part of the Earth can affect plants and animals many miles away. A great "web of life" connects all plants and animals on Earth. The sun shines and plants use the sun's energy to make oxygen. Animals breathe oxygen. Some animals eat plants and some animals eat other animals. Animals give off carbon dioxide as they breathe. Plants use the carbon dioxide to make oxygen. Animal and plant wastes provide food for life forms such as mushrooms, worms, and insects. When part of this chain is interrupted (such as when animals die because their habitat is destroyed), other parts of the web are affected as well. Animal habitats in mountain, desert, woodland, and wetland areas around the world have been damaged or lost.

The following is a starter list of endangered or threatened animals for children to investigate. The habitat listings should be considered as general starting categories since some habitats overlap and some animals may cross habitats.

Desert
-Desert tortoise
-Fringe-toed lizard
-New Mexico ridge-nosed rattlesnake
-Desert slender salamander
-Bactrian camel
-Giant armadillo
-Desert rats
-Mhorr gazelle (North African desert)

Mountain/Cliff
-California condor

-Timber wolf
-Black-footed ferret
-Gray wolf
-Brown bear
-Grizzly bear
-Gorilla

Prairie
-Atwater's prairie chicken

Woodland/Forest/Jungle
-Red wolf
-Oregon silver spot butterfly
-Cheetah
-Hawaiian hoary bat
-Spider monkey
-Jaguar
-Blank rhinoceros
-Indigo macaw
-Organutan
-Giant panda
-Tiger
-Asiatic lion
-Clouded leopard (Southeast Asian rain forest)
-Macaque monkey
-Tahitian lory bird

Wetland/Coastal/Water
-Whooping crane
-Polar bear
-Northern fur seal
-Redheaded duck
-Florida panther
-Everglades kite
-Bald eagle
-Blue whale
-Arizona trout
-El Segundo blue butterfly
-Guadalupe fur seal
-Florida manatee
-Brown pelican
-Wyoming toad
-American crocodile
-Devil's Hole pupfish
-Kemp's Ridley sea turtle

Additional endangered and threatened species information can be found in many encyclopedias that are available at school and local libraries.

c. One Important Environment — The Rain Forest

By looking at the issue of the shrinking rain forests, children can see both how we affect an environment far from home and how we rely on that same environment. A rain forest is a tropical woodland near the equator which receives 100+ inches of rain each year. Rain forests are found in Central and South America, Asia, Africa and parts of Australia. Rain forests give us 40 percent of the world's oxygen and are home to one-half of the plant and animal species on Earth. Rain forests are being destroyed at an alarming rate. Some statistics say that over 100 square miles a day are lost. They are cut down to create new farmland, to build cities and roads and to provide fuel and building materials. Once they are cut down, they cannot easily be grown back. Replanting takes years and in the meantime, plant and animal life forms can be lost.

d. How We Can Help Animals and Plants

What are we doing and what can we do to help plants and animals on our Earth? Think about these things:

- We can and have adopted laws to limit hunting of animals and to limit the amount of pollution manufacturers and factories create.
- We can enter into treaties with other countries to help us all develop Earth-safe habits.
- We can create wildlife preserves and sanctuaries to provide safe, protected homes for plants and animals.
- We can be careful consumers and not buy products if rain forests or wild animals are hurt to obtain the products.
- Animal organizations such as zoos can work on breeding programs designed to increase the numbers of endangered animals in the wild.

Project Directions

1. Water Pollution and Conservation

The ideas here provide hands-on methods for children to explore the water cycle, groundwater contamination, water treatment and their own families' household use of water.

a. The Portable Water Cycle

In this project children make terrariums from plastic soda bottles. The simplest method is to cut the bottle in half, drop a few small rocks in the bottom to promote drainage, put in 2" of potting soil and place a small plant, cutting or seeds in the soil. Water lightly and use masking tape to fasten the top half of the soda bottle to the bottom. Place in a sunny location. Soon the water in the soil will begin to evaporate and then condense on the sides of the bottle. As it collects, it begins to drip like rain and fall back to the soil below. The water cycle is seen in action. Pothos, ivy, geraniums, succulents, sunflower seeds and radish seeds are good things to grow in the terrariums.

To make a prettier terrarium to use as a gift after you watch the water cycle at work, cut only the top 2" to 3" off the soda bottle. Then remove the bottle from its plastic base by running hot tap water over the base to loosen the glue. The plant is planted in the plastic base in the same way you planted the terrarium above. After the plant is watered, the open end of the bottle is pushed down into the base to make the closed terrarium environment. Decoration can be added to it by letting children use puffy plastic fabric paints to make designs on the plastic base or by gluing Spanish moss and dried flowers to the domed top in a decorative way. Tacky glue works best for this gluing project.

b. Explore Groundwater Contamination

The simplest way for children to explore this issue is to visualize a dumping site and how such sites have caused contamination of groundwater. This can be done in two ways, but regardless of which method you use, draw a simple picture on the blackboard to show what groundwater is and how it sits below the Earth we walk on.

- For this first landfill project, you can dig a hole in ordinary soil. This hole approximates the kinds of dumps that were used before the advent of modern landfill technology (as a result of which new dumping sites are lined with clay). Ask children to imagine that the hole is a tiny dumping site. Dump sites are open air facilities into which rain and snow fall. This precipitation falls into landfill waste and can eventually mix with chemicals in the landfill and seep slowly into the ground below. This can even happen in landfills that are lined with clay and other materials because over time, land shifts in some places can lead to cracks through which leachate can seep.

Place a tablespoon of granulated fertilizer into your "landfill." The blue crystal types that are easily water soluble work best. Fill the hole with a quart to a half-gallon of water. Gradually, the water seeps into the soil. On the first or second try (depending upon the type of fertilizer used) the fertilizer begins to dissolve as the soil absorbs it. Ask the children to think about where the fertilizer crystals went. Did they really disappear? Tell children that just as the fertilizer crystals mixed with the water and disappeared into the soil, so does the soil beneath a dumping site adsorb chemicals in the dump's waste. If groundwater levels under or near a waste site are high, these toxins can reach groundwater more easily and contaminate it. Even in toxic waste dump sites which have special protective linings, seepage like this can occur over time.

- For the second project you will use sand, a plastic sink, a colander, food coloring, and water to show how this seepage works. In this project, you simulate a modern, lined landfill but show how seepage can work through cracks and breaks that may develop over time. Place 2" or 3" of sand in a plastic sink. Pack a 1" layer of wet sand on the inside of your colander. The colander is like the landfill lining, but tell the children it has developed some breaks in it. Place ten drops of red or blue food coloring in the bottom of your landfill. These are the chemicals in the landfill. Then slowly (one-half cup at a time) and gently pour water over the space where the food coloring is. This is the rain and other precipitation that will occur over time. Gradually, the sand beneath the colander will begin to color as the food coloring leaches its way into the sand. Tell the children to imagine that the groundwater sits below the layer of sand. What do they think will happen to the groundwater?

Ask children how they think they can help solve this problem. Some possible ways are:

- Use natural, biodegradable cleaners and household supplies.
- Try to find natural, nonchemical ways of combatting pests.
- Follow directions for proper disposal of chemicals.

c. Making Water Safe to Drink

To help children understand part of the process of cleaning water, have children make a water filter in one of these two ways.

1. Make a miniature filtration system using pie tins or Styrofoam meat trays, paper towels or cotton fabric (such as terry cloth, knit or muslin), dirt and water. For best results, this project needs to be done carefully. In one tray, mix a quarter to a third of a cup of dirt with a cup of water. Roll a piece of paper towel or use rolled fabric pieces. Place one end of paper towel or fabric in the tray holding muddy water. Place the other end of the towel in the clean tray. The tray holding the water is held above the empty tray in a stair step fashion. The paper towel quickly absorbs the muddy water but filters the particles of dirt so that as the water soaks into the towel and travels down toward the second tray the water is cleaned. Clear water begins to appear in the second tray. The paper towel strips work more quickly than the cloth strips.

2. Do a water filter demonstration using a clear bottle, strainers or funnels, paper towels and rocks and sand. In a strainer or funnel, layer paper towel, then small pebbles or aquarium gravel, and finally sand. Put your homemade "filter" across the top of a wide mouth bottle or a plastic liter bottle with the top cut off. In a small clear bottle with a lid, mix two cups of water with one-half cup of dirt and shake. Pour part of the water into the filter. Shake the dirty water and pour more into the filter as it absorbs each dose of water. Repeat until you have poured about half of the dirty water into the filter.

    Slowly the dirty water will work through the filter's layers and water will begin to drip into the clear bottle underneath. When the filter stops dripping, look at the filtered water. Give the dirty water a shake. Is the filtered water cleaner than the unfiltered water? This filter will not get the water completely clean but it will give students the idea of how filtering works.

    Depending upon the age level of your students, you might want to supplement a water filtering activity with a cooperative learning group project. Divide children into groups of no more than six to create water treatment charts. Have children research the processing steps in a water treatment plant. Each group member works on exploring one part of the process and explaining it by words and pictures on the chart.

d. Water Conservation Begins at Home

Have children explore personal and family water usage. This can be done in several ways.

• Ask children to fold a blank sheet of paper into quarters. Children draw a picture of one way in which they use water in each square and describe that usage in a sentence or two. For older children, you might ask them to make a map of their house, instead. They should label each room in the house and write in the center of each room how they and their families use water in that room. In some rooms usage may be limited to drinking, but even in living rooms, periodic rug shampooing and uphol-stery/curtain cleaning may result in water usage. Ask children to think of ways in which they can cut down on water use. They can write water-saving tips on the back of their drawings.

• Another way for children to explore water usage is for children to do household water surveys. Using the Home Water Survey Activity Sheet at the back of this chapter, each child analyzes his family's habits. As a related activity, children can use the Saving Water Activity Sheet, also at the back of this chapter. This activity also stimulates thought about ways in which the child and his family can change household habits in order to save water. This is a good "family" project.

    Encourage children to work with their families to talk about usage and estimate amounts used.

• Perhaps some of the children would like to test their toilets for leakage. By placing 10 to 15 drops of blue or red food coloring into the tank and letting the toilet sit without flushing for 15 to 30 minutes, children can find out if their toilet is leaking and wasting water. If the water in the bowl becomes colored by the food coloring, it leaks. Some leaks can be repaired with a simple trip to the hardware store to get the correct materials; others might require a plumber's help.

• Find out if there is a small area around your school in which the children can plant a drought garden. In this activity, they explore the kinds of plants they can grow in their own yards that will require only limited water. Plants such as cacti, succulents and geraniums will grow from small pieces, and are drought resistant as well. If you live in a part of the country in which these plants are common, ask children to bring in pieces from their yards. Children should then look over the plant pieces to see what they have and try to plant the pieces in the designated area with some sort of plan in mind. Children can create sketches of garden design before planting begins.

2. Air Pollution

There are several different activities that students can undertake to explore the quality of the air where they live and the various ways in which our Earth's air becomes polluted. Some possibilities are:

a. Petroleum Jelly Air Samples

Smear a quarter-inch of petroleum jelly on the insides of white or clear margarine tubs or whipped topping containers. Mark the exterior of the container with the address at which the sample will be taken. Ask children to take home the prepared tubs and place them outside for two weeks to a month to test whether the dust in the air near their homes is clean or dirty. Place the containers high on a fence or in a tree so that dirt scuffed up by foot traffic does not get into them directly.

b. Air Test Strips

Cut 2" x 5" strips of posterboard for children. Punch a hole at one end and insert a string for hanging. Then in three locations on the strip, hole punch areas that are about 3/8" to 1/2" in diameter. Down one side of the strip run a length of clear adhesive or cellophane tape so that the three groups of holes are covered on one side only with the tape. Hang these strips in different locations around the children's homes, the school or local businesses to test for the amount of dust in your local air. Mark each strip with the address or place at which it will be hung. Leave the strips in their locations for one to two weeks. Then collect them and have children review the results. The collected strips can be mounted on a bulletin board map of your community, if you choose.

c. Smudge Tests

Give each child two sandwich size plastic bags or envelopes, each with a cotton ball inside. Ask children to choose two locations (either home, school or business) from which to collect dust smudge samples to test the air residues in the local community. Children should try to locate window seals and ledges which are not dusted often from which to collect their samples. Samples are collected simply by rubbing the cotton ball over the dusty area and returning it to the plastic bag or envelope. Caution children to work with an adult when collecting samples from an area not recently painted or which might be splintered. On the envelope or bag, the child should write the location from which the sample is collected.

These samples can simply be mounted on posterboard with the address indicated or, if you have the time, you can mount them on a bulletin board map of your community. To do this, draw several major cross-streets and landmarks on your map. Then glue the samples on the board in their approximate locations in the community. The resulting display may show places in your community in which dust residues are dirty and in which they are relatively clean. Near major freeways, roads, and factories dust samples will probably be dirtiest.

d. Fiber in the Air

Many things get into our air every day. Some of them are chemicals, some are poisons, and some are simple fibers. Fibers can end up in the air as a result of textile manufacturing, insulation manufacturing and handling, or by simple daily tasks such as drying clothes in a dryer. Ask a few children to sample the air that comes out of the dryer vents at their homes. By placing a net, cheesecloth, or tulle with a string or rubber band over the vent opening for two to three dryer loads, children learn about another source of fiber and dust in our air. While not necessarily toxic, such fibers do contribute to the quality of air in a community.

Perhaps children have seen painters or gardeners wearing small painters' masks over their noses and mouths as they work. They do this to keep many kinds of fibers, dusts and fumes out of their lungs. Some of these are wood fibers and paint dust from sanding, dust, wood and leaf fiber from gardening and false nail dust and glue fumes from beautician activities. Seeing first-hand some of the fibers produced at home from ordinary activities may help children see how the problem of dusts and fibers in the air gets serious when we add up all the activities of all the different people in a community.

e. "To Market, To Market" Emissions Charts

Ask children to work in cooperative learning groups to explore the sources of air pollution in the process of getting a consumer product to market. This exercise helps children begin to understand the complexity of the air pollution issue. The results of each group's work can be displayed in a flow chart. Examples are:

- Gasoline - Exhaust-producing vehicles are used in the process of pumping oil from the ground. Oil is sent by pipeline to refineries. Refineries create emissions. Refined oils and gas are transported by exhaust-producing vehicles to gas stations. We "gas up" and drive exhaust-producing vehicles to go to work and to run errands.
- Bananas - Bananas are picked and transported by exhaust-producing trains to distribution centers at shipyards. The bananas are loaded onto exhaust-producing ships and transported around the world. At their destination, they are unloaded from ships and loaded onto trucks for distribution to local produce markets. Grocers drive exhaust-producing trucks to market to pick-up bananas and deliver them to stores. We buy the bananas and drive home in exhaust-producing cars to eat them. As an added air pollution problem, pesticides or herbicides may be used on plants in the growing process creating more chemical by-products in our air.

f. Comparison Shopping To Help the Air

Ask each child to visit the market with mom or dad to do some comparison window shopping. Ask students to talk with their parents about the things that they regularly use and buy in spray or aerosol form. These things include laundry preparations such as spray starch, household cleaners, pesticides and weed killers, hair sprays, deodor-

ants, and even cooking non-stick sprays. Can people buy the desired product in both a spray and non-spray form? For example, deodorants come in sprays, roll-ons and sticks. Can people buy the product in aerosol and pump form? For example, hair spray comes in both forms. Can people use a spray and "by hand" method to do a particular household or cooking task? For example, to grease a pan you can use a non-stick cooking spray or grease the pan by hand. For another task, can you use both a petro-chemical spray and a natural substitute? For example, petro-chemical ant pest sprays sometimes work no better than rinsing a counter top with vinegar. So many daily habits we take for granted. Can we change one household buying habit to help the environment? Ask each child to try to identify at least one household buying habit that could be changed or that is currently used specifically to help the environment.

3. Recycling and the Landfill Problem

These activities help children understand how the things they do each day can affect the environment and specifically help deal with landfill issues.

a. Garbage Analysis

Ask several children to collect trash from household trash cans and bring it to school. (Suggest that they not use the kitchen trash can which can be full of very messy wastes.) Take the trash the children bring together with your classroom trash and analyze it. Spread newspaper on the floor and dump out the contents of this trash collection. Ask some of these questions:

- Which things are recyclable?
- What is biodegradable?
- Are any of the items quickly biodegradable?
- How much non-recyclable trash is packaging?
- Could this packaging trash be reduced if manufacturers sold the products in a different way?

Organize the trash into piles according to recyclability, biodegradability and the like. Have children decide how much of the trash could be eliminated if recycling were done or buying habits changed.

b. Biodegradability Study

To do a biodegradability study, you will want to choose a variety of things that will be buried for varying lengths of time. Depending upon your interest, burial space and available study time, you can do one burial or you could choose to do several burials early in the school year and unearth them at two to three month intervals to check the progress of the decomposition.

To do this project, collect an assortment of small items - paper, whole and broken fruit, pencils, paper clips, Styrofoam, pennies, aluminum. Place some paper and fruit inside plastic bags to see how this affects the decomposition process. Bury these items for at least one month. If you choose to do successive unearthings throughout the year, have three sets of burial items with each set being approximately the same as the others so that children can easily compare results. When you unearth the items, place them on newspaper or butcher paper so the students can view them easily and analyze which items show signs of decomposition, which ones have not changed and how items were affected by encasement in plastic. If you plan unearthings later in the year, keep these items in a box for later comparison or take photos so children can remember what the earlier unearthings looked like. If students are keeping an environmental journal, have them record the results of their investigations, perhaps item by item. Have them conclude with which things are quickly biodegradable and which things are not.

c. Comparative Shopping Waste Demonstration

Much of the trash that goes into our landfills is packaging waste. Comparative food shopping is an easy way to show children how they can reduce waste by shopping carefully and perhaps changing their habits a little. Either you (or students and their families) can do some comparative shopping and share results with the class. Microwavable and other types of convenience foods are often packaged in multiple layers. Even though these foods are touted as convenience foods, sometimes a careful look shows that there is little difference in time to prepare something packaged more simply.

Some comparative shopping ideas are:
- Compare canned chili and microwave chili. What is the difference in preparation time? Which packaging can be recycled?
- Compare various rice packaging methods. Bulk rice purchases, boxed rice and specialty rices come in different layers of packaging.

Microwave packaging is usually the most wasteful.
- Compare specialty lunch packaging such as individually packaged applesauce cups versus jarred applesauce sent to school in reusable plastic containers.
- Which lunch drinks come in containers that can be recycled? Should we try to buy lunch juice in recyclable containers rather than throw away containers?

d. Landfill Relief

Children seldom see a landfill. Make a model of one. City planners and waste managers often locate a landfill in a large natural depression surrounded by rolling hills. Start with a plywood board for best results. Use crumpled newspaper placed on and around Styrofoam cups and taped to the base to form the hilly terrain. This can be covered by papier-mâché (newspaper strips dipped in starch or equal parts glue and water. Remember that an access road must lead to the dump site and that a community often surrounds the landfill. Perhaps you would like children to fill the dump with mock waste. Small pieces of paper, miniature toys, tires from miniature trucks are all good examples of the kinds of things that end up in a landfill.

As an adjunct to this project, ask one or two children to investigate where trash goes in the local community. To start this investigation, they can call city hall, their local city councilperson's office or the local waste management office. Review telephone etiquette with students who volunteer to make these calls.

4. Endangered Species and Habitat Loss

These activities help children to understand the interrelationship between all living things and to explore specifically the very important and ever shrinking rain forest.

a. Create a Class Web of Life

Have your class make a web of life display.
- In the center of the board place four cards or pictures labeled air, sun, soil and water. In a circle around these central labels, place pictures of animals or plants drawn by the children. Each child receives a three by five card or a 5" paper plate on which he or she draws the life form he or she chooses to depict. These

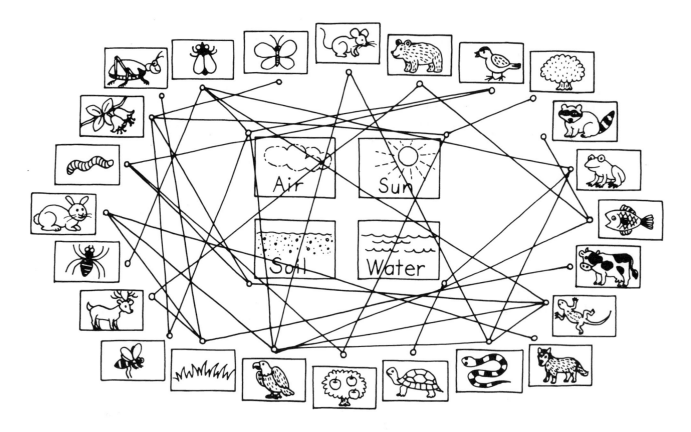

pictures are stapled onto the board in a circle around the four central labels. A push-pin is placed by each picture and by the four central labels. Each child connects his or her picture to another picture on the circle with a piece of white yarn or string. For example, if one child draws a bird and another draws a tree and another draws a beetle, the bird can be linked with the tree (bird's home) or the beetle (bird's food). The beetle could be linked to "water" as all creatures need water. Soon a web-like structure is created by the yarn as each picture is linked to at least one other on the board. Some sample animals and plants for depiction are:

Grasshoppers	Cow
Grass	Oak Tree
Lizard	Spider
Beetle	Sparrow
Crow	Eagle
Hawk	Bee
Butterfly	Geranium
Honeysuckle	Worm
Fly	Snake
Deer	Rabbit

Raccoon	Turtle
Fish	Bear
Toad	Frog
Apple Tree	Wolf
Mouse	

• Use these discussion guidelines to introduce the "web of life" concept to your class and to help them understand and make sense of the complicated interrelationships between living things on Earth.

Have you thought about what you need to live?
Air, water, food, shelter
Can you think of anything else that needs these things to live?
Animals, insects, plants
Think about animals. What do they need?
Think about plants. What do they need? Do plants need shelter?
Sometimes they are shelter to animals and insects.
What about insects? What do they need?
Do we all need the same things?

Talk about a few specific animals. What does a snake need?

What does a bird need?

What does a bear need?

This chain of animals eating other animals and plants is the food chain.

Can you think of some things in the world that are bad for us and animals?

Litter, chemicals, smog, loss of homes/ habitat.

Sometimes things that people do break this chain or break the web between animals. Tell the story about DDT:

At one time farmers used DDT, a pesticide, to kill bugs on corn and other crops. This pesticide killed the bugs but it got into the soil, rivers picked the chemical and took it to the ocean. Pelicans who lived around ocean water consumed the DDT by drinking the water and eating fish living in the water. It made the shells on their eggs so thin that the eggs could not hatch and the pelicans started to die off. We no longer use DDT and the pelicans are doing much better now. If we had not stopped our use of DDT, we might have broken the web and killed the pelicans forever.

What happens if one animal becomes extinct? Does it matter?

What if we lose birds of prey?

Then they are not there to eat rodents who then eat up too many plants and the plants die off.

Can what we do in one place affect what happens someplace else?

Yes, because all living things are tied together. It's like a great big web holds us together.

b. Adopt an Animal

Have each child "adopt" an animal that is currently endangered or threatened. You can guide the children's choice by using the animals in the background information of this chapter as a starting point, or by directing children to this information in classroom encyclopedias. Children do a mini-report on their adopted animal. The report should contain the following types of information:

• Name the animal

• Identify its animal group (i.e., reptile, mammal, bird, fish, insect, amphibian)

• Describe its appearance

• Where it lives

• What it eats

• How it reproduces

• Life span

• Why it is endangered

• How can we help

If you choose, children can instead use the Endangered Creature Report Activity Sheet at the end of this chapter for their reports.

Each child should draw a picture of the adopted animal. The reports and illustrations can be collected to make a class book of endangered animals. For a suggestion as to how to expand this report and drawing project to encompass creative writing, see Item 5 of the writing activities section of this chapter.

c. Build a Habitat

Have each child create a diorama of a habitat for either his adopted animal or another animal of his or her choosing. Some sample habitats are desert, mountain, wetlands, coastal, meadow, woodland, and prairie. Ask each child to bring in a shoebox or other small box. Children might want to approach the task as follows:

• Cut a piece of white paper the size of the interior of the box and paint a wash for the background with watercolor paint.

• Using an appropriate ground cover for the habitat (e.g. sand for wetlands or desert, dirt for other habitats) paint a layer of glue on which to affix ground cover.

• Make the animal from paper or clay.

• Use pieces of plastic, silk, or real plants to recreate greenery needed. Use plasticine clay or florist's clay to hold plants upright.

• Add rocks and other items as appropriate.

d. Make a Living Habitat

Building a living habitat is very exciting for children. An obvious classroom habitat is a fish tank. Another is an aquarium with gravel, sticks, large rocks and a water bowl for a hermit crab. Still another habitat, albeit a temporary one, can be made by taking some pond water (an inch or so in an aquarium or plastic sink) from a local pond together with a few tadpoles and raising the tadpoles in class. They can be fed on a diet of boiled lettuce and so long as you add water to existing pond water as it evaporates the tadpoles should be able to survive. Place a few rocks in the container holding the pond water to make it more of a natural environment.

Perhaps the best environment of all, though, for classroom creation is a reptile habitat for an anole or chameleon or other inexpensive pet shop reptile. Use an old aquarium with a removable screen or mesh lid. Mound up soil and place live local plants in it. Place a water bowl in the environment. Add crickets from a pet store or small insects the children bring in to feed the reptile. Place the aquarium in a reasonably warm part of the room. Mist the environment occasionally, as reptiles drink from dew drops left on leaves in the early morning. Put in a potato peel, piece of apple or rabbit food pellets for crickets to eat. This project is very exciting for children, who become excellent and concerned caretakers for their habitat and its guest.

e. Make a Rain Forest Mural

Have children use markers or paint to create a bulletin board size mural of the rain forest. All children should be able to participate. The information needed is available in many non-fiction texts on the rain forest. Children should depict and label the levels of the rain forest—i.e., herb, shrub, understory, canopy, emergents and the like. These exist in layers from bottom to top. Children can also include animals that populate each layer of the rain forest. National Geographic, Ranger Rick, and Earth Day issues of children's Scholastic News are good sources of animal pictures. They can be cut out and used on the mural or used to inspire student-drawn animals.

f. The Shrinking South American Rain Forest

Use the Shrinking Rain Forest Activity Sheet at the end of this chapter to explore where rain forests are today in South America and where they have been in years past. In this way, children can see where rain forests are located and how dramatically they have shrunk. Have them make up their own keys for their maps with colors and/or cross-hatch designs to show rain forests then and now.

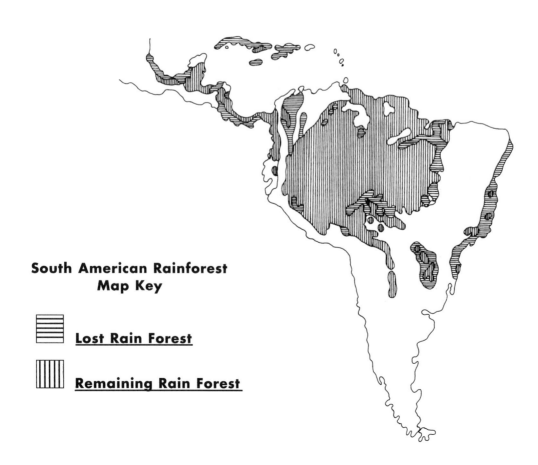

South American Rainforest Map Key

▤ **Lost Rain Forest**

▥ **Remaining Rain Forest**

Writing Activities

The suggested writing activities cover a number of different environmental subject areas. Some of them can be integrated into the lesson or craft activities suggested elsewhere in this chapter.

1. Chapter Vocabulary

Use some of these suggested words in conjunction with word activities for this theme:

Environment
Toxicity
Energy
Resources
Water Filtration
Conservation
Litter
Emissions
Groundwater
Leachate
Pesticides
Biodegradable
Endangered
Threatened
Habitat
Pollution
Ecology
Landfill
Extinction
Species
Smog
Acid Rain
Rain Forest
Deforestation
Oil Spills
Compost
Ozone
Environmental Protection Agency
Name of state or local environmental protection agency
Phosphate
Atmosphere

2. Create a Water Conservation Pamphlet

Using an 8 1/2" by 11" sheet of white writing or construction paper, ask children to create a pamphlet that encourages people to save water. Children should think both about their written product and the aesthetic qualities of the pamphlet. They need to consider:

- The pamphlet should be folded in an interesting manner. Pamphlets are often folded in thirds. Writing and/or art should be planned for each folded surface.
- Written information should be written in complete sentences. The written material should explain to people why water is important, why we need to conserve it, and ways in which we can change our habits or make household changes to help save water. Some writers may want to include "water facts" that they research. This includes information such as how much water is wasted by leaky faucets or how much water is used in showering and bathing.
- Graphic art ideas and design should be included as part of the pamphlet project. If possible, collect some water-saving pamphlets from your local water company before this project so the children can see how some professional pamphlets are put together. These should be available at no cost by making a call to the education or public affairs department of your local water utility.

3. Write a Political Action Letter

One thing we can all do to help the environment is to take the time to let our elected officials or major corporate executives know how we feel about environmental issues and/or corporate practices that affect the environment. Depending on the age and sophistication of your class, you can choose to have children write individual letters seeking some environmental action, or you can write a class letter which is then typed up and signed by all the students. If you choose to write to a government official, choose a local city councilperson, state legislator or congressperson. Local representatives tend to respond in writing more quickly than people higher up the political ladder.

Consider the following letter subject ideas:

- If you want to ask for environmental action at the city level (e.g. request for commencement of a local recycling program or express concerns about a planned landfill site or manufacturing operation), write a letter to a local official in the city or county government.
- If you want to request action on a state or national level (e.g. participation in international environmental treaties or a request for protection of particular animal, location or habitat), direct your letter to a state or federal government representative, such as state assemblyperson or senator or a congressional representative.
- If you have identified an environmentally unsound consumer practice, direct your letter to a company that engages in the practice you would like to change. Direct the letter to the chief executive officer of the company or the company president. One example of a problematic corporate practice concerned the foam packaging of food products by some fast-food chains. Consumer pressure led to change. Another example was the wasteful packaging of compact discs in boxes. Consumer and internal management pressure made record companies rethink and change the wasteful practices. Can children think of a marketing practice that should be changed?

4. Rain Forest Report

Ask children to investigate the rain forest problem and write a report. Tell them to write a simple report using the five-point method. This method requires an introductory statement in which the child states the subject to be covered, three statements about the subject area and a closing statement that summarizes what has been discussed. Possible rain forest subjects are:

- Why is the rain forest important to us? Reasons to be explored are that 40 percent of the Earth's oxygen is created in the rain forest, important drugs are created from rain forest plants, rain forests are home to one-half of the world's animal and plant species and impor-

tant products we use everyday come from the rain forest such as rubber, cocoa, vanilla, teak and mahogany.
- Why are rain forests being destroyed? Reasons to be explored are urban growth and the need for farm and cattle grazing lands.
- What are [one to three] products we get from the rain forest and why are they important to us? Examples are rubber to make tires, tool handles, hoses and surgical gloves, plants to make cancer drugs and other prescribed medicines, plant fibers such as ramie from which we make clothes and string and rope, and foods such as bananas, coffee, sugar, pepper and teas.

5. Create a Tri-nimal

If you make the endangered or threatened species book suggested in Item 5 of the art and craft activities section of this chapter, you might want to ask children to pick parts of three different animals and make up a fantasy endangered animal. For example, the fantasy animal could have the head of a tiger, the body of a gorilla and the feet of a whooping crane. Have children write a paragraph or story about their animal—where it lives, what it's called, what it eats and how it entertains itself.

Example:

Yesterday I met a tirillane. This animal was very strange. It had the head of a tiger, the chest and arms of a gorilla and the skinny legs of a whooping crane. Being part tiger, this animal can run very fast but it looks very funny as it does because its legs are so thin. The tirillane likes to eat fish. It hatches its babies from small eggs. Sometimes the other animals make fun of the tirillane and say he looks funny. When they do this, he just lets out a whoop and flaps his hairy arms.

6. Earth Haiku

Have children write environmentally-themed haikus. A haiku is a Japanese poem that has three lines. The first line has five syllables, the second line has seven syllables and the third line has five syllables. The lines need not rhyme. They can be separate sentences or the poem can express one thought.

Examples:

I fear for the Earth
Because we give it no care
And go on our way.

Today is Earth Day.
Tomorrow is Earth Day, too.
Every day is Earth Day.

Perhaps your class would like to collect its poetry and some Earth facts and create a publication to distribute to parents or other classes. You could call it "Earth Thoughts" or another name of the class's choice. If you have a parent volunteer with a computer and newsletter software, such a publication can be completed very easily. Better still, more and more classrooms are now equipped with computers and software that allow children to directly input and create newsletters. Perhaps children can create the complete newsletter themselves on a classroom or school computer. Either way, children feel a great sense of pride in the creation of a published product that they can share with others.

Art and Craft Activities

1. Design Water Conservation Posters.

Using half sheets of posterboard, ask children to use markers to design posters to encourage the school community to save water, both at school and at home. The poster should include a written idea or theme and a graphic art idea. You could invite other classes to participate and then hold a poster contest. Invite the principal or a community representative to judge the posters. Display posters around the school in prominent places.

2. Environmental Banner Bulletin Board

Here are several ideas for a striking classroom bulletin board with an environmental message. Start with a piece of paper about the size of your board. Then each child can work on a piece of art which will be glued or stapled to the board.

• Bird Board - Have each child make a single origami bird from a 7" or 8" square of paper cut out of an old magazine. This way, the paper children use to create the art is being recycled. Glue one wing of each bird on the board. Arrange birds in a random fashion to simulate the look of a flock of birds in flight in the sky. Save space on the board for an environmental message such as "Save Our Birds—Stop Using Pesticides." A simple origami bird suitable for this project is shown in the illustration on this page.

• Tree Board - Another attractive board can be made using kirigami trees or blow-art trees. Kirigami trees are made using a triangle of green paper and a small rectangle of brown paper. V-cuts are made out of two sides of the triangle and kept. The triangle is glued to the banner above its trunk and then the V-cuts are glued back into the triangle leaving 1/4" space between the triangle and the cut-out.

Blow art trees are made by having children blow brown tree trunks and branches onto the paper with a straw and thinned brown tempera paint. To do this, a small amount of paint (about one teaspoon) is placed at the bottom of the paper. The child blows through the straw to spread the paint into a form resembling a trunk and branches. Crushed green tissue in assorted shades can be used to decorate the branches. This environmental message could be "Help Our Air— Plant a Tree" or "Save the Rain Forest."

3. Recycled Art

Children can recycle ordinary trash into sculptures or make recycled art paper.

• Have children collect trash materials from their homes that they typically do not recycle. Talk about these in class. How could they avoid creating this trash — e.g. could they buy products with less packaging or could they buy different products? How could they reuse or recycle the trash to avoid sending it to a landfill? After this discussion, ask children to take an assortment of the trash and create something else with it. Ask them to think about something that they could use again. As an example, large bags and string sometimes become toys such as doll purses or useful items such as coupon holders.

Alternatively, ask children to bring in some larger trash such as boxes, together with other recyclable and non-recyclable trash. Have children work in cooperative learning groups to make large trash sculptures between two and four feet in height. Place these structures in an empty room or auditorium in an aesthetic way to create a temporary sculpture garden. Invite other classes to visit your sculpture garden. Remind children to title and label each piece and to list the name of each student sculptor as well. Perhaps the sculptures could be displayed in a school office, the local library or an office in a city building.

• Make recycled paper from old newspaper. To do this, you will need newspaper strips, water, rolling pins or canned foods, old towels, twelve 5" by 7" plastic needlework grids (enough for six students to work at one time). Boil the newspaper in a pot of water. Mash the paper with a potato masher and boil for 20 to 40 minutes until it has been reduced to pulp. Let pulp cool. Dip plastic grid into pulp. Pull some pulp up from the water on the grid, holding the grid flat. Place on an old towel. Top with a second grid and roll water out with rollers or cans. (Note: Before you press water out you can decorate pulp with bits of colored tissue, ribbon or cotton yarn.) Remove second grid and peel paper off the first grid. Let dry overnight. Press with iron when dry, if necessary, for paper to lay flat. This is a very easy way to make paper. Five to six students can work at one time. Even kindergartners can make paper with this method.

4. Rhythmic Recycling

Using recyclable as well as non-recyclable trash, make instruments with which to create "recycling rhythms."

- Rasps - Several bottled water products come in bottles with ribbed sides. When a pencil or dowel is rubbed over these sides, the bottles become excellent rasps.
- Drums - Make drums from empty coffee cans and other cylindrical containers with plastic lids. Cover the outsides of the containers with decorated construction paper. A fancier drum to make, but one that requires parent help, is one in which the drum heads are made from circles of inner tube. Cut off both ends of the coffee can. Cut two circles of inner tubing, each with a diameter four inches larger than the diameter of the coffee can. Poke holes every two inches with a knife (adults only) around the edges of each circle. Place one circle on each end of the can and lace them tightly with heavy string through the holes so that two drum heads are created. This makes a very sturdy and good sounding drum.
- Rattles - Fill small plastic bottles with beans, rice or paper clips to make rattles. Rattles can also be made from toilet paper rolls or aluminum cans filled with beans, taped shut and covered with construction paper. Old aluminum containers such as pie plates or stiff paper plates can serve as tambourine-type instruments. Using plastic bag ties, yarn or pipe cleaners, attach three or four metal pop tops, water bottle or beer bottle caps (through which holes have been drilled or punched by adults) to each of six points on the plate. Make sure the caps move easily on the ties so that when you shake the "tambourine," they rattle.

Use these instruments in conjunction with environmental chants, cheers or slogans the children create themselves. Older children might want to take turns sharing the instruments with children in younger classes and teaching them their Earth cheers or simple Earth songs such as those listed below. Younger children might want to stage an Earth parade with instruments and cheers.

Here are sample environmental songs to teach the children. They are simple enough that older children can easily teach them to younger children.

To "Jim Along Josie"
The Earth is ours. We must protect it.
Do your part. Let's start today.

Name the problem. Find an answer.
Step by step, let's start today.

Let's clean up, now. Don't be careless.
No more litter. Change today.

Change your habits for our Earth, now.
Do your part. Let's start today.
© Pamela A. Marx 1993. Used with permission.

To "Happy Birthday to You"
We love our Earth
We love our Earth
Please help us take care of it
You know what to do
© Pamela A. Marx 1993. Used with permission.

To "Yankee Doodle"
Mother Earth has lots of problems
Careless hands have caused them
So it's time for us to act
Let's make a helping hand pact

Help the Earth
Do what you can
Make recycling your plan
Help the Earth
Look here and there
And show how much you care
© Pamela A. Marx 1993. Used with permission.

Older children may want to put their own lyrics to a well-known tune.

5. Endangered Animal Class Book

Have each child draw an endangered animal of his or her choice but with a twist. The animal is drawn on an 8 1/2" x 11" sheet of paper that has been divided into thirds by two horizontal black lines. The head of the animal is drawn in the top section, the torso of the animal is drawn in the middle section and the legs and feet of the animal are drawn in the bottom section. If your students wrote endangered species reports as suggested in the lesson activities section of this chapter, they can write some key information about the animal on the back of the bottom section of the picture.

The class book is assembled simply as follows:

- Each child's animal is given a number. He writes the number on the right hand side of each section of his picture. This will be the picture's page number.
- If the book is to be assembled with brads, each picture is then cut into thirds on the black lines. The pictures are placed in order, 1,2,3 and so on. Each picture is hole punched at two places on the left hand side of each section. An uncut but hole punched cover is placed on the front and back of the pictures and the six brads put in place.
- If the book is to be assembled with a spiral binding machine, a cover should be placed on it and the binding completed next. Then each picture is cut into thirds after the book is bound.

Children can flip through the book to learn about the endangered animals the other children investigated. They can also use the book to do the creative writing project suggested in Item 5 of the writing activities section of this chapter. To do this, each child chooses a head, torso and legs/feet, each from a different animal. He or she can use the information provided in the bottom section of the animal pictures to get ideas for the creative writing exercise.

6. Make Rain Forest Rainsticks

Rainsticks are percussion instruments made from bamboo, wooden pegs and seeds. When turned upside down, they simulate most incredibly the sound of falling rain. Children can make their own rainsticks using five toilet paper rolls, posterboard scraps, barley, tape and construction paper. Cut four circles the size of the end of the toilet rolls from stiff posterboard. Cut two of these circles in half. Tape the half-circles onto the ends of four of the rolls. Then tape a whole circle to one end of the remaining roll and one of the first four rolls. Place a handful of dry barley in one of the rolls over which a whole circle as been taped. Tape the five rolls together with masking tape in the manner shown in the illustration here. Cover

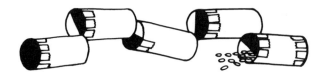

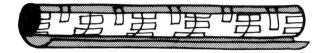

the tube with brown construction paper or strips of masking tape. Children can decorate the paper or tape to look like wood. Tilt the completed rainstick slowly and turn it to create the rain sound.

7. Create Rain Forest Art

The rain forests of the world are inhabited by many different peoples. These people decorate baskets, clothing and tools with designs. Have children recreate some of these designs using pastels or colored chalk on dark construction paper.

To do this, ask children to research information about indigenous rain forest peoples and use the patterns they find in books to create their artistic designs. Have children draw their designs on scratch paper first if they like and then, once satisfied, transfer them in pencil onto the dark paper. Stylized geckos are a favorite tropical animal design. Children can finalize the designs with chalk or pastels.

8. Hat Day

Have children use small boxes, cut-off gallon size plastic milk and juice bottles or real hats upon which to attach recyclable things to make creations for a hat day. Children can make the hats at home and bring them in on your designated hat day. Pick a time and have all the children parade around the room and view each other's creations. Then place the hats in the room on display and have children vote for most original, funniest, and most-recycled materials used.

9. Rain Forest Flora and Fauna

Turn your room into a rain forest with these ideas for birds and tropical flowers.

• Using an enlarged version of the bird shape shown here, have children make brightly colored toucans to hang around the classroom. Use fluorescent paints, feathers and crepe paper streamers to create the colorful birds. Have children explore the math concept of symmetry with this project.

This can be a several-step project. Children cut two bird shapes out of black paper. Using brightly colored tempera paints, they paint one side of each cut bird with beak and wing markings. Since birds are symmetrically colored, the painted sides should be mirror images of each other. If you would like to add real feathers to your birds, these can be glued on the next day. (Craft feathers are expensive, but discount outlets often sell very inexpensive feather dusters that have brightly colored feathers. These can be easily detached and used for craft projects.) The last day the bird is stuffed with newspaper, stapled together, a crepe paper streamer tail added, and a hole punched to thread fishline for hanging.

• Make tropical flowers to decorate your walls. These are very simple to make. Start with a 9" x 12" piece of white paper. Mix one part glue and one part water. Have children cut about 9 tissue petals in 6" x 8" oval shapes. Some small pieces of another colored tissue can be cut, crushed and used to create the center of the flower. The child paints some glue mixture onto the paper and places petals around a circle he has drawn in the center of the sheet. Then three or four petals are gathered at one end and the gathered ends glued around the center of the flower to add another dimension. Lastly, the other tissue pieces are added to complete the center of the flower. These flowers are showy and easy to make.

• Rain forests are also home to myriad butterflies. On any color paper, cut out a butterfly shape. By painting these butterflies, children explore symmetry, this time using a modified "squish" paint method. Have pie plates with three colors of paint available. In each plate, have four 18" strings. The ends of the strings remain outside of the paint. Children fold their butterflies in half and then open them flat. They dip the mid-points of two strings in paint and lay the folded painted parts on one side of the butterfly. The free wing is folded on top of the string. While folded, the string is pulled out from between the wings. The result is a symmetrical string painted butterfly for mounting on a wall or hanging. You can also try the ideas for geometric butterflies in the art and craft activities section of Chapter 2.

Food Activities

These cooking ideas can be used to spark discussion about environmental issues. Some of the recipes rely on tropical foods which grow in or near rain forest regions. These will allow you to easily incorporate in class discussions the rain forest's relationship to our daily lives.

1. Good Earth Cake

Good Earth cake is an ideal cooking exercise for this theme. To make this "cake" you need the following ingredients:

2 20-ounce packages of creme-filled dark chocolate sandwich cookies
2 3-ounce packages of vanilla pudding
1 8-ounce package of cream cheese
3/4 cup powdered sugar
3 1/3 cups milk
1/2 cup margarine

Let cream cheese and margarine soften. Mix cream cheese with powdered sugar and margarine until creamy. Mix pudding mix with milk and let thicken. Mix the pudding gradually into the cream cheese mixture. Crush cookies with a rolling pin. In an 8" clay flower pot lined with plastic or waxed paper or a deep casserole dish, layer crushed cookies, pudding mixture, crushed cookies and so on ending with a crushed cookies layer. You can also save one cookie per flowerpot and cover the bottom hole with that. Refrigerate. "Plant" an artificial green plant on top or decorate with some gummy worms around the top to "aerate the soil." You may need two "planting" containers to hold all the good Earth ingredients generated by this recipe.

Use this cooking project as another opportunity to talk about soil. What makes it healthy for plants and animals? What makes it unhealthy? What things pollute the soil? What can students do to make a difference?

2. Greens Soup

Make this soup in celebration of the green theme of protecting the environment. To make it easy, start with four cans of chicken broth or have students make broth according to directions using water and bouillon cubes. Season to taste with salt and pepper. Have children bring in assorted green vegetables. These may include green beans, broccoli, snowpeas, zucchini, celery, green onions, green cabbage, bok choy, and green bell peppers. Children can dice vegetables into small pieces. Add vegetables to hot broth and boil or simmer for fifteen to twenty minutes, or until vegetables are tender.

3. Green Sandwiches

Ask children if they have ever had green sandwiches before. Children might want to try a version of an English tea treat by making cucumber sandwiches. For the sandwiches you need bread, margarine, soft or whipped cream cheese, rice vinegar and peeled and thinly sliced cucumbers. (Ask parents to pre-peel the cucumbers at home.)

To make the sandwiches, spread each slice of bread with margarine (if desired) and then cream cheese. Slice peeled cucumbers thinly and marinate in rice vinegar for a few minutes. Place a layer of drained cucumbers on the spread cream cheese. Top with second layer of prepared bread. Quarter each sandwich and serve.

4. Rain Forest Treats

A number of foods we take for granted grow in rain forest areas or are associated with tropical climates. Some rain forests foods are bananas, Brazil nuts, cashews, coconut, sugar, cocoa, and vanilla. Pineapple is also associated with tropical climates like Hawaii. As you make a chosen treat with children, remind them that some of the things they are eating come from rain forest areas or similar tropical climates.

Rain Forest Refresher
20 bananas, finely mashed or pureed
1 quart passion fruit or guava drink, cold
1 can coconut milk

Mash bananas in large salad bowl or a punch bowl with potato masher. Slowly add coconut milk beating with a hand mixer. Then add juice a little at a time until the drink has the proper consistency - i.e., that of a fruit smoothies drink. Serve immediately.

This smoothie style of drink can be made even more easily and effectively in a blender if you have one available for classroom cooking.

Tropical Sundaes
Vanilla ice cream
Chocolate sauce
Chocolate chips
Cashew bits
Flaked coconut
Drained crushed pineapple or, if available, fresh cut papaya, mango or guava
Give each child a scoop of vanilla ice cream. Each child can top with his or her choice of tropical toppings.

Rain Forest Delight
3 large packages instant chocolate pudding
Milk as needed to make pudding according to directions
1 6 ounce package of chocolate chips (preferably mini-chips)
1/2 cup flaked coconut (optional)
2 8-ounce cans of crushed pineapple, drained
8 cups whipped topping
Start with two large bowls and spoons. In one bowl, make up instant pudding according to directions. Add chocolate chips and stir. In the other bowl, mix coconut, pineapple and whipped topping. In clear plastic cups (so children can see the layers), spoon in a layer of chocolate mixture and then a layer of cream mixture. Top with a dollop of chocolate mixture. Serve immediately.

Candy Carnivale
1-8 ounce cream cheese
3 cups powdered sugar
1/2 teaspoon vanilla
1 cup flaked coconut
1/2 cup finely diced cashew bits
Cocoa powder

Mix first three ingredients in a bowl. If too dry, add a little water. If too sticky, add a little powdered sugar. When well mixed, add coconut and cashews and mix. Take by teaspoons and roll into balls. Roll balls in cocoa powder. Store in cool area or eat immediately.

Art Masters—Old and New

The works of two artists are suggested for exploring art masters in conjunction with your classroom environmental activities. The two artists are Henri Rousseau and Georgia O'Keefe. The projects are designed to inform students about the work of famous artists and to offer them techniques to create an art piece in the style of each artist.

Background Information

1. Henri Rousseau

Rousseau was a French painter in the Impressionist period of the late 1800s. Some of his most famous paintings were inspired by the jungles and jungle creatures of exotic rain forest-type environments.

2. Georgia O'Keefe

O'Keefe was an artist of the 20th century. She was born in 1887 and died in 1986. Born in Wisconsin, she grew up in a family that encouraged women to be educated. In her early years she studied art in the eastern United States, living for a while in New York. Eventually she settled in the Southwest and used its dramatic desert landscapes as much of the inspiration for her work. She did a very famous series of paintings based on flowers. A single flower was often painted on a large canvas and it alone more than filled the canvas.

Project Directions

1. Rousseau's Exotic Jungle

A Rousseau-like jungle scene can be recreated by students in this manner:

• On a sheet of black paper approximately 12" x 18", the child pencil sketches the outlines of his or her jungle scene. This sketch is of the basic outlines only.
• Once completed, the child goes over these pencil lines with white glue.
• When the glue is dry, the child completes the picture with pastels or colored chalks using mostly cool colors such as greens and blues

except when depicting animals. The finished product has the now famous look of Rousseau's jungle artwork.

2. O'Keefe's Bigger-Than-Life Flowers

Since much of O'Keefe's inspiration came from nature and since one of her most famous series is of flowers, exploring her art in conjunction with studies on protecting the natural environment makes sense. To do this project:

• Have child begin with a 9" x 12" piece of white construction paper. The flower the child creates should fill most of the page and several of the petals should "fall off" the edges. In the center of the sheet, the child draws a 1" or 2" diameter circle or oval.
• Using two or three similar shades of tissue paper (colors that might be found within a single flower as it blooms), ask children to decide on a petal shape and cut seven or eight such petals from the tissue. Each petal should be the same shape and the shape should be approximately 5" or 6" long and 2" or 3" wide.
• Once cut, the child paints a glue mixture (equal parts white glue and water) onto the white paper and places his or her petals on the page around the space marked in the center area. Petals can overlap one another as they might in a flower and not all petals need to be used. Any part of a petal that falls over the edge of the paper will be trimmed later.
• When dry, children can use dark paint (black, dark blue, purple) and a fine tipped brush (or dark markers) to do simple outlining around some of the petals. Other colors can be used to dab in a dotting manner the center of the flower. The petal parts that run off the page can be trimmed. When the project is complete, the child will have recreated the feeling of a Georgia O'Keefe flower painting.

Sharing Activities

1. Spirit Banner Project

This can be a class project or it can be shared with other classes in the school. If done within the classroom, each banner is created by a group of students in a cooperative learning setting. The spirit banner project works like this - each day of the designated week a banner is hung in the entrance area of the school so that all students, teachers and parents can see it as they arrive. The banner states a simple environmental message or encourages a particular environmental behavior or activity for the day. Some ideas are:

• Litter Hurts - Do your part every day
• Conserve Water - Every drop is precious
• Lost Habitats mean Lost Homes
• Reduce, Reuse and Recycle
• Walk More, Drive Less - Combine Errands
• Help the Air - Plant a Tree

Spirit banners can be painted or made with markers. Members of the school community begin to look forward to the next day's message and to join into the spirit of the students' efforts.

2. Alphabet Walk

Have your class divide up the letters of the alphabet to create an environmental alphabet. For each letter of the alphabet, an environmental message is created.

Example:

A is for acid rain which hurts plants and buildings and people.

B is for biodegradable products. They help our Earth.

C is for composting which helps save landfill space.

and so on.

Each child transfers his or her message with art or graphics to a poster. These posters can be hung down a school hallway to create an alphabet walk for the environment. In this way, students share their environmental lessons with other students in the school. Other classes in the school may want to visit the alphabet walk with their teachers to talk about the environmental messages stated on the posters or members of the sponsoring class can invite other classes on a guided tour of the poster walkway.

3. Take a Step for the Earth

This project can be done by one class or each class in the school can be invited to participate. To create the Earth Walk, every child in the class traces his feet onto colored paper and cuts them out. On each foot, the child writes his or her name and one thing he or she can do for the environment. The footsteps are then glued onto long banners and hung around the school to remind the school community to "take a step in the right direction for our Earth" or to encourage "Earth-wise walking." Children can also trace around their hands, cut them out, and write couplets, slogans, or Earth cheers on them. These can also be glued on the banners for decoration.

Examples:

Couplet -   *Make the scene.*
            Work for green.

            Lend a hand.
            Save the land.

Slogan -   *Think green.*

            Give the Earth a new birth.

            Earth work is worth it.

4. Recycled Art Show

Host a recycled art show for the school. Ask students to create creatures from recyclable materials. This is becoming a relatively common activity at community fairs and events so children may even have seen a few recycled creatures before. Most of the creatures created look a little like space creatures, and they are all entertaining and fun. Ask the principal or a community person to judge the art entries. Give out certificates to participants and winners.

5. It's a Wrap

In conjunction with a recycled or other Earth-themed art show, make an artistic environmental statement in the style of Christo as described in the art masters section of Chapter 5. Choose a hedge, tree trunk or other natural part of the school campus to "wrap" in fabric or material that students bring in. Old sheets and large fabric scraps as well as sheets of plastic covering can be stapled together and used to wrap some part of the school. Near the display you might put a poster explaining the work—i.e., "… in the style of Christo, this living sculpture celebrates nature and reminds us that caring for nature is a daily obligation."

6. Plan an Assembly

A single class can very easily put on an informative and interesting assembly for the school with only a small time commitment. Here are some ideas:

a. You might want to ask a community representative to speak. Consider local school officials who could speak on the district's environmental efforts, city government officials in charge of local recycling and water treatment or conservation efforts, the school principal who could speak about the school's efforts or a representative from a local environmental protection group such as Treepeople, the Humane Society or the Audubon Society.

b. Ask one or two students to present their reports about the rain forest or an endangered animal.

c. Ask students to research "Earth facts" to present at the assembly. These can be presented in a "Did you know?" format.

d. If children made environmental alphabet posters, these can be presented.

e. Divide the class in half and memorize and present one or two selections from *Joyful Noise: Poems for Two Voices* listed in the resources section of this chapter. These poems celebrate the insect world, a much maligned but important part of every ecosystem.

f. Children could sing one or two songs with an environmental theme. These could be the songs suggested earlier in this chapter or a popular song such as the Beach Boys' "Don't Go Near the Water," John Denver's "Trees" from his Amazon album or another of your choosing.

7. Plan a Poster Contest and/or Calendar Sale

Ask children in your class to make small 8 1/2" by 11" water conservation or environmental posters. You could also invite other classes to participate and make it a contest. The twelve chosen winners will be used to make a calendar that will be printed up and sold to raise money for a local environmental cause, a zoo animal adoption or other Earth-safe program chosen by the class or school. A local printer might be willing to photocopy a sufficient number of the calendars so that each child in your class can sell three or five to help earn money to save the Earth through your chosen cause.

If the calendar idea seems too complicated for a fundraiser because of the problems finding free or inexpensive printing, consider having your class sponsor an aluminum can recycling drive or even a bake sale. Then donate the proceeds to a worthy environmental organization.

Name: _____

**CHAPTER 1
ACTIVITY SHEET**

Home Water Survey

Room of the House/Yard	How is Water Used	Number of Times per Day	Estimated Amount of Water Used
_____	_____	_____	_____
_____	_____	_____	_____
_____	_____	_____	_____
_____	_____	_____	_____
_____	_____	_____	_____
_____	_____	_____	_____
_____	_____	_____	_____
_____	_____	_____	_____
_____	_____	_____	_____
_____	_____	_____	_____
_____	_____	_____	_____
_____	_____	_____	_____
_____	_____	_____	_____
_____	_____	_____	_____
_____	_____	_____	_____
_____	_____	_____	_____

Name: _____

CHAPTER 1
ACTIVITY SHEET

Saving Water

I can save water in my household.

Room/Yard	Suggested Change in Habit	Estimated Water Savings
_____	_____	_____
_____	_____	_____
_____	_____	_____
_____	_____	_____
_____	_____	_____
_____	_____	_____
_____	_____	_____
_____	_____	_____
_____	_____	_____
_____	_____	_____
_____	_____	_____
_____	_____	_____
_____	_____	_____
_____	_____	_____
_____	_____	_____
_____	_____	_____

Name: _____

Endangered Creature Report

Use complete sentences to write your report.

Name of Creature: _____

_____

Animal Classification: (mammal, reptile, etc.) _____

_____

Appearance: _____

_____

_____

Habitat: _____

_____

_____

Foods: _____

_____

_____

Reproduction and Lifespan: _____

_____

_____

Reason for Endangerment: _____

_____

_____

How can we help? _____

_____

_____

_____

Name: _____

The Shrinking Rain Forest

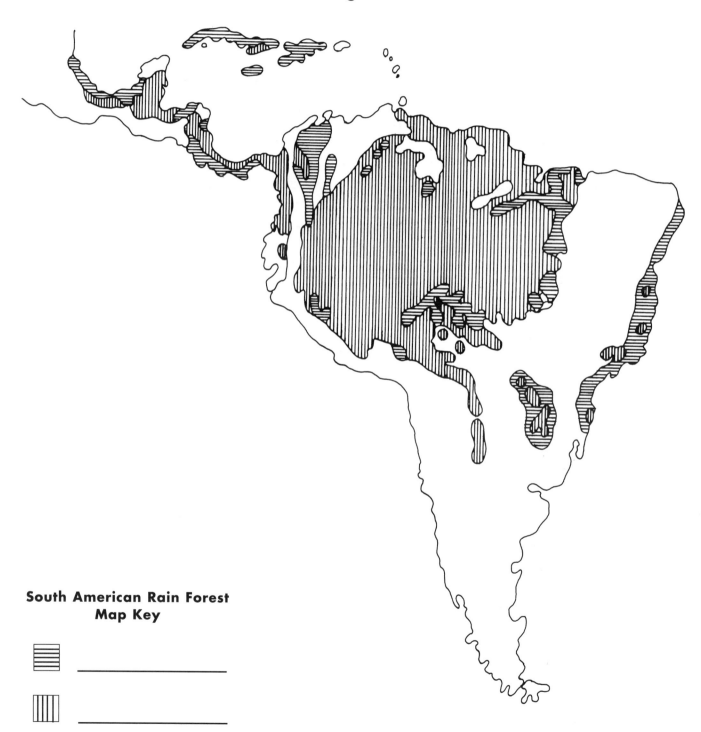

**South American Rain Forest
Map Key**

_____

_____

Resources

1. These factual resource books can be used by students as they engage in theme-based activities.

The Earth Book for Kids by Linda Schwartz published by The Learning Works (1990).

Great Lives: Nature and the Environment by Doris and Harold Faber published by Charles Scribner's Sons (1991).

One Day in a Tropical Rain Forest by Jean Craighead George published by Crowell (1990).

A New True Book: Endangered Species by Lynn M. Stone published by Children Press (1984).

Wildlife Alert! The Struggle to Survive by Gene Stuart published by the National Geographic Society (1980).

2. The following literature books work well with an environmental curriculum theme.

The Great Kapok Tree by Lynne Cherry published by Harcourt Brace Jovanovich (1990).

The Wump World by Bill Peet published by Houghton Mifflin (1970).

Brother Eagle, Sister Sky by Chief Seattle published by Dial Books (1991).

Who Really Killed Cock Robin? by Jean C. George published by Penguin Books (1984).

A River Ran Wild by Lynn Cherry published by Harcourt Brace Jovanovich (1992).

The Lorax by Dr. Seuss published by Random House (1971).

Joyful Noise: Poems for Two Voices by Paul Fleischman published by Harper & Row (1988).

The lessons in this chapter are designed to instill in children an appreciation of the large part math plays in our daily lives, and how useful and enjoyable working with numbers can be. One way to use the ideas and activities in this chapter is as a year-opener to excite children about math concepts they will later explore in more detail and to give them insight into the reasons these skills are important. Or you may want to set aside one day a month as Math-A-Mania Day to challenge children with a set of math activities over and above their regular course work.

More and more, jobs of the future will rely on a person's ability to solve math problems and to deal with issues which require an understanding of mathematical concepts. Simple, rote math skills become less meaningful in the job market as the use of calculators and computers becomes more widespread, but the ability to think about math remain a creatively issues will valued skill. Encourage creative math thinking with the activities in this chapter.

Lesson Activities

The Lesson Activities in this chapter include learning activities that build strength in estimating, sorting, measuring, and "real world" computing skills.

Writing Activities

The Writing Activities provide writing opportunities that explore geometric concepts through poetry and offer creative writing opportunities that use numbers as the catalyst for the creative effort.

Art and Craft Activities

The Art and Craft Activities use classroom art activities to reinforce geometric principles as well as symmetry and sequencing.

Food Activities

The Food Activities focus on having children work with recipes to halve them and double them and to work with fractional and geometric concepts in creating food snacks.

Art Masters—Old and New

Art Masters - Old and New provides background information on Pablo Picasso, Georges Braque, and Liubov Popova, three artists who either inspired or were inspired by the Cubist art movement. Project directions give two different ways to explore Cubist art in the classroom.

Sharing Activities

The Sharing Events section provides several ideas for fun math-related events with a focus on helping children appreciate the importance of numbers in their daily lives and enjoying the numbers that they use every day.

Lesson Activities

Background Information

Most of the math activities in this chapter require no background information. In a few cases, limited information might be useful to refresh the memory or to serve as a quick resource on certain points. These areas are covered briefly below.

- **Three Ms**. In exploring numbers as suggested by some of the lesson activities described below, you may be able to cover the concepts of mode, mean and median. The mode is the number of each item that appears most often. For example, if a bag of colored candies contains two yellow candies, two green candies, two red candies, three brown candies, and four orange candies, the mode is two. The mean is the average number of individual things which is determined by adding up the number of things in each category and dividing this number by the total number of categories. The median is the number that occurs in the middle with an equal distribution of numbers greater and less than the median number.

- **Volume and Mass**. Volume (also called mass) is the amount of space something takes up. Weight is the manifestation of a mass in a given gravitational field. Hence, a person of a certain mass weighs more on Earth than he or she does on the moon where the gravitational pull is less. Mass is the only constant; it stays the same regardless of pressure or gravity.

- **Shapes Everywhere**. Children explore a variety of two dimensional shapes as part of math curriculum. There are shapes with no straight lines such as circles and ovals. There are three sided shapes and four sided shapes. Within the classification of four sided shapes, children can explore many different types of four-sided figures and analyze their similarities and differences. Some of the key two-dimensional shapes in this category to explore are:

Trapezoid: a four sided figure having only two parallel sides
Trapezium: a four sided figure having no two parallel sides
Parallelogram: a four sided figure with opposite sides parallel and equal in length
Rectangle: a parallelogram whose sides are all joined at right angles. All rectangles are parallelograms. Not all parallelograms are rectangles. A diamond is a parallelogram that is not a rectangle; it is a non-square parallelogram all of whose sides are the same length.
Rhombus: an equilateral parallelogram the angles of which are usually not right angles
Square: a parallelogram whose sides are all equal and which is composed entirely of right angles
Polygons such as hexagons and octagons are other two-dimensional shapes that older children explore.

There are also three-dimensional shapes to explore such as *spheres*, *pyramids*, *cylinders*, *cones*, *cubes* and *polyhedrons*.

Project Directions

1. Numbers Everywhere

This series of activities is designed to demonstrate to children just how much of the world is organized by mathematical principles. If they can begin to see numbers as more interesting than the rote memorization of addition, subtraction and multiplication facts, they may begin to value math more and see how important it is.

a. Numbers Survey

Give each child a copy of the Numbers Survey Activity Sheet at the end of this chapter. Have each child analyze his or her daily activities in terms of numbers. Ask children to talk to parents and ask how parents use numbers daily—checkbooks, purchases, driver's license numbers, vehicle license numbers, the child's social security number, job tasks. Ask them to think about the things they do each day—tasks in which they count, sort or organize by size and type. These tasks include sports scoring, games, clothing and bedroom organization. All these things involve math skills. Require that students find at least five numbers in each category. To encourage a thorough response, you might want to make a contest of the survey form with the children who come up with the most uses receiving small prizes.

When the survey is complete, have children pair up and compare the numbers they found. You might then talk about the survey results with the class as a whole. Finally, ask children to take a number that is part of their lives, such as an address or telephone number and make up five to ten equations or word problems that utilize the numerals in that number. Encourage students to create problems that use different operations on each side of the "equals" sign (e.g. 9 x 4 = (3 x 3) + (3 x 3) + 9 + 9).

Example:

333-0949
$3 + 3 + 3 = 3 \times 3$
$309 \div 3 =$
$4 + (3 \times 3) = 3 + 3 + 3 + 4$

You can complement this activity by using some of these same numbers as the source numbers for a number collage or a number picture. To make a numbers collage, children use the newspaper, magazines, scissors and paper to find or write and cut out specific numbers of their choice. Then they glue them to a sheet of paper in an artistic and abstract way of their own choosing.

b. Candy Bar Day

Ask each child to bring in his or her favorite candy bar (regular size, not a mini-bar from a bag) marked with his or her name. You can use them to explore the numbers used on the wrapper and what they mean as well as engage in some basic graphing exercises.

First, use the bars as an opportunity to have children explore how numbers are used on candy bar wrappers. This shows students just one example of how numbers are used on all food product packaging. The candy bars which seem to have the most thorough numerical information are those manufactured by Mars Co. and the Hershey Foods Corporation such as Snickers, Milky Way, and Hershey's bars. Numbers are used in a variety of ways on food packaging. In many candy bars, these ways include:

- Weight of the bar
- Serving information - i.e., serving size equals 1 bar
- Bar code with its attendant numbers that many cashiers now use to code price into their cash registers
- Caloric data
- Nutritional information - percentage of daily nutritional requirements.
- Legal information - 36 USC 380 refers to federal law
- Date before which bars should be eaten/sold
- Manufacturer's lot number to help with identification and recall when necessary

Children should explore this information and record it on the Candy Bar Numbers Activity Sheet at the end of this chapter. Children might want to work in pairs to do this since each candy bar will not necessarily provide the same information. If one child's bar has less information than some of the others, the partner's bar is likely to have more information so that both students get to fully explore these numbers.

Once this activity is complete, you might want to create a class pictograph using the wrappers to show the favorite candy bars among the students. Or you could create a class bar graph based upon the different weights of the candy bars.

Before enjoying the candy as a snack, consider using the candy as the basis of the art project described in Item 1 of the art and craft activities in this chapter.

c. Meal Planner

By doing restaurant or meal planning activities, children experience first-hand how often they and their families use math each day. This can be done in either of the ways suggested below.

- Have your class explore the concept of ordering a meal at a restaurant. To do this, ask a local restaurant if you can have enough take-out menus so that each child has one or can share. Have children order a meal from the menu and figure out how much it will cost. You might also have children figure tax and tip.

• Another idea is to ask children to plan a meal or snack and then try to figure out how much it would cost to buy the ingredients. To prepare for this activity, ask children to bring in the food sections from the local paper for several weeks before you plan to do the project. In this way, you should have handy a good selection of food advertisements.

Once children have decided on the snack or meal they want to prepare, they must think about the foods they will need to make this meal. Have them discuss with their parents food prices and ingredients for their chosen snack ahead of time. Once prepared, have students use the food section of the local newspaper for advertisements and "buy" the ingredients for their meal or snack based upon the prices in the advertisements in the newspaper. Let children know that they can modify their planned meal if they can find no advertisements or price information for the items they first chose. Pretty consistently, the food section will include advertisements for meats, produce and snack foods. This project would work well for cooperative learning groups. If some of the students have calorie counters at home, they could bring them in and try to figure out how many calories they would consume in the snack or meal of their choice.

2. Sets Within Sets

Help children understand that people sort and organize in their daily lives. Create sorting jars from which students can sort sets and subsets. For example, large jars can each be filled with several kinds of dry pastas, dry beans, paper clips, colored buttons and other small household objects. Let children take turns or work in groups to sort jar contents into sets and subsets. For example, ask children to sort within a set to create subsets, such as subsets of buttons. There are blue buttons and white buttons; there are square buttons and round buttons. There may be square blue buttons and round blue buttons. Have children think about how they are sorting the objects. What characteristic are they relying on to make their sorting decisions? As they sort, each child can keep a record of sorting and counting results. How much of each kind of thing is there?

An additional activity with these jars would be to use their contents to exercise the students' estimation skills. Fill differently sized jars to different levels with differently sized objects. Children estimate the number of items in the jar and check their answers. Ask a parent to help with the time-consuming task of counting contents. You might want to use small containers such as baby food jars, small Tupperware® containers or old yogurt containers so that the activity preparation can be completed more quickly than it can with larger containers.

3. Estimate

Have children explore the concept of estimation through some combination of the activities suggested here. Understanding the concept of estimating and learning to use the skill to approximate results can really help a child develop math confidence.

Estimating games can be used in many ways through the school year. The sorting jar concept described above is one such estimation skill game that can be used again and again. Have a different jar or different contents each week. Ask for parent help to supply the weekly guessing jars and counted contents.

Another easy estimation game is to pick designated spaces of different sizes and ask children to estimate how many students can fit in the space. Variations are standing students, seated students and prone students. After each child makes his estimate, the children see the space filled with students and students "count the contents" of the space.

With the specific estimating activities suggested below, children can also explore concepts of arithmetic mean (average) and mode as well as work on graphing skills. As the children do the investigations below, integrate some of these concepts. For example, children can find which color in a bag of Skittles® is the mode (the one that occurs most often) or the average number of pieces of candy by color.

a. How Many Candies in the Bag?

Using small bags of Skittles®, M&Ms®, Gummy Bears® or other small candies, ask children to work in groups or individually as they guess how many candies are in their bags and how many candies are of each color. (To save on expense you may want to use the mini-bags that are packed in larger bags for sale.) Skittles® are probably the preferred candy to use here since the additional factor of flavor can be explored. Children can engage in the bag exploration using the How Many - Estimate, Guess-timate! Activity Sheet at the end of this chapter.

The following sequence of activities is suggested but can be completed over several periods since the information needed for the later activities is recorded on the Activity Sheet in the initial investigation.

- The child estimates the total number of candies in his or her bag and the number of each color in his or her bag. The child's estimate is made using a combination of methods—touching, counting, multiplying and prior experience.
- The child then opens the bag and counts the actual number of total candies in the bag and the number of each color of candy in the bag.
- At this point make a class bar graph on the board or on butcher paper on the colors of the candies in the bags. To do this, list the colors on the board—green, yellow, red, orange, purple, etc. So that it goes quickly, ask each child to call out the number of each color of candy in his or her bag and record the information by tallies under the proper color column on the board. In this way you can quickly count up the total number of each color of candy. As an alternative, children can write their color information on the board as they complete their counting and sorting tasks. When you have the totals of each color, make the class bar graph of the color distribution of candies in the class.
- Now that the children know what the bar graph should look like, ask them to make a bar graph of the candy colors in their individual bags, this time using the Graph Paper Activity Sheet at the end of this chapter. If children are at an appropriate stage in their mathematical development, they could translate their bar graph results into a pie graph on the reverse side of the Graph Paper Activity Sheet.
- An additional activity is to have students work in cooperative groups of at least four students each to find averages (means), and modes of colors or numbers of candies for the group's bags.
- As a class, you might want to have children vote on their favorite flavors, assuming you

use Skittles® or some other small fruit flavored candy. You can make a class pictograph with this information. A pictograph is like a bar graph except that pictures are used to relay information. To do this you cut out construction paper circles in the appropriate fruit colors in advance. Children could draw an "S" in the middle of their colors and glue their Skittles® flavor on the appropriate line of the graph. If you have experimented with vertical graphs before, you may want to try a horizontal graph with this one, or vice versa.

b. Animal Cracker Activity

These same kinds of activities can be done with boxes of animal crackers or bags of Teddy Graham® crackers. In this version of the activity, children explore the numbers of crackers of each animal in their boxes (or the number of bears in a particular position—i.e., arms up, arms down, etc.). This is also a good math activity to use as an adjunct to life science explorations of animals and animal groups.

c. Is Your School Average?

Have children collect data on the number of children in different classes, the numbers of boys and girls in classes and any other information of interest and then determine average information for your school such as average class size, average number of boys and girls in classes, the median class in your school in terms of student ages/grades and the like. Use the Is Your School Average Activity Sheet at the back of this chapter.

4. Measure Meant for Kids

Measuring activities are fun for children and can be used at various ages to reinforce the importance of basic math skills in daily life. Children can do measurement in just metrics or in a combination of metrics and the customary system of inches, feet and yards.

a. Measurement Treasure Hunt

Have children go on different measurement treasure hunts. Tell the children they have to find and measure the lengths of different specified items around the room which you have previously identified and listed on the Measurement Treasure Hunt Activity Sheet at the back of this chapter. Measurement items can even be simple numbered strips of paper of varying lengths that you can cut out and tape around the room. You can give each child who completes the measuring activity a sticker or small token for their "treasure." This is a good free time activity for children to work on as they complete other work. It is also a good activity for children to do as pairs - the more advanced child can help the one struggling with measurement concepts.

For a greater challenge, have children measure in one method (e.g., inches) and then mathematically convert their inches to centimeters or vice versa. You can also use the measurement treasure hunt concept to have children find perimeters, circumferences, radii and square inches/centimeters of different items such as book covers, cupboard doors, globe bases and the like. The measurement treasure hunt concept can be used over and over again with different emphases depending on the math concepts being studied at any given time. Or, children can measure cut-outs of geometric shapes such as squares, circles and rectangles for which students need to find perimeters, area and circumference.

b. Measurement Olympics

Recreate the Olympics for your class with a measurement theme. Create about six events. Consider these ideas: 1) paper plate discus; 2) wrapping paper tube javelin; 3) standing broad jump; 4) hop-hop-hop triple jump (child does three jumps in a row to see how far from the starting position she or he can get); 5) "touch the wall" high jump; and 6) crushed tissue paper or newspaper shotput. Each child participates in each event.

Upon completion of each child's effort at an event, the child estimates the distance completed and then measures it. Children can record their results on the Measurement Olympics Activity Sheet at the back of this chapter. Measurement can be done in customary units and/or metric, as you choose. If your students' skill level permits, you could have them save their sheets after measuring in one system so they could mathematically convert their measured figures to the other system.

5. Weights and Measures

Try some activities that allow children to explore the concepts of weight, mass (or volume),

and density and to practice weighing. Here are some ideas:

a. Same Size, Different Weight

Using a cup (such as a measuring cup) as your vehicle of measurement, have children bring in a "cupful" of different things. These can be marshmallows, water, kitty litter, cotton balls, flour, hamster litter, sugar, peanuts, oatmeal, honey - whatever. You might ask some of the children to bring in cupfuls of items that, when combined, create a snack food such as Goodie Gorp described in the food activities section of this chapter. After children measure out a cupful of each item, ask them to estimate weight on the Looks the Same Activity Sheet at the back of this chapter. They then weigh each cupful and record the results for each item. Ask them why some things weigh more than others even though each has the same volume (i.e., takes up the same space).

b. Different Size, Same Weight

The inverse of the preceding project is to ask children to go on a one-pound or a half-kilogram shopping expedition at local grocery stores and/or hardware stores. Each child brings in one pound of something - flour, sugar, bananas, beans, nails, fiberfill, cotton balls. Again, as with the previous project, ask children why a pound of one thing has different volume than a pound of another thing. Conclude the activity by having children write their observations and conclusions in a written paragraph.

c. Let's Weigh It

Have children work in cooperative learning groups to use simple classroom scales. If you have simple balance scales, consider the following approach. Talk about how business was transacted before the advent of modern weights and measures. Purchases might have been made in a village marketplace by customers buying a stone of this and two stones of that. Have children create the measuring base for their scales and then weigh things on their scales. Perhaps they could even role-play marketplace activities. Each item in the measuring base, such as a small rock, should be nearly the same size as all the others so the measuring system "works" fairly and accurately. Children can "buy" small items such as buttons, paper clips, erasers and the like while other children weigh out the proper amount—i.e., "I'd like two stones of buttons, please."

6. Fraction Fun

Explore fractions in one of these ways:

a. Paper Plate Fractions

Using inexpensive paper plates, cut and label fraction shapes. For example, you cut the plate in half for halves, into six even pie-shaped pieces for sixths, and so on. Have enough sets so that children can overlay fraction pieces and thus understand in a hands-on way that four-eighths equals two-quarters equals one half. For a complete experience, children should be able to work with halves, quarters, eighths, thirds, sixths and twelfths. Have upper grade students make the paper plate fractions themselves and use them to work with lower grade children. This will reinforce fraction concepts for the older group and introduce the younger children to fraction concepts. Older students can invite lower grade children to a "Fun with Fractions Hour" and use the Fraction Fun Activity Sheet at the back of this chapter with the younger students. The upper grade children could even make up their own worksheets for the younger children to use.

Paper plate fractions are a great way to introduce and reinforce fraction concepts. They are especially helpful to children who are struggling with basic fraction concepts. If used by the older children as a teaching tool with younger students, the older child's understanding grows with the teaching experience.

b. Counting Musical Notes

Reading and playing music is based on counting fractional parts of whole notes. Explore fractions through music using 4/4 time. 4/4 time means that a quarter note gets one count and that there are four counts to the measure. The number of counts in the measure is the top number. Four counts to a whole note is indicated by the bottom number. Use the Counting Musical Notes Activity Sheet at the back of this chapter to introduce these counting and fraction concepts. Have some or all students clap out their sample measures. With younger children, do not develop the eighth note concept as it can get confusing.

As a closing activity, explore musical counting through class clapping and percussion exercises. This can be done as follows:

- Break the class into four groups.
- The first group "plays" a whole note by rolling their tongues or buzzing for four counts and repeating.
- The second group "plays" half notes with their fingers on the table hitting the table on alternating counts (i.e. counts 1 and 3).
- The third group "plays" a half note and a quarter note by making a humming sound. The half note hum is held for two counts, rest one count, hum one count, repeat sequence.
- The fourth group claps four quarter notes to each measure—1, 2, 3, and 4.

The rhythm looks like this in chart form.

If you have different percussion instruments available, you can give each of the four groups different instruments to use to make their rhythm sounds.

7. Shapes, Shapes Everywhere

Shapes are also part of math. They are the children's first introduction to geometric concepts. For younger children, explore the different kinds of shapes. Older children can also explore them in terms of types and subtypes or sets and subsets.

a. Shapes All Around Us

Have children take a shape survey of their homes or classrooms. After you have introduced the subject of two and three dimensional shapes, have children locate as many different basic geometric shapes as they can in the rooms and places they frequent everyday. Have children do shape surveys of their homes. They can list by rooms in their homes the shapes they see. You might limit them to two or three basic rooms to explore such as kitchen, bedroom or living room and bathroom. Ask children to think about which shapes appear most frequently. Why do you think this is? (Circles are useful tools when used as wheels; square corners are structurally strong.)

b. Geometry Puzzles

Using five or six wooden tongue depressors for each child, have children create their own geometry puzzles which they can reuse to reinforce the names and characteristics of geometric shapes. Each puzzle is made as follows:

- Lay five or six tongue depressors side by side to create a square or rectangular shape. Then run a strip of masking tape down each side to hold the puzzle pieces together. Children can work in pairs to do this.
- Using old gift boxes or lightweight posterboard, cut out a selection of geometric shapes appropriate to your math curriculum to be traced onto the puzzles. Ask a parent volunteer to do this at hone. The optimal situation if you are going to be making your puzzles all

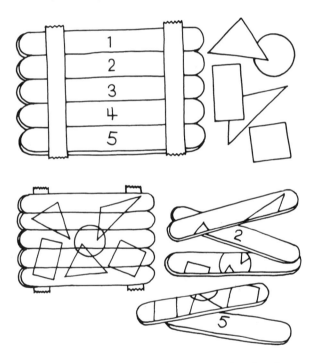

at the same time is to have enough of each shape so that each group of two or three children can share a complete set of the shapes you choose to use. Each shape should be between 1" and 2" in size.

- Children use pencils to trace shapes onto their puzzle form. Have them use all the shapes on their puzzle, but the arrangement of shapes is up to them. Also, remind them to try to place each shape so that part of it is on two different pieces of the puzzle. This makes putting the puzzle together more fun and interesting.

- Children can color in each shape using crayons or markers.
- Number the back of each puzzle piece so that the students can turn pieces over for guidance if they have difficulty putting their puzzles back together.
- Write the child's name on the back of each puzzle piece. Remove tape, mix up pieces and put the puzzle back together again. Give each child a rubber band to keep puzzle pieces together.

As children become experienced with their own puzzles, have them swap and try to put classmates' puzzles together. You can also have informal contests in which children compete against themselves or others to see how fast they can put a puzzle together.

c. Which Shape is Which?

Have children explore four-sided figures. How many different kinds or shapes are parallelograms? How many different kinds of trapezoids can they make? Give each child a sheet of graph paper on which to explore these shapes and classify them.

d. Grow a Geometry Garden

Third and fourth grade students may want to grow a geometry garden. Line one or two cookie sheets (with sides) or cookie sheet size gift box lids with foil. Place several layers of wet paper towel or 1/4" sponge on the bottom. Cover with a thin layer of potting soil. Cut large geometric shapes which you are studying out of paper and place them on your garden. They should be in the 4" to 6" size range depending upon shape.

After this preparation, planting begins. Use two types of fast sprouting seeds such as rye grass and alfalfa (available in health food stores) to grow your garden. Thickly sprinkle rye grass seed on the uncovered areas. Remove the paper shapes and sprinkle the shape areas with alfalfa seeds. Cover with a thin layer of potting soil. Water with the finger sprinkle method. Cover with plastic wrap for the first day or two. Then water and leave open. The geometric shapes should be visible within a couple of days, and the garden will look its best at about six to seven days after planting.

8. Banking Day

Have a banking day at school. You can use play money, but get real blank deposit and withdrawal slips from a local bank and make bank checks and mock bank books by photocopying the forms provided on the Banking Day Activity Sheets in this chapter. Have children pair up and role play acting as tellers and customers. Banking is one of the most basic ways we use math as adults. Tell children that they have each just received a $500 paycheck and that they must each deposit the check into a checking account. To do this, they explore the forms you give them from the local bank.

Follow this exercise up with a check writing activity that reinforces banking, writing and basic math skills. If you want to use the "Post Office" idea mentioned below as part of the banking day activities, ask for a student volunteer to make a cardboard box post office with a wide slot or make sure that you have allotted time for you or a helper to complete this project before your class Banking Day. Use the Shopping By Mail Activity Sheet in this chapter and have children engage in the activity as follows:

- Each child peruses the mail order catalog page on the Shopping By Mail Activity Sheet. He or she may spend up to the $500 in his or her checking account. Although in a real order all items ordered would be paid on one check, you might tell children to write a check for each item they order so that they get experience filling out the check and deducting (subtracting) from their checking accounts.
- When the child decides what to order, he or she writes a check for that amount and deducts the amount of the check from his or her activity sheet bankbook. If your students have the skills, you might want to have them figure tax and a percentage handling charge for their orders before they write their checks.
- Using the related writing activity suggested in Item 4 of the writing activities section of this chapter, the child completes his or her order and puts it in an envelope. Once addressed, the order is dropped in the class "post office" which is simply a box with a slot in it that sits by the teacher's desk.

9. Math "Jeopardy"

As a fun classroom exercise which you may want to repeat from time to time throughout the year, play a math version of the television game show "Jeopardy." The teacher gives an answer such as "56" and children raise hands with the answer "What is 7 x 8?" You can limit the children's answers to equations using addition, subtraction, multiplication or division or require that they use a combination to come up with an answer. As an added game component, you could use plus, minus, times, and divided by as categories. Children pick a category and must come up with a question using that operation. This game can be played at any skill level. The class can be divided into groups to play or students can take turns playing against each other.

You can even turn this into a pencil and paper game by requiring that students give you a division question for larger numbers. As an example, in response to the answer "56" a child could answer "What is 1336 divided by 6?" The teacher can quickly check the equation questions with a calculator. This version of the oral game improves children's facility with numbers and their understanding about how multiplication and division functions relate.

10. Mental Math

Another classroom math activity that can be effectively used in small increments of time such as five to fifteen minutes is "mental math." Simply make up word problems that use a variety of math functions with which your students are familiar. The children try to figure them out in their heads and raise their hands to give the answers. If a child gives the correct answer, ask him or her to explain the answer.

Writing Activities

Written exercises explore math through geometric shape, numbers of lines and meter.

1. Chapter Vocabulary

The following are some math-based words to include in regular vocabulary or to use for a theme-related vocabulary exercise.

Survey
Graph
Pictograph
Pie graph
Bar graph
Line graph
Percentage
Serving size
Bar code
Advertisement
Set
Subset
Estimate
Arithmetic mean
Mode
Average
Median
Customary system of weights and measures
English system of weights and measures
Metric system of weights and measures
Weight
Measure
Plane
Timeline
Cube
Cone
Cylinder
Triangle
Circle
Square
Rectangle
Rhombus
Trapezoid
Parallelogram
Fraction
Volume
Mass
Tangram
Symmetry
Sequence
Cubism

2. Explore Geometric Poetry

Choose a topic area that dovetails with some study area. Ask children to write a diamond poem or a word circle.

a. Diamond Poem

The diamond poem is so called because it has five lines with an increasing and then diminishing syllable or word count. You can also use this exercise to have children explore certain parts of speech by requiring them to use adjectives, adverbs, sentences, etc. in the appropriate number of words or syllables for certain lines.
Examples:

Word Count Diamond Poem
Line 1 - One Word (topic word)
Line 2 - Two Words
Line 3 - Three Words
Line 4 - Two Words
Line 5 - One Word (synonym for topic word or general adjective)

or

Line 1 - One or Two Words
Line 2 - Fours Words
Line 3 - Eight Words
Line 4 - Four Words
Line 5 - One or Two Words

Examples:

Flowers
Daisies, Roses
All different colors
Smell Nice
Lovely

Autumn
Leaves turn.
Cold winds blow.
Leaves fall.
Changes

Wind
Blow cold and icy
Howls in the valleys and over hills
Harsh child of winter
Frightens me

Syllable Count Diamond Poem
Line 1 - One or two syllables
Line 2 - Three or four syllables
Line 3 - Eight syllables
Line 4 - Three or four syllables
Line 5 - One or two syllables

My home
I like my home.
My family is there for me.
We play games.
They care.

The sun
helps flowers grow
as its golden rays fall to earth
and spread warmth.
Shine on.

b. Word Circle

A word circle is a writing project through which children can explore the multiple meanings of words and/or free association of words in a "geometric" framework. First the student or teacher picks a topic word. Then, in eight to ten sentences the students go from that word to others and back again by stating that one word reminds them of another and so on.
Examples:

Thanksgiving reminds me of eating turkey.
Eating turkey reminds me of stuffing.
Stuffing reminds me of pillows.
Pillows remind me of night time.
Night time reminds me of sleep.
Sleep reminds me of dreams.
Dreams remind me of wishes.
Wishes remind me of Christmas.

Christmas reminds me of eating turkey.
Eating turkey reminds me of Thanksgiving.

Pioneers remind me of covered wagons.
Covered wagons remind me of bumpy rides.
Bumpy rides remind me of amusement parks.
Amusement parks remind me of hot dogs.
Hot dogs remind me of catsup.
Catsup reminds me of tomatoes.
Tomatoes remind me of farms.
Farms remind me of farmers.
Farmers remind me of hard work.
Hard work reminds me of pioneers.

A word circle can be written in a circular format starting at the center of the circle and writing in a spiral shape until complete.

3. Number Stories

Ask children to write a story using certain numbers such as one through five or one through ten. In plotting the story the child needs to use each number at least once. The story could be structured like a children's counting book or it could be a story that employs different numbers as part of the plot, such as a sports story that involves scoring or a fanciful story like the example below. If children want to create counting books, have them write and illustrate them, bind them with a binding machine and donate the completed books to the school kindergarten or preschool. This math-based literary project could then also serve as a service project.

Example: (using numbers 1 through 10)

Once upon a time there was a princess who owned one beautiful silver necklace. Her father gave it to her before he died and told her never to take it off. The princess also had ten gray cats and lived in a castle haunted by two witches.
The witches wanted the necklace and tried three different plans to get it. The first time they tried to get it, they sent four bats to the princess's castle to pluck the necklace from her neck while she slept, but the windows were closed. The bats failed. The next time they sent five mice to steal the necklace from her neck, but the castle workmen had just boarded up all the mouse holes so the mice could not get it. The last time the witches sent six spiders to drop from the ceiling and steal the necklace. They failed

too, when the castle cleaning woman swept them away with her broom.

At this point the witches gave up. One cried seven tears and the other cried eight tears in sorrow. But then they heard about a prince in the next county who had a silver belt buckle with nine diamonds on it. They decided to move to his castle and come up with devious plans to steal the buckle. In the meantime, the princess lived happily ever after with her one silver necklace and her ten gray cats.

4. Shopping by Mail

Use the Banking Day Activity Sheet activities in this chapter as an opportunity to reinforce letter writing skills, including envelope addressing. Each child writes a letter to the mail order company to enclose his or her order, addresses the envelope, stuffs it with the letter and check and drops it off in the classroom post office.

5. Recipe Writer

Ask children to think about a favorite simple snack and use it as the basis for this writing exercise. The snack can be anything from a peanut butter sandwich to a boiled egg to a bowl of popcorn. First, the child thinks about the ingredients necessary to make the treat and how much of each ingredient is needed. After this is done and written down, the child must think about all the utensils necessary to make the food, the steps taken in the proper sequence to prepare it and how many servings the recipe makes. At this point the child writes step by step directions on how to make the snack. In this project, children think about amounts, measuring, and sequencing.

An alternative but similar writing project is to have children create a recipe for the "perfect" candy bar. Again, they must identify ingredients, amounts, how many servings the recipe makes, and the step by step directions. Make sure they remember to name their new candy bar. This may be the part they enjoy the most.

6. 1-4-2 Couplets

Have children use iambic form to write poetry couplets. These are two lined poems with a meter and count that goes like this:

—/—/—/—/

—/—/—/—/

Ask children to use at least one number as a word that is part of the poem.
Example:

I saw six cats go walking by.
I called "hello" but they were shy.

While this example is a form of iambic tetrameter, trimeter or pentameter could also be used.

7. Travel Itinerary

Starting from the city you're in, have students choose a destination in another part of the United States or any other place to which they can travel by car and write an itinerary for their car trip. To do this they will figure out how many miles they will travel each day before stopping, where they will stop and how many days overall it will take them to get to their destination. This written project can be short, only a paragraph or so, but it should incorporate the information described above. This project involves map reading skills, mathematical calculation based upon vehicle speed and writing skills.

8. Place an Ad

Have children peruse the newspaper classified sections to see how advertisements for selling homes, cars, or pets are written. Have them think about all the mathematical things that can be included in such ads in addition to price. For example, for houses, these things include number of rooms - baths, bedrooms, square footage, distance to local schools or parks. For pets, information may include how many puppies/kittens are for sale, how many weeks/months old the animals are, when to call, and the phone number to call. Have them write an advertisement to sell an imaginary home or their own home, a car, or a pet that includes at least four characteristics that use numbers.

Art and Craft Activities

1. Candy Bar Sequence Drawing

If you have a candy bar day as suggested in the lesson activities section of this chapter, you might want to include this art project as part of that day's activities. It allows children to create a series of pencil drawings in sequence to show the process of eating a candy bar. This is a relatively time-consuming project. The art can be created in three or four stages as you choose. For example, the first picture is of the unopened candy bar, the second picture is of the end opened and one bite gone, the third picture is with more paper torn away and the bar half gone, the last picture is with the bar gone and the paper wrapper left. The child should create each picture in the series on a square of white paper 4" to 6" square or on a three by five card.

At each stage in the opening and eating process the child stops to create one complete picture. Tell children to try to be thorough. Ask them to create a picture not on what they assume the candy bar looks like; they should draw exactly the shapes they see. If they really do this, the drawing at each stage will take time, but the finished project is quite rewarding to the child who finds that his or her drawing looks much more realistic than his or her usual creations. Children as young as second grade can achieve excellent results with this project. Children should mount the finished pictures in sequence on a larger length of construction paper.

2. String Pictures

This project is sometimes called "space spiders." Give each child a 4" to 6" square of black construction paper and a square of graph paper the same size. The graph paper is glued to the construction paper. On the graph paper the child plots dots at a right angle for two sides of a square that fits within the confines of the paper (about three squares in from the edge). Then using needle and bright colored thread (heavy thread such as embroidery thread works best) the student begins by connecting the last dot of the line on one side of the angle with the dot closest to the

corner on the other line. The next thread connects the next to the last dot on the first line with the dot next out from the corner on the second line and so on.

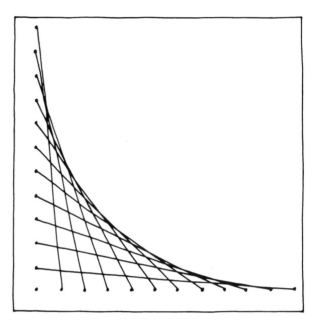

This process should be illustrated on the blackboard before you begin so children get the idea before they start. This striking art project helps children see how circles are formed geometrically since the completed picture will form the arc of a circle. Children can make a complete circle if you are so inclined and have available class time. Or they can make several arcs of different sizes.

3. Multiple Patterns

Using the Math Patterns Activity Sheet in this chapter, have children use different math patterns to create designs. For example, what design do they get if they color every tenth number blue? What if they color every third number green? This can be done for every combination 2 through 10. If each child completes each pattern on a separate sheet it can be kept and referred to from time to time to reinforce multiplication skills.

4. Butterfly Symmetry

Symmetry is the correspondences of parts, designs and color on opposite sides of a center line. This is a mathematical concept that has many examples in nature. Butterflies, insects and people are all obviously symmetrical. Have children make butterflies with symmetrically designed wings to explore this concept. Some ways to do this are:

a. Window Butterflies

Children fold paper in half to cut out the double-winged basic butterfly shape. With butterfly still folded, they then cut out shapes in the wing areas. When the butterfly is unfolded the open spaces on each side mirror each other. Tape colored pieces of cellophane, tissue paper or multiple layers of colored plastic wrap into the corresponding part of each wing and tape butterflies to your windows.

b. Geometric Butterflies

Have children fold black sheets of paper to cut out a double-winged butterfly shape. Using bright colored construction paper scraps, have them cut out pairs of geometric shapes - circles, diamonds, squares, trapezoids and the like. They open the butterfly wings and glue one set of shapes to one wing in a pattern and glue the other set symmetrically on the other wing.

c. Squish Butterflies

Children cut out a symmetrical butterfly shape. They dot tempera paint in colors of their choice on one wing, press the wings together and press all surfaces of the wing so that the paint is "squished" and transferred to the second wing. Open wings and let symmetrically painted butterfly dry.

5. Number faces

Have children create faces with crayon or marker using only numbers to create the pictures. For example, zeros are the eyes, a "7" is the nose and a series of "3s" is the mouth. These pictures have a silly look that children enjoy.

6. Reflecting With Numbers

Have each child decide on several numbers of significance in his or her life. A good choice for numbers is the child's month, day and year of birth. On a 9" x 12" paper folded in half the long

way, children create mirror images of the numbers they choose and then color them in to make a design. On one side of the fold, the child writes his chosen numbers in black crayon. The child must press hard to make the numbers very dark. Then the paper is folded closed and the child presses both sides together (again, very hard) so that some of the crayon markings are transferred to the other side of the fold line. The child then goes over these faint markings to reinforce them. The child can then color in the design. Encourage her to explore symmetrical color patterns. The child should color the corresponding parts of the picture on each side of the fold in the same way so the entire picture is symmetrical when completed.

This same project can be done using the children's names written in cursive.

7. Triangle or Tangram Time

Each child takes a square sheet or two (approximately 8" square) of colored construction paper. The child then folds the paper until he or she has outlined squares of about 2" in size. They cut out their squares as neatly as possible and then cut each square in half diagonally to create triangles. All the triangles can be put into a pot and children can choose as many triangles as they cut out to create an animal or other triangle picture. Children explore shapes and how they combine to make other shapes through this art project.

Older children might want to explore the possibilities in the old Chinese tangram puzzle using the Chinese Tangram Puzzle Activity Sheet in this chapter. The puzzle designs on the puzzle activities sheet have solutions shown on the answer key at the back of this book.

8. My Timeline

Teach children about time and chronology by having each child create a personal timeline on a 6" x 18" sheet of construction paper. First, explain what a timeline is by drawing one of your own on the blackboard. Then ask students to create their own timelines showing key dates in their lives. Students can also illustrate the key dates with pictures.

9. Dot-to-Dot Art

Each child starts with a piece of white paper. The children in the class count off and each gets a number. Each child writes his or her number in a random location on the paper of every other child in the class. When each child's paper has all the numbers, the child connects the dots (in a 1, 2, 3 fashion). After the dot-to-dot picture is completed, the child colors in the picture. The result is an abstract, fun picture.

10. Newspaper Numbers Collage

Have children explore the newspaper and magazines and cut out as many numbers as they can find. This will include advertisements, dates, stock reports, sports scores and weather information. Have children use the numbers to make a number collage on bright-colored construction paper. This activity helps children appreciate the diverse ways in which numbers are used in the newspaper and also to become familiar with the different sections of the newspaper.

11. Geometry Picture

Each child chooses a single geometric shape (triangle, rectangle, etc.). He or she then cuts out the shape from colored paper in any variation of the shape and as many times as he or she chooses. The students glue the shapes to another piece of paper to create a picture.

Food Activities

1. Let's Double Up Twice

Have children quadruple the ingredients to a recipe. Before you decide upon who will bring what ingredients, tell children that the recipe will need to be doubled and doubled again to feed the class. Have them determine what proportions will be necessary. You can use this idea with any recipe, but consider using it with this or a similar punch recipe:

x4 Fruity Floats
2 cups of a favorite cranberry juice drink
1 cup of orange juice or lemonade
2 cups of lemon-lime soda
1 pint orange sherbet
Mix first three ingredients in punch bowl quadrupled in amount as discussed above. Spoon scoops of sherbet into each glass and fill with punch. Serve in large cups with spoons.

Another recipe doubler you might try is one for making snack mix or granola, but in this case the children are merely doubling the recipe included below. Some of the ingredients could be brought to class as part of lesson activity Item 5a described earlier in this chapter.

Goodie Gorp
2 cups small animal-shaped snack crackers such as tiny bear graham crackers or a bite-sizes breakfast cereal of choice
2 cups mini-marshmallows
1 cup flaked coconut
2 cups honey-coated nuts or unsalted nuts
1 cup raisins
1 cup chocolate buttons
Mix all ingredients in a very large bowl. Serve up in five ounce cups.

2. Cut It Down

The inverse way of having children adjust recipes is to have them cut a recipe in half. Again, this can be done with any recipe you choose, but here's a good chocolate chip cookie recipe for halving. When halved, it should bake up one oversized cookie for each child, or several smaller ones.

Chocolate Chip Plus Cookies

2 12-ounce bags of chocolate chips
2 six-ounce bags of butterscotch chips
3 cups vegetable shortening or margarine
2 cups granulated sugar
1 cup brown sugar, packed
6 eggs
3 teaspoons vanilla
7 cups flour
3 teaspoons baking soda
3 teaspoons salt

Children halve the ingredients. Preheat oven. Mix shortening and sugars until smooth. Add eggs and vanilla and beat until smooth. Add dry ingredients and stir slowly. Add chips and mix. Drop by heaping tablespoons onto greased cookie tray. Bake at 375 degrees ten to fifteen minutes or until lightly brown.

3. Quarter Creatures

Each child receives a small paper plate, a plastic serrated knife, one quarter of an orange, a trimmed stalk of celery, a square slice of American sandwich cheese and his or her choice of decorator items so long as the child takes four of each item chosen. The decorator items can be olives, peanuts, mini-marshmallows, chips and the like. The child must cut the celery in quarters and the cheese into four equal pieces by cutting the whole first in half and then each piece in half again. Once this is completed and the child has chosen his or her decorator items, the child is free to create a creature with his chosen food on his paper plate. Everything used is in multiples of four or, as with the orange, a quarter of a whole or one of four.

4. Cylinder Sandwiches

The crust is trimmed off enough slices of bread so that there is one slice of bread for each child. Each slice is buttered lightly on one side with soft margarine. (This step can be omitted if your cream cheese mixture is very spreadable.) Mix four eight-ounce packages of softened or whipped cream cheese with one/half cup diced black olives or chopped pimiento, as you choose. Add a tiny bit of milk or water if necessary to thin the mixture so children can spread it. Spread a layer of cream cheese mixture on each slice of bread. Roll it up and toothpick it closed in two spots. The shape of the resulting sandwich is a cylinder.

You might decide to have a sandwich day and do at least one other geometric sandwich such as a triangle sandwich. Perhaps the triangle sandwiches could be peanut butter and jelly.

Ask children if anyone would like to take home the leftover crusts to feed to a pet or wild birds. Encourage them not to view food projects as creating unnecessary waste.

5. Domino Treats

Using a double batch of your favorite brownie recipe or two mixes, make brownies that the children turn into dominos with miniature chocolate or other chips and a contrasting color of frosting. Perhaps the easiest way to do this is to ask two parents to each bring in one batch of brownies cut into rectangles like a real domino shape. Then the children can frost and decorate their dominos as a food activity. Remind them that a domino has two numbers represented by dots, one on each half of the domino.

This activity can also be done using graham crackers and regular sized chips or mini-marshmallows as you choose. If you use marshmallows, use chocolate frosting for contrast.

Art Masters—Old and New

The art master lessons in this section relate to students' exploration of geometric mathematical concepts. Children will explore the Cubist style of art prevalent in the early 1900s.

Background Information

The art master lesson for this chapter focuses on the Cubist style of painting as an extension of some of the geometric issues that come up in math. The Cubists were a group of painters in the early 1900s led by Pablo Picasso and Georges Braque who saw their subjects in terms of a multitude of flat planes. As they viewed their models and transferred them to canvas, they elongated, stretched or otherwise changed the shape and order of the planes they saw. A famous Russian female painter, Liubov Popova, also spent part of her career exploring this artistic style.

1. Pablo Picasso

Picasso was born in Spain in the late 1800s. During his long career he explored many different artistic styles and was an accomplished artist in many media. He, along with French painter, Georges Braque, pioneered the style of art called Cubism. It flourished in the early part of the 1900s and influenced many modern painters of this century.

2. Georges Braque

Braque was born in France in 1882 and became a leading proponent of the Cubist style of art along with his artistic peer, Pablo Picasso. He was also an early creator of collages. Sometimes he painted with textures that simulated wood and stone surfaces. The geometric designs of African wood carvings and sculptures influenced his work.

3. Liubov Popova

Popova was born in Russia. She used dramatic colors and geometric shapes to explore and expand the Cubist style of painting she often used. She became a leading Russian painter in the Cubo-futurist style. Before women became artistic leaders in Europe and America, she gained stature as a leading artist in Russia during an artistic movement that helped restructure the roles of men and women.

Project Directions

1. Cubist Still Life

A still life is a picture of a group of objects such as flowers, fruit, vases, writing instruments and paper, and so on. Use this project to help children see how a Cubist painter viewed his subject or subjects and twisted the spatial relationships of each of their parts.

Place a basic still life composition (such as a large bowl of fruit) in view of the children. Tell children that, while they may draw the entire bowl of fruit on their paper, they may also focus on just part of the fruit bowl. Before beginning, remind children that the picture must be drawn largely so that the bowl and its fruit fill most of the paper. Remind them to draw from the model, not just what they think the bowl looks like. If a child creates too small a picture the project will not be effective, so ask those whose focus is too small to turn the paper over and start again, this time drawing large images.

On a 9" by 12" page of white construction paper, have each child draw his still life in pencil. Then he or she colors the picture in with crayon. Make sure that the child draws a table line into the picture to show that the bowl and the fruit are sitting on a table rather than flying in space. Suggest that they fill in the background with color as well. Then the child folds his picture in half and in half again, up to a total of four times so that, when opened, the picture is divided into eight or sixteen folded rectangles. The child then cuts on the fold lines. Once cut, the picture is reassembled in an abstract way on top of another sheet of white construction paper 9" x 12" in size. Perhaps children want to put the pieces down on the second sheet with the drawn sides facing down so that they are not tempted to put the picture back together the "regular" way. Once all the pieces are on the page face down, they are turned over and the child sees his or her "Cubist" work. After adjusting the order of the pieces modestly as desired, the pieces are glued down to the second sheet and the "Cubist" work is complete.

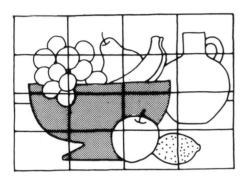

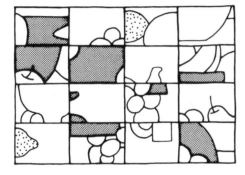

2. Cubist Portrait

This is a little more advanced way to explore the Cubist style, but it is truer to the original artistic endeavors of the Cubist painters. Cubists saw their subjects in terms of flat planes. When they painted the subjects, they altered the shape of each plane so that a geometric, abstract look resulted. Best results will be had with older elementary children as this is a little more difficult to recreate.

Your students can explore this in the following way. Have students think about the structure of a face in terms of individual planes or areas. Starting with a 9" by 12" sheet of white construction paper, children fold the paper in half the long way. Children then unfold the paper and, holding the paper so the long side is vertical, fold it in thirds horizontally. Students draw a portrait using the entire sheet. In the top third the forehead, hair and eyes (at the bottom of this third) are depicted. In the central third of the page symmetrically from the mid-line, the cheeks, ears and nose are

drawn. In the bottom third of the sheet, the mouth, chin and neck are drawn. The face should fill the page with only about a 1" to 2" border around the edges. This drawing will serve as the child's model as he attempts to divide the face into five or six planes or areas and alter them in some fashion for the final product.

Give each child a second sheet of 9" x 12" white construction paper. Again the paper should be lightly folded or marked in the six equal parts into which the first sheet was divided. Looking at the planes or facial areas he identified on the first sketch, the child draws each of those six areas on the second sheet of paper in a slightly different shape (and perhaps place) than that part of the face appeared in the first sketch. Each plane or facial area has angular edges. When each plane of the face has been reconstructed in pencil on the second sheet of paper, then the child can color the Cubist portrait in with watercolor, chalk or crayon, as you choose. As the child places each part of the face on the second sheet of paper, remind him or her that the eyes, nose and mouth may be moved out of order.

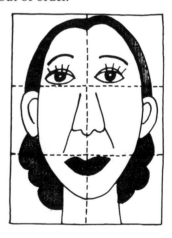

Sharing Activities

1. Bingo Party

Plan a bingo party for an afternoon (or evening) with your class and invite the parents. Use one of the commercial mathematics bingo games as the basis for your event. They come in versions for addition, subtraction, multiplication and division. You could also ask parents to bring snacks and drinks to make a real party out of it.

2. Game Day

Many games that children play at home have a mathematics component. Set aside a day in which children bring a game from home that can be played at a game "hour" on game day. Each child has to explain to the class how math is involved in playing the game he or she brings to school. (You can make this explanation a writing activity in which children explain in a paragraph how math concepts and math skills are used in playing the game. This could be done as homework.) Only those games that use math qualify for game day. Also, depending upon the number and types of games brought in, you might choose several of the most math oriented games to be played or have the class vote on which games to play. Any games that are not played could be displayed with the text written by the student explaining how math is used in playing the game.

3. Fundraiser Fun

To reinforce counting skills and particularly money counting skills, your class might want to sponsor a "penny project" for your school. The object of a penny project is to have students bring in pennies and other small coins for a week to raise money for a chosen cause, such as an environmental organization or other worthy group. Before the project begins, your students deliver a shoebox, oatmeal carton or plastic container to each participating class and explain the project to the other class asking those students to participate. Students in each class deposit their pennies each day in these containers. Your students collect the contributions from each class each morning and count them. The classroom will sing with the sound of coins as this project gets underway and the children will gain valuable experience from sponsoring the event and handling the money.

4. Math Day

Have your class act as the host for a Math Day in which another class visits your room to participate in math-related fun stations. Some of these might be:

a. Number Patterns Station

The project at this station is the one described in the art and craft activities section of this chapter. The Math Patterns Activity Sheet is included in the back of this chapter. The host students encourage visitors to try different patterns.

b. Paper and Pencil Game Station

Another station could be one in which students complete geometric shapes such as squares using the Pencil and Paper Square Game Activity Sheet at the back of this chapter. Played by two children, each takes turns connecting dots. The object in connecting dots is to complete squares. If you complete a square, you can claim it with your initial regardless of who started the square. The child who completes the most squares wins.

c. Three-D Shapes Station

Children build three dimensional geometric shapes such as cubes and pyramids using toothpicks and miniature marshmallows.

d. Number Memory Game Station

One or two children in your class could make number memory games to play with visitors. Each game set is made as follows: Cut fifteen three by five cards in half. Number each set of cards 1 through 15 or with related math facts or equations and answers (e.g. 8 x 7 and 7 x 8; 8 x 7 and 56; 2 x 6 and 4 x 3). The cards are placed face down randomly and players take turns turning over pairs of numbers to find matches. If a player makes a match, he or she gets the pair and gets another turn. The player who gets the most pairs wins. This game can also be played using regular playing cards. To do this take the number cards from each of two suits and use them as the number cards to be matched. The numbers are the same; only the suits are different.

e. Tangram Station

Have children work with matching tangram designs at this station. The materials can be made using posterboard or construction paper and the Chinese Tangram Puzzle Activity Sheet in this chapter.

f. Buzz Game

Have children play the buzz game in pairs. As they count they say buzz when they get to a multiple of a given number such as three, four or five. Once one person says buzz, it is the other person's turn to count until he or she reaches a number to "buzz" on. This game can also be played with students saying "buzz" on any number that contains a chosen number such as 7 or 5.

g. 1 to 10 Games

This game requires 10 small square cards, numbered 1 through 10, and two dice. The child can play against him- or herself or with a partner. The cards are laid on the table face up. The object is to roll the dice and use the resulting two numbers to create a math equation that will equal a number from 1 to 10. If the player can come up with an equation using the numbers showing on the two dice, then he can take the number card that is the result of the equation. For example, all the cards are up and the dice roll is 6 and 3; the player says "6 minus 3 equals 3" and takes the "3" card. If the player cannot come up with an equation to equal a number left, then he or she gets no card and it is the other person's turn. If the child is playing against him- or herself, he or she tries to see how few turns he or she can take to remove all the number cards. If he plays against another person, the winner is the one with the most number cards.

h. Fraction Station

Have one station based on the paper plate fraction activity described in the lesson activities section of this chapter.

5. Math Bee

Hold a math bee with your class. Run it like a spelling bee but use math equations. Give equations appropriate to your students' level. They can answer them on the board if necessary, but it is preferable to use the math bee to encourage students to work out problems mentally. The bee can be done as a way to reinforce multiplication tables, addition/subtraction math facts, or more complex word problems. Give children a five to ten second limit to come up with the answer, depending upon the type and complexity of equations used.

Name: _____

Numbers Survey

1. List personal numbers of family members such as age, height, weight, driver's license number, birthdate, social security number, and the like. Use only those personal numbers your family chooses to list. _____

_____

_____

_____

_____

2. List home numbers such as telephone number, address, clocks, games, number of rooms in house, dials, appliances, electronics, etc. _____

_____

_____

_____

_____

3. List car/vehicle numbers such as license plate, speedometer, odometer, radio dial, mileage gauges, make and year of car, serial number, etc. _____

_____

_____

_____

_____

4. List school numbers such as room, grade, clocks, number of students, desks, work areas, play areas, and the like. _____

_____

_____

_____

_____

Name: _____

Candy Bar Numbers

1. Weight: _____
_____

2. Serving information: _____
_____

3. Bar code numerals: _____
_____

4. Price: _____
_____

5. Calories: _____
_____

6. Nutritional information: _____
_____

7. Legal information: _____
_____

8. Date: _____
_____

9. Lot number: _____
_____

10. Other numbers: _____
_____

Name: _____

How Many - Estimate, Guess-timate!

1. How many total candies are in the bag?

Estimate   **Actual**

_____   _____

2. How many candies are the color   **Estimate**   **Actual**

a. _____ ?   _____   _____

b. _____ ?   _____   _____

c. _____ ?   _____   _____

d. _____ ?   _____   _____

e. _____ ?   _____   _____

f. _____ ?   _____   _____

In the next section, you will need to work in cooperative groups. Working with your group, find the following:

3. What is the average number (arithmetic mean) of candies in a bag? _____

4. What is the average number of a particular color of candy in a bag? _____

5. Is there a color of candy that occurs most often in your bag? If so, it is the mode color. What color is it?

_____

6. Pretend your group has 6 bags of candy. In 3 bags, red candy appears most often. In 1 bag, yellow candy appears most often. In 2 bags, green candy appears most often. What would the mode color in these bags be?

_____

7. Is there a mode color of candy for the bags in your group? If so, what is it?

_____

Is Your School Average?

Total number of students in school   _____

Total number of boys in school   _____

Total number of girls in school   _____

Total number of classes in school   _____

Find the average number of students in a class   _____

      the average number of boys in a class   _____

      the average number of girls in a class   _____

Total number of students, boys and girls in your classroom.

Room	Total Number of Students	Total Number of Boys	Total Number of Girls

How does your class compare to the school averages?

_____

_____

Can you think of some other averages to find in your school? Use the reverse side of this paper to find another average in your school, such as the average number of desks or chairs in each classroom.

_____

_____

Is there a median grade in your school? If so, what is the median grade in your school?

_____

_____

Name: _____

Measurement Treasure Hunt

What to Measure	Customary System Inches	Metric System Centimeters
1. _____	_____	_____
2. _____	_____	_____
3. _____	_____	_____
4. _____	_____	_____
5. _____	_____	_____
6. _____	_____	_____
7. _____	_____	_____
8. _____	_____	_____
9. _____	_____	_____
10. _____	_____	_____

Name: _____

CHAPTER 2
ACTIVITY SHEET

Measurement Olympics

	Estimate	Actual
1. Paper Plate Discus	_____	_____
2. Wrapping Paper Roll Javelin	_____	_____
3. Touch-the-Wall High Jump	_____	_____
4. Hop-Hop-Hop Triple Jump	_____	_____
5. Standing Broad Jump	_____	_____
6. Crushed Paper Shot Put	_____	_____

Name: _____

Looks the Same . . .

	Estimated Weight	Actual Weight

One cup of:

1. _____ _____ _____

2. _____ _____ _____

3. _____ _____ _____

4. _____ _____ _____

5. _____ _____ _____

6. _____ _____ _____

7. _____ _____ _____

8. _____ _____ _____

9. _____ _____ _____

10. _____ _____ _____

Name: ____________________

CHAPTER 2
ACTIVITY SHEET

Fraction Fun

1. _____ 1/2s make a whole circle.

   How many 1/8s in 1/2 circle? _____

   How many 1/4s in a 1/2 circle? _____

2. _____ 1/4s make a whole circle.

   How many 1/8s in 1/4 circle? _____

   How many 1/8s in 3/4 circle? _____

3. _____ 1/8s make a whole circle.

   2/8s is the same as _____

   2/4s is the same as how many 1/8s? _____

4. _____ 1/3s make a whole circle.

   How many 1/6s in 1/3 circle? _____

   How many 1/6s are the same as 4/8s? _____

5. _____ 1/6s make a whole circle.

   How many 1/6s in 2/3 circle? _____

   How many 1/6s in 1/2 circle? _____

6. _____ 1/12s make a whole circle.

   How many 1/12s in 2/3 circle? _____

   How many 1/12s in 3/4 circle? _____

**CHAPTER 2
ACTIVITY SHEET**

Counting Musical Notes

1. $\frac{4}{4}$ This is a _____ note. It has _____ counts.

2. $\frac{4}{4}$ These are _____ notes. Each note has _____ counts.

3. $\frac{4}{4}$ These are _____ notes. Each note has _____ count.

4. $\frac{4}{4}$ These are _____ notes. Each note has _____ count.

Sample musical measures. Can you clap them out?

Make up three measures of musical notes in 4/4 time.

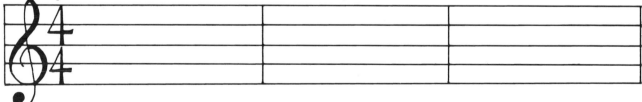

Name: _____

Banking Day - Checks

Three blank check forms

Name: _____   No. _____

Address: _____   Date: _____, 19___

         _____

Pay to the order of _____ $ _____

_____ dollars.

Memorandum _____   _____

                                              Signature

Account No. _____

Name: _____   No. _____

Address: _____   Date: _____, 19___

         _____

Pay to the order of _____ $ _____

_____ dollars.

Memorandum _____   _____

                                              Signature

Account No. _____

Name: _____   No. _____

Address: _____   Date: _____, 19___

         _____

Pay to the order of _____ $ _____

_____ dollars.

Memorandum _____   _____

                                              Signature

Account No. _____

Name: _____

Banking Day - Checkbook Record

Balance Forward _____

Date	Check Number	Description of Transaction	Payment/ Debit (-)	Deposit (+)	Balance

Name: _____

Shopping by Mail

Catalog

Item No.	Item Description	Price
01	Tennis Racket	$38.00
02	Baseball Glove	21.00
03	Baseball Bat	27.00
04	Roller Skates	29.00
05	Roller Blades	42.00
06	Camera - 110	15.00
07	Camera - 35mm	53.00
08	Digital Watch	18.00
09	Walkman	39.00
10	Video Game	23.00

Order Form

Item No.	Quantity	Description	Price

Total Order _____

Tax (5%) _____

Handling fee (7%) _____

Total Due _____

**CHAPTER 2
ACTIVITY SHEET**

Math Patterns

1	2	3	4	5	6	7	8	9	10
11	12	13	14	15	16	17	18	19	20
21	22	23	24	25	26	27	28	29	30
31	32	33	34	35	36	37	38	39	40
41	42	43	44	45	46	47	48	49	50
51	52	53	54	55	56	57	58	59	60
61	62	63	64	65	66	67	68	69	70
71	72	73	74	75	76	77	78	79	80
81	82	83	84	85	86	87	88	89	90
91	92	93	94	95	96	97	98	99	100

Chinese Tangram Puzzle

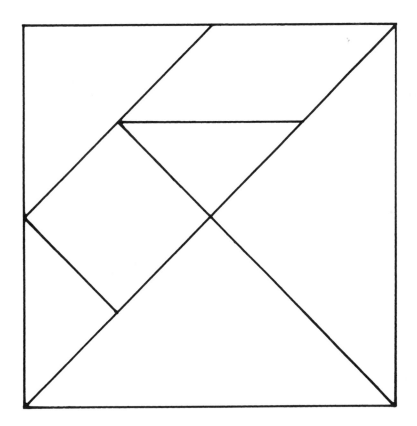

1. What shapes can you find in the tangram puzzle piece? _____

_____

2. Can you make a square using 3 pieces of your tangram puzzle?

3. Can you make a tall house using 6 pieces of your tangram puzzle?

4. Can you make rectangles two different ways using 5 pieces each time?

Name: _____

Chinese Tangram Puzzle

Using all seven pieces, can you make:

1.

a nesting bird?

2.

an anteater?

3.

a tent?

4.

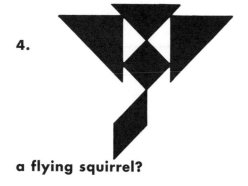

a flying squirrel?

5.

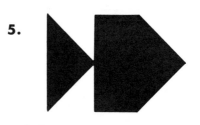

a fish?

6.

a submarine?

7.

a ship?

8. **Make up your own design.**

Name: ______________________________

CHAPTER 2
ACTIVITY SHEET

Pencil and Paper Square Game

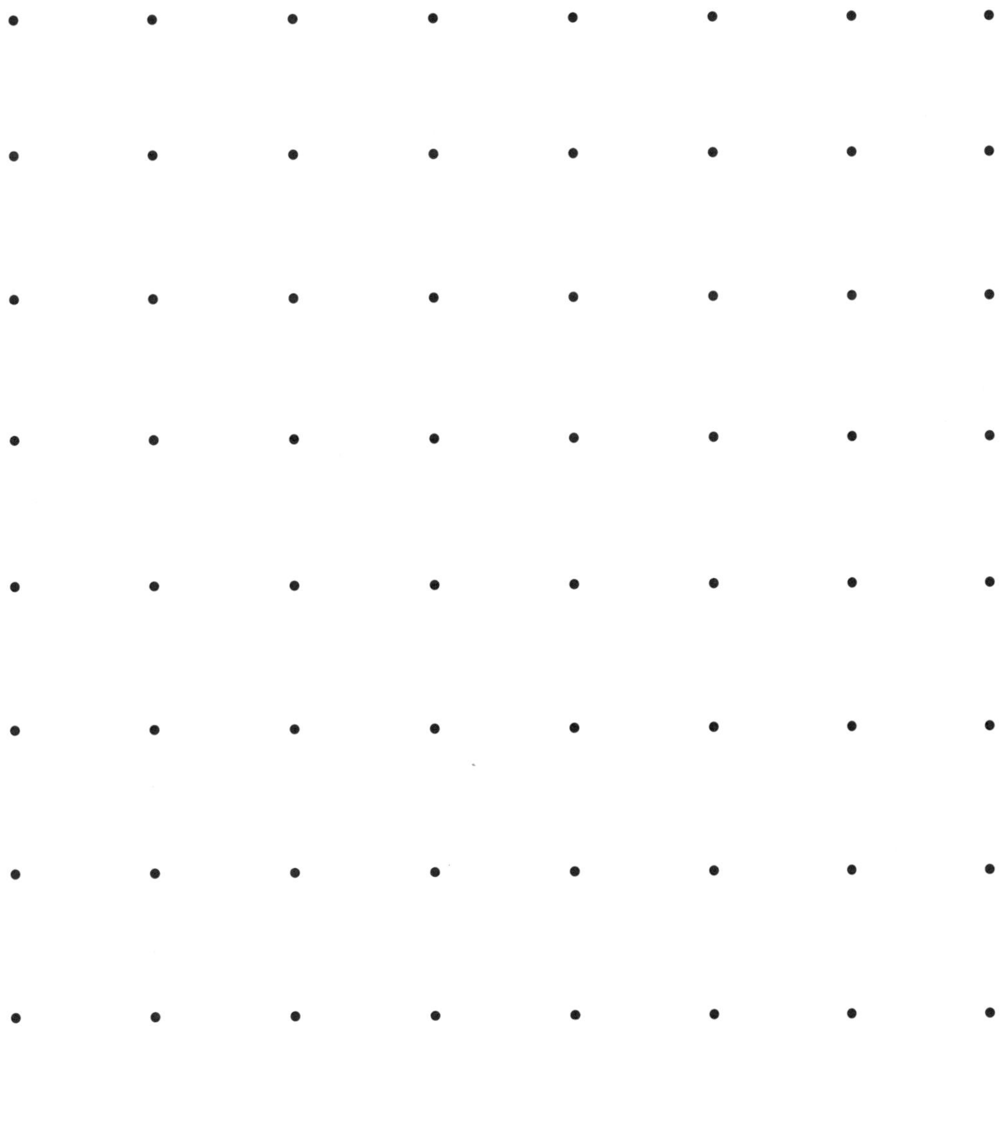

Name: _____

CHAPTER 2
ACTIVITY SHEET

Graph Paper

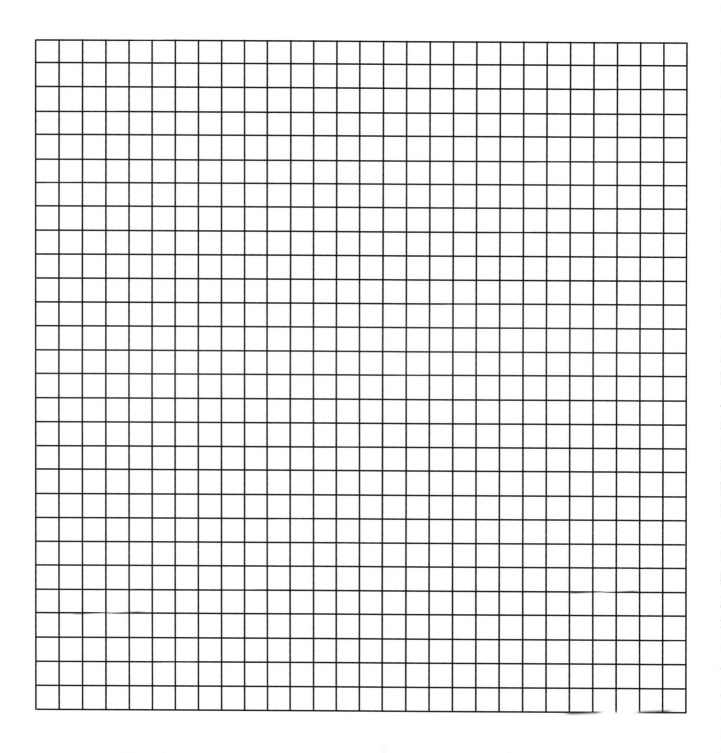

Resources

1. A selection of literature books that deal by title and to some extent by theme with numbers are:

500 Hats of Bartholomew Cubbins by Dr. Seuss published by Random House (1989).

The Hundred Dresses by Eleanor Estes published by Harcourt Brace & Jovanovich (1944).

Seventeen Kings and Forty-Two Elephants by Margaret Mahy published by Dial Books (1987).

2. A good selection to introduce Pablo Picasso to children is *Picasso* by Mike Venezia published by Childrens Press (1988). This book is part of the Getting to Know the World's Greatest Artists series published by Childrens Press. Another book for elementary school children is the Picasso book which is part of the Art for Children series written by Ernest Raboff and published by Harper & Row. Books in this series are titled by the artist's first and last name.

3. Several books which deal with the concept of numbers in one way or another and that should be enjoyed by younger students are:

How Much Is A Million? by David Schwartz published by William Morrow & Co. (1985).

If You Make A Million by David Schwartz published by Morrow & Co. (1989).

Freckle Juice by Judy Blume published by Four Winds Press (1971).

Children will also enjoy the math puzzles and problems in *Sideways Arithmetic* from Wayside School by Louis Sachar.

4. Some excellent computer programs are available to help elementary students understand "real world" math applications. One such program is "Labs for Learning". For more information about this program contact Learning Quest, Inc., P.O. Box 61, Corvallis, Oregon 97339, (503)753-6474.

TECHNOLOGY AND OUR SHRINKING WORLD

We often think of technology as the development of more and better machines to save us the time and labor of difficult jobs. This is largely true, although today we also talk in terms of specific technologies, such as biotechnology (in which living organisms are investigated and altered in an attempt to improve health). In any form, technology is still the development of ways to improve life.

Technological developments also seem to ever shrink our world by tying us daily not only with our next door neighbors but with our neighbors around the world. In the development of transportation and communications, this power of technology to bring the people of the world together is especially clear. In many respects, the developments of this century in transportation and communication can be seen as related because through transportation and now high-tech communications, vast numbers of people in one part of the world are able to visit and communicate with people across oceans. In this chapter, children can explore a technology continuum that will help them see how technology has changed the way people live through the years.

Lesson Activities

The Lesson Activities in this chapter help children trace the history of technological development and begin to understand the way in which need leads to invention. Since technology is intertwined with scientific exploration, several activities are suggested that are really science experiments by nature. Their inclusion here, however, helps children understand how inventions are developed by trial and error, and sometimes purely by accident.

Writing Activities

The Writing Activities provide a diverse range of ideas for writing exercises that complement the lesson activities. These include factual written explorations of inventors, as well as creative writing adventures that encourage the students to do some technological dreaming of their own.

Art and Craft Activities

The Art and Craft Activities provide ideas for using the materials and products of technological advances such as wires and Styrofoam to create craft projects with a mechanical and sometimes "high-tech" look. The projects focus on creation of images or sculptures of transportation vehicles, be they land vehicles, boats or planes.

Food Activities

Food Activities provide suggestions for many fun snacks and treats which are generally in the shape of a plane, boat or car.

Art Masters—Old and New

Art Masters - Old and New provides classroom art project ideas based on the work of three different artists of the last 100 years: Paul Klee, Louise Nevelson and Marcel Duchamp. These artist either did series on subjects related to the lessons of this theme or their work used the discards of modern technology in creative ways.

Sharing Activities

Sharing Activities provide several ideas for transportation-based contests as well as community display ideas.

Lesson Activities

The lesson activities in this chapter are designed not only to familiarize children with the basic social studies topics of transportation (and hence geography), but also to help children really understand how developments in transportation and the related area of communications have changed our lives from the way our parents and parents' parents lived. As children investigate these study areas, they are encouraged to see the many ways in which the world seems smaller, and in fact is smaller, from the world of their grandparents and great-grandparents.

Background Information

1. Early Machines

The basis for many technological advances on which we rely daily is one or more of the six basic machines. These are the wheel and axle, screw, inclined plane, lever, pulley, and wedge. These simple machines are used together with other machine components to make complex machines. When they are used in this way, they are called machine elements.

The earliest complex machines date back to about A.D 900. Some of these early machines were probably powered by water such as grain mills. Other early complex machines include forges for blacksmithing and sawmills. The true Age of the Machine, however, did not begin until the Industrial Revolution at the end of the 19th century.

2. Quick History of Technology

The developments of technology over the ages are too numerous to name. Several resource books are suggested in the resources section of this chapter to give you in-depth information on the major technological developments of history. As a quick resource, however, a brief timeline of well-known and well-used technological developments is provided for classroom convenience and use.

Beginnings of farming/first grain harvests - 10,000 b.c.

Sheep and goats domesticated - 8500 b.c.

Use of donkeys and oxen as work and transport animals and to pull sledges - 5000 b.c.

Discovery of the wheel - 3500 b.c. (not widely used until 500 years later) (Use of wheel spread as follows: 2500 b.c. in India, 1400 b.c. in Europe, 1300 b.c. in China)

Sails and sailboats - 5000 b.c.- 3200 b.c.

Horses tamed - 2000 b.c.

Sundial - 500 b.c.

Extensive system of paved roads - 300 b.c. to a.d. 200

First paper - 150 b.c.

Mechanical clock - a.d. 725

Development of horse-based transportation and vehicles (rigid horse collars) - a.d. 800 to a.d. 900

Invention of gunpowder - a.d. 1000

Invention of compass - 1125

Invention of moveable type printing press - 1454

Improvements in ocean going vessels that made long ocean voyages more common - late 1400s

Invention of spinning wheel - 1530

Invention of flying shuttle loom - 1730

Steam engine developed - 1700s

First aerial voyage in history (via hot air balloon) - 1783

Invention of cotton gin - 1793

Bicycle without pedals introduced - 1816

Successful steam train transportation - 1825

Practical telegraph service begins - 1840s

Dirigible aircraft development - 1852

Invention of telephone - 1876

Invention of phonograph - 1877

Invention of incandescent light bulb - 1879

Invention of the internal combustion engine - 1880

Invention of internal combustion automobile - 1890

Invention of X-rays - 1895

Long distance radio transmission - 1897

First photocopy machine - 1900

Motor-powered one-person airplane successfully flies - 1903

Louis Bleriot flies across English Channel - 1909

Successful television transmission occurs - 1920s

Talking movies introduced - 1926

Charles Lindbergh flies solo across Atlantic - 1927

Amelia Earhart flies solo across Atlantic - 1928

First large analog computer - 1930

First commercial jet airlines begin service - 1950s

First telecommunications satellite in orbit (Telstar) - 1962

Unmanned moon landings - 1966

First human lands on the moon - 1969

First flight of reusable rocket shuttle (space shuttle) - 1981

Some of the dates and locations listed above are approximations made by scholars and historians. Others reflect developments when they occurred in a certain part of the world and may be no reflection on whether similar technological advances were occurring elsewhere in the world at the same time.

3. History of Transportation
a. Land Transportation

Obviously the first means of land transportation for people was their own feet. Walking was and still is a basic form of transportation, but people developed ways of going long distances and moving heavy or awkward loads.

The first real development in this regard was learning to use animals such as donkeys and oxen (circa 5000 b.c.). As people and animals pulled loads from place to place they learned to put them on sledges and then rollers to make the job of moving the cargo easier. In the Middle East sometime around the 3500 b.c., the first wheel was probably invented, but its use spread slowly at first. Nonetheless, it was a simple machine which changed the course of history and one we still rely on daily.

As use of the wheel spread, people also learned how to make more effective harnesses and collars so that horses and other animals could pull wheeled vehicles without choking. Around the world, people developed wheeled coaches, carts and chariots to carry people and things from place to place. Most of these were animal powered, although some, such as pedicabs, relied on human muscle. Stagecoaches were one example of animal powered carriages; they came into common use in North America in the mid-1700s.

By the 1700s the steam engine was developed and improvements in engine design and power sources continued from there. Successful railroad operations occurred in the early 1800s. Advances in the wheel led to the bicycle in the 1880s as well. By the 1890s, gasoline-powered engines had been placed on coach-type bodies and the dawn of the automobile age was in sight. By the 1920s, automobiles had replaced the horse to become the primary means of passenger transportation in the United States.

b. Water Transportation

The first "boat" was probably a log that fell into a lake or river. A person sat atop it and may have used a stick to push him or herself to the other side. Real boats were made when people began to take those logs and hollow them out so that the log could hold people and things. These "dug outs" are still made today. In parts of the world in which large logs were not available, people tied together reeds or other plant branches to make rafts. Still others made and waterproofed large basket-like structures (called coracles) in which they could sit and move across a small body of water. Inflated animal skins that worked like pontoons and woven leaves also served as boats in some parts of the world. Paddles and oars soon developed. These early boats and small boats today are for traveling rivers, lakes and streams and perhaps near the ocean shore.

These early boats relied exclusively on human power and any available water current to make them go. The Phoenicians and Egyptians made early use of sails. In Mesopotamia, sails appeared in 5000 b.c. probably in conjunction with oars. The Egyptians began using sails in 3200 b.c. These early sail boats used large square sails.

Most of these early boats were used to traverse inland waterways. It was not until sometime in the 1400s that ship-building technology had progressed to the point that sailing ships from Europe were able to embark on long sea voyages for exploration. However, historians believe that hundreds of years before this the islanders of the South Pacific migrated between the Polynesian Islands in the open ocean in raft-like boats far simpler than the complicated sailing vessels of the European explorers.

In the mid-1800s American shipbuilders developed a new, faster sailing ship called the clipper ship. A clipper used multiple sails and a streamlined body. This type of ship was used for the fast transport of cargo for about 50 years. At this time, they were replaced by steel, steam-powered ships.

Today there are many kinds of boats in use around the world. Small boats still rely on human power such as kayaks, canoes, rafts, dugouts and coracles. Paddles and oars guide and move these boats. Some hobbyists enjoy small sailboats and sailing yachts. Steamboats and paddle wheelers still traverse riverways, largely for tourists. Larger boats such as cruise ships, tankers, cargo ships, and warships are powered in a variety of ways from fossil fuels to nuclear power.

While warships, submarines and cruise ships seem to capture our imagination more often, the most important ships today are probably the cargo ships that transport products to and from places the world over. Many cargo ships are now designed as container cargo ships. Large rectangular containers containing products to be shipped are loaded onto these ships. The cargo is then unloaded at its destination and placed on a truck bed to be transported to its final destination.

c. Air Transportation

Throughout human history, people have dreamed of flying. The reasons were less practical than those that fueled developments in land and water transportation. To fly like a bird was an end in itself. Today, of course, airplanes and jets are used to transport cargo as well as serving as routine people transportation. We still dream of conquering the heavens as countries around the world pursue space programs—launching rockets, satellites, and space stations to investigate the possibilities beyond our Earth.

The first real aerial voyage was made by hot air balloon in the late 1700s. But balloons are not easily controllable and could never be designed to go very long distances. Accordingly, dreamers still looked for a flying design that was more bird-like in structure. People developed gliders, kites and parachutes in an effort to learn more about the power of air and how to keep objects in flight.

Sir George Cayley is often called the father of modern aeronautics. He was a wealthy Englishman who experimented with flying models and full size aircraft and wrote down his findings. He pioneered the idea of fixed (non-moveable) wings on airplanes. Before Cayley, people designed flying machines with moving flaps like birds' wings.

Otto Lilienthal, a German mechanical engineer, was a pioneer of air-powered flight. He designed, built and flew gliders with fixed wings and tail structures. His activities occurred in the last half of the 19th century. He died in a glider accident.

By 1903, the pioneering efforts of those before laid the groundwork for Wilbur and Orville Wright to build the first powered plane that successfully flew with a man aboard. After this beginning, developments were rapid. Within a few years, planes were routinely used as evidenced by their widespread use during World War I. Today, air transportation is taken for granted, and people regularly fly around the world for business and pleasure.

Still the dream of flight lives on in the human heart. Today, the destination is space. With the development of space flight in the 1950s, air travel took a dramatic turn. Today the National Aeronautics and Space Administration has space shuttle programs, space station plans, and exploratory missions throughout the solar system.

4. History of Communication

Communication is the transmission of information from one person to another. Basic interpersonal communication is done through talking, writing, sign language, body language, and facial expression. But through history, people have had the desire to explore places far from home to find out if people inhabit those places and what those people have to say. Since technological advances of the last few hundred years in both transportation and communication have allowed us to fully explore the Earth's continents, today we wonder if intelligent life inhabits space and we want to communicate with that life if it exists.

Early developments in transportation facilitated communication and transference of ideas and information between peoples from otherwise isolated parts of the world. Of course, the exchange of things like crops, resources, animals, plants, and technologies occurred along the way as well.

In addition to the technological developments in transportation, fast-changing improvements in communication technologies themselves have spurred the exchange of ideas in recent years. As a result of the widespread and rapid communications systems available today, rapid development of other technologies has occurred around the world.

Let's look at some of the changes in communication throughout history. First, communication was sign language, gesturing and ultimately spoken language. Information was passed from generation to generation through stories and songs. Methods of communication over distances were limited to sending and receiving signals by smoke, drum, flags and bells or personal delivery, whether by human foot or animal foot.

The development of written language, however, allowed people to preserve their stories and information. Early writing was pictorial, usually paintings and etchings on rock. For many languages, alphabets developed so that writing became more precise. Written and then printed words such as letters and books allowed for the recording of specific ideas and information and exchange of those ideas between people and between generations of people.

Letters were an early way of transmitting information to people living far away from you. Methods of getting letters from one place to another developed along with developments in transportation. In some ancient civilizations such as the Inca Empire of Peru, letters (sent only to the rulers) were hand-carried by fleets of runners over 1000 miles. As transportation technologies developed, ships, horses, stagecoaches, pony expresses, and railroads have all been among the methods of transporting letters.

Still, the messages traveled slowly. People kept searching for ways to communicate more quickly - indeed, to communicate instantly. In the 1800s, a new age of communications was beginning. The telegraph and the telephone realized the dream of a new era of instant communications.

In the 1900s wireless radio transmission was being tested. Only a few years later (by the 1920s) radio became a popular form of entertainment. Large scale television developed in the 1940s. The first telecommunications satellite was launched into orbit in 1962 and the age of immediate worldwide live communications had arrived.

These new telecommunications technologies have changed how we perceive the world and our place in it. Today, wars can be seen as they happen on the television in your house. These events no longer seem so far away. The world has become smaller as our ability to be spectators to events as they happen across the globe has grown.

Project Directions

1. What Is Technology?

Use the discussion guidelines below to introduce or reinforce for students the ways technological advances change daily life. Many of the machines that we use and rely on each day are scarcely 100 years old. Many of these modern machines, however, rely in significant part on the six simple machines from antiquity. Help students to understand this and how the combination of these machines and other components in complex machines and the development of technologies such as electricity and the automobile have made their lives so different from what life was like 100 years ago.

a. Technology Awareness Discussion Guidelines

Let's talk about some of the things we do every day and see if we can identify how the technological developments of the last 100 years have changed our lives.

Before we start, can we define what technology is?

Technology can be described as using science and scientific methods to solve practical problems and meet people's needs for shelter, care and food and comfort. In other words, technology is the creation of machines, medicines, and any other things that people need or want.

What are some technological developments that you can think of?

Invention of the wheel, building of the first boat and the development of boat and ship construction, the discovery of and development of uses for electricity, the invention of the telephone, the printing press, the spinning wheel, television and the like.

The list of technological developments is almost endless. Can you think of some inventions or machines that have been developed that affect your daily life?

Let's think about technology and how developments and changes in the last 100 years affect us everyday.

[Note: Each time a child mentions activities related to an electric-powered device or automobile-related transportation, write that item up on the board. Use the following questions or similar ones to elicit discussion about equipment and activities that we take for granted. Discussion should bring up common household appliances, vehicles, electric lighting, television, computers, etc.]

How did you wake up this morning?

What did you get dressed in? How was it made? How was it washed?

What did you eat this morning? How was the food grown, brought to your house, cooked or processed at home? How many machines were involved?

How did you get to school? Did you walk or ride a bicycle, bus or car? Did you rely on a machine to get you to school?

What is your room at school like? How do you light it? What machinery or equipment is in your school? Do you use paper and pencil? Do you use books? How were they printed?

What do you have for lunch? Where was that made? Is it cooked?

How will you entertain yourself when you get home tonight?

b. Six Simple Machines

The six simple machines form the basis or are integral parts of many machines we all use every day. The wheel because of its significance in land transportation is one of them which will be explored at length in the lesson activities on land transportation. The others are the lever, the inclined plane, the wedge, the pulley and the screw. Describe one or more of these machines and have students think about how these simple machines are at use around them everyday. Have examples of them available to show students. Wheels, screws and inclined planes may be the easiest for children to identify with and discuss. One very common use of the inclined plane, for example, is in access ramps for handicapped persons and loading ramps for delivery of goods.

Ask children to build a model of one of these machines to share with the class. This project can be done at home since common materials such as cardboard and foil can be used to make it. Examples are an aluminum foil screw or a cardboard inclined plane.

2. Make a Technology Timeline

Using your bulletin board or a long sheet of butcher paper, create a class technology timeline. Keep your timeline project simple. You may want to use it to mark in dates for development of major technological advances that come up in a class discussion. To make the timeline, ask children to show by picture and simple sentence description a major technological advance of their choosing. They will do this on a three by five card or a piece of paper sized so that all the students advances can be placed on the timeline. The year of the development should be written in marker on the card. The cards will be placed on the bulletin board in chronological order. If a few children choose advances from ancient times (and you should encourage this), the timeline will graphically show children how the pace of technological changes has increased in the last few hundred years.

Some of the technological advances you might want to have handy for plotting your timeline are listed in the background information in this chapter. Many of the dates provided relate to developments in transportation, but there are also other dates relating to significant inventions. Ask children to pick one item from this list or one invention or development of their choosing that they would like to include on the timeline.

After each student has plotted a development on your class timeline and drawn a small picture to illustrate it (as described above), ask each student to write a paragraph or short essay about why he or she chose that particular development. Why does the child believe it to be an important technological advance for people? Does the child think the development is still important today?

3. History of Transportation

The development of transportation technologies throughout the history of the world has had a major impact on the development of the world and the histories of peoples around the world. These issues come up in curriculum from kindergarten on. Columbus's expeditions and the Pilgrims' voyage, for example, involve sea transportation. The importance of transportation developments is in many ways the basis for upper grade explorations of world history since so much of history was affected by humans' ability to reach and explore places not reachable before.

The activities in this section are designed to help children understand advances in the three key areas of transportation - land, sea and air. The activities provided are short class discussion tools and hands-on activities that allow children to explore the scientific and technical aspects of creating a working vehicle, whether a wheel, a boat or an airplane.

a. History of Land Transportation

This section includes three activities. One is a brief discussion tool. One is a role-playing of the creation of the first wheel. In the third activity children undertake a scientific investigation (just as any real inventor or scientist would) in an attempt to discover a technological advance - in this case, a new synthetic rubber. The latter two activities taken together allow children to jump chronologically from the first wheel to pretend they are modern scientists trying to find a new rubber substitute with which to make wheels today.

- **Discussion Guidelines.** This is a short discussion guideline to introduce the wheel role-play.
  How would early people have moved themselves from one place to another?
    Walking
    Riding an animal once animals were tamed
  What if a person wanted to move things from one place to another? How would the person do that?
    Carry them
  What if a person wanted to move bigger loads than he or she could carry? What would you do?
    You might put the object(s) on something and drag it.
  Would you try to think of easier ways to move things? Why?
    Yes, because you want to make your work easier.
  What would you think of that might help you move things more easily?
    You might see something in nature around you that rolls, such as a rock. You might try to make something round that you could put your load on as you dragged it.

  Gradually, the idea for rollers and then the wheel would develop.

  Think of vehicles that use the wheel today to help us get ourselves and things from one place to another. What are some of these?

  [Note: The following are listed in order of probable development.]

Carts - human or animal powered
Horse-drawn and human-powered coaches
Trains
Bicycles
Automobiles, buses
Subway trains
Airplanes, jets

• **The All-Important Wheel.** In this interactive classroom activity, children will try to visualize how and why early peoples came up with wheel-like devices. From early times, humans looked for simple machines to help them with work. These simple machines included the inclined plane, the lever and the pulley. A major development that eased man's work was the development of the wheel. It led to human- and animal-powered carts and other vehicles, and later to more complex machines and transportation vehicles.

Ask children to try to visualize the world before wheels. To do this, ask them to think about the labor intensive job of building ancient pyramids. Much of the work on ancient pyramids such as those in Egypt was done before the wheel or with wheel proto-types. Students will recreate the hauling of a stone block from the quarry to the building site. As they role-play their attempts to move a massive block, they will think about ways to make the job easier.

To act this out, you will need twenty feet of rope, a large box to be your pyramid stone, two large, flat pieces of cardboard taped together (your sledge) on which to place the "stone," and a heavy cardboard carpet or newsprint roll sawed into three segments. (Check with local carpet dealers to get castoff carpet rolls. Check with local newspaper pub-lishers to see about getting empty newsprint rolls.) Using these props, children will try to recreate the creative human thinking that led to use of round or cylindrical objects to move the stone. Children can explore the creation of the early wheel or its forerunners as described below.

First you set up a creative thinking sce-nario. Ask children to imagine that they are asked by a pharaoh or ruler to move two-ton quarried stones from the quarry to the build-ing site. The trip might be a mile or more long. How would they do it? How many peo-ple would they need? Remind them they have no horses, no cars, no tow-trucks, to help. Also, to get a better feel for the task, brain-storm—how heavy is two tons? What else weighs two tons? Can children imagine carry-ing or pulling an elephant? a pick-up truck?

Have children start with a large box (or an ice chest) and ask them to pretend it is as heavy as two cars. How would they move it through the sand and dirt? Could they push it? They might try, but could they push it a whole mile? Would they try to pull it? They could tie ropes to it to try to pull it. What else might they try? Would they have oxen or other draft animals pull it? This would be a good idea, but draft animals were often considered too valuable by the pharaohs for the tedious work of pyramid building, especially when they had so many human slaves available.

Perhaps they could place the block on a sled-like piece of wood. Place your "stone" on a two-thickness piece of cardboard so the

stone will not sink as easily into the dirt or sand. Would this work well enough even with ropes around the stone which ten to twenty people pulled and several people pushed? What else can be done to make this job easier?

What if the stone and sledge could be placed on wooden logs or rollers? Place three or four cardboard rolls under the block. As the stone is moved forward, one or two workers has to continuously move the released rollers from the back of the sledge to the front of the sledge so that the stone remains over the rollers. There were no wheels on axles yet. So even with rollers (perhaps these were the first wheel prototypes) the job of moving the stones remains difficult. But the rollers made the job a little easier. Perhaps this is one of the ways people thought of making wheels. This is how development in technology works even today.

As they role-play this scenario, children see how many people it took to move one stone. How many are needed to move the rollers? How many might have been used to pull? How many helped by pushing? Additional people were also needed to pour water or milk on the sand or dirt to make it more firm as the sledge rolled over it. Perhaps 12 or more men were needed to move each stone.

Ask children how they think wheels may have developed from this primitive beginning. Draw their discussion to wheeled carts, human- and animal-drawn vehicles, human-powered bicycles, and finally independently-powered vehicles.

• **Be a Transportation Scientist.** In this activity, children will test a classroom-made "synthetic rubber" substance to see if this substance would be a satisfactory alternative to the rubber currently used to make tires for so many land transportation vehicles. They will act as scientists to test the properties of this new substance. Let the children decide if the substance will result in a technological advance for wheel production or not.

To set the stage, remind children that tires for many land vehicles are made from rubber. Rubber comes from tropical rain forest areas of the world. Tell children that, as these areas shrink, we will need to find alternatives to rubber such as a human-made or synthetic rubber to meet our tire needs. In this case, children will create their manmade rubber by following a recipe that requires white glue, borax and water, or you can make the rubber ahead of time and have it ready for them to

test. You can make it a day or two ahead of time and it will still be good for the classroom exploration if you keep it in a covered container. After several days, however, it may begin to mold.

Synthetic Rubber Recipe
4 cups white glue
4 teaspoons Borax, Borateem or Boraxo
4 cups water

Put white glue in a bowl and have a large stirring utensil such as a metal or wooden spoon handy. Mix the borax product with four cups of water in a separate container. Pour this water mixture slowly into the glue stirring constantly. Almost immediately the glue begins to get stringy and rubbery. Keep stirring until you have gotten rid of any remaining areas of glue which have not had contact with the water. Not all of the water will absorb into the glue. When the glue has turned into a soft ball, remove it from extra water and pat dry carefully with cloth or paper towel. It may be a little sticky at first. Knead the glob for several minutes. Then divide it into equal parts so that each student has a small piece with which to experiment.

Borax used with Elmer's® white glue probably makes the most elastic synthetic rubber; however, it can sometimes be a bit too elastic, almost to the point of being sticky. Other white glues tend to make a stiffer "rubber." You might want to make the stiffer synthetic rubber for this particular lesson activity or you may want to have several different forms of the putty available (i.e., ones made with Elmer's® glue and ones made with other white glues), including some samples of Silly Putty®. Some students can work with one substance, some students with another.

To begin the investigative activity, divide students into cooperative learning groups of four to six students. Make sure each group has some actual rubber substances such as old pieces of tire, latex surgical gloves, rubber bands, erasers and rubber balls. Ask them to bring in rubber items that they might have at home. Now they will test their synthetic rubber against the real rubber to find out if they have discovered a new substance for making tires or a substance with another altogether different use. Have children explore elasticity, bounce, and strength of the synthetic versus real rubber using the Be-A-Transportation Scientist Activity Sheet at the end of this chapter.

Ask students who finish investigating their substances and discussing their findings within their groups to reach a consensus on whether the synthetic rubber would make good tires. Ask that each group report to the whole class as though presenting their findings at a scientific convention. Have the students explain why the substance would or would not make a good tire. If the classroom consensus is that the substance is not suitable for tires, can the students think of another use for the substance? Perhaps the experiment will not improve tire technology, but will result in an unexpected technological advance of another kind. This is how things often happen in science in real life.

b. History of Water Transportation

Use the discussion guidelines here to spark the children's thinking about the development of water transportation. Then use the lesson activities to help children explore questions about why boats float and water displacement.

Discussion Guidelines

How do you think people started going over or across bodies of water?

Swimming or floating on a log or some other object that floated.

Why do you think people started going over or across bodies of water?

To get away from danger, to find food or shelter, to explore new places, to conquer other lands, to transport cargo from one place to another.

Think about the first boat. What do you think it looked like? What was it made of? Was it simple or complicated?

The first boats were probably hollowed out, carved logs such as Native American groups used. In places without large trees, they were probably made from groups of reeds and small branches or grasses tied together. They might have been waterproofed with sap, animal fat or skins.

How were the first boats powered? What made them move? How could the person control where the boat went?

Human power such as hands, oars, paddles or sticks (to push along the bottom of the lake or river).

What power did people harness next in making their boats go and go quickly?

Wind power, with sails

What other power sources have been developed for vehicles that transport people and things in water?

Steam, fossil fuels, atomic energy

What kinds of boats or ships can you think of that are used today or have been used in the past?

Sailboats, warships, submarines, steamboats, motor boats, rafts, canoes, cruise ships, cargo ships

In what different ways are these boats powered?

Wind, fossil fuels, steam, human muscle, nuclear power

Use these discussion guidelines to lead the children into an exploration of boat making as described below.

• **Boat Float Contest.** Ask each child to make a boat using simple household items and scraps such as wood pieces, foil, toilet paper tubes, masking tape, pint size plastic juice bottles, pint size dairy cartons, plasticine clay, disposable cups and plates. Masking tape, plastic wrap and foil can be used to waterproof the boats as needed or desired. Encourage the children to bring boat making materials from home, but let them know that prepackaged boat models and toy boats will not be acceptable. This is really a boat made from recycled materials.

Let children know that you will have a contest to see which boat can carry the most cargo without sinking. If children make their boats in class, have several dishpans filled with water available for children to test the "floatability" of the various items they bring in. Tell children that their boats may be no longer than eight inches.

Once all the boats are completed, set aside another period to have the boats tested for cargo capacity. For this, have metal washers or nails available to test the boats by putting one item in the boat at a time while the boat floats in a plastic dishpan. When the boat capsizes or sinks, you stop and move on to the next boat.

In this activity children learn about the respective densities of items and water as they test materials to use for their boat and decide on which ones to use. They learn about water displacement and how boats float partially above the water line and partially below.

3. History of Air Transportation

Through the activities in this section, children explore the history of flight and experiment with air pressure and aerodynamics to reach conclusions about the technological development of air transportation.

Discussion Guidelines
Why do you think people want to fly?
The answer here is not so simple as why people might have wanted to cross a body of water. Use the ancient Greek legend of Icarus to explain the timeless human desire to be like a bird. Icarus made wings to soar to the sky, ignored his father's warnings and flew too close to the sun. The wax on his wings melted and he plummeted to earth.
What do you think were the first flying machines that carried people?
The first aerial voyage by man was in a hot air balloon in 1793.
How were the first vehicles that people flew in powered?
Air power for gliders, hot air for ballooning
How many different kinds of flying machines can you think of that are in use today?
Airplanes, jets, helicopters, hot air balloons, gliders, rockets, space shuttles
What do we use flying machines for today?
Air transportation, shipping cargo, war jets, space exploration and placing satellites in space, glider hobby activities, hot air ballooning
How many different ways are these machines powered?
Petroleum-derived fuels for airplanes and jet engines, air currents for gliders, hot air for balloons

• **Explore the power of air.** Much of the early investigation and testing of airplane prototypes was based upon learning about what structure could best utilize air pressure to lift the device off the ground. Take a class period to help children explore air pressure at different classroom work stations or by different demonstrations that students can also do at home. As the experiments are performed, have children use the scientific method to help them think about what they see. For each experiment or demonstration, have them write down their hypothesis about what they think will happen and what actually does happen and why? For this, they can use the Scientific Hypothesis and Results Activity Sheet at the end of Chapter 9 or simply record this information in a journal or on a piece of paper. Here are a few ideas for air pressure experiments:
-**The ruler trick.** Set a wooden yardstick or yard-long piece of thin wooden molding half on and half off a table. Strike it quickly. What happens? It flies off the table. Try this again but this time lay a large piece of construction paper or lightweight posterboard over the portion of the ruler that sits on the table. Slowly push on the ruler. The part of the ruler with paper on it will move the paper. Since you are pushing on the stick slowly, the air above the paper is displaced and the ruler moves without breaking. Now strike the ruler quickly. Often it breaks. Why?

Even though we can't see air, it has weight. When the ruler is not covered by the paper, the small size of the ruler can easily displace air allowing the ruler to fall from the table when struck. But when a large sheet of paper is placed over the ruler, air pressure is exerted over all parts of the paper (and thus the ruler) and this pressure cannot be as quickly displaced. If you push on the ruler slowly, however, you can displace the air without breaking the ruler.
-**The balloon blowing tricks.** These three activities further demonstrate that air has pressure or strength even though we cannot see it.
i. Place a balloon inside a glass soda or water bottle. Fold the edges of the balloon's opening over the mouth of the bottle. Try to blow up the balloon. Can you? No, because the mouth

of the bottle is sealed by the balloon so the air inside the bottle has nowhere to go, and can't allow the balloon to expand. (Another way to demonstrate this is to jab the side of a potato with a paper straw. If you do not hold a finger over the end of the straw, the straw breaks. But if you hold the end of the straw shut, the air pressure in the straw is strong enough to allow the straw to penetrate deeply into the side of the potato.)

ii. Another balloon activity is to place a balloon under one or two books and try to blow it up. The air in the balloon is strong enough to make the books move up. The air on the top side of the books is strong but it is displaced by the slow movement of the books.

iii. Hang two balloons side by side with eighteen to 24 inch strings. The balloons can be hung from a yardstick, doorway or a table. Hang the balloons ten to twelve inches apart. Blow the air between the balloons. The balloons will move toward each other, but most children think they will move apart if they have not seen the experiment.

Why do the balloons move toward each other? Moving air has less pressure than stationary air. Accordingly, since the air on the outsides of the balloons is stationary and the air between them is moving, the air on the outside of the balloons pushes the balloons together. This principle is used in the design of airplane wings which are rounded on top and flat on the bottom. The rounded top of the wing creates more air movement as air travels over the wing. The air beneath the wing has more pressure than the air above the wing. Thus, this wing design helps lift the plane.

-If you use these air pressure experiments, the suggested hypothesis questions to use on the Scientific Hypothesis and Results Activity Sheet are:

Ruler Experiments
-Will the uncovered ruler break when you hit it?
-Will the paper-covered ruler break when you push slowly on it?
-Will the paper-covered ruler break when you hit it?

Balloon Experiments
-Will the balloon in the bottle expand when you try to blow it up?
-Will the balloon raise the books when you blow into it?
-Will the balloons move away from each other when you blow the air between them?

• **Explore Wing Design.** Give each child a plastic straw, a small round balloon and a rubber band. The child affixes the balloon to one end of the straw with the rubber band so that the balloon can be blown up through the straw. Then using construction paper and clear tape, the child cuts out two pairs of identical wings to tape onto the straw. One set is taped on top of the straw and one set is taped on the bottom. Then the ends of the wings are taped together.

Children then blow up their propulsion systems (the balloons) and let them go. Have children measure the distance that each aircraft goes. When every one has flown his or her aircraft, line up the five to ten "planes" that flew the furthest. Have the children look at them and try to decide on similarities in wing shape, design and placement on the straws. Ask them to write about their conclusions about the best wing design and placement for flight. You might want to let the children know in advance about this project to encourage them to test designs at home first.

• **Map Measurement.** This lesson activity can be incorporated into study of any form of transportation, whether air, land or sea, but is provided here as an adjunct to the air transportation activities because it can help children see how much faster air travel allows us to get from one place to another.

Challenge children's math skills by asking them to figure out how long it will take you to get to a chosen destination using different methods of transportation. When they undertake this project they will use a map, its key, and their analytical abilities to determine what equations to use to find the information. You might want to assign this project in conjunction with the travel brochure writing project suggested in the writing activities section of this chapter.

General travel speeds by method are:
- Walking you can go 3-4 miles per hour or 5-6 kilometers per hour.
- Biking you can go 10 miles per hour or 16 kilometers per hour.
- By car you can go 55 miles per hour or 88 kilometers per hour.
- By train you can go 85 miles per hour or 140 kilometers per hour.
- By jet you can go 550 miles per hour or 885 kilometers per hour.

• **Reaching into the Solar System.** You can use a variety of learning activities to help children think creatively and learn to draw analogies while learning about space travel, space exploration and outer space itself..

An easy-to-use and interesting "must" as a classroom handbook for exploring space is the paperback book, *The Planets in Our Solar System*, by Franklyn M. Branley. With this single inexpensive resource book, children can create a variety of classroom displays that make your classroom come alive with the planets, their orbits, distances from the sun and the like. Divide the class into different groups, each of which will explore space and space travel in a slightly different way. Have each group make an oral presentation of its finished work. The groups are as follows:

i) Distance from the Sun. This group uses the Branley book or another resource with the same information to plot the relative distances of the planets from the sun on a 15-foot sheet of butcher paper. Encourage the children to also reflect in their banner project the relative sizes of the plants if they so choose. Have this group present short oral reports and pictures on four or five of the planets and the group described below can be responsible for short reports on the remaining planets.

ii) Big and Little Planets. Ask one group to demonstrate either by poster, mobile, or model the relative sizes of the planets. Again, the Branley book provides students with an easy to use resource to complete this project. The students in this group also report on the planets not assigned to the first group described above.

iii) Sun So Hot. Ask another group to make a poster display on the sun. This group will reflect in its display different facts about the sun such as solar flares, sunspots, temperature and its place in our solar system. Ask the group to find and identify ten facts about the sun that the students think would interest the class.

iv) Systematic Circles. Ask one group to chart and discuss the orbits of the planets of our solar system. The group should identify the shapes of the orbit paths, the number of days/years it takes the different planets to complete their orbits and whether any orbit paths intersect (i.e., Pluto/Neptune).

v) Probing Space. Ask another group to use clean trash such as cups, Styrofoam, foil, string, tape and the like to create models of human-made spacecraft such as space stations, satellites, shuttles and rockets. Each student in the group could do a different vehicle and the group's presentation could focus on the similarities between the structures, especially those made to carry people. For example, manned spacecraft need food preparation space, laboratory space for conducting experiments, sleeping quarters, restrooms and the like. Most spacecraft also have cameras on board, holds for the film, transmission and reception panels and the like. Encourage students to identify basic features of the different types of spacecraft.

vi) A Star Can Be a Sun. Ask one group to explore the kinds of stars that exist in the universe. Have them also discuss three to five constellations that can readily be seen in your part of the sky during different parts of the year.

Some of these students might want to create constellation gazers as part of the classroom presentation. To make a constellation gazer, students need black paper, masking tape, foil, a toilet paper tube, and a small flash light. Students choose a constellation to recreate for the class from any book showing the different star formations. The Branley book on stars listed in the resource section in this chapter is one such book. The toilet paper tube is wrapped in black construction paper. Three or four layers of aluminum foil are folded into a square slightly larger than the end of the paper tube. The points of the constellation are placed with pencil on the foil. Holes are then pressed through the foil with round toothpicks or small nails. The constellation-pierced foil is carefully placed over one end of the tube and taped on so that the end of the tube is sealed except for the star holes. Check the foil holes with the toothpick or nail. Turn off the lights, place the flashlight at the open end of the tube and cover any escaping light with your hands or a cloth. Aim the stargazer at the wall and a faint vision of the chosen constellation should appear. You may need to get fairly close to the wall to view the stars, but this method usually works and students can do it without adult help.

vii) An Endless Frontier. Have another group explore the endlessness of space through creation of a large three by seven foot mural of some of the galaxies of our universe. If black paper is available for this project, it would be helpful. To do this project, children explore the features of the universe - its spiral galaxies, black holes and the like. Make sure students remember to include our own galaxy, the Milky Way. Ask them to describe for students a variety of space phenomena such as black holes, meteors and the like.

Each group should include some oral and written report component with its presentation. Facts need to be researched and shared. When all the classroom presentations are complete, the children will have been presented with a good overview of space travel and related space issues.

4. The History of Communication

This theme provides a discussion tool to introduce developments in communications. It also provides a telecommunications class activity.

a. Discussion Guidelines

These discussion guidelines are designed to help children understand the importance of transmitting messages quickly over long distances and how this technology has developed. To do this, a reverse chronological discussion method is suggested by which the students try to figure out how they would get a message to a far outpost of their country or an empire, both now and in the past.

If you were a leader of a nation, such as the President of the United States, and you had a message today that you wanted to get quickly to someone in another country, how would you get that message to him or her?

By telephone, telegram, fax

Communication today can be completed immediately. But a few years ago, all these technologies were not available. If you were President in 1880, what would be the fastest way to get a message across the country?

Telegraph. Even telephone lines were not common yet, as the telephone was developed by Alexander Bell only four years earlier in 1876.

If you were the President and it was 1850 to 1860 (example: President Lincoln trying to communicate with his generals during the Civil War), how would you send an important message?

Someone could be dispatched by horse to deliver it in a letter. After the transcontinental railroad was completed, the railroad was also a way to send information. For a little over a year in the mid-1800s , the Pony Express carried letters across the country more quickly than other available means.

But before railroads and without horses, how would you get a message a long distance if you were a leader?

In the ancient Inca Empire in Peru, communications were made by a system of runners who carried the messages. Runners ran from hut to hut. At each hut a new runner took over and carried the message about two miles. In about 400 b.c. in the Greek Empire, messages were sent from hilltop to hilltop by coded torch light.

Native Americans passed messages by smoke signal from one mountain top to another to warn of danger or communicate other messages.

If you had no telephone, no car, and no telegraph, how would you get information somewhere quickly? As with the Native Americans and the Incas, you would use materials at hand such as smoke and animal skins, your own feet, drums or a domesticated animal.

Close by asking children to think about the fact that "instant" communication has been available scarcely 100 years. Today we take it for granted, but not so long ago, people could not even send a letter across country quickly. Receiving a letter was a big event.

b. Classroom Newscast

Modern communication technologies which use space satellites allow us to transmit live events from around the world. We can now watch wars, space launches and other newsworthy events as they happen. We can see suffering and joy taking place in parts of the world we might not otherwise think about. In this way, newscasts of events from one part of the world can influence people's actions and events in another part of the world as never before.

Have children watch the national and international news and think about the kinds of stories told by the reporters. They will be about people in other parts of our own country and in other countries of the world.

Children can use this experience as background as they work in cooperative groups to recreate a newscast. The total "air time" should be only about five minutes per group but can include segments on weather, national, and international events. Remind students that most newscasts utilize on-the-scene reports from reporters who work in the field covering events live. Every child can have a part.

The students should script the newscast before their performance and rehearse it several times. The writing and rehearsal should be completed with three twenty-minute sessions of the children meeting in groups. At the first meeting, they decide which stories to cover in their newscast and who will play which parts. At the second meeting, they discuss and begin writing their stories. Writing can be completed at home. During the third meeting, they rehearse their newscast and the reading of their news reports. At this meeting, they should also plan where they will be located in the classroom for "cutting" to live reports from news scenes.

Remind children as they prepare for this activity how orbital satellites and radio transmission technologies have made modern news reporting possible.

Writing Activities

In addition to the writing activities incorporated into the lesson activities above, consider the following writing projects to extend and reinforce the lesson activities.

1. Chapter Vocabulary

Suggested words and terms from which to choose for theme-based vocabulary activities are:

Technology
Machines
Machine elements
Complex machines
Simple machines
Power source
Fossil fuels
Steam power
Wind power
Air pressure
Float
Displacement
Ballast
Timeline
Invention
Sledge
Transportation
Communication
Engine
Radio transmission
Telegraph
Transport
Vehicle
Synthetic
Scientific convention
Dugout boat
Raft
Coracle
Sailboat
Oars
Steamboat
Cargo ship
Atomic power
Hot air balloon
Dirigible
Glider
Aerodynamics
Propulsion

2. Inventor Biographies

Study people who have helped make technological advances. Ask children to do a five-point report on an inventor or other individual who has contributed to advancement of some technology. The technology may, but need not be, related to transportation or communications. Encourage the children to include in their reports the person's name and birthdate, childhood facts, education, training or jobs, accomplishments and how the person's activities and/or invention helped the world and people today. If you prefer, you can have children do their report on the Biography Report Activity Sheet at the end of Chapter 4.

3. Be an Inventor

Help children engage in some free, creative thinking. Ask them to pretend they are inventors. What would they invent and why? Children can write a brief essay on their invention identifying its name, what it does, how you make it, and why we need it. Encourage children to draw a picture of their invention or, if you have time, to make a model of it using things they find around the house.

4. Silly Travel Poem

Let children have some fun with letters and sounds using this sample format for a non-rhyming "travel" poem. The child fills in the blank in each line with a word that starts with the same letter as his or her name or, another name the child chooses. A children's dictionary is a good source of words if children get stuck as they go.

Here is a sample format for the poem although other sentences about what the child saw and did can be added:

My name is _____.
I went on a trip to _____.
I traveled on a _____.
We saw a _____.
We ate _____.
We brought home a _____.

Examples:
My name is Butch.
I went to Brazil.
I traveled in a boat.

I saw a bear.
I ate bread.
I brought home a book.

My name is Jonathan.
I went on a trip to Java.
I traveled on a jet.
I saw a jaguar.
I ate jam.
I brought home a jacket.

5. Create a Travel Brochure

Have each child create a travel brochure to a place of the child's choice. Use this as an opportunity to have children explore the travel section of the local newspaper. Also, try to pick up some sample brochures from a local travel agent to give the children the idea of what a brochure can look like. (Ask travel agents or local consulate offices if they can send you travel posters to use as classroom decoration.) You might suggest that the child's chosen travel destination be in the United States or let children go worldwide depending upon what fits best with the rest of your curriculum.

To create the brochure, ask that each child research the cost of as many methods of transportation as possible to reach his or her destination (i.e.,, bus, train, air and ship). They can write about foods, hotels, and sight-seeing spots in complete sentences, and include maps if possible.

To obtain background information, children can use encyclopedias and the travel section of the newspaper, but can make up names of hotels if they like. They should try to research foods and sights in the travel spot of their choice. Travel resources are available at many local libraries. Since a really thorough brochure could entail quite a bit of research, you may want to have children work in pairs.

To further incorporate cross-curricular subjects into this project, have children plot their travel brochure vacation spots on a bulletin board map of the United States or the world, as appropriate to your assignment. Run yarn from your city to the chosen travel destinations around the world and then ask children to write along the path of the yarn how many miles it is from your city to their travel destinations.

6. What Would It Be Like Without...

Ask children to imagine a day in their lives without three technological advances that they take for granted. You might require that at least one of these advances be chosen from this group: electric light, running water, telephone, or automobile. Things like television, tape players and washers and dryers are also good choices. Ask children to consider what they would do differently, what would take much longer, what changes in their schedules would be necessary, and how they would entertain themselves.

7. Found Poem

Using Mother Goose travel rhymes or your choice of poems from children's poetry collections, have children create "found" poems of four to six lines that have traveling themes. A found poem is an unrhymed poem made by taking phrases from other poems. Ask children to use at least two- or three-word phrases from the source poems. Clearly, the found poems will be silly or nonsensical to some extent. Let children use prepositions with their found phrases to help them create poems with some story or meaning.

Source: Mother Goose Rhymes

Dr. Foster
Goosey Goosey Gander
Teeth & Gums
Thirty White Horses
To Babylon
The Derby Run
I Saw a Ship A-Sailing
Winken, Blinken and Nod
Dapple Gray
A Ship's Nail
Duke of York
Old Woman of Harrow
Willy Boy
Three Wise Men of Gotham
Going to St. Ives
Ride Away to See an Old Lady upon a White
    Horse
To Market
The Flying Pig
Banbury Cross

Example:

Ride away, ride away
To Banbury Cross
To buy a fat pig.
The pig flew up in the air.
Jiggety jig, jiggety jig.

rt and Craft Activities

1. Wire Sculptures

Using old bell wire or inexpensive wire from the hardware store, have children create sculptures. Sometimes a telephone repairman will give you a "hunk" of used wire if you ask. Otherwise, inexpensive wire can be purchased from the hardware store. Copper wire, thin plastic coated wire and green floral wires are all good. You can either let children make anything they like with this product of modern technology or you can ask them to create a vehicle of some sort with it—a bicycle, car, truck, airplane or ship. The special direction this project takes is up to you.

2. Watercolor Wash

Let children explore the technique of watercolor wash by combining this background with one of several types of transportation images superimposed upon it. First, have children choose whether they want to place sailing ships or airplanes against the wash background. If the child chooses sailing ships, the child should "wash in" sky in the upper two-thirds of the paper and ocean in the lower one-third of the paper. If the child chooses a plane or rocket picture, the entire paper can be covered in the wash of a sky.

The ship and/or airplane can be created in any number of ways. One way is to have children cut out ship bodies and square sails to glue onto the wash. The sails can be connected to the hull of the ship and given a three-dimensional effect by "flying" them on toothpicks before gluing them down. Airplanes or rockets can be made using aluminum foil. To do so, fold a 28 to 32 inch sheet of foil in half twice (so that you have four thicknesses) and press flat. With pencil, draw a large outline of an airplane. The child cuts out the plane shape or shapes and glues it on the sky wash. Another way to create an image on the wash is by using brightly colored toothpicks and forming the shape using the toothpicks, which are then glued onto the wash. Any of these methods can result in very striking pictures.

3. Transportation Prints

Collect foam meat trays (or use foam disposable plates) that have some flat, unprinted surface. When you have collected one meat tray for each child, ask children to draw shapes of ships, planes, cars, trains, wheels or any vehicle or simple machine onto the meat tray with pencil. They can even press detail into their shapes with their pencils or toothpicks. Each shape should be about two by two inches in size. Use a sticky adhesive or glue to affix the shapes to scraps of wood or old blocks. Have children print their stamps with ink pads or by painting them with a thin layer of paint and then pressing them onto a sheet of paper. Ask them to explore some sort of repeating pattern or design with their prints so that they are not just randomly placed on the page. You might also use these stamps to decorate your technology timeline should you choose to do one.

Consider other kinds of printing for a technology art project as well. For example, children can do track printing. Using either old toys with wheels or by making their own rollers, ask children to make track prints. A simple way to make a rolling track print is to tape string around an aluminum can. Children paint the side of the can with tempera paint and roll the can over paper to create track prints. The wheels of a discarded toy could also be painted and rolled to make a print.

4. Soap Carving

Ask each child to bring in a bar of Ivory® soap to carve a vehicle of his or her choosing. Using only plastic knives and round toothpicks, children carve the shape of a boat, car or airplane out of a bar of soap. This project allows children to explore a different medium and a different method for creating three-dimensional art and can provide them with a potential hobby interest.

5. Marble Art

Let children explore marble art as another way to create track-like artwork. To do marble art you need marbles or one inch rubber balls, slightly thinned tempera paint, plastic butter containers and plastic spoons, cut off boxes or box lids and paper. The child places one sheet of paper into the box lid or cut-off box. Then the child dips one or two marbles out of the plastic paint containers using the plastic spoons. He drops the marbles on the paper and then rolls the marbles across the paper by gently tilting the box lid this way and that. Have at least three colors of paint and marbles for each color available for the students' designs.

6. Recycled Rockets

Collect toilet paper rolls, cardboard, meat trays, egg cartons and other small boxes and paper items. Ask children to cut, glue and fold the materials to create rockets and airplanes. Then cover the aircraft with aluminum foil to create model airplanes and spacecraft. Use their creations to decorate countertops or to hang from ceilings.

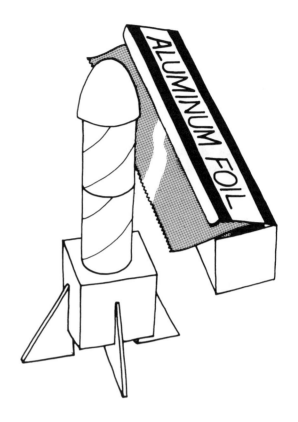

Food Activities

1. Car Snacks

As a fun and nutritional classroom food activity have children use vegetables, crackers, peanut butter, and other snack food to make edible, healthful cars. Here are two ways cars can be made:

a. Cracker and Celery Car

Fill two three-inch pieces of celery stalk with peanut butter. "Glue" the two stalks together using the peanut butter they contain. Use peanut butter to stick four wheels to the car body. The wheels can be made from any of the new mini-circle crackers of your choice such as Ritz® minis.

b. Cream Cheese and Celery Car

Fill one three-inch stalk of celery with cream cheese. Using two round toothpicks and four circles of carrot, insert the toothpicks into the celery and attach the carrot wheels at the four points. Now you have toothpick axles and carrot wheels. Children can put passengers into their snack cars by using cream cheese to attach a large and small marshmallow to the top of the car. Dip toothpicks in food coloring to dot on eyes and mouths.

2. Cracker and Candy Traincars

Here are two ideas for making edible trains.

a. Graham Cracker Train.

Have students make a graham cracker cargo train with graham crackers, small candies and prepared frostings. Each child will need five cracker halves to make a topless box car. Attach pieces to one another with frosting and use frosting to affix small candies. Small, hard, flat, round candies, lifesavers or mini-Oreros can be used as wheels and attached with frosting as well. Place the box cars one after another to create your train on a counter or long table.

b. Candy Choo-choo

Another kind of train to make is a candy train. If each child can bring in a pack of gum and a roll of Lifesavers®, this train can be made at nominal expense. It is fun to make and can serve as a gift

for penpals, siblings or dads. To make each train, the child needs a pack of gum, a roll of Lifesavers®, four hard, flat, round candies, one caramel square and one candy kiss. The Lifesavers® are glued to the gum; the four candy wheels are glued to the four corners of the gum pack. The caramel square is placed on one top end of the Lifesavers® roll and the kiss is glued onto the other top end of the roll. The train is complete. Use white glue or a low-temperature glue gun for this project.

3. Boats Times Three

You and your class could make any one of three kinds of boats - a tuna boat, a baked potato boat or a banana boat. Use these food activities as an opportunity to talk about food groups and nutritional eating. Depending upon the ingredients used, each of these snacks can serve as an all-in-one meal which incorporates three, if not four, food groups.

a. Tuna Boat

Each tuna boat is made by placing about three tablespoons of tuna salad on top of half a hot dog bun and topping this with two triangular tortilla chips which serve as sails. Combine drained tuna with diced celery, green onions, boiled egg, diced or grated cheddar cheese, pickle relish, and mayonnaise or salad dressing to make your salad. Five large cans of tuna and one jar of mayonnaise should provide the base for enough salad to make tuna boats for a class of 30 to 35 students.

b. Hot Potato Boats

To make each boat you need one small baked potato, a wooden barbecue skewer, one slice American cheese cut in half to make two rectangular sails, and potato toppings of your choice. To bake the potatoes, oil them and poke holes in the skins with forks. Bake at 350 to 375 degrees for one hour or until soft. The cheese slices are cut in half and the two rectangular "sails" woven onto the barbecue skewer. The potato is topped with the student's choice of grated cheese, diced broccoli flowerets, chopped green onions, butter, and sour cream. The sail can be placed on top of the potato before eating.

c. Banana Boats

To make each banana boat, slit a banana open in its peel with a metal knife. Both the peel and the banana are split in half so that it can serve as a bowl. Stuff the banana boat with tasty cargo such as granola, chopped fruit, yogurt, nuts and perhaps whipping cream. It would make a healthful breakfast treat.

4. Airplane Snacks

Here are a couple of ideas for snacks that use the airplane transportation theme.

a. Banana Plane

Each plane is made with a peeled banana, two apple slices for wings, chocolate chips pushed into the sides of the banana for passenger windows, and banana chips, almond slivers or more apple slices for tail fins. Give each child a paper plate on which to create an edible airplane. For greener bananas, use a plastic knife to make a slit in the banana, and push the wing or tail fin into the slit.

b. Peanut Butter Dough Planes

Use edible peanut butter dough to make small planes, the wings of which are made with sliced almonds or pieces of banana chips. An easy recipe for peanut butter dough is:

1 medium size jar smooth peanut butter
1/2 cup honey
1/4 cup toasted wheat germ
2 cups dry milk

Mix ingredients together to make consistency of Play Doh®. If too sticky, add more dry milk. If too dry, add a tiny bit of water or honey.

Children roll a tablespoon of dough to make the body of the plane. They add the almond or banana chip wings and decorate plane with windows and the like by making indentations with a toothpick.

5. Space Age Smoothie

Many foods that we take for granted today were the result of experiments to find appropriate foods for space travel. One such food is Tang® breakfast drink. Remind children about how experimentation in one area, in this case space travel, can lead to technological improvements in areas that benefit all of us. Here is a recipe for using Tang to make a refreshing drink.

Tang® drink mix
20 bananas
1 quart vanilla ice cream, softened

Mix up four cups of Tang® drink accordingly to directions. In a large bowl, mash bananas with potato masher or puree in a blender. Pour orange drink slowly into bananas, beating with an electric hand mixer. Add one scoop of ice cream at a time. Continue beating until smooth. Serve up in individual cups for a cool drink treat. Smoothies can also be made in a blender by mixing the Tang®, bananas, and ice cream in batches.

You can substitute several bags (about four) of frozen strawberries for the bananas if you are using a blender with ice crushing capability.

Art Masters—Old and New

Art lessons in the style of several different artists are provided for this chapter on technology and transportation. Most of the artists are from modern periods whose art reflects the technological developments of the age.

1. Paul Klee

Klee (pronounced *klay*) was a Swiss artist whose major works were completed in the first half of the 20th century. He was one of a group of artists called the Weimar (pronounced *vy-mar*) artists who were greatly influenced by the tragedy of World War I. Klee painted many works in geometric and abstract styles. He also did a series of pen and ink drawings which included a work called *Harbor at K* in 1939. This and the other pen and ink works are very reminiscent of a child's naive drawings.

2. Louise Nevelson

Nevelson was an American artist who had a long career and was active in artistic creation through the 1960s when she died. Nevelson began as a painter, but one day after many years work as an artist she was inspired in a new direction. She looked at a wooden packing crate divided into spaces to hold the objects inside. When she saw the square holes, she was inspired to fill them with pieces of wood and other small articles. She then sprayed the creation all one color. Her early works were sprayed black. Her later works were sprayed white. These sculptures became known as "art in a box" and were the creations in her career that finally made her famous.

3. Marcel Duchamp

Duchamp was a French artist of the Dada period. Although Dadaism began in 1916, works created by Duchamp as early as 1913 reflect the spirit behind this art style. Dadaists were part of a movement that might be called anti-art. They were dissatisfied with the way things were in the art world and in the world generally. They were concerned about the developments of technology and the changes urbanization was making in people's lives. They took everyday things from homes, factories and businesses and put them together in strange ways to create sculptures and painted canvases. Sometimes there were pictures of gears with words. One of Duchamp's famous early works was a sculpture of a bicycle wheel stuck upside down into a wooden stool. This is the kind of art that many people of Duchamp's time looked at and said "That's not art" or "I don't get it." This is perhaps why the Dadaist movement was called an "anti-art" art movement.

Project Directions

1. Paul Klee Harbor Mural

Use a bulletin board to recreate a Paul Klee style mural of a harbor scene. With white paper as the background, children use black markers to recreate a busy harbor scene. Have children look at books that contain pictures of harbors and the types of ships, vehicles and equipment that populate them. Talk with children about the life and work of a harbor. Ships come and go. They must be loaded with cargo and unloaded, counterbalanced as necessary with ballast. There are tug boats, dinghies, and cruise ships. On land, there are trucks, cars and cargo-loading equipment. There might be small marinas nearby with hobbyists' sailing ships and motor boats.

The teacher (or students, depending upon their skill level) provides the basic harbor shape or outline with thick black marker. Each child creates at least one ship or boat design for the mural, but since the mural should be full when complete you may ask children to do more than one design shape depending upon the size of your board. Children should create outlines as Klee did—with only his or her pen and ink. This is done with black marker on small pieces of white paper. Each child cuts out her design leaving the black lines showing. The designs are stapled or glued to the board in appropriate places.

2. Art in a Carton

Louise Nevelson saw a crate and made sculpture. The crate was just an ordinary shipping crate, but she saw its artistic potential and filled its spaces with odd and ends from life around her. Children can experience these famous boxes of art by using cardboard egg cartons as their starting point. Remove the top of the carton and glue the bottom part onto a piece of posterboard not much bigger than the carton. Ask children to collect small things from their daily lives to glue into the egg holding compartments. Have them focus on articles that have been created by modern technology (i.e., machinery) rather than items from nature. These items can include pieces of pasta (wheels, corkscrews, etc.), washers, pieces of straws, toothpicks, sponge, erasers, parts of broken toys, bottle caps, paper clips and the like. Glue them with white glue into the carton compartments. When dry, spraypaint the completed sculptures a solid color. An adult can do this part of the project. Complete the spraypainting outdoors.

3. Dada Art

Children can explore the anti-art concepts of Dadaist artists such as Marcel Duchamp in a number of ways. One way is to take found objects such as straws, toothpicks, cotton swabs, corkscrew and wheel pasta and create small sculptures on pieces of cardboard by gluing them together with white glue. You might want to at least partially spraypaint over the final project.

Another way to explore this art form is to have children lay out the items of their choice on paper in a design of their choosing. The design is then spraypainted and the articles removed to leave their images on the canvas. To do this, have children place a 9" by 11" sheet of light colored construction paper on a large piece of newspaper. They then lay their objects out. When complete, an adult (or student if appropriate) spraypaints over the paper. When paint is dry, the objects are removed, leaving their imprints. Caution: Never use spray paint during the school day inside the classroom, as the fumes can be a problem.

The latter version of this project works very well on solar graphic paper or dark blue construction paper and the issue of spraypainting is then avoided. Solar graphic paper for making sun prints is now available at much more reasonable prices than when it was first introduced. If using solar graphic paper, follow package directions. If using construction paper, the project must be done on a hot, sunny day and left to sit in the sun for several hours. The sun will fade most construction paper where it is left uncovered.

Sharing Activities

Here are some ideas for ways to share your class activities with the school or to just provide a focal point to culminate your explorations of technology and how it changes our lives.

1. Bookmark Contest

Using the theme of traveling to new worlds through books, hold a bookmark design contest. Either as a class or inviting other classes to join in, ask children to create a travel theme bookmark to encourage children to read and visit the local library. Give children pieces of white paper 2" by 8 1/2" to create their bookmarks using only dark pencil, black, or blue ink. Encourage children to come up with catchy slogans as well as illustrations. Sample slogans are "Travel the World Through Books" or "You can go to the store by car or to the capitol by plane, but you can travel anywhere by books" or "Your local library—check it out. Travel there by car, by bike, by foot, but travel there."

Ask the principal or a local librarian to select a given number of winning bookmarks. Mount them side by side on a sheet of 8 1/2" x 11" paper and have them photocopied. Cut them apart on the paper cutter and donate them to the local library to pass out to school children who visit the library. Or distribute them at your school library. Make enough copies so that each child in the school can receive a bookmark on weekly class visits to the school library. Bookmarks encourage discussion of good book-care habits, too.

2. Inventor Day

Ask children in your class and other classes as well to imagine something they would like to invent and then make a model of it. This can be organized as a family project so that all members of the student's family are welcome to participate. Suggest that models of inventions may be no larger than 12" x 24". A three by five card should be completed for the model that states the name of the invention and its purpose. Examples of inventions can end up being as diverse as a proposed new amusement park ride or an elaborate mouse-trap. Encourage children to use their imaginations. Inventions can be real or fanciful. If you choose to make a contest of it, ask a local business such as a book store or art supply store to donate gift certificates to winning students.

3. Flight Day

Paper airplane making may not be new, but it can be both fun and educational. This activity is similar to one of the lesson activities in this chapter but anticipates children making complete airplanes from paper–totally of their own design. If you plan a paper airplane contest, invite another class to participate with you.

Let children know about the contest in advance and encourage them to look up designs in books at the local library. Should planes be weighted? If so, where? What fold design works best? Perhaps they will experiment at home before bringing their "best" design to school for the flight contest. On the day of the contest, children fly their planes to see which go farthest. Children can also do the flight measurements and record them in inches and/or centimeters. Display the five or ten designs that fly the furthest so that children can see the similarities and differences between these planes. You might have children pair up or work in cooperative learning groups to write up their observations and conclusions on design of the far-flying planes.

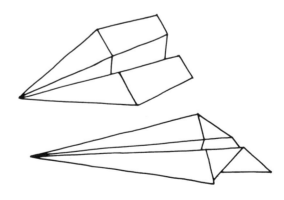

Name: _____

**CHAPTER 3
ACTIVITY SHEET**

Be-A-Transportation Scientist

Do each of these activities with both a real rubber item and synthetic rubber. For items 1, 2, and 3, use a rubber glove, rubber band, or balloon. For items 4 and 5, use a rubber ball.

1. Is it elastic? When you stretch it slowly, stop and let it go, does it return to its original shape? If so, how quickly?

        Synthetic Rubber   Rubber

      _____   _____

2. What happens when you stretch it slowly and hold it in the stretched position? Does it hold its shape?

        Synthetic Rubber   Rubber

      _____   _____

3. When you pull it quickly, does it break?

        Synthetic Rubber   Rubber

      _____   _____

4. When in ball or sphere shape, does it bounce? Which bounces higher?

        Synthetic Rubber   Rubber

      _____   _____

5. Does it hold its shape in a ball

        Synthetic Rubber   Rubber

after one minute?   _____

after 5 minutes?   _____

after 10 minutes?   _____

after 60 minutes?   _____

6. Would this synthetic rubber be a good material for making car tires? Why? Why not? If not, what practical use might it have? (Write answer on the back of this paper.)

Resources

1. Basic reference works that can give you detailed timeline information on technological advances are:

The New York Public Library Book of Chronologies by Bruce Wetterau published by Prentice Hall Press (1990).

The Timetables of History, 3rd Revised Edition by Bernard Grun published by Touchstone Books (1991).

2. Some good books on flight and space that might be helpful resources for classroom activities are:

Flight Through the Ages by C.H. Gibbs-Smither published by Thomas Y. Crowell Company, Inc. (1974).

The Planets in Our Solar System by Franklyn M. Branley published by Harper Trophy (1981).

The Sky is Full of Stars by Franklyn M. Branley published by Harper Trophy (1986).

Living in Space: A Resource Guide with Activities for Elementary School Teachers by Sheila Andrews and Audrey Kirschenbaum developed by Science Weekly, Inc. and available through the Superintendent of Documents, Government Printing Office, Washington D.C. 20402 (free or nominal cost).

Elementary School Aerospace Activities: A Resource for Teachers EP-147 by National Aeronautics & Space Administration (1977) available through Superintendent of Documents, Government Printing Office, Washington D.C. 20402, Stock No. 033-000-00693-4 (free or nominal cost).

3. Many core literature selections can be used in conjunction with a technology and specifically transportation theme. Some good ones are:

By the Great Horn Spoon by Sid Fleishman published by Joy Street Childrens (1985).

Trouble River by Betsy Byars published by Penguin (1989).

The Ox-Cart Man by Donald Hall published by Viking (1979).

Journey to America by Sonia Levitin published by Atheneum (1970).

Long Way to a New Land by Joan Sandin published by Harper & Row (1981).

The Glorious Flight Across the Channel with Louis Bleriot by Martin and Alice Provensen published by Viking (1983).

Magellan: First Around the World by Ronald Syme published by Morrow (1953).

Daedalus and Icarus by Penelope Farmer published by Harcourt Brace Jovanovich (1971).

The Wonderful Flight to the Mushroom Planet by Eleanor Cameron published by Little, Brown (1954).

The Mouse and the Motorcycle by Beverly Cleary published by Dell (1965).

The Railway Children by Edith Nesbit published by Philomel (1990).

Seafaring Women by Linda G. DePauw published by Houghton Mifflin Co. (1982).

The Long Journey from Space by Simon Seymour published by Crown (1982).

4. Related biographical readings can be found in:

Great Lives: Exploration by Milton Lomask published by Charles Scribner's Sons (1988).

Great Lives: Invention and Technology by Milton Lomask published by Charles Scribner's Sons (1991).

A WALK AROUND THE WORLD

This chapter is designed to provide teachers with a framework for exploring multicultural traditions and for helping children see the ideas, feelings and traditions that are common to people around the world. The lesson materials provide children with an opportunity to explore folk traditions in both story and music and the other chapter activities introduce children to craft, food, and art traditions from different parts of the world.

Lesson Activities

The Lesson Activities in this section provide children with an opportunity to identify their own cultural roots and explore them. Additional lessons help children see the similarities and differences in people from different cultures by examining the similarities in folk traditions from around the world. Specifically, the lesson activities provide methods and educational tools for exploring similarly themed folk tales from different parts of the world. Lastly, the activities include ways for children to explore the theme of peace around the world.

Writing Activities

The Writing Activities offer suggestions for children to explore poetry forms that originated in other countries, as well as providing ideas for reports and creative writing activities consistent with the theme of exploring the peoples and cultures of our world and the issue of peace.

Art and Craft Activities

The Art and Craft Activities provide simple craft ideas from some of the countries on each of the populated continents.

Food Activities

In the Food Activities section, a virtual recipe book of international dishes is provided to give children an opportunity to cook and enjoy foods from around the world. An effort has been made to provide recipes from countries such as Vietnam and Korea. Large numbers of people from these countries have immigrated to this country in recent years.

Art Masters—Old and New

The art masters explored in this chapter are the famous Mexican muralist and painter Diego Rivera, Spanish painter Joan Miro´, and the famous Chinese painter Tung Ch'i-ch'ang.

Sharing Activities

The ideas provided for sharing events are folk dance festivals, international songfests and multicultural potlucks.

Lesson Activities

Background Information

The background information in this chapter is limited to information about the United Nations and its peace-making activities around the world. Since the lesson activities in this section are geared toward providing a teacher with ideas on how to structure and organize each student's exploration of his or her own heritage or the student's personal exploration of an unfamiliar culture and country, no other background information provided in a book of this type could be particularly useful.

The United Nations

People try to find peace in their lives in many ways. In order to be happy, productive members of society we need to find peace within ourselves, our families, our communities, our country and our world. Peacemaking is a skill children need to learn. They learn it through making compromises when working in cooperative learning groups. They learn it through finding solutions to problems they have with siblings and mom and dad. They learn it (or learn its opposite) from watching other role models within the community, country, and world in which they live.

Peace is made by learning how to talk through differences and seek solutions, often in the form of compromise. The United Nations is an international peace organization which many children have heard of because of its role in world crises such as the Gulf War of 1991, upheavals in eastern Europe, the plight of Somalia's poor and hungry, and the Rwandan refugee situation. While not always successful, the methods used by the United Nations to find peaceful solutions can be instructive to children.

The United Nations came into being about fifty years ago. Why was this and what does the United Nations do?

War has been a frequent blot on human history through the ages. Wars have been fought over many things—power, money, land, religious principles, oppression. As wars were fought, people developed more and more sophisticated ways to kill each other in an effort to win the war for their side.

One of the great wars in world history, World War II, occurred not so long ago. People fought in Europe, Africa, Asia, and the South Pacific. The frightening atomic bomb was dropped for the first time during this war. The United States dropped this bomb on two cities in Japan in an attempt to hasten the end of the war. The devastation was like none ever seen before.

Even before this bomb was dropped, people knew it was being developed and they knew that it was important that there be no more great wars like World War II. A group of people, leaders in their own countries, decided to create an organization that would try to keep peace in the world. In 1945, people from several countries met to make a plan for how a world peace-keeping organization would work. They decided to call it the United Nations or the U.N.

Many countries were asked to join this effort and on October 24, 1945, enough countries had agreed to join for the U.N. to begin its work. That is why October 24 each year is designated United Nations Day.

The United Nations meets in New York City. Flags of the member countries fly in front of the U.N. building. Representatives from member countries around the world meet to try to solve world problems and to settle arguments when they arise. When a dispute arises, how does the United Nations try to solve it? The U.N. has a special committee called the Security Council that meets when serious world arguments threaten war.

The United Nations knows that as long as there are rich and poor people in the world, peace will be difficult to maintain. The United Nations has groups that send teachers, scientists, doctors, and farmers all over the world in an effort to have rich nations help less fortunate nations learn how to become self-sufficient, literate, and healthy.

Project Directions

1. Exploring Me

The exploration of a personal family history is the starting place for any child in his or her effort to discover the world and his or her place in it.

a. Family History Report

The report should include:

- A family tree
- Description of a favorite relative
- Favorite ethnic recipes from the family's cultural heritage
- Brief description of the countries from which each side of the family emigrated
- Description of one or two family traditions, whether from the "old" country or from the child's own nuclear family

Children should try to find out the approximate years in which family members came to the United States.

In addition to the usual assignment of writing a family history as described above, this section provides additional ideas for family interviews and other ways to make the exploration of the child's cultural heritage come alive.

b. Family Interviews

As part of an assignment to write a family history, ask that the child interview at least one family member about his or her life and perhaps some of his or her most interesting memories. Children can use the Family Interview Activity Sheet at the back of this chapter as a starting place for conducting the interview but should be encouraged to make up several questions of their own. Children should try to get their interviewees to describe experiences before the child's birth and which the child is likely to study in school, such as World War II, the Korean or Vietnam War, the moon landing, the civil rights movement, or the 1960s anti-war movement.

c. Around-the-World Bulletin Board

After children have learned a little about the countries of their origin, use this bulletin board idea to have children begin to understand the geography of their family's travels. First, ask each child to design a flag that represents her family. (Most children will need to make several copies of

their flags as discussed below so remind children to keep flag design simple.) Each child's personal flag might reflect colors from flags of his or her countries of origin, symbols of his or her family life such as pets, sports enjoyed, etc. The child makes several copies of the flag on 1" by 2" pieces of white paper. These flags are then pinned to a bulletin board that holds a large map of the world. Each child pins his flags on one or more countries of origin.

Make a map key at the bottom of the board. Each child's flag design is placed in the key at the bottom of the bulletin board next to his or her name. Arrange children's names alphabetically in the key. This way, children can look up other students' flags. The activity helps reinforce map reading skills.

d. Reports from the Mini-United Nations

Have each child select one country from his heritage upon which to do a short report. Subjects could include location, size, population, geography, agriculture, climate, form of government, way of life (food, lifestyle, holidays, religion, clothing) and industry. If time is limited, have children do a simple five-point report in which a child merely identifies the country, lists three facts or characteristics, and closes. Older children, however, should be encouraged to make this short report a little more extensive.

e. Mapamatics

Using a flat world map, have children find out how many miles it is from the school or community in which they live to one or more of their countries of origin. To do this, they must measure the distance, read the key, and compute the number of miles.

You might want children to take this process a step further. After they have found their distances, they could find out how long it would take to get to their country of origin in a car, in a plane, or train, or some combination thereof. Cars travel 55 to 60 miles per hour. Planes fly 550 miles per hour. Trains travel 85 miles per hour.

f. Countries-of-our-Class Cookbook

Ask each child to bring in a recipe that relates to the family's cultural heritage. For some families who have not recently immigrated to this country, traditional family recipes may not reflect their original countries of origin. In such cases, children might want to look up a recipe that does relate to a country of family origin. If this is not possible, the child can use a traditional recipe used within the family; in this case, however, the student should try to obtain the story about how the recipe got to be a family tradition.

Have each child write the recipe neatly in black ink. The child can illustrate the recipe if you like. You might want each recipe to fit on a half sheet of paper to cut down on duplicating time and expense. Then assemble the recipes in a book format, have the children design their own covers on construction paper or cardstock and let each child take home an international recipe cookbook that helps them understand the ethnic origins of their classmates.

You could even ask children to include basic information about the country from which the recipe comes as part of the recipe page format. If you choose to do this (which increases the informative and educational aspect of the cookbook), you may want to use the Recipe Activity Sheet in the back of this chapter.

2. Exploring Folk Story Telling Traditions

Around the world, throughout history, people have told stories. If we look at folk stories from different parts of the world, we begin to see similar themes, similar characters, similar plots. Some things are different, though. Sometimes animals differ in stories in one part of the world from stories in another part of the world. Sometimes different terrain or foliage is described. All these things reflect those things that are unique about the area or country in which the story originated.

Here are some famous and relatively available selections of different folk story types to use to explore this cross-cultural activity. Under the generic story types, you might be able to find other books that involve similar themes by checking with your local children's librarian.

Cinderella Stories
France
Cinderella or The Little Glass Slipper translated from Charles Perrault illustrated by Marcia Brown and published by Charles Scribner's Sons (1954).

Cinderella by Paul Galdone published by McGraw-Hill Book Co. (1978).

Korea
The Korean Cinderella by Shirley Climo published by HarperCollins (1993).

Native American
The Rough-Face Girl by Rafe Martin published by Scholastic, Inc. (1992).

China
Yeh-Shen A Cinderella Story from China retold by Ai-Ling Louie published by Philomel Books (1982).

Egypt
The Egyptian Cinderella by Shirley Climo published by Thomas Y. Crowell (1989).

Russia
Vasilissa the Beautiful by Elizabeth Winthrop published by HarperCollins Publishers (1991).

Little Red Riding Hood Stories
France
Little Red Riding Hood translated from Charles Perrault by Beni Montresor published by Doubleday Dell Publishing (1991).

Little Red Riding Hood retold by Trina Schart Hyman published by Holiday House (1983).

China
Lon Po Po, A Red Riding Hood Story from China by Ed Young published by Philomel Books (1989).

Impending Disaster Stories (i.e. "the sky is falling")
England
Henny Penny by Paul Galdone published by Seabury Press (1968).

Henny Penny by Henny Penny published by Little, Brown (1976).

India
Foolish Rabbit's Big Mistake by Rafe Martin and Ed Young published by G.P. Putnum's Sons (1985).

Africa
Why Mosquitoes Buzz in People's Ears by Verna Aardema published by E.P. Dutton, Inc. (1975).

Prince in Disguise Stories
Germany
The Frog Prince by Paul Galdone published by McGraw Hill (1975).

France
Beauty and the Beast by Jan Brett published by Clarion Books (1989).

Norway
East of the Sun and West of the Moon by Kathleen Hague published by Harcourt Brace Jovanovich (1980).

East of the Sun and West of the Moon by Mercer Mayer published by Four Winds Press (1980).

Korea
"The Toad Bridegroom" from *Sun and Moon Fairy Tales* from Korea by Kathleen Seros published by Hollym International Corp. (1982).

Vietnam
The Fisherman and The Goblet by Mark Taylor published by Golden Gate Junior Books (1971).

Riches From Ordinary Things Stories
Ireland
Tim O'Toole and the Wee Folk by Gerald McDermott published by Puffin Books (1992).

India
The Magic Cooking Pot by Faith M. Towle published by Houghton Mifflin Company (1975).

China
"The Old Jar" from *The Rainbow People* by Laurence Yep published by Harper & Row (1989).

England
Goose that Laid the Golden Egg by Geoffrey Patterson published by London (1986).

Child-Snatching Witch Stories
Germany
Hansel and Gretel by Ruth Belov Gross published by Scholastic, Inc. (1988).

Hansel and Gretel by Jacob Grimm published by William Morrow (1979).

Russia/Eastern Europe
Bony Legs by Joanna Cole published by Four Winds Press (1983).

Special Talent Stories
China
The Five Chinese Brothers by Claire Bishop published by Coward-McCann (1938).

The Seven Chinese Brothers by Margaret Mahy published by Scholastic, Inc. (1990).

Russia
The Fool of the World and the Flying Ship by Arthur Ransome published by Farrar, Strauss & Giroux (1968).

Mexico
The Riddle of the Drum: A Tale from Tizipan, Mexico by Verna Aardema published by Four Winds Press (1979).

Mean Ogre/Small Hero Stories
Germany
The Valiant Tailor by Kurt Werth published by Viking Press (1965).

The Brave Little Tailor by Jacob Grimm published by Doubleday (1982).

Ireland
Molly Whuppie by Walter de la Mare published by Farrar, Strauss & Giroux (1983).

England
The History of Mother Twaddle & The Marvelous Achievements of Her Son, Jack by Paul Galdone published by Seabury Press (1974).

Jack and the Beanstalk by Steven Kellogg published by Morrow Junior Books (1991),

Jack and the Beanstalk by Lorinda Bryan Cauley published by G.P. Putnam's Sons (1983).

Sleeping Beauty Stories
About Sleeping Beauty by P.L. Travers published by McGraw-Hill Book Company (1975) (contains five sleeping beauty stories from Germany, France, Italy, Ireland and India).

Thumb-Sized Child Stories
Japan
Inch Boy by Junko Morimoto published by Viking Kestre (1986).

Germany
Tom Thumb by Tom Thumb published by Atheneum (1973).

England/Germany
Tom Thumb by Margaret Hillert published by Follett Publishing Co. (1982).

Denmark
Thumbeline by Hans Christian Andersen published by William Morrow (1980).

Nice Girl/Mean Sisters Stories (Cinderella variant)
Greece
The Twelve Months by Aliki published by Greenwillow (1978).

American Folk
The Talking Eggs by Robert D. San Souci published by Dial Books for Young Readers (1989).

Have children work in cooperative learning grounds to explore two or three folk stories of the same "type" originating from different places. For example, one group explores two of the thumb-sized children stories—one from Japan, the other from Germany. Another group reads two special talent stories, one from China, the other from Mexico. These folk stories can be enlightening in a variety of ways and can lead to further cultural explorations about the countries they come from.

a. Exploring the Stories Themselves
Here are several ideas to help children explore the folk stories and the countries from which they come.

- First children in the learning group must read the stories. You might have them read them softly aloud to one another. As one child reads, the others take notes on characters, environment, props, transportation, historical time, and dress. Children need to be paying attention and focusing on these subjects because they will be comparing these subjects

as between the stories. The Facts in the Folktale Activity Sheet and the Folk Story Analysis Activity Sheet at the back of this chapter will help children take notes and identify characteristics of the stories.
- Once all the stories have been read and notes taken, have children use a Venn diagram to identify the similarities and differences between the stories. Children can also identify similarities and differences using the information on the two activity sheets. Each member of the group should write a paragraph to one page report (as time permits) on the similarities and differences between the stories.
- Each group should choose one of its folktales to reenact in some fashion. (For this activity, encourage children to choose a less familiar version of the story—e.g., most children are familiar with Little Red Riding Hood while fewer are familiar with the Chinese version called "Lon Po Po.") Each group can decide how it wants to reenact its story. Possible ideas are through skit, puppetry, or a choreographed storytelling with sound effects and hand motions.

  Have the audience class members take a few minutes to write a paragraph or two summarizing the folk story reenacted by each group to be sure that they are listening to and thinking about the folktales. This will allow each child to have a short book of folktales from around the world when the entire project is complete.
- Ask children to make some tangible recreation of the story they reenact. These could be in the form of a story quilt, a diorama, a table model, designing a book jacket for the folktale or creating a movie poster for the folktale (children pretend that their folktale has been made into a major motion picture). Some of this work can be done in class and some (such as the story quilt) can be done in pieces at home and assembled at school.

b. Each learning group chooses a country from which one of its stories comes and explores that country in detail
It usually makes sense to suggest that the country chosen for this project be the country of origin for the folktale reenacted. The children do a group

report on the country they adopt in this project. Children assign each other research and investigation into some or all of the following subject areas:

> Agriculture
> Music
> Art Dress
> Foods
> Language
> Customs (major holidays/festivals)
> Industries
> Climate
> Terrain
> Flora and Fauna
> Religion
> Form of Government

The report each child submits to be included in the group report need not be long. Suggest a paragraph to a page depending on the requirements of other classwork.

You might ask that children present their country reports briefly orally before they reenact their folktales so that the audience has some sense of the place from which the folktale comes. These presentations can include maps, posters and artifacts if the children so choose.

3. Exploring Folk Music Traditions

Music is often called the universal language. Most people easily relate to the rhythms and melodies of music from other parts of the world. Explore other countries by exploring some of their musical traditions. Dance, song or rhythm can be explored.

a. Step Left, Hop

Basic folk dance music is often available from local libraries, or a general library of folk music may be available from a school or district resource center. While music is not provided here, step directions or dance ideas are provided for a few well known dances or types of dances which may or may not be available in your local library.

- **Chinese Ribbon Dance.** Using toilet paper tubes covered with construction paper, staple four two and one-half to three foot lengths of crepe paper streamers to one end of the paper tube to create your dancing ribbon. Make up a simple routine using the ribbons. These can

include figure eights, diagonal movements across the body and swishing the ribbon back and forth across the body while moving from a squat to a standing position. If you cannot find Chinese folk music at your local library, perform the dance to an instrumental piece of your choosing.

- **Maori Poi Ball Dance (New Zealand).** The poi ball dance comes from the Maori group in New Zealand and is one of many well known Polynesian dance forms. Children love working with the poi balls. Poi balls can be made by using 8 to 9 inch fabric squares, yarn or fish line, clothesline rope and toilet paper. Cut clothesline into 28" to 32" lengths. Knot each end. Wrap 40 sheets of toilet paper around one knot of the clothesline. Crush to size of

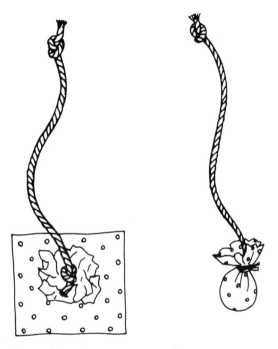

fist and lay this mass into a fabric square. Gather fabric up around the paper mass and knot. Then tie the fabric very tightly around the clothesline with yarn or fish line. Tack excess cloth to clothesline with needle and thread, if possible. Perhaps each child can take his or her poi ball home to complete this small sewing task. If the poi balls are not tacked, they may occasionally need to be retied.

To use the poi balls, make up a routine in which each child uses only one poi ball and in which each movement is done for counts of eight. A sample routine would be circles on the right side for eight counts, circles on the left side for eight counts, circles on alternating sides for eight counts, circling overhead like a helicopter for eight counts, alternating again for eight counts, body slap (holding poi ball in front of body you throw it gently around your body letting ball "slap" your back changing directions each time) for eight counts. Perform dance to a drum beat or claves beat of your choice if no Maori Polynesian music is available from your local library.

- **Israeli Hora.** This dance requires no props and is easy to learn. It can be danced to any traditional lively Israeli music. Right foot steps to the right. Left foot crosses over right foot. Step right with the right foot and jump on the right foot. Step down on the left foot and jump on the left foot. Repeat sequence again and again as you dance. Dance in a circle formation.

- **Mexican La Raspa.** This is a well-known Mexican folk dance. You may already know the beat and steps. Here are some directions to serve as a reminder.

    Partners face each other. One partner puts the left heel forward on the floor, then the right heel forward on the floor, then the left heel forward on the floor, in time with the music.

    The dancer repeats this action once, but this time he or she starts with the right foot.

    The entire six-step sequence is then repeated once.

    The other partner does the same steps simultaneously.

    Partners then join right or left arms at the elbow and turn in a circle to the music for about eight counts, clap, and then change arms and reverse direction for about eight counts.

    The music segment you use guides how the sequence is repeated. The melody and rhythm is one of the most familiar Mexican folk dances.

b. Sing a Song

Children enjoy learning songs from other countries, including songs in other languages. Here are some well-known examples. Additional international song resource books are listed in the resources section of this chapter.

"Frere Jacques" (French Folk) (Older children sing it in rounds.)
"Alouette" (French Folk) (Older children sign it in rounds.)
"Au Clair De La Lune" (French Folk)
"Dona Nobis Pacem" (Give Us Peace) (Latin)
"Las Mananitas" (Spanish)
"The Hand Clapping Song" (Mexican Dance)
"La Cucharacha" (Mexican Dance)
"Greensleeves" (English)
"Mayim, Mayim" (Water, Water) (Jewish)
"Had Gadya" (One Little Goat) (Jewish)
"Jim Along Josie" (American Folk)
"Shortenin' Bread" (Southern Folk)
"It's A Small World" (American Popular)
"I'd Like to Teach the World to Sing" (American Popular)
"Let There Be Peace on Earth" (American Popular)
"Des Colores" (Mexican)
"Pearly Shells" (Hawaiian)

"Pearly Shells" is both a song and a hula, primarily to be performed by girls or women. The song is done in an echo format with one student or group leading and another repeating. Students can perform it sitting on their knees and making motions to illustrate the song's story.

c. Rhythm Makes the World Go Round

Percussion instruments are those which provide the beat and basic sound for the many different kinds of music that people make in different parts of the world. Nearly every music tradition has certain percussion instruments (often drums or rattles) that provide the basic beat. This section gives you ideas on how to recreate some of these percussion traditions from the far corners of the world. You might also try to check out some music from countries around the world and let children tap along with the beat so they begin to understand the important part percussion plays in any musical tradition.

- **Drum.** Drums can be made in a variety of ways, from covering oatmeal boxes with paper to more elaborate versions made from coffee cans with their tops and bottoms cut off and heads made from innertube laced between the top and bottom heads with heavy string.

- **Rasp.** Rasps are rough surfaced objects over which a stick is rubbed to a beat. Ribbed plastic water bottles with dowel or pencil sticks make good rasps.
- **Maraca.** Maracas are often gourds or carved wood spheres that contain seeds or small pebbles and are shaken. They can be made with aluminum cans filled with a half-inch of dry rice, beans or barley or a few paper clips. The maraca is then sealed shut with masking tape and covered with decorated construction paper.

3. Peace Among Many

An additional focus for an exploration of peoples around the world is to explore world cultures from the view of creating a peaceful world in which to live. There are many turns such an exploration can take. Both a personal and an international perspective are offered here.

a. United Nations Security Council

Have children look through the newspaper and talk to their parents to come up with an international dispute, current or historical, which your students could discuss and attempt to resolve peacefully. Whether you choose a historical dispute or a current one depends upon available information as well as your class curriculum. Clearly, information on historical disputes may be more readily available from libraries but current disputes serve as an introduction to obtaining information from newspapers, news magazines and newscasts. Assuming students bring several "dispute" subjects to school, have them vote on the one they want to discuss as a class. Alternatively, you can "make up" a simple dispute such as one country taking another's best farmland so that the invaded country threatens war. The invaded country, however, had taken valuable mining lands from the invading country 10 years earlier.

To prepare for the class discussion or debate, have each student research the dispute and write a 5-point report about the dispute which includes a suggestion for how it should be resolved.

To roleplay the United Nations at work, have the children divide up so that some represent the countries involved in the dispute and others represent neutral member nations of the U.N. The children representing the hostile nations sit in the front of the classroom and present their respective sides. The member nation representatives sit at their desks and can ask questions of the hostile countries. Then all students can suggest possible peaceful resolutions which you might want to post on the board. (Each party has to give up something and get something.)

If your class is using a current international dispute and it is appropriate to the issue debated by your class, have children individually or as a class compose a letter to the United States Representatives to the United Nations or to a congressional representative stating your class's proposal for resolving the dispute.

b. Peace Leader Paper Quilt

Using some of the names in Item 3 of the writing activities section of this chapter, have children adopt a world peace leader from history or current events and create a portrait of the leader or a picture of a major peace event in that leader's life along with the leader's name, years of birth and death, country of origin or in which the person's work was done, and brief description of his or her work for peace. The portraits can be mounted onto a large paper "quilt" and used to decorate a bulletin board or wall as a peace quilt. You can use small yarn ties or bows at various corners to recreate the look of a real quilt.

c. Parents - Center Stage

Perhaps several parents would be willing to come and visit over a two or three week period to make short presentations with artifacts such as flags, sculpture, costumes and jewelry to tell about a country of the parent's origin, a country they or a friend have visited or a country they lived in at one time.

d. One World Globe

Children can make their own class globe. Inflate an oversized balloon (available at science specialty stores) or even a large beach ball and papier-mâché over it using starch or equal parts glue and water and newspaper strips. When it is dry, have children recreate the ocean and continents on it with tempera paint. Some labeling can be done with marker when the paint is dry. This project will help reinforce the geography of the earth.

Writing Activities

1. Chapter Vocabulary

Vocabulary words and phrases suggested by this theme are:

- Peace
- United Nations
- Compromise
- Cooperation
- World hunger
- Relief
- Resolution
- Solution
- Discrimination
- Hostility
- Prejudice
- Enemy
- Folk art
- Retaliation
- Continents
- Europe
- Asia
- Australia
- North America
- South America
- Africa
- Famine
- Drought
- Peace-keeping force
- Equality
- Opportunity
- Folktales
- Similarities

2. Write Your Own Folktales

After completing the investigation into folk story traditions around the world, ask children to write their own folktales. Each folktale needs to have characters, conflict and resolution.

3. Peace Leader Report

Either as a stand alone project or in conjunction with the making of the peace leader quilt described in the lesson activities in this chapter, have children do a biographical report on a world peace leader of their own choosing. Children can use the Biography Report Activity Sheet at the end of this chapter if you like. To provide a starting point, consider these well known people:

Anwar Sadat (Egyptian leader who made a peace pact with Israel in 1977)

Bishop Desmond Tutu (South African leader and Nobel Peace Prize winner who led the crusade to end apartheid)

Mohandas Gandhi (Indian independence leader who preached peaceful civil disobedience)

Mother Teresa (Albanian-Indian Nobel Peace Prize winner who works in India helping the homeless, orphans, and lepers)

Martin Luther King (American civil rights leader who advocated peaceful protest and winner of Nobel Peace Prize in 1964)

Jimmy Carter (American President who facilitated 1977 peace meetings between Menachem Begin and Anwar Sadat)

Menachem Begin (Israeli leader who met with Anwar Sadat and made a peace pact with Egypt)

Mikhail Gorbachev (Soviet leader who promoted political change that led to the end of the cold war)

Aung San Suu Kyi (Burmese speaker and leader and Nobel Peace Prize winner who helped in movement to remove cruel national leaders)

Oscar Arias Sanchez (Costa Rican president and Nobel Peace Prize winner who drafted peace plan in 1987 to help facilitate end of Central American civil wars)

Henry Kissinger (Past American Secretary of State and Nobel Prize winner in 1973)

Lech Walesa (Polish union leader and Nobel Peace Prize winner in 1983)

Dalai Lama (Tibetan religious leader and Nobel Peace Prize winner in 1971)

Willy Brandt (West German leader and Nobel Peace Prize winner in 1971)

Mairead Corrigan and Betty Williams (peace leaders of Northern Ireland and joint Nobel Peace Prize winners in 1976)

Javier Perez de Cuellar (Peruvian diplomat who began service in 1982 as the United Nations secretary-general)

Trygve Lie (Norwegian diplomat who served as first secretary-general of the United Nations from 1946 to 1952)

Dag Hammarskjöld (Swedish leader who served as United Nations secretary-general and died in United Nations service while on a peace-keeping mission in Zaire (then known as the Congo))

Nelson Mandela (South African leader of the anti-apartheid movement who spent many years in prison for his efforts)

Theodore Roosevelt (American President and Nobel Peace Prize winner in 1906)

Woodrow Wilson (American President during World War I and Nobel Peace Prize winner of 1919 who founded the now defunct League of Nations)

Linus C. Pauling (American scientist and winner of 1962 Nobel Peace Prize)

Jane Addams (American worker for poor and underprivileged and winner of 1931 Nobel Peace Prize)

Ralph J. Bunche (American peace leader and winner of 1950 Nobel Peace Prize)

Albert Schweitzer (Nobel Peace Prize winner in 1952)

Danny Kaye (American actor and international advocate for UNICEF)

Audrey Hepburn (Belgian/American actress and international advocate for poor and under-privileged)

George C. Marshall (American political leader and drafter of rebuilding plan after World War II and winner of 1953 Nobel Peace Prize)

Some organizations the students could investigate and report on that have been past winners of the Nobel Peace Prize are: United Nations Peace-Keeping Forces (1988); International Physicians for Prevention of Nuclear War (U.S. 1985); Office of United Nations High Commissioner for Refugees (1954, 1981); United Nation's Children Fund (UNICEF) (1965); Amnesty International (1977); International Labor Organization (1969); and the International Red Cross (1944, 1963).

A reasonably current complete listing of Nobel Peace Prize winners can be found in *The New York Public Library Book of Chronologies* published by Prentice Hall Press (1990).

4. New Year Many Ways

New Year events are celebrated around the world at different times and in many different ways. There are many books available at most libraries to detail how the New Year is celebrated in different countries. Give each child a continent and ask the child to write a report about a new year celebration from some country on that continent. By assigning the project in this way, the child also has to investigate each continent a little to find out what countries are on that continent as well as researching the report itself. The report can be either a paragraph or page in length, as you think appropriate.

You could pick other festivals such as harvest festivals or winter festivals generally, but there is usually a wealth of new year information available and comparative research into the same holiday yields interesting opportunities to compare and contrast cultures.

5. International Recipe

If you do international cooking as suggested in this chapter, have each child write down the recipe ingredients and their own directions for making each dish cooked in class. If you do several recipes, each child will then have a mini-cookbook of international dishes.

Alternatively, have each child write the recipe and directions for one dish from his or her cultural heritage. These can be put together to make a class cookbook as described in the lesson activities in this chapter.

6. Japanese Haiku

Have children learn to write Japanese haiku. A haiku poem is one with three lines. The first line has five syllables, the second line has seven syllables and the third line has five syllables. The poem is unrhymed, relates to themes in nature and must contain one "season" word. The season word can be the actual name of the season or it can be a word that clearly reminds the reader of what season it is, such as "snow," which reminds the reader of winter.

Examples:

Hot dusty winds come
To blow off the memory
of budding green trees.

The deer steps gently
On the crisp new fallen snow
In search of a leaf.

I see a white cloud.
The spring cloud floats like a sock.
Then strong winds pull it.

7. Limerick Lines

A limerick is a humorous poetry form from Ireland. The poem contains five lines, a rhyme scheme of *aabba* and the following metrical patterns:

-/-/-/
-/-/-/
-/-/
-/-/
-/-/-/

Example:

There was a whale named Jim.
For a whale he was too slim.
Milkshakes he drank
But then he sank
For Jim could no longer swim.

8. Simple Sonnets

For elementary school children, sonnets are not so simple. Shakespeare wrote a great many of them. The poetry form is of Italian origin. A sonnet's lines are usually in iambic pentameter (i.e., -/-/-/-/-/) and written according to a designated rhyme scheme such as *abab cdcd efef gg*.

Example from Shakespeare:

Lo, as a careful housewife runs to catch
One of her feather'd creatures broke away,
Sets down her babe, and makes all swift despatch
In pursuit of the thing she would have stay;
Whilst her neglected child holds her in chace,
Cries to catch her whose busy care is bent
To follow that which flies before her face,
Not prizing her poor infant's discontent;
So runn'st thou after that which flies from thee,
Whilst I thy babe chase after thee afar behind:
But if thou catch thy hope, turn back to me,
And play the mother's part, kiss me, be kind:
So I will pray that thou mayst have they Will,
If thou turn back, and my loud crying still.

Sonnets are often about love but can be written about any subject or emotion the children might like to explore. A poem like this is a major project for a child and is probably best limited to advanced upper-grade children. Children could be encouraged, however, to write a fourteen line poem on a subject of their choosing with a rhyme scheme that might be easier for them to handle such as aa, bb, cc, etc.

9. Peace Poems

Ask children to write couplets or longer poems on the subject of peace using an *aa, bb, cc*, and so on rhyme scheme.

Example:

Show you care.
Always share.

The beauty of a flying dove
Speaks to me, 'the world needs love.'
Let's all try to do our part.
Join hands today to make a start.
Give to others every day
And peace will surely come our way.

10. Penpal Project

Contact an international penpal agency to see if you and your class can start a letter writing project to a child or children in another part of the world. Prepare for this project in advance of the school year by contacting one of these organizations. Here are some penpal resources:

Student Letter Exchange
630 Third Ave., 15th Floor
New York, NY 10017
(212)557-3312

World Pen Pals
1694 Como Avenue
St. Paul, Minnesota 55108
(612)647-0191

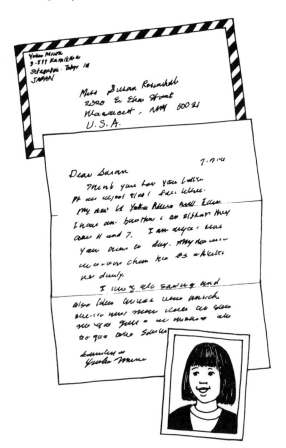

Art and Craft Activities

1. Exploring Me

As a craft activity to relate to the family history project, ask each child to create a family shield and attach a decorative personal acrostic to it. A large shield shape (i.e., 9" x 12") should be cut out of construction paper in a color of the child's choosing. A smaller shield shape is cut out of white paper. On this white sheet, children engage in a modern version of heraldry by creating their own family shield. The shield can use family name initials in a decorative way as well as symbolic images of things the child identifies with his family such as foods, sports, pets, home and the like. The decorated white shield is glued onto the colored shield. On another sheet of construction paper about 9" x 12" (or smaller if desired) the child will glue a sheet of white paper on which he or she has created a personal acrostic based on his or her family's last name. For each letter of the last name, the child thinks of a characteristic of him- or herself or family that begins with that letter.

Examples:

G   Good person
A   Artistic
R   Reader
C   Caring
I   Industrious
A   Athletic

Make two hole punches in the bottom of the shield and two in the top of the acrostic and tie the two together with yarn or ribbon. Hang on a bulletin board or decorate class walls.

2. Exploring Folk Traditions

The art and craft ideas suggested here are based on folk art traditions from around the world. These craft activities are designed to let the children see how art traditions overlap around the world as well as the fact that some art traditions are uniquely tied to a culture through religion, availability of materials or otherwise.

As you will see as you peruse the section, while materials and styles differ, folk art from any given area usually relies on patterns from nature such as animals and plants. Geometric designs are also seen in many cultures. Similarity of design is not the only crossover in crafts from different cultures.

Particular types of art and craft forms have appeared in many cultures. These art forms include mask-making, mosaic, and papier-mâché sculpture.

a. North and Central American Arts and Crafts

- **Southeastern Native American Quilting.** Directions for the creation of a fabric-like design similar to that created by the Seminole Native Americans of the Southeast are provided in Item 1 of the art and craft activities section of Chapter 7.
- **United States Traditional Crafts.** Directions for traditional and colonial American arts and crafts can be found beginning in the art and craft activities section of Chapter 6.
- **Mexican Eye of God (Ojo de Dios).** This craft symbolizes good luck. It is bright, colorful and easy to make. Use two popsicle sticks or wooden barbecue skewers and brightly colored yarn. Cross the sticks at their mid-points so that they are perpendicular to each other. Starting with an 18" piece of yarn, cross the yarn over and around the two sticks at their intersection in an "x" design to hold the sticks at right angles. Take the remaining yarn and cross it over and around each stick, then the next and the next. As you wrap your yarn around each stick, place the new wrap next to the prior wrap so that the eye grows. To change yarn colors, simply tie on a new color of yarn and continue your wrapping.

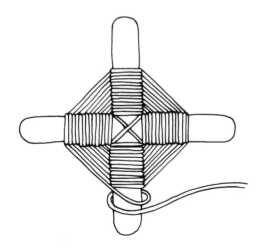

- **Mexican Bark Art.** Using a torn piece of heavy brown paper bag to simulate bark, ask children to create simple but brightly colored designs with oil pastels or pastel chalks on this mock bark. In the traditional craft from Mexico the designs are painted with bright pastel colors and usually reflect flowers or animals in a fairly stylized way. To help children keep their designs simple, have them first outline a design in pencil, fill it in with the pastels, and perhaps outline it in a darker color as a finishing touch.
- **Mexican Papel Picado.** This is a paper cutting craft which uses brightly colored tissue paper. Any design can be cut into the tissue which is folded and refolded in an "accordion" manner or it can be folded in much the same way that paper is folded to cut a snowflake. With papel picado the folded designs can be cut from rectangles (12" x 9"), squares (12" x 12") or circles. One interesting way to display papel picado is by attaching the finished pieces to string, end to end, and hanging them in streamer fashion from the ceiling or along a wall.

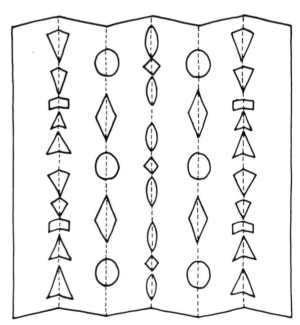

- **Guatemalan Worry People.** A Guatemalan tradition is using tiny yarn-woven dolls to dispel troubles and woes. According to the tradition, once a trouble is told, it becomes the responsibility of the doll. A rather oversized worry doll can be made using a one-piece wooden clothespin, yarn, two toothpicks, and markers. The legs of the doll are the two clothespin shafts. They are wrapped tightly with yarn, the yarn ends being tucked under the wraps with a toothpick. Wrapping continues up the torso of the doll—about halfway up the joined shaft of the pin. The two toothpicks are placed on the side of the pin to resemble arms. Wrapping continues up the torso of the doll and includes the top half of each toothpick. The wooden ball at the top of the pin is the head. The face is decorated with marker, and yarn can be glued on the head if desired or hair can be drawn on with marker.

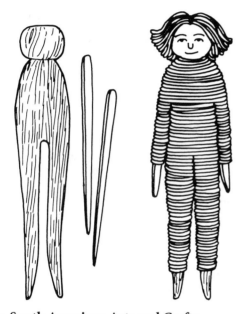

b. South American Arts and Crafts

• **South American Clay Animals.** In many South and Central American countries, clay pottery and figures are made and sold. They are painted in a variety of designs and glazes depending on the area in which they are made. Exploration of multicultural arts and crafts provides a great opportunity for students to work with clay inspired by the folk art from another part of the world.

Children in South American countries such as Venezuela make toys from clay while their parents make pots for sale. Toy pots and banks are popular. Often they are in animal shapes such as birds or turtles. Use a terra cotta colored clay to have children explore this art form. Have children mold their animals and then give them texture by using toothpicks as their tools.

Encourage children to pull the limbs, head, and other features of their animal from the central lump of clay. This helps eliminate problems with parts falling off. If children do want to add parts with separate pieces of clay, remind them to score the joint area of both pieces of clay before joining them. This helps the joint stay together. Then the joint should be smoothed.

Allow the clay to dry completely before firing in a kiln. For small animals (4" to 6" in size), drying can take seven to ten days. Glazing is optional. If students do glaze, try to have resource books available that show glazing styles from different South American countries.

• **Colombian/Venezuelan Rope Coiling.** In the countries of the northern part of South America, many items are made from coiling rope such as hemp. Hot pads, mats, and rugs are made from coiling rope. Designs can vary from simple repeating geometric patterns such as repeating circles or diamonds to more complicated animal designs.

Have children recreate rope coiling on posterboard using hemp string, another string that is flexible but made from natural fiber, or roving yarn. If you use a natural-colored string, have students dye some of the string in food coloring or fabric dye if you have time. Roving yarn, which is available in many schools, comes ready to use in a variety of colors. Have children draw the outline of their designs. The student fills the design in by painting a layer of glue in the design upon which he or she coils the string until the design area is completely filled in.

This kind of hanging, often using a simple repeating geometric design such as repeating circles, is also made by people in certain parts of Africa.

• **Brazilian Carnival Masks.** Each year in Brazil, a huge festival is held just before the beginning of the Lenten season. This festival is called "Carnival" and is similar in some ways to Mardi Gras celebrations in New Orleans. People celebrate with parades, feasting and fancy disguises or costumes. Elaborate, colorful, and shiny masks are part of this festival. Make Carnival masks with your class.

To make the masks, cut slightly oversized half-face masks from posterboard. The tops of the masks can be scalloped or zigzagged to add interest. If desired, eye holes can be cut with exacto knives; have parent volunteers do this part at home in advance. If you choose not to cut eye holes, simply have children draw in the eye holes with marker. Masks can then be decorated with tempera paint (including fluorescent colors), feathers, sequins, glitter, buttons, and plain and colored foils. You can roll and tape a 6" x 12" piece of posterboard into a cylinder (or dowel) and attach it to the side of the mask for holding and carrying.

c. Australian and Polynesian Arts and Crafts

- **Maori Poi Balls.** A craft from the Maoris who live on the island of New Zealand off the coast of Australia is the poi ball used in performing traditional dances. Directions on how to make these balls and how they are used is included in the lesson activities section of this chapter.
- **Aboriginal Art.** A method for recreating art in the style of the native peoples of Australia is suggested in Item 7 of the art and craft activities section of Chapter 1.

- **Polynesian Tapa Cloth.** Traditional tapa cloth was made from pounded or pressed bark or by treating and pressing fibrous plants to make cloth. This cloth and its geometric linear designs are well recognized. Usually the designs were painted white, black, brown and reddish-brown tones. Using squares or rectangles of either brown bag or brown construction paper, have children recreate the designs of Polynesia using chalk or oil pastels or tempera paints in the colors described above. Ask children to find resource books in the library to help them recreate the design and look of tapa cloth.

d. Asian Arts and Crafts

- **Indonesian Shadow Puppet.** Roll and tape 6" x 18" pieces of posterboard to create 18" cylinders. Your puppet will be attached to one end of the cylinder. Have children create a 10" jointed figure out of posterboard or tagboard. The central part of the puppet may need to be reinforced with a longer cylinder if you use lighter weight cardstock, but use of lighter weight cardstock such as posterboard makes cutting and hole-punching much easier.

The head and torso (and legs) can be one piece. (The upper arms and lower arms should be separate. Upper and lower legs can also be separate, if you so choose.) Hole punch each piece at its ends and attach to related pieces with brads. To provide the lacy shadow effect seen in many of these puppets, have children hole punch around the edges of the pieces. Children may want to attach a dowel or straw to each hand. A puppeteer can use these dowels to move the arms in specific ways.

Again, take advantage of resource books in the local library to help children create shapes and designs that reflect the traditional Indonesian puppet art.

Children can create a shadow parade of their puppets for each other to enjoy to see how their puppets look in shadow form. A shadow theater can be created with a flashlight and suspended sheet or other lightweight fabric or tissue paper.

• **Oriental Greetings Scrolls.** The new year is one time of the year when colorful scrolls in red, orange, and white decorate doorways and shops. Have children explore the artistry and beauty of Chinese or other Asian language letters (called characters) through creation of small greeting banners. First, have children bring in books from the school or local library that contain examples of characters from one or more Asian languages. Many books should be available that show Chinese and Japanese characters. Other languages are probably available as well. Local newspapers printed in an Asian language would also provide good source material.

Using strips of colored tissue paper about 5" across and 12" long (torn or cut to suit the artist's tastes), ask students to write oriental characters vertically. They can do this by dipping a cotton swab in a small amount of bleach, tapping off excess bleach, and drawing the characters of their choice on the tissue. The bleach immediately takes the color out of the tissue leaving the written design. Use caution with this project and do it only with sufficient adult supervision as you do not want children wiping bleach in their eyes or getting careless with their clothes. Mount the tissue design on a rectangle of light colored construction paper slightly larger than the tissue or, alternatively, frame the tissue with construction paper and hang in a window.

Another way to do this project is to use strips of white construction paper and dip the cotton swabs in black tempera paint to create Asian characters. Have students sign the artwork in the traditional way by writing their names in a vertical fashion in the lower corner of the greeting and stamping a red circle over the name. This can be done by using a cut carrot or radish and a red stamp pad or red paint. Mount the white strips on slightly larger strips of red or orange paper.

• **Origami.** The Japanese art of paper folding is fun for children of all ages and can be easily taught using squares of construction paper or squares cut from pages of old magazines. Use the origami idea suggested in the art and craft activities section of Chapter 1 or check out a book on simple origami designs from the local library.

• **Kirigami.** This art project is a Japanese paper cutting craft. For more directions on how to use this idea, refer to the illustration here and the art and craft activities section of Chapter 1.

• **Carp Windsock.** Use brightly colored, coated butcher paper. Cut two simple fish shapes of the same size. The fish shapes should be about twenty-four inches long and eight to nine inches wide with an open mouth. Glue sides closed, but leave both ends open. Decorate body with large scales drawn with markers or painted with tempera. Punch holes at either side of the mouth and hang with yarn. This is a decoration that can be seen in many Asian countries such as China, Vietnam, Japan, and Korea. The carp windsock, for example, is flown in Japan on Boy's Day.

• **Batik.** Batik is a well-known eastern craft and art form practiced in many countries. While it is presumed to have originated in Indonesia, it is done in many countries including India and countries in Africa. It is the art of applying wax to fabric in a design and then dyeing the fabric, after which the wax is removed. Usually batiking is done on fabric, but a form of it can be done on paper. Several classroom batik crafts are suggested below.

i. **Paper Batik.** Have a plastic wash pan available to hold a dark fabric dye such as red or

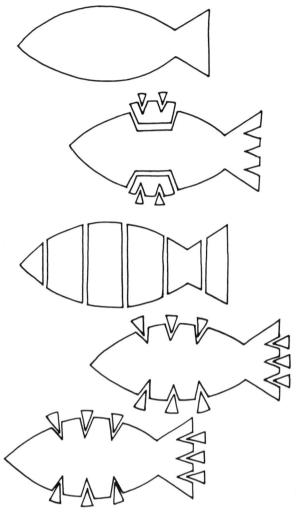

blue. Rit® dye dissolved in water works well. You will use this darker dye in the first stage of the project and a lighter dye such as yellow in the second stage of the project, if desired. An electric stew pot or other deep pot can be used for melting the wax. The wax is placed inside a metal or glass container which sits in hot water in the surrounding larger pot. Caution students and adult helpers about working with wax. The wax need not be made extremely hot. Wax will melt and be usable if you heat it to warm (i.e., a temperature at which it barely melts). Paraffin or old white votive candles can be melted to make wax. The wax goes a long way. The wax from four or five votive candles will probably be more than enough for the class batik project.

Give each child a 10" square of butcher paper and a sturdy paper hot drink cup. The child then dips the cup into the wax and

places the dipped end of the cup on his or her paper. This is done several times to create a wax design. The wax is then allowed to harden, the paper is gently crinkled and uncrinkled, and the waxed paper dipped into the pan of the dark colored dye.

Let the paper dry overnight and then let children iron off the wax with adult help. To do this set the iron on low to medium temperature and, with adult help, iron the wax off the picture by placing it between two sheets of paper towel.

If desired, dip the dyed paper into a second lighter dye (such as yellow) and let dry for final product. The squares can be mounted on a large classroom paper quilt.

ii. Fabric Batik. Repeat the project in the steps described above but use muslin or other inexpensive white or off-white cloth. If you have a volunteer who can sew backings onto the batik fabric, you might want to make pillows out of them. Stuff with polyester fiberfill. Alternatively, children can batik pieces of fabric 12" x 36" in size to create table runners. Finally, you can choose to merely mount the fabric batik designs on construction paper and hang for display.

e. European Arts and Crafts

• **French Straw Art.** A traditional French craft is making animals and designs using straw. This is common in other countries as well such as Poland. To recreate this craft in the classroom, give each children a nine by twelve inch sheet of posterboard. Using either natural flat toothpicks, wooden barbecue skewers (which can be cut or broken to different lengths), or actual straw (obtained from feed stores), have children create an animal or flower design on the paper. They do this by gluing the toothpicks or straw to the paper in designs of their choice.

Most traditional crafts involved stylizations of things from nature such as animals and plants. This is another cross-cultural aspect to folk art that you might want to share with students—that is, that traditional crafts from around the world are inspired by similar subjects—e.g., subjects from nature—but different materials and styles are used to translate the subject to the art form, depending upon resources available in a particular region.

- **German Paper Cones and Egg Craft.** In some parts of Germany, children customarily receive paper cones full of small candies on the first day of school. Make and decorate paper cones with your class and if you have a few wrapped candies to drop into each the child probably won't mind. Paper cones can be made simply out of construction paper and glued or stapled together. Before assembling cones, however, have children decorate the outside of the cones with designs of their choosing.

Another German craft is dyeing eggs using brown onion skins to create a wood-like effect. For directions for creating this egg art, see Item 2c of the art and craft section of Chapter 5.

- **Ukrainian Egg Art.** Beautifully painted geometric designs grace the eggs of Ukrainian egg crafters. These designs are created in bright colors with precision tools, beeswax, and dye. They are often seen at Easter or springtime in shops and craft shows. To recreate this craft with your students, have students recreate the linear geometric pattern of these designs on egg shapes cut from meat tray foam. They do this by pressing the design into the foam with round toothpicks. Use a gummy, removable adhesive to attach the completed design to a small piece of wood for printing. This eliminates the problem of fingers spoiling the design. Press the egg stamp onto a black ink stamp pad and print it onto a sheet of 9" x 12" construction paper. Students should put about five egg prints total on their papers, placing them as they choose. Students can print their own egg five times or print their own and those of four other students so that their picture has a variety of egg designs. This also enhances the cooperative nature of the project. When the prints are dry, the spaces between the black ink can be colored in with crayon, pastels or colored pencils.

Another way to do this project is to give each child an egg shape cut out of black construction paper. With a pencil, the child creates the outline of the Ukrainian geometric design he or she chooses. The designs are then filled in with oil pastels leaving 1/4" spaces between all the filled in space so that the design is outlined in black over the entire egg.

- **Spanish Tile.** Spanish tile was much influenced by the arrival in Spain of the Moors from North Africa where tiling and mosaic were extensively used in building and decoration. Students can recreate Spanish tile designs by creating square tiles on graph paper. Designs are simple floral patterns and geometric shapes in brown, blue, green, yellow or rust. The tiles can be colored with crayon or colored pencil. Ask children to research pictures of Spanish tile to give them design ideas or provide some examples yourself. Have students create their tile designs using a square shape cut from a copy of the Graph Paper Activity Sheet at the back of Chapter 2.

f. African Arts and Crafts

- **African Tie-Dye.** Tie-dye is a well-known fabric dyeing method. While used extensively in many countries today, some sources say it was first developed in western Africa. Using several plastic pails filled one-third full with different colors of dissolved fabric dye, have children tie-dye t-shirts, old or new. To make the tie-dye design, children wrap rubber bands or string around clumps of t-shirt fabric and then dip different parts of the tied shirt into different colored dyes. Make sure children wring the excess water out of their shirts before moving to a new bucket and make sure the dyes are not too warm for the children to use.

Another way to do tie-dying is to have children complete the string or rubber band wrapping of their shirts in the same way described above. The dying is done a little differently, however. Put liquid dye in the primary colors into small squeeze bottles with small openings. Children gently squeeze a little dye onto different tied parts of the shirt, letting the colors bleed together somewhat. The effects will be striking. Let set in a plastic bag for several hours before removing bands.

- **Egyptian Scarabs.** A scarab is an artistic version of a beetle and was considered symbolic of eternal life in ancient Egypt. Scarabs were carved out of stone and kept as fetishes or worn as jewelry. Children can make their own scarabs out of salt dough made from a recipe of 4 parts flour, 1 part salt, and 1 1/2 part water. To make salt dough scarabs, make an

egg-shape out of crushed foil approximately 1 1/2" long and 1" wide. Cover the shape with a quarter inch layer of salt dough and shape smoothly into an oval shape. This is the stylized beetle. Make indentations with toothpicks to recreate the scarab designs found in ancient Egypt. Bake at 325 degrees for one hour. When cool, children can paint the scarabs with blue and green watercolor or food coloring.

- **West African Printed Fabric.** Indigo is a popular dye in many parts of the world. Popular in India, it became common in Africa and then in North America in denim and other fabrics. In parts of Africa, indigo dye has been printed onto plain cloth with squash and melon rinds and other available plant material

that was cut into simple shapes and then used as the printing tool. A wavy combed pattern for water was popular in some places and might be combined with stylized leaf and flower designs.

To recreate blue printed fabric with your class, give each child a square of meat tray foam. Make these squares as large as possible, but all students' pieces should be the same size if you want to make a paper quilt with them upon completion of the project. Children then create a design with shapes from nature. As indicated above, wavy lines (perhaps signifying water), small repeating leaf and petal patterns and the like are good. These repeating designs are first sketched on a piece of paper and then imprinted onto the foam with a dull pencil or round toothpick. Use a brayer or paintbrush to apply a thin coat of indigo colored paint (preferably acrylic) to the foam print board. The design is then printed on

either white paper or white fabric. Children can mount their completed print projects individually, or they can be used in a class project to create a large paper quilt with the different blue designs.

Another way to do this project is to give children pieces of meat tray foam or a disposable foam plate. Students cut small design shapes from the foam. They use a gummy adhesive to affix foam shapes to wood blocks. The design is made by pressing the small foam print blocks onto a blue ink pad and then on white paper to create a "fabric" design.

• **North African Fabric Craft.** North African fabric and rug designs have often have a geometric look, not dissimilar to Native American designs in North America. Have children use resource books to recreate a picture of such designs on graph paper. These can be done in pencil, crayon or marker and should be in natural tones and black. Students can use the Graph Paper Activity Sheet located at the back of Chapter 2.

3. Exploring Peace Through Arts and Crafts

Have the class make a community "people of the world" sculpture. Sculpture is many things and takes many forms. Sometimes it is carved from wood. Sometimes it is molded from clay. Sculpture can be created from an endless variety of materials. Some works of art are always changing like our world and the people in it. The sculpture suggested here can be continually changed as well.

Have each child create a small head that represents either him- or herself or another person on our planet. The heads can even be somewhat fanciful if desired by the child. The head could be carved with plastic knives and toothpicks from bars of Ivory® soap or they could be molded from commercial clay or salt clay. Heads made from salt clay are created in the same way as the Egyptian scarabs described earlier except that a head shape is molded around the foil. Any clay that requires

firing should be fired if it is to be included in this project; otherwise, it is likely to break.

The second part of this project is the creation of a peace cloth. Each child designs a symbol of peace to be included on the cloth which should be 36" to 44" square. The cloth can be white or light blue. Individual peace designs are then placed on the fabric. Children can do this by drawing with crayon or permanent marker directly on the fabric. If blue cloth is being used, peace symbols and designs can be painted onto the cloth using bleach and cotton swabs. (Rinse fabric thoroughly after all designs are placed on fabric.)

When the heads and cloth are complete, the sculpture is assembled to represent the unity of the people of the world. One way to do this is to use an old pot (solid color preferably and no more than eight inches in circumference such as a terra cotta gardening pot). Fill the pot two-thirds full with crumpled newspaper and then press your peace cloth into the top of the pot around the paper draping over the side as well so that the heads can be placed on it, both at the opening of the pot and on the cloth draped on the tabletop at the side of the pot. After the cloth has been arranged, ask each child to place his or head on the sculpture. The heads can be examined and moved. This is a living sculpture, changing all the time. The class may want to give it as a gift symbolizing peace in the school or peace in the community to the principal or a local city office or library.

Food Activities

This section is intended to provide teachers with a mini-international cookbook of foods that can be prepared in a classroom setting. Most of these foods should be greeted with favorable nods although a few of the recipes which use lemon to sour them may be a little strong for some tastes. The first food activity, unlike the rest, provides the children with the opportunity to explore flags of the world in an edible art activity.

1. Edible United Nations

Have children explore international flag designs using graham crackers and colorflow frosting. Colorflow frosting is made by mixing powdered sugar and water to a consistency that will allow children to paint the crackers with small tipped water color brushes. Color the frosting yellow, red, and blue (leaving some white) and let children mix colors to get the secondary colors they need to paint their flags. Give each child a small paper plate to use to make a palette of the colors he or she needs. When dry, children can eat their flag cookies as they celebrate designs and symbols from flags of countries around the world.

2. Mini-International Cookbook for Classroom Cooking

a. Asian and Middle Eastern Foods

Middle Eastern Salad
3 cans chick peas (drained and mashed)
1/3 cup tahini (sesame seed paste) thinned with a little water (optional)
2 lemons or 1/4 cup lemon juice concentrate (to taste)
1/3 cup olive oil
2 minced garlic cloves or 1/2 teaspoon crushed garlic (from a jar) or 1/4 teaspoon garlic powder
Salt and pepper to taste
3 tablespoons fresh parsley (minced) or 2 tablespoons dried parsley
Pita bread triangles
Mix thinned tahini with mashed chick peas, lemon juice, and olive oil. Add garlic, parsley, and salt and pepper to taste. If too thick, thin with a

little water or olive oil. Serve with pita bread triangles. If you can't find tahini, you can substitute a little peanut butter or omit it entirely.

Greek Meatballs

2 pounds ground beef or turkey
1 egg, slightly beaten (optional)
3/4 cup bread crumbs (optional)
6 green onions (diced)
1 tablespoon red wine or apple cider vinegar
1 teaspoon oregano
1 teaspoon mint leaves (minced fresh leaves preferred)
1 tablespoon parsley (minced fresh leaves preferred)
1/2 teaspoon salt (to taste)
1/4 teaspoon pepper (to taste)

Mix all ingredients. Have students make teaspoon size meatballs. The meatballs can be fried in oil on medium high heat, but an easier way to cook them is to preheat a soup pan of water and boil them until done. By using this method you avoid concerns about splattering grease and you can put the meatballs in the pan as they are made without having to worry about burning them. A large soup pot can hold sixty to seventy boiling meatballs. Serve two to three meatballs to each child, depending on size and number made. Serving the meatballs skewered on toothpicks makes for easy serving and eating.

Tabouli

1 cup kasha or bulgur prepared as indicated on package (generally, bulgur is easier to use because it can be prepared by soaking in water)
1 cup minced fresh parsley
3 medium or 2 large tomatoes (diced)
6 green onions, finely diced
1/4 lemon juice (less or more to taste)
1/4 to 1/3 cup olive oil
Salt and pepper to taste
1/2 cup minced fresh mint leaves (optional)

Mix all ingredients except lemon juice and olive oil. Blend lemon juice and olive oil by shaking a tightly closed container, whisking in a bowl or whipping in a blender. Pour over salad while stirring ingredients so that dressing is thoroughly mixed with salad ingredients. Refrigerate until served.

Rosh Hashanah Treat

Sliced apples and bread chunks
Honey

Apples and bread are cut into slices or chunks, dipped into honey, and eaten. This is a Jewish New Year custom. The eating of the foods dipped in honey symbolizes the desire for a sweet and harmonious new year.

Easy Oriental Eggrolls

1 package pre-shredded cabbage coleslaw
Eggroll wrappers (in refrigerated Oriental food section of market)
4 diced green onions
1/4 cup to 1/3 cup diced water chestnuts
1 teaspoon minced garlic or 1/2 teaspoon garlic powder
1 1/2 tablespoon soy sauce
1 teaspoon minced fresh ginger (or 1/2 teaspoon ground ginger)
1 egg, beaten
Oil for frying

Stir-fry all ingredients except wrappers and egg in one tablespoon oil until cabbage is just slightly limp (between one and two minutes). Drain off any excess liquid. Put heaping tablespoon of mixture in center of wrapper. Fold eggroll according to directions on wrapper package and seal shut with dab of beaten egg. Fry until golden brown in an inch or two of oil heated over medium heat.

Chinese Egg Drop Soup

4 cans chicken broth (or make 8 cups of chicken broth with bouillon cubes)
1 to 2 cups water (as needed to make enough servings)
3 eggs, beaten so that whites and yolks are broken and mixed
1/2 to 1 cup diced green onions

Bring broth and water to a boil. One person stirs slowly while another slowly pours egg over the tines of a fork into the hot soup. The soup must be stirred constantly during this process. Add onions right before serving. If served in Styrofoam cups, students can even enjoy this soup without a spoon.

Korean Vegetable Skewers

Fresh small mushrooms (or quartered larger
mushrooms)
Green onion cut into 1" pieces
Another vegetable of your choice cut into bite-size
pieces
Wooden barbecue skewers
Oil
Flour
4 eggs, beaten with a little water to break up yolk
and white

Dipping Sauce

1/3 cup soy sauce
2-3 tablespoons oil
2-3 tablespoons sugar
1/4-1/2 teaspoon garlic powder

Have enough pieces of vegetable, mushrooms
and onion so that each mini-skewer can have two
pieces of each.

After vegetables are cut, push or thread onto
each skewer two mushrooms, two onions and two
pieces of any other vegetable you choose to use.
Roll each skewer in the egg mixture and then the
flour to coat. Fry for two to three minutes in hot
oil until vegetables are tender and coating is light
brown. Drain and serve. Drizzle dipping sauce
over skewers right before serving.

Of course, chunks of chicken or beef can also be
used on these skewers. If you choose to use meat,
use the dipping sauce as a meat marinade, too.

Indonesian Opor (Chicken Stew)

2 medium onions, chopped and sautéed in oil
3 to 4 potatoes, diced
2 cups cooked, diced chicken (canned chicken is
fine)
1 can coconut milk
1 teaspoon mild curry powder (more if desired)
6 cups water (more if necessary)
Salt and pepper to taste

Place all ingredients in covered pot over medium heat. Stir occasionally and add water as necessary to keep from drying out. Cook until potatoes
are tender—approximately twenty to thirty minutes depending upon potato size.

Vietnamese Sweet Rice

Sticky rice is the base for this sweet treat and is
eaten throughout Vietnam and in many neighbor-
ing countries. It is sometimes made into croquettes,

fried and seasoned for snack eating. In this recipe,
it is a sweet treat.

Make enough sticky white rice in a rice cooker
to feed your class. For every cup of rice mix in
about 1/4 cup brown sugar. Toast coconut flakes
by browning it in a dry pan. Serve up spoonfuls of
rice sweetened to taste and top with flaked
coconut. You can eat it warm or cool.

If you cannot make sticky rice or have no access
to a rice cooker, you can substitute a white minute
rice although the flakiness of the rice diminishes
the authenticity of the treat.

b. African Foods

African Pumpkin Soup

3 medium onions, diced
1 cup butter
1 can chicken broth (or 2 cups broth made with
bouillon cubes)
2-12 oz cans evaporated milk
1 large can pumpkin
1/2 teaspoon salt (to taste)
1/4 - 1/2 teaspoon pepper (to taste)
3 - 4 tablespoons flour or cornstarch (optional)

Sauté onion in butter, add other ingredients
(except flour) and simmer for ten to twenty minutes. If thickening is necessary, mix flour or cornstarch with some of the soup broth until smooth
and add to soup slowly.

Easy Senegalese Soup

3 cans cream of chicken soup prepared according
to directions
1 - 1 1/2 teaspoons mild curry powder (to taste)
2 cup diced canned chicken

Combine ingredients over medium heat and
serve warm.

East African Sweet Potato Stew

2 cups canned pumpkin
2 medium to large sweet potatoes, peeled and
diced (or one large can yams)
2 medium onions, diced
2 tablespoons butter
1 tablespoon lemon or orange juice (optional)
1/4 teaspoon cloves
1/2 teaspoon cinnamon
1 can coconut milk
salt to taste

Peel and dice sweet potatoes and onion into small pieces. Brown in butter and juice. Add remainder of ingredients except pumpkin. Cover and cook over medium low heat for ten to twenty minutes stirring and checking occasionally so that stew does not dry out. If it begins to dry out, add a little water. When sweet potatoes are tender, add pumpkin and heat thoroughly. Serve with crushed peanuts on top if desired.

For a faster way to make this stew, substitute canned yams for sweet potatoes. Dice the canned yams before using.

North African Sweet and Sour Carrots
10 to 15 carrots, scraped and cleaned
1 cup diced onion or 2 medium diced onions
*   (substitute 6 diced green onions if desired)*
1/2 cup (1 stick) butter or margarine
1/4 - 1/2 teaspoon nutmeg
1/3 cup vinegar
1/3 - 1/2 cup brown sugar (higher amount if
*   deemed more palatable by children)*
1/2 - 1 cup raisins

Grate or dice carrots. Melt butter and brown carrots, onions and nutmeg together. Pour in vinegar and cover. Simmer until carrots are done. Soak raisins in 1 1/2 cups warm water. When carrots are done, drain raisins and add to carrot mixture together with the brown sugar. Heat through and serve hot.

Nigerian Fried Pastries (also called Chin-chin)
1 cup softened butter or margarine
1 cup sugar
3 eggs, slightly beaten
1/4 cup water
4 1/4 cups flour (add enough so dough is not sticky)
1/2 teaspoon baking powder
1/2 teaspoon nutmeg
1 tablespoon grated orange peel
Dash of salt
Oil

Cream butter and sugar and add eggs slowly (one at a time). Then add water. Mix in remaining ingredients except oil and add slowly to creamed mixture. Add more flour if dough is too sticky to work with. When dough is no longer sticky, place it on floured area and knead with flour-dusted hands until smooth. Roll or press dough out to 1/4" thickness and cut into 2" x 4" strips. Fry in 1" medium hot oil until lightly browned. Drain. Dust with a little sugar, if desired. Serve immediately.

Raita
4 cucumbers
3 cups plain yogurt
2 tablespoons fresh mint, minced OR 1/2 teaspoon crushed cumin and 1/2 teaspoon minced garlic

This side dish is made in many countries with slight variations in ingredients. It is eaten in South Africa, India, the Middle East, and Armenia, for example. The Armenian version often includes mint leaves. The Indian version excludes mint and includes garlic and spices and sometimes minced produce such as tomato and onion.

Peel and dice cucumbers. If using mint leaves, mince them. (You might want to ask that children bring cucumbers to school already peeled as peeling them is not easy for children.) Then mix all ingredients together and serve cold. This is a very refreshing salad, but a little tart for some children. Serve with pita chips or pita bread triangles.

c. European Foods

Tuna and Tomato Sauce with Pasta (Italy)
Any small pasta (such as corkscrew, elbow, or shell) precooked in a quantity so each child can have about one heaping tablespoon of cooked pasta with sauce

Sauce
3 tablespoons oil (preferably olive oil)
2 medium onions or 1 large onion, diced (diced green onion can be substituted if this is easier for children to handle)
1/2 teaspoon garlic powder or minced garlic clove
3 16-ounce cans crushed tomatoes
3 7-ounce cans drained tuna
1 1/2 teaspoons crushed oregano
1 tablespoon sugar
1/2 teaspoon salt
1/4 teaspoon pepper
1/4 cup diced fresh parsley or 2 tablespoons parsley flakes
1 small can sliced black olives (optional)
1/4 teaspoon of any other seasonings you like such as basil, marjoram, thyme, or rosemary

Sauté onions in deep pan in oil until translucent. Add remaining ingredients to pan and cook over medium heat for 15 to 20 minutes stirring occasionally. Add cooked pasta and stir. This is a dish that is popular all over Italy and can be served with any kind of pasta.

Italian Stuffed Peaches

8 peaches
20 macaroons
1 cup raisins
1/3 cup sliced almonds
Powdered sugar

Peel, dice and mash two peaches with a potato masher. Cut remaining peaches in six slices each. (You may need more peaches depending upon the number of desserts you need to serve the class). Place raisins in a bowl covered with warm water. Break up macaroons and place in bowl with mashed peaches and almonds. Mash these ingredients together adding a little water as necessary to help mash into paste. Add a tablespoon or so of powdered sugar and continue to mash. Drain raisins and add raisins and mash to make a paste filling. Mixture should be stiff enough to spread onto a peach slice. To prepare dessert, spread a small amount of macaroon mixture onto each of the peach slices. You can top each peach slice with a second slice if you have enough peaches. Top with a dollop of whipped cream or whipped topping if desired.

Polish Cabbage Roll Casserole

1 small head of cabbage (shredded) or 1 16-ounce
*   package shredded cabbage*
1 pound ground beef or turkey, browned and
*   drained*
2 medium onions, diced and sautéed with ground
*   meat*
2 cups quick rice, cooked (quick rice can be brought
*   from home pre-cooked)*
1 teaspoon salt
1/2 teaspoon marjoram
2 15-ounce cans tomato sauce
3/4 cup brown sugar (the sugar can be adjusted to
*   taste)*
Butter or margarine

Cabbage rolls are a traditional dish in several different countries. Poland is a well known home to this hearty dish. Cabbage rolls are also a traditional food in many Jewish homes for the Succoth harvest holiday.

The ingredients described above will fill a 9 x 13 inch casserole dish. In the greased casserole dish, students will layer the ingredients for this casserole. Before you begin to assemble the casserole, mix rice, meat and spices together. Then mix tomato sauce and brown sugar. To layer the casserole, start with a layer of the meat mixture, then the cabbage, then the sauce. Repeat if pan can hold a second layer of the casserole. Bake at 375 degrees covered for 45 minutes or until cabbage is tender.

d. Australian/New Zealand Foods

Pavlova

6 egg whites
2 teaspoons vanilla
1/2 teaspoon cream of tartar
2 cups granulated sugar
3 boxes strawberries (or other berries)
6 kiwi fruit, peeled
Whipped topping of your choice

This recipe is a modified version of the traditional fruit meringue dessert from New Zealand called pavlova. Individual meringues are made by children which are filled with a few pieces of fruit and topped with sweetened whipping cream.

Beat room temperature egg whites with vanilla and cream of tartar until you get soft peaks. Use a metal or glass bowl which has been recently cleaned with boiling water or in a dishwasher. Then slowly beat in sugar until stiff. Place heaping tablespoon size dollops on waxed paper on a cookie sheet. Flatten them slightly with a spoon. You will need to use two cookie sheets. Bake at 275 degrees for about 55 to 60 minutes.

While this part of the dessert is baking, have children dice strawberries (or other berries) and kiwi fruit. Just before serving, whip whipping cream with a little powdered sugar and vanilla until stiff. Do this right before serving. Serve each meringue topped with a spoonful of fruit and a dollop of whipped cream. You can substitute pressurized canned whipped cream or refrigerated whipped topping, it you prefer. It makes preparation a bit easier.

Australian Cook-Out Bread

4 cups flour
4 teaspoons baking powder
1/4 teaspoon salt
1 3/4 cups water

Stir all ingredients until dough is formed. If too dry add a little water. If too sticky to handle, add flour a little at a time. Divide dough into two pieces. Flatten each piece into a greased 8" to 9" pie plate. Bake in oven at 375 degrees for about 30 minutes or until golden brown. You can make individual biscuits on a cookie sheet, if you prefer. In this case, shorten cooking time to 10 to 12 minutes before serving. Children might enjoy it served with butter or jam. This is a bread sometimes made over a campfire by people when camping in the Australian bush.

e. North American Foods

Gazpacho (Mexican Cold Vegetable Soup)

1 24-ounce can V-8® juice
6 diced tomatoes
3 diced onions or 1 bunch green onions, diced
1 diced green sweet pepper, if desired
1 peeled, diced cucumber
1/4 - 1/2 cup diced fresh cilantro
1/8 teaspoon black pepper
1/4 - 1/2 teaspoon garlic powder

Mix all ingredients together in large bowl. Serve cold in small cups with dollop of sour cream if desired.

- Recipes for Native American dishes from North America can be found in the food activities section of Chapter 7.
- Recipes for historical "American" dishes from colonial to pioneer to depression days are provided in the food activities section of Chapter 6.

f. Central and South American Foods

Corn Tortillas

Tortilla flour (masa)
Water

Mix up enough tortilla flour according to the directions on the tortilla flour package to make the desired number of tortillas. Mixture should be stiff enough to handle without being too sticky. Add more masa if too sticky. Take teaspoon or tablespoon of corn mixture (as you like) and roll into ball. Place on a plastic bag on tabletop. Cover with a second plastic bag and press with bottom of pie plate. Peel off plastic and bake on hot, dry skillet or griddle. To make enough for a class quickly it is best to make each tortilla from about a teaspoon of mixture and cook three or four at the same time. Cook for a minute on each side at the most. Remove from heat and pile on top of each other until ready to serve. Serve with pat of butter, beans, or salsa.

Paraguayan Squash Casserole

2 pounds yellow or summer squash, diced
1/2 cup butter, chunked
1 cup cornmeal
4 tablespoons sugar
1/2 pound grated or diced mild cheddar such as
*   longhorn*

Boil squash in salted water until tender. Drain, mash and mix with next three ingredients. Mix in cheddar, put mixture in greased casserole dish, and bake at 375 degrees for 30 to 40 minutes.

Ecuadoran Black Beans

3 large cans black beans
2 medium onions, diced
8 slices bacon
2 teaspoons crushed, minced garlic

Sauté bacon and diced onions until onions are translucent. Remove bacon, cool, and break into small pieces. Add garlic and drained black beans. Heat and mash with potato masher. Add in bacon bits and serve.

Brazilian Chocolate Treat

2 cans sweet condensed milk
2 tablespoons + 2 teaspoons cocoa powder

Candy Covering
2 heaping tablespoons powdered sugar
1 heaping tablespoon cocoa powder

Mix first two ingredients in a saucepan and heat over medium heat until consistency becomes thicker, like pudding. Remove from heat, cool, and serve in small cups with spoon. This treat is very rich—a little goes a long way.

The alternative way to serve this treat is to let it cool and drop it by teaspoonfuls onto powdered candy covering. Roll in the powdered mixture and set on waxed paper. This recipe should make about 30 to 36 pieces.

Art Masters—Old and New

Background Information

1. Tung Ch'i-ch'ang (doon chee-chang)

Born in 1555 in the Ming period of China, this artist was both a painter and a great scholar. His art and distinctive style opened up new directions for Chinese artists that followed him. While his contemporaries in the art world were interested in naturalism, he was interested in structure and modeled his work on ancient designs and calligraphy. He greatly influenced artists that came after him.

2. Diego Rivera

Rivera was born in Guanajuato, Mexico in 1886. He became famous for his murals that portrayed Mexican life and history. He was controversial because of his attacks on the Catholic Church and because his political beliefs were viewed as radical. He developed his own style of large, simplified human figures and bold colors. One of his finest works in the United States is a mural at the Detroit Institute of Arts that celebrates science and industry.

3. Joan Miro´

Miro´ was a famous Spanish artist. He was born in 1893 and lived until 1983. He developed a highly abstract style in which he used simple forms and shapes to portray fantastic creatures and objects. Some of the works showed a story or scene from a story. He developed his distinctive style in the late 1920s and early 1930s. Geometric forms and shapes outlined in thick black lines and points were highlighted with bright colors. Miro´ also did ceramic work, sculpture, and lithography.

Project Directions

1. In the style of Tung Ch'i-Ch'ang

Students can create a watercolor or mixed media art project in the style of this artist by using the technique described here. Graceful lines, serene colors, and a feeling of harmony with nature are characteristic of Ming period works of Chinese art.

To help children understand something of the structure of these works, have students adhere to a three-part structure, each picture will be wonderfully different from the next. Give each student an 18" x 12" sheet of white construction or watercolor paper. Use the paper vertically. The picture will be based upon three points of interest.

First, the child needs to draw three irregularly shaped (rock-shaped) points of interest on the sheet of paper. The smallest is in the top third of the page, the next largest is in the middle third, and the largest is in the bottom third. They should range in size from a dime at the small end to a quarter or fifty-cent piece on the large end. Have them place these marks in a non-linear, zigzag manner on the sheet. This can be done with pencil. Each of these rock shapes will be the focal point for creating one of three mountains. The one at the top of the page is furthest away from the viewer. The bottom one is closest to the viewer. Before any further drawing is done, the child puts a watercolor wash on the entire surface of the paper and then lets it dry.

From the three different points of interest, three mountains will emerge. For each mountain start at a top point of the rock shape and draw with a colored pencil or crayon a slightly wiggly curved line around and downward, fading off at the end. This movement is repeated from the top side of the rock until a mystical looking mountain is formed that seems to drop off into a fog. When each mountain has been completed, the child can add forests with green pencil or crayon. The forests on the farthest mountain are depicted as mere dots. The trees on the nearer mountains are still small but more specifically drawn. Teachers can use this project to discuss perspective and draw the parallel from the three-point style of this picture to the three-point structure of other items of Oriental design such as certain styles of floral arranging.

As a final touch when the pencil part of the drawing is complete, the child can add a river meandering through the mountains. To do this, the student paints the river area with water first, and then paints a single line of blue paint over the wet area. This paint will bleed out, making the river wider and graceful looking. Let dry.

2. Rivera-Style Mural Art

Making a mural in the style of Diego Rivera can be an all-class cooperative project. Before starting, children should review reference works that show Rivera's style and subject matter. A typical scene might be of a peasant farmer or young woman. The woman might wear a long skirt, shawl, and bare feet. The class mural should probably hold no more than two people and an animal together with some flowers or crops harvested from the fields. Lines should be sketched in simply using rounded lines. If children fail to fill the paper with the figures, have them start again. Everything should be drawn a little larger than life. Children have a tendency to draw smaller and smaller and this defeats the purpose of this mural.

Once the pencil outlines are in, every member of the class can help paint it in with bright tempera paints. Students might want to outline each figure with a thin line of brown paint to set off the design from the background.

3. A Miro´ Fantasy

Have children think of figures or objects they would like to paint. Have each sketch his chosen object on scratch paper. Tell children to sketch only basic outlines and to think about a nonsense or fantasy version of the creature or object. Once they have decided upon their designs, the children transfer their sketches in pencil to white construction paper. Mix black tempera or powdered paint into white glue. Each child goes over the basic outline of the picture with the blackened glue. Children can do this best by using glue squirt bottles to lay on the black line. This part of the picture is left to dry.

When dry, students fill in the picture outlines with brightly colored paints or pastels emphasizing the three primary colors. The completed project is a dramatic fantasy creature or object in the style of Miro´.

Sharing Activities

1. Folk Dance Festival

A folk dance festival is an event appropriate to many times of the year - United Nations Day in October, May Day in the spring. Your class could invite other classes in the school to participate in a multicultural dance event in which each class would perform a dance from a different country.

2. International Songfest

If your class learned a variety of ethnic or international songs, share them with other classes in the school by performing them at an assembly. Close the program with a sing-along. Ask children in the audience to join in with any that all the children might know such as "Frere Jacques" or "Alouette." If you want to, you can project words for group singing on a screen using an overhead projector.

3. International Potluck

In conjunction with a simple song and dance fest in which students from your class (and perhaps others) perform two or three songs and/or dances and perhaps read a haiku or two, have an international potluck. Ask children to bring a dish from their heritage and invite parents to join in and attend this lunch-time event. Also, ask all students to dress in some ethnic costume, either from their heritage or from another. This is a lot of fun and more fun when the adults dress up, too. This event is very easy to prepare since the students bring all the food and only paper plates, napkins, and utensils need to be provided. It can be a good event for a year opener as parents and students have an opportunity to talk and mingle.

Another way to hold a meal event is discussed in Item 1 of the sharing activities in Chapter 5. Groups of children adopt parts of the world and food is served on tables organized and decorated by children to reflect the country or part of the world for which they are providing food. The tables can be decorated with placemats, table runners, flags, and flowers, most of which children can create with construction paper and tissue paper. If this type of event is used, children research and prepare foods from the assigned part of the world instead of providing foods from their own heritage.

4. International Storytelling Event

Ask the local community or school librarian if he or she would be able to present some folktales from different cultures around the world. Parents can be invited to such an event and children who choose to can reenact the folktales they adopted as part of the lesson activities in this chapter. This kind of event can also be coupled with the international potluck luncheon described above.

5. Peace Assembly

Ask children to present a peace assembly in conjunction with Martin Luther King's birthday, United Nations Day, Armistice Day or Memorial Day. Children could present posters, recite sections of Dr. King's "I Have a Dream" speech, and sing several of any number of peace songs. Some recommended songs are:

"Dona Nobis Pacem" (Give Us Peace)
"Let There Be Peace on Earth"
"I'd Like to Teach the World to Sing"
"It's a Small World"
"Everybody's Beautiful"
"We Shall Overcome"
"Go Down, Moses"
"One Tin Soldier"
"The Universal Soldier"
"Abraham, Martin and John"
"Hymn to Freedom"
"If I Had a Hammer"
"Simple Gifts"
"You Have to Be Carefully Taught"
    (from South Pacific)
"Blowin' in the Wind"

Many fairly contemporary songs from the 1960s and early 1970s have peace themes, so you may be familiar with many other very singable pop songs that you would like to have the children sing.

6. Working for Peace

As you discuss issues of peace and peace-making, children will begin to realize that inequities in food distribution, shelter, health care and the like can lead to serious obstacles in finding peace. All people have basic needs to be fed, to be healthy, to have shelter and to see their families thrive. Your students may want to organize a fundraising effort to raise money for an organization that helps in the fight for world peace by helping the poor and hungry of our world.

One fun way to do this is to have one or more classes sponsor a penny project in which each classroom is provided with a decorated milk carton and students are asked to bring pennies and small coins for a week to help raise money for the chosen project. One class collects the coins each day and counts them. A parent volunteer can be asked to arrange for deposit of the money or perhaps your school's parent-teacher organization can help. Children get the additional benefit to their math skills of dealing with the money received from the project.

Some organizations which you might want to contact for more information about their work and for fundraising ideas are:

CARE
660 First Avenue
New York, New York 10016

Heifer Project International
P.O. Box 808
Little Rock, Arkansas 72203
(sends live animals to needy communities so that the gift given continues to produce food and sustain families; provides curriculum packets at a nominal fee on the issue of world hunger)

Salvation Army World Service Office
1025 Vermont Avenue, NW
Suite 305
Washington, D.C. 20005

U.S. Committee for UNICEF
331 East 38th Street
New York, New York 10016

World Vision Relief Organization
International
919 West Huntington Dr.
Monrovia, California 91016.

For more information about the issue of world hunger, contact:

The Hunger Project
802 Rhode Island Avenue NE
Washington DC 20018
(202)269-0200

US Committee for World Food Day
1001 22nd Street NW
Washington, DC 20437
(202)653-2404

If you or your students prefer to work on a more local scale for peace in the community, your class might want to sponsor a food or clothing drive for needy families, arrange to work in a local soup kitchen, or work at a food bank.

Name: _____

Family Interview

1. **What is your name?** _____

2. **How are we related?** _____
_____

3. **When and where were you born?** _____

4. **When did your ancestors come to the United States and from what countries did
they come? [Question for interviewees who were born in the United States.]**
_____

5. **What major event(s) of history have you lived through?** _____
_____
_____
_____

6. **Which one is most important to you and why?** _____
_____
_____
_____

7. **When you were my age, what kinds of things did you do? [Examples: How did
you get to school? What did you play with? What music did you like?]**
_____
_____
_____

8. **Make up your own question.** _____
_____
_____
_____

Name: _____

Recipe

Country of Origin: _____   **Continent:** _____

Language: _____   **Population:** _____

Terrain: _____   **Agriculture:** _____

Industry: _____

Recipe

Name of Dish: _____

Appetizer ☐   **Salad** ☐   **Side Dish** ☐   **Main Dish** ☐   **Dessert** ☐   **Drink** ☐

Ingredients: _____

_____

_____

_____

_____

_____

_____

Directions: _____

_____

_____

_____

_____

_____

_____

By: _____

_____

Name: _____

Facts in the Folktale

Type of Shelter: _____
_____
_____

Type of Clothing: _____
_____
_____

Food: _____
_____
_____

Recreational Activities/Work: _____
_____
_____

Landforms: _____
_____
_____

Climate: _____
_____
_____

Local Animals: _____
_____
_____

Local Plants: _____
_____

Name: _____

Folk Story Analysis

Story Title	Country of Origin	Locale/Setting of Story (forest, desert, etc.)	Human Characters	Animal Characters

Foods	Transportation	Shelter	Dress

Name: _____

Biography Report

Write information in complete sentences.

1. Name _____

2. Date of Birth _____

3. Childhood facts _____

_____

_____

4. Education or Training _____

_____

_____

_____

5. Jobs _____

_____

_____

_____

6. Accomplishments or Awards _____

_____

_____

_____

7. How the person or the person's work contributed to society. _____

_____

_____

_____

Resources

1. The comparative folktales described in the lesson activities in this chapter provide good literature selections and ideas for curriculum activities on multicultural concerns. These books can be read to the class by the teacher as part of the classroom read-aloud program, or they can be read by the children in groups as part of their reading and social studies curriculum.

2. Several books for younger children that explore the cross-cultural similarities between peoples of the world are listed below:
Everybody Cooks Rice by Norah Dooley published by Carolrhoda Books (1991).

They Put On Masks by Byrd Baylor published by Macmillan Publishing Company (1978).

The Way to Start a Day by Byrd Baylor published by Macmillan Publishing Company (1978).

I Hate English! by Ellen Levine published by Scholastic Inc. (1989).

3. Several resources on the issues of peace and inter-cultural understanding are:
The Big Book for Peace edited by Ann Durell and Marilyn Sachs published by Dutton Children's Books (1990)

Molly's Pilgrim by Barbara Cohen published by Lothrop, Lee & Shepard (1983).

Let the Celebrations BEGIN! by Margaret Wild and Julie Vivas published by Orchard Books (1991).

4. Several songbooks that have a good selection of folk songs from around the world are:
Children Sing Around the World by Jerry Silverman published by Mel Bay Publications, Inc. (1991).

Folksongs from the Far East by Peter Gritton published by Faber Music (1991).

Folksongs from Africa by Malcolm Floyd published by Faber Music (1991).

5. Some modern-day versions of traditional fairy and folktales that children will enjoy in conjunction with their investigation of multicultural folktales are:
The True Story of the Three Little Pigs by Jon Scieszka published by Scholastic Inc. (1989).

The Frog Prince Continued by Jon Scieszka published by Viking Penguin (1991) (combines elements of Sleeping Beauty, Snow White, Hansel and Gretel, Cinderella and the Frog Prince).

Snow White in New York by Fiona French published by Oxford University Press (1986).

The Stinky Cheese Man and Other Fairly Stupid Tales by Jon Scieszka published by Viking (1992).

FOODS, FITNESS AND OUR GROWING BODIES

This chapter is designed to provide activities to teach and reinforce information about the systems of the human body and what our bodies need to be healthy and strong. A main lesson focus is helping children see that the things they eat each day and the things they do each day can help them to be healthy both today and in the years to come. In this context foods, nutrition, and exercise via sports activities are discussed.

Lesson Activities

The Lesson Activities in this chapter cover three primary areas—the major systems of the human body, healthful foods for growing bodies, and exercise.

Writing Activities

The Writing Activities section provides ideas for poetry that incorporates the lesson themes and some ideas, in addition to those suggested in the lesson activities, for short reports about foods, exercise, and how the body works.

Art and Craft Activities

The Art and Craft Activities take several different turns. Some of them use images of parts of the body to create art (e.g., suggestions for hand art). Others provide opportunities for students to explore healthful eating pictorially.

Food Activities

As you might imagine, Food Activities in this chapter focus on dishes that utilize most or all of the food groups and simple healthful snacks as alternatives to junk food.

Art Masters—Old and New

The Art Masters - Old and New section provides children with the opportunity to explore any one of several famous artists from the last thirty years. Pop artists such as Andy Warhol used Madison Avenue images of food and other consumer products in repetitive ways to make their artistic statements. Art project ideas to explore these Pop Movement concepts are provided. A project relating to the art of Christo is also provided based upon some of his early work covering ordinary containers.

Sharing Activities

Sharing Events from this chapter involve coordinating events that involve sports, foods, and guest speakers.

Lesson Activities

This information and the suggested activities are designed to help children become more familiar with how their bodies work.

Background Information

1. The Human Body, Its Systems, and How They Work

The human body is made up of many different systems that work together to make us function as we do. These systems include the nervous system, the skeletal system, the muscle system, the circulatory system, the respiratory system, the digestive system, and the body's network of endocrine glands.

Each of these systems is made up of millions of the body's building blocks. These building blocks are called cells. There are skin cells, nerve cells and bone cells, among others. These microscopic cells work together within their own system and with the other cells in other parts of the body to allow us to breathe, eat and digest food, think, run and play.

a. The Human Cell - The Building Block of the Body

While the cells in different systems of the body are uniquely made to do the work they are required to do, there are some common features of human cells. Each cell has a nucleus. The nucleus is like the command center or brain of the cell. It directs the cell's function. The cell contains a substance called cytoplasm and has a cell membrane (or wall) to contain the cytoplasm. Most cells also have vacuoles which are tiny spaces inside the cell's cytoplasm that hold fluid. Mitochondria are also found in cells. These are long bodies that help the cell breathe. They can be rich in fat, protein, and enzymes. There are tiny ribosomes that help produce protein. There are lysosomes which are roundish bodies that contain enzymes.

b. The Systems of the Body

This chapter provides ideas for exploring seven different systems of the human body. These are the nervous, respiratory, circulatory, digestive, skeletal, endocrine, and muscular systems.

• The Nervous System

The nervous system of the body is like a huge, complex telephone system that sends and receives messages all over the body. What kind of messages does it send? It sends messages telling the body to breathe, to digest food, to read, to run and play. Anything we do, even the things we don't think about, like breathing, is controlled by our nervous systems.

The nervous system is made up of two systems that work together. One is called the central nervous system. The other is called the peripheral nervous system.

What makes up these systems and how do they work?

The brain and the spinal cord comprise the central nervous system. Because they are so important to making the operations of the body run smoothly, they are well protected by the skeletal system of the body. The skull protects the brain. The vertebrae of your back protect your spinal cord.

The other nerves and nerve endings in your body that connect to the brain and spinal cord make up the peripheral nervous system. This peripheral system sends and receives messages (called nerve impulses) to and from the organs of the body. Without this peripheral system your senses would not work. Your hands could not feel. Your eyes could not see. Your ears could not hear.

The nervous system is an amazing thing. Some of it works without you ever thinking about it. Do you think about taking each breath you take? Do you think about telling your stomach to digest the food you eat? These and the actions of the circulatory, endocrine, digestive, and reproductive systems work automatically with the brain always in control. They are the part of the nervous system that is called the autonomic nervous system.

How does the nervous system send and receive messages?

Tiny electrical impulses pass through the nerves to relay the brain's messages. Neurons, the cells of the nervous system, make up half of the nervous system. The brain alone contains about 112 billion of them. They are present in all parts of the body and are the messengers that send the messages through the nervous system to the brain and back. They are unlike other cells in the body because they do not multiply as the body grows. The body cannot make new neurons as it can new skin cells or new blood cells. An adult has the same number of neurons as he or she did when born except for those that might have died or been destroyed.

Each neuron or nerve cell contains a nucleus, dendrites and an axon. The dendrites are fibers that extend through the cell body to transmit sensation. A single axon in the cell extends beyond the cell walls to facilitate the transmission of information between nerve cells.

• **The Skeletal System**

What would we look like without our skeletons? Would we stand tall or would we be a jelly-like mass of soft tissue? Our muscles are strong, but without the bones that make up a skeleton, the muscles could not do their work and we would not be able to stand or move as we do. Bones have a hard outer covering and a soft inside called marrow. The joints of our body are where the bones meet. Ligaments hold the bones together at the joints.

The skeleton is the framework and support of the body. It does many important things. It provides protection for our soft internal organs. For example, the skull protects the brain and the ribcage protects the heart and lungs. It provides a system of levers that, together with the body's muscles, allow us to move in many ways. Red and white blood cells are manufactured in the bone marrow of certain bones. The making of blood cells is a very important job. The bones also store minerals such as calcium and phosphorous which the body needs for good health.

The adult skeleton consists of 206 separate bones. When we are babies, though, we have nearly 300 bones. As we grow, some of these fuse together to form stronger bones.

• **The Muscle System**

The network of muscles in the body does very important work. Every time the body moves, our muscles are at work. They are like engines. They convert the energy in the body (which is provided by the food we eat) into movement. If it weren't for muscles, nothing in the body that moves could do this work. We could not breathe, we could not swallow, and we could not blink our eyes. Our hearts would not beat, our jaws would not chew, our lungs would not fill with air. We would never be able to take a step or catch a ball or play the piano without our muscles.

The body contains 656 different muscles. Depending on a person's overall weight and physical condition, muscles make up about 40 to 50 percent of total body weight.

There are three types of muscles. These are skeletal, smooth and cardiac muscles. The skeletal muscles are the muscles that are attached to our bones and move them. Smooth muscles are in our internal organs, blood vessels and skin. The cardiac or heart muscle makes the heart beat and pump blood. It is tireless. This muscle never rests, pumping blood through a person's entire life.

All the muscles of the body have nerves. This means that they work all the time with the nervous system of the body as they contract and stretch to do the work of making our bodies move.

Since all of our muscles work with the nervous system to know what to do, let's think about how this works. Do we think in our brains about all the muscles in our bodies and making them do their work? No. Some work automatically like the muscles of our heart, lungs and other internal organs. These are our involuntary muscles. Others like the skeletal muscles are voluntary. We decide whether or not to put them to work. We decide to walk to the kitchen. We decide to ride the bike. We decide to chew gum.

Sometimes an injury makes it impossible for the nerves to tell a muscle what to do. When this happens, a muscle becomes paralyzed; the muscle cannot move.

• The Digestive System

The digestive system includes all the organs and glands involved in bringing food into the body and eliminating it. This means it involves the mouth, esophagus, stomach, pancreas, small intestines, and large intestines (colon). The digestive system's job is to process food so that the body can use it for energy.

Part of the work is done mechanically and part of it is done chemically. Food is first broken down mechanically by chewing in the mouth. Enzymes in the saliva in the mouth are integrated into the chewed food and, as the food is swallowed, they begin to chemically break down the food as well. Fluids are excreted from the stomach and pancreas to further break down the food so that it can be absorbed into the blood system which will distribute the food's energy into the body.

Muscles in the walls of the stomach and intestines move what's left of the food (the body's waste) through the system so that it can be eliminated.

The large and small intestines of an adult are about 23 to 27 feet long all together.

• The Circulatory System

The circulatory system feeds the various parts of the body and takes wastes out of the body. It is made up of the heart, blood vessels and lymphatic glands and, of course, the blood cells themselves. The blood cells do the important job of transporting oxygen, food and waste to and from organs and cells of the body.

The heart is a muscle which pumps the blood cells through the body. The heart never gets a rest or vacation from pumping. A system of artery vessels carries oxygenated blood cells to the body to feed it. After delivering the important cargo of oxygen, the blood cells pick up carbon dioxide and waste and return to the heart in a system of vessels called veins. The blood's round trip from the heart and back takes only about a minute.

Blood cells themselves are made inside bone marrow. Bone marrow is the soft inner tissue of the long bones of the body. This marrow is the manufacturing center for new blood cells that enter the blood stream to take the place of old cells as they die.

The lymph glands of the body produce other cells which are distributed in the blood stream. These cells act as filters to keep bacteria and other particulate from entering the blood stream.

• The Respiratory System

The lungs and the respiratory passages make up the respiratory system. The respiratory passages include the nasal cavities, the mouth when open, pharynx, larynx, trachea, and the bronchi.

Air is taken into the body through the nose and mouth. The air moves into the pharynx to the trachea which then divides into two tubes called bronchi. One bronchus feeds each lung. The lungs expand as oxygen-containing air comes into them. They contract to expel carbon dioxide.

Blood cells then pick up oxygen from the lungs to finish the work that the respiratory system starts. This is the work of feeding the body oxygen.

• The Endocrine System

To call the endocrine glands a system may be somewhat misleading. A variety of glands throughout the body are called endocrine glands although they each have different names. What these glands have in common is that they produce internal secretions that are discharged into the blood or lymph and carried throughout the body. The secretion of each gland, however, performs a different service needed by the body for proper development from childhood to maturity. The body's changes from infancy to childhood to puberty and adulthood are controlled by chemicals called hormones. These hormones are produced and secreted into the bloodstream by the endocrine glands.

The endocrine glands work as a system in that the hormones secreted by the individual glands all circulate in the bloodstream. They do not function in isolation from one another. As they circulate, they affect the rate at which all the individual glands secrete the hormones they make. They work to achieve a balance of hormones needed by the body.

The main endocrine glands are the thyroid, parathyroid, adrenal, pancreas and pituitary glands and the testes in men and the ovaries in women. The endocrine glands are ductless glands. They are called ductless glands because they discharge their secretions directly into the bloodstream instead of utilizing ducts or small canals to transport their secretions from one part of the body to another.

The thyroid gland is located in the neck, in front of and slightly below the so-called Adam's apple. It helps control normal growth of the long bones of the body. The pituitary gland really consists of two separate glands attached to the base of the brain. It secretes at least six different hormones. The anterior pituitary gland is the most important and regulates overall growth of the body. The posterior pituitary gland controls uterine contractions during the last stages of pregnancy and controls the release of breast milk from a mother.

The parathyroid glands are the smallest glands in the body. They are located on the lobes of the thyroid gland. There are four parathyroid glands, two on each lobe. These glands secrete a hormone called parahormone which controls the amount of calcium and phosphorus in the blood stream.

The pancreas is sometimes referred to as part of the digestive system and sometimes as part of the endocrine system. This is because the secretions it makes are digestive juices that are secreted into the small intestine. The pancreas itself is a flat gland about six inches long. It is located below the stomach. It secretes insulin and glucagon. It helps control the amount of glucose in the bloodstream.

The adrenal glands sit on top of the kidneys. There is an inner and outer part to each gland. The inner part is called the medulla and the outer part which completely surrounds it is called the cortex. The medulla secretes two hormones. These secretions prepare the body for emergency conditions by giving it a sudden rush of energy or strength. The adrenal cortex regulates the body's use of carbohydrates and proteins. It regulates the amount of mineral salts and water in the body and helps reduce inflammations.

2. Healthful Foods and Your Growing Body

The traditional nutritional eating concept of four food groups (meat (protein), fruits and vegetables, dairy, and grains) has undergone some rethinking and refocusing in recent years. Some health organizations have redefined the four groups into four "new" food groups which are fruits, vegetables, grains, and legumes, thereby deleting entirely meats and dairy products. Others such as the United States Department of Agriculture have modified the concept of food groups somewhat and their suggestions for daily servings.

The United States Department of Agriculture has adopted a new healthful eating concept which includes five food groups if you consider fruits separately from vegetables. This new nutritional concept is called the Food Guide Pyramid. In a food pyramid, the food groups are organized by the number of servings per food group that a person should eat each day. The food group from which we should eat the most servings is the base of the pyramid and the food group from which we should eat the fewest servings is the top of the pyramid.

The Food Guide Pyramid looks like this:

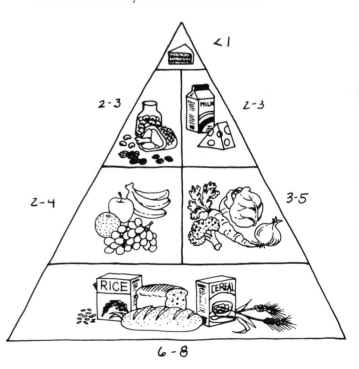

Different versions of the pyramid seem to indicate different serving amounts to meet daily needs, but all versions are consistent as to the level of each food group. The most foods to be consumed daily are grains and the least are meats.

3. Daily Exercise Needs of the Human Body

In addition to healthful eating habits, daily exercise habits contribute to the healthy bodies of both adults and children. Children should be encouraged to spend their free time in a mixture of activities which includes an active play or exercise component. Sedentary activities, such as television watching, do not contribute to strong muscles and a healthy body. Through the activities in this section, children are encouraged to analyze how they use their free time and the amount of exercise they get each day and to engage in fitness activities in a fun and enjoyable setting.

There are several different kinds of exercise that your body needs. Stretching exercises are important to keep your back and limbs flexible. Muscle strengthening exercises such as sit-ups, leg raises, push-ups and pull-ups increase the strength of individual muscle groups. These exercises should be increased in number gradually to allow muscles to increase in strength without injury. Aerobic exercise is important to the health of your heart and circulatory system. Some of these exercises are jumping rope, brisk walking, jogging, running, swimming, cycling and active running team sports such as basketball.

When you do aerobic workouts, you want to exercise your heart without hurting it. To do this, you exercise at a target heart rate for a sustained period of time. For adults this period is often suggested to be 20 minutes at least three times a week. As an adult, you find your target heart rate by adding your age to your resting heart rate. Subtract this figure from 220 and multiply the result by 0.6. Add this figure to your resting heart rate.

When you exercise, your body uses the energy it gets from the foods you eat. It burns calories. All foods contain a certain number of calories. As you go about your daily activities the body burns calories. It burns them faster when your activities are more strenuous such as in sports or exercise. You can figure out how many calories you need to eat each day to stay the same weight by multiplying your body weight times 15.

Project Directions

1. The Human Body, Its Systems and How They Work

a. Building Blocks.

Cells are the building blocks of the human body. Each system in the body is made up of millions of microscopic cells. Using microwave meal lids, pie plates, small box lids or cut off bottoms of milk or juice containers, have children create models of a human cell of their choice. Using plaster as the cytoplasm, have peanuts, jelly beans, candy-coated licorice, and gumballs to provide the three-dimensional visual effects of vacuoles, ribosomes, nuclei, and mitochondria.

Here are some examples of items to use to reflect the different cell parts:

Ribosomes - 1 inch segments of licorice or vines

Mitochondria - Peanuts in the shell

Vacuoles - Shelled almonds

Nucleus - Sour balls, jelly beans and corkscrew macaroni

Cells vary a little in size and look depending upon whether they are blood cells or skin cells so have children decide ahead of time what kind of cell they plan to make for their model. They should look at pictures in encyclopedias or other resource books to get ideas for how they want to design their cell models.

Since plaster sets up quickly, have children pick the "decoration" for their cells and what each item will be before plaster is mixed and poured. Pour 3/8" to 1/2" layer of plaster into the container and then remind children to place their nuclei, vacuoles and mitochondria quickly. Make up plaster in batches large enough to do this for about ten children at a time. Those who are waiting their turns for plaster can work on making small paper labels for each cell part to glue onto the model once it is dry.

Children can also use toothpicks to help recreate aspects of the cell in the plaster. They can be used to make impressions and markings in the cell cytoplasm before the plaster sets.

b. All Systems Go

Use these discussion guidelines to introduce the study of the human body through exploration of its numerous and complex systems. The systems explored will be those covered by the background information above and the purpose of these discussion guidelines is to both help the children understand the individual systems and to see how they work together. Each system is introduced by a few questions and most of these introductory questions include a teacher's note that suggests a visual way to dramatize the system to make this introductory exercise as interesting as possible.

In addition, to ensure that children remain on task during the discussion, you might want to give each child a copy of the Build A Body System Activity Sheet at the back of this chapter. A separate activity sheet can be completed by students for each system discussed.

On the Activity Sheet, experiments are suggested to enable students to explore several of the key body systems a bit further. These hands-on activities can be undertaken in conjunction with class discussion of the relevant body system.

Discussion Guidelines

- **Introductory Discussion**
  Let's name some parts of our bodies.
  Bones, teeth, heart, lungs, muscles
  How would we be different if we did not have bones?
  We could not stand up or move around the way we do.
  How would we be different if we did not have teeth?
  We would not be able to chew to eat so we would have to eat very different things or much, much more slowly.

  Let's see if we can identify some basic parts of the body and how they work.
  Bones - There are many bones. The bones work together with other bones making up a system of bones called the skeleton.
  Muscles - There are many muscles in the body. Anything that moves in your body moves by muscle power. There are muscles that work without you thinking about them like muscles in your lungs, muscles in your digestive system, and your heart muscle. There are muscles that work when you decide to make them work like your leg muscles and arm muscles.
  Heart and Blood - The heart and a network of blood vessels are at work all the time carrying oxygen to all the parts of your body and taking away wastes.
  Lungs - Oxygen comes into the body through the nose and mouth and is delivered to the lungs. The lungs, with the help of the diaphragm muscle, contract and expand as we breathe.
  Digestive System - The digestive system of the body is the group of organs, muscles and bones which allows you to eat and to process the food you eat. The food is used by the body to make energy so that the body can function and do its work.
  Endocrine System - The endocrine system is the system of glands within the body that secrete fluids needed for bodily functions. The glands include the pituitary gland (secretes fluids needed for growth), thyroid gland (secretes fluids needed for the body to metabolize food), and adrenal glands (secrete adrenaline which the body uses for quick energy in case of crisis or danger).
  Brain - The brain is the control center of the body and specifically the nervous system. Through a system of nerves in the body, the brain is constantly sending messages to other parts of the body to tell those parts of the body to do their jobs. The nerves also send back information to the brain about what is happening on the outside—is it cold, did you touch something hot, are you in danger? This is the work the brain does when it receives and processes information provided to it by your five senses.

- **The Nervous System**
  Since the brain is the part of the body that directs all the body's activities, let's start there.
  [Note: To help children visual the brain and relate to it, bring in another object of some sort that is approximately the same weight as a brain (a little less than 1.5 kilograms/3 pounds). A 3-pound item of produce such as a small cabbage or cantaloupe is a good choice. Additionally you might want to bring in an

object that feels the same as brain tissue. Some examples are cold oatmeal, soft Jell-O® or a water-filled balloon. Finally, in your description of the nervous system, a good analogy to make is that the brain is like a telephone switching station that receives and transmits messages.]

What is the brain?

The brain is the communications center for the body. It regulates and coordinates all the body's activities. It weighs about 1350 to 1400 grams or about three pounds. It has three parts - the cerebrum, cerebellum and medulla.

How does it control the body's activities?

The brain is connected through the spinal cord to nerves that run throughout the body. These nerves are constantly sending and receiving messages. This system involving the brain and nerve cells is called the nervous system.

What makes up the nervous system?

The nervous system has two main parts— the central nervous system and the peripheral nervous system.

What kinds of messages are sent?

Some messages are autonomic (involuntary) and some are volitional. Thought, memory and emotion are all centered in the brain's activities.

What are autonomic messages?

These are messages by which the brain directs the lungs to breathe, the heart to pump and the organs of the body (such as the digestive organs) to work without us thinking about them. These messages go on constantly without us realizing it consciously.

What are voluntary messages?

Anything we actively choose to do such as talk, walk, throw a ball or play piano is directed by the volitional part of the brain. For example, when we choose to throw the ball, the brain sends messages which are transmitted nerve cell to nerve cell to the hands, arms and so on to tell those parts of the body what to do to make the ball go.

How are these messages sent?

The messages are sent back and forth through a complex system of nerve cells located throughout the body. These nerve cells make up the peripheral nervous system. Some of them pick up data from the outside world which they collect from the five senses—taste, sight, hearing, smell, and touch.

What other systems of the body might the nervous system work with?

As the control center or captain of the body's operations, the brain and the nervous system work with all parts of the body to make sure they are doing their jobs.

• The Respiratory System

[Note: To help children visualize part of this system, simply blow up a balloon or have a child do so. Compare the balloon to the lung sacs that expand and contract as they take in and expel air.]

What makes up the respiratory system?

The lungs, diaphragm and the air passages make up this system. The air passages include the nasal cavities, pharynx, mouth (when open), and trachea.

How does the system work?

Oxygen is inhaled into the system.

How does oxygen get into the system?

Air is taken in through the nose or mouth and the lungs expand. Oxygen is absorbed and carbon dioxide is exhaled as the muscles of the lungs contract.

What happens to the oxygen?

It gets picked up by blood cells and transported to other parts of the body.

How do the lungs and blood cells know what to do?

The brain and the nervous system tell them.

What systems might the respiratory system work with?

Muscle System - The lungs expand and contract by the work of muscles. The diaphragm muscle helps the lungs work.

Circulatory System - The oxygen brought into the body by the respiratory system is distributed to the rest of the body by the circulatory system.

Nervous System - The brain, the captain of the nervous system, tells the lungs to breathe.

• **The Circulatory System**
[Note: To help children visualize and understand the heart and the muscular nature of its tissue, bring in a raw chicken or beef heart and liver. When they touch the heart, they see how strong the heart muscle tissue is. By contrast, when they touch the liver, they see just how soft organ tissue can be. Ask them to think about the size of a chicken compared to its heart. Tell them to make a fist and to think about the fact that their hearts are about fist size.]

What makes up the circulatory system?
It is made up of the heart, blood, blood vessels and lymphatic glands.
What does the heart do?
It is a muscle that pumps blood to the body.
How often does it do this?
Constantly.
How long does it take for blood cells to make the whole trip from the heart to the body and back again?
About a minute.
How does the heart get the blood to the rest of the body?
Through a network of blood vessels, blood cells full of oxygen travel throughout the body, deliver their oxygen, pick up carbon dioxide and waste and go back to the heart to pick up more oxygen. Arteries carry blood from the heart to the tissues of the body. Veins carry unaerated blood to the heart.
We said the circulatory system includes the lymphatic system. How does this work?
The lymph glands in the body produce cells that act as filters keeping bacteria from entering the blood stream. They work to keep the blood circulation system clean and healthy.
Which systems might the circulatory system work with?
Respiratory System - Oxygen comes into the body through the lungs where it is picked up by blood cells and distributed to the rest of the body. Blood cells deliver carbon dioxide back to the lungs to be exhaled.

Muscle System - The heart is the most important muscle in the body. It makes the circulatory system work and the circulatory system is the system that feeds the oxygen to all the other parts of the body.

Skeletal System - Blood cells are made in the bone marrow of certain bones.

• **The Digestive System**
[Note: To keep children's interest in this discussion bring in a piece of rope or hose that is the length of the large and small intestines (23 to 27 feet). Remind them that this length of intestine is coiled up in the lower digestive tract.]

What is the digestive system?
The digestive system includes all the organs and glands involved in bringing food into the body and eliminating it. This tract goes from the mouth to the rectum.
How does the digestive system work?
It breaks food down both mechanically (by chewing) and chemically (by the enzyme action of the organs in the gastrointestinal tract). While salt, simple sugar and water can be absorbed into the body unchanged, other foods like fats, proteins and starches must be chemically changed by the stomach and the intestines.
After the chewing and swallowing is done, how do the enzymes work to break food down further so the body can use it?
The stomach and the pancreas secrete fluids which contain digestive enzymes that help break down the chemical composition of food so that the body can absorb the food and use it for energy. The muscles in the walls of the stomach and intestines keep the food moving as necessary to process it.
Where does food go after the stomach?
First the digesting food goes into the small intestines, then the large intestines (colon), then the rectum where the waste is excreted.
How big are the intestines?
The large and small intestines together are about 25 feet long (7.3 meters). The small intestine itself, according to some sources, is about 10 feet (3 meters) long.

What other systems might the digestive system work with?

Muscle System - Muscles make the esophagus, stomach, and intestinal walls contract so that food can be processed through the system and excreted.

Circulatory System - The oxygen in the blood vessels feeds the muscles and organs that work the digestive system.

Skeletal System - Jawbone together with connective muscles make the jawbone move so food can be chewed to aid in its digestion in the stomach.

Nervous System - The brain tells the digestive system to do the "involuntary" work of digesting food.

• **The Skeletal System**

[Note: Bring in cleaned chicken or beef bones leftover from a meal. Have some of the bones cut in half so that children can see that some bones are not solid but have soft marrow tissue inside.]

What makes up the skeletal system?

Bones, 206 of them, make up the human skeleton. This is the framework that holds the body in place.

The bones are located approximately as follows:

Head - 29
Torso, vertebrae, ribs, sternum - 51
Arms, shoulders, wrists, hands - 64
Legs, hips, ankles, feet - 62

What do the bones do for the body?

Bones protect soft organs and tissue. Bones help the muscles work. Inner bone called marrow makes blood cells.

How do bones work together with each other?

Some bones such as your vertebrae are connected by a fibrous, elastic material called cartilage. (Your nose and ears are made of cartilage.) Other bones are connected at joints by ligaments.

What is a joint?

A joint is a place where two bones in the body meet. There are three main kinds—hinge joint, ball and socket, and saddle. A hinge joint works like a door. The knee is an example. The ball and socket joint is like your shoulder and arm and gives the bones more rotation. (You can simulate this joint by placing the fist of one hand in the curved cup of the other hand.) An example of a saddle joint is the joint where your thumb joins with your hand.

What other systems of the body might your bones work with?

Muscle System - Muscles work with the bones, contracting and expanding, to allow you to make voluntary movements like walking, chewing, jumping, and sewing.

Circulatory System - The inner part of the bone (marrow) makes new blood cells.

• **The Muscle System**

[Note: Muscles expand and contract. Bring in thick rubber bands or balloons. Stretch them and let them contract to provide an analogy for how the muscles work.]

What makes up the muscle system?

Three types of muscles make up the muscle system. Smooth muscles and the cardiac muscle make our organs do their work without our having to think about it. Skeletal muscles allow us to make our voluntary movements.

What do muscles do?

If it moves and it is a part of the body, it's a muscle. Everything that moves in the body is a muscle.

Where are muscles?

Everywhere. Muscles in the lungs allow us to breathe. Muscles in the digestive tract allow us to digest and use food. The heart muscle pumps blood. Muscles in our arms and legs allow us to write and walk. Muscles in our eyes allow us to see in different directions without turning our heads.

What other systems of the body might your muscles work with?

Skeletal System - Your voluntary muscles (the muscles you choose to move) work with your bones to allow you to throw balls and play the piano.

Digestive System - Muscles in the walls of your stomach, intestines and colon move food through your body and help make the digestive system work.

Respiratory System - Muscles in your lungs help you breathe.

Circulatory System - A big muscle, your heart, pumps blood through your body and never rests in doing its job.

• **The Endocrine System**
[Note: In introducing the endocrine system and helping children to identify with the way in which endocrine glands secrete fluids our bodies need, have them think about how they felt the last time they were in an emergency situation. This could have been when a car they were riding in had to slam on its brakes unexpectedly or when an earthquake occurred if you live on the Pacific Rim or when they got into a scary situation on a bike or skates. Did they feel flushed and a little shaky? Did they start to sweat a bit? If so, they were feeling their adrenal glands kick into gear to pump adrenaline into their blood streams to help them deal quickly with the anticipated emergency. In addition, in a very rough way, squeezing a wet sponge gives children some idea of the secretion process in a ductless gland.]

What makes up the endocrine system?
Different glands throughout the body that secrete important fluids make up the endocrine system.
What glands are these and where are they found?
Thyroid gland in the neck affects metabolism.

Adrenal gland in the brain area helps us respond to danger.

Pituitary gland in the brain area affects growth.

Testes (male)/Ovaries (female) affect development of adult sexual characteristics such as beards and chest hair on men.

These glands don't work together so much as they help different parts of the body work as they are supposed to.

What other body systems might the endocrine system work with?
Circulatory System - Needed bodily fluids are carried to other parts of the body through the blood stream.

Nervous System - The brain and nerves send messages to the glands to send out the necessary fluids.

When you have completed introductory discussion of all the systems, you might have children complete the Name That System Activity Sheet at the back of this chapter. The answer to each question is pretty easy for children to decipher from the fact provided but the facts themselves should be of interest to the students and are the primary reason for using the activity sheet. They tend to spark interest in the subject.

c. It's Your Check-up
Using an actual pediatrician check-up form or the It's Your Check-Up Activity Sheet at the back of this chapter, talk about what happens when the children go to the doctor for a regular physical examination. What is the doctor looking for? Why does the doctor ask the questions he or she does? You can use the activity sheet to stimulate some class discussion about the things doctors look for when we visit.

Children can work in pairs to measure heights, weights and resting pulse rates. Have weight scales and a measuring tape on the wall that children can use. Ask a local pediatrician if you can have a copy of the height/weight chart used to determine the tallness or shortness of boys and girls for their respective ages. Remember to ask for charts for both sexes. Have children plot their height and weight and use the percentile information to complete the activity sheet.

Some of the things doctors look for in well-child check-ups are:

Ears: Punctured eardrum, infected ear, wax
     build-up
Eyes: Retinal attachment
Mouth: Cavities, tonsil infection
Chest: Clear air passages
Lower Torso: Organs that are sore or swollen,
     size of appendix
Reflexes: Nervous system response
Walking/Jumping Activities: Balance and
     coordination/ inner ear and nervous
     system health

If possible, arrange to have a nurse or physician speak to your class about what health care professionals check for during routine annual check-ups.

d. Build a Body System

Divide children into cooperative learning groups. Each group will explore in detail one of the body's systems. (Basic information about these systems is included in the background information above.) The exploration of the "adopted" body system can be structured as follows:

- The group completes a group written report. The group can use the Build A Body System Activity Sheet at the back of this chapter if you choose. This report should explain what parts of the body comprise the system, what the system does for the body, and how the system works with other systems of the body.
- The group creates a human size model of the system by tracing around one member of the group and creating a life-size body upon which the system is drawn. To do this, two copies of the traced version are cut out. On one (or both if you want the final models to be two-sided), the group members work together to depict the system on which the group is reporting. Children should use library, textbook and other resource books to help them recreate the system visually. (It should be noted here that some systems such as the endocrine system are easier to artistically recreate than others and you may want to consider this when assigning the student groups their systems to explore.) When the system is fully depicted on the first paper body, the students staple the second paper body to it, stuffing it with newspaper as they

go. The result is a somewhat three-dimensional representation of the system.
- The group makes an oral presentation to the class describing the system it has researched. To do this, the group can use the written report, the paper model and any additional materials the students desire such as charts and posters.
- If you choose to let students use the Build A Body System Activity Sheet for their group reports, encourage the children to write their reports in dark pencil neatly so that the reports can be photocopied for each student in the class. Each student will get a copy of each group's report so that students can compile individual books on the systems of the human body. In addition, this book can contain, if you choose to, the children's notes and activities for each system—i.e., completed Build A Body System Activity Sheets filled out in conjunction with introductory classroom discussions, Name That System Activity Sheets and the like.

e. People Graphing

As a way to integrate mathematics into your human body curriculum, your class could create graphs on the distributions of hair color, eye color, and heights and weights in your class. They could pursue this further by finding the average height or weight of children in the class. If height or weight are sensitive issues for older children, they could each write their height or weight on unidentified slips of paper which are collected and graphed so that individual information is anonymous.

2. Healthful Foods and Your Growing Body

a. Build a Food Guide Pyramid

As a class project, have children explore the Food Guide Pyramid. Using corrugated cardboard from large discarded boxes, cut a square base and four triangles. Before constructing the pyramid, have children measure the height of the triangle, divide the total number of inches by four, and measure and draw horizontal lines on the sides of the triangles so that the sides are divided into four equi-distant areas. Masking tape the bottom edge of the triangles to the sides of the square base. Pull up the triangles to meet at the top, masking tape the point and the sides where the triangles meet. A small group of children should be able to complete this project.

Once the pyramid is built, have children bring in labels from foods in the different groups, dried foods such as macaroni, rice, beans or corn that fall within certain groups, pictures from magazines and representations of food cut out of construction paper. These will be pasted on the appropriate level of the pyramid to reinforce eating proper amounts of food group items. You might also want to write onto the appropriate level of the pyramid the recommended number of servings per day.

b. Personal Meal Diary

Ask children to chart everything they eat for one day. They can use the Personal Meal Diary Activity Sheet at the back of this chapter to chart their eating for the day. Once each child has completed the meal survey, they should check their servings against the serving suggestions of the food pyramid and check their daily intake of junk food servings.

You may want to have children do this activity one day a week during each week of the curriculum unit so that they can increase their personal awareness of their ordinary eating habits.

c. Menu Planner

Using the serving information they have learned from the Food Guide Pyramid, have children make up a complete healthful menu for a full day. If this is too much, ask them to plan a complete specific meal such as breakfast or lunch. Encourage them to bring to school the recipes for some of the dishes they include on their menu.

Younger children (third or fourth grade) might enjoy making this project an art project. Using a paper plate they can cut out construction paper food items or use magazine pictures or actual food such as dried beans or rice to show their suggested meal pictorially. They can even complete this project by mounting the plate onto a paper placemat and gluing plastic flatware to complete the setting. If you like, you can use this activity as an opportunity to reinforce table etiquette such as table setting and courteous table manners.

d. Breakfast with a Capital B

Children and adults often hear advice that they should start the day with a good breakfast, but many do not heed the advice. Many adults just have very bad breakfast habits, substituting coffee or perhaps coffee and toast for a nutritional meal. Children have to take the lead from the adults in their family and often get little breakfast because of time crunches or adult disinterest.

After reminding children how important breakfast is in terms of providing basic energy for the body to start doing its work each day, ask children to work either individually or in groups to create an "advertising" poster with a snappy slogan to try to convince America or at least their families and friends to start the day with a healthful breakfast meal.

e. Nutritional Analysis

Most families buy cereal from time to time. Three to four weeks in advance of this project, ask children to bring in empty cereal boxes. It is helpful if they can bring in more than one in the event some children do not bring in any. Using the Nutritional Analysis Activity Sheet at the back of this chapter, each child will examine a cereal box to determine its good and questionable nutritional points.

f. Grocery Store Treasure Hunt

Ask children to visit the produce section of the local grocery store and list five items they have never tried before. Have them write a little information about each such as where it is grown, what part of the plant is eaten, how it is prepared to eat and its nutritional value. Much of this information may be gathered directly from the grocery store's tagging information on or near the produce or from a dictionary or encyclopedia. Different greens, roots, flowers, and melons may be among these unfamiliar foods. Encourage children to bring in a sample of one of their "untried" produce selections to share with the class.

3. Daily Exercise Needs of the Human Body

a. Exercise Survey

Using the Exercise Survey Activity Sheet at the back of this chapter, children can track the amount of physical exercise they get each day for a week. At the end of the week, they can see at a glance how much exercise they got each day. What portion of their daily activities was spent jumping rope, walking, playing running games, playing ball, biking or skating? Children can use the activity sheets to reach conclusions about when and how they could increase their daily physical activity. Use this as an opportunity to talk with students about television viewing as an activity choice.

Remind children of activities they might forget to list such as walking to school. Also, you may choose to have them keep the survey forms at school to complete each day right before going home. In this way they will get lost less frequently and be completed more often.

b. Sport Day

Have a sport day for children during which they try certain physical exercises and activities and log in their results. Provide awards for each event and participation awards for each child who completes all the activities. You can make circle-shaped posterboard medallions as your awards and tie them to ribbons so they can be hung around the neck like an Olympic medal. Alternatively, use two-inch wide ribbon or construction paper ribbons glued to the bottom of the medallion as the award. Don't forget to ask parents to help you make these awards and to man the sporting event stations. Children can record their results on the Sport Day Activity Sheet at the back of this chapter.

Some possible event activities are:
1) Basketball free throw toss
2) Baskets made per minute
3) 50-yard dash
4) Quarter mile walk or run
5) Jumping rope (length or uninterrupted jumping or complexity of jumping)
6) Standing broad jump
7) Softball distance toss
8) Softball accuracy throw
9) Jump and touch (child jumps as high as he or she can and marks wall with chalk)

c. Fitness Day

To stress cardiovascular fitness, host a fitness day at which students choose three aerobic activities to engage in and measure their own heart rates. In this activity, children increase their awareness of how aerobic exercise works the circulatory system. Students should work in pairs for this event. Partners help each other take and record pulse rates and time or count the cardiovascular activity, as appropriate. Use the Fitness Day Activity Sheet at the back of this chapter for this activity.

Suggested aerobic activities are:
• Jumping rope for two to three minutes
• Running a 50-yard dash
• Speed-walking an age appropriate number of laps
• 100 jumping jacks
• Running in place or jumping in place for one to two minutes

Writing Activities

1. Chapter Vocabulary

The suggested vocabulary words and terms for this chapter from which you might want to choose are:

Nervous system
Skeletal system
Muscle system
Circulatory system
Respiratory system
Digestive system
Endocrine gland
Cell
Cytoplasm
Nucleus
Neurons
Central nervous system
Peripheral nervous system
Involuntary muscles
Contract
Expand
Digestion
Enzymes
Arteries
Veins
Secretions
Hormones
Nutrition
Fitness
Exercise
Calories
Energy
Aerobic
Carbohydrates
Proteins

2. Pick a Part, Any Part

Have children write, at minimum, a five point report about a part of the body. Students can use the Pick-A-Part Report Activity Sheet at the back of this chapter to provide a framework for this short, focused report. Perhaps they want to write the report about an organ or body part which starts with the same letter as either their first or last name. An alphabetical listing of human organs or body parts is provided to serve as a starting place should you choose to assign this report on this alphabetical basis.

A Adrenal glands, appendix, arteries
B Brain, bones, bladder
C Colon, capillaries, cartilage
D Denticle, disk, diaphragm
E Esophagus, epidermis, ear, eye
F Fingers, femur
G Gland (of your choice), ganglion, gums
H Heart, hair
I Intestines, incus bone
J Jaw, joint
K Kidney, knees
L Liver, large intestines, lungs, lymph nodes
M Muscles, mucous membranes
N Nails, nose
O Optic nerve, ovaries
P Pituitary gland, pancreas
Q Quadriceps (large thigh muscle)
R Rectum, ribcage
S Stomach, spleen
T Teeth, tongue, tendon
U Uterus, ulna bone
V Vessels, vertebrae, ventricle, vein, villi
W Wrist
X Xiphoid (bottom of sternum)
Y Y ligament (y-shaped band covering upper, front hip joint)
Z Zygomatic bone (cheekbone)

3. Over the Cytoplasmic Sea

Children can engage in a creative writing activity that grows out of their newly acquired knowledge of cell structure. Ask children to write a story about shrinking so small that they are able to take a journey through the inside of one of the cells in their bodies. The cell could be a bone cell, blood cell, nerve cell or a generic cell. They would chart their ride over the cytoplasmic sea, to stop at the nucleus or take a break on a floating vacuole or mitochondrion. To give students an idea of how to go about writing this kind of story, you might refer them to *The Magic School Bus Inside the Human Body* by Joanna Cole published by Scholastic, Inc. (1989).

4. Five Senses Poem

Ask children to write a five senses poem. A five senses poem is an unrhymed poem about the effect of a certain stimulus on each of the senses. In writing a five senses poem children can explore simile.

Example:

Summer and Me

Summer feels like the hot sun upon my skin.
It smells like a smoky backyard barbecue.
It looks like a delicate flower wilting at noon.
It tastes like cool, sweet watermelon.
It sounds like waves crashing on the seashore.

5. Hawking Healthful Foods

If children watch morning television any day of the week, they have seen numerous advertisements for every kind of sugar coated cereal imaginable. Give children the opportunity to give a new twist to such advertisements. Children can work in cooperative learning groups to create mock television advertisements for healthful eating. The advertisement could include use of a graphically designed poster, hand puppets and/or role-playing. The children would need to write the script for their presentation on a cooperative basis. No advertisement should be reenacted until the children have produced a written script for their finished product.

The subject of the advertisement could be as general as healthful multi-food group eating or "no more junk food" or as specific as why people should start the day with a healthful breakfast. After the children have presented their ads to the class, some of them might like to present them to younger classes who may just be learning about these concepts and who would benefit greatly from role modeling by older students.

6. Oranges, Oranges Everywhere, But Not a Drop of Juice

Have children bring in a fruit or vegetable of their choice. This object will be the inspiration for a series of creative writing activities.

a. Fruit and Veggie Riddles

In this exercise, children place the fruit or vegetable on their desks so they can see it clearly and at close range. The writer's job is to write a paragraph riddle explaining in detail what the food looks like without stating what it is. They should write about its shape, colors, texture, and size. The paragraph is written in the third person and should start describing the object by saying "It is …" and end with "What is it?" The writer should then include an answer line that states what the described object is. You might then want to collect the writing samples and read them without identifying who wrote them or what the fruit or vegetable is and let the class guess the answer to the riddle.

Example:

It is round like a ball and yellow orange in color. It is waxy to the touch and looks like it has been pricked with toothpicks all over its surface. It is a little shiny. It is the size of a baseball. What is it?
Answer: *An orange.*

b. Tasty Autobiography

Ask children to imagine that they are their fruit or vegetable. Now they must write their life story starting from seed and continuing to salad or whatever the fulfillment of their ultimate purpose in life. Some children might even choose to have their food object remain uneaten only to wither, mold, and die. Ask the children to write the story as an autobiography using the first person. If you have classroom encyclopedia resources or if children are told in advance to do a little research, they could include in their autobiography reference to the geographic location in which they might have been grown and harvested.

This project allows children to think in an ordered fashion about the growing process as well as the entire distribution process that takes a vegetable from soil to store.

c. Food Sense Poem

Use the five senses poem to have children explore their fruit or vegetable through this written exercise.

Example:

A Nectarine

A nectarine smells like candy.
It feels smooth as a bald head.
It sounds like a slurp when you bite it.
It tastes juicy.
It looks like a baseball when it rolls.

7. Healthful Foods Restaurant Menu

Even though most children probably eat more often at a fast food restaurant than at one of the many types of healthful foods restaurants that have sprung up in recent years, it is fun for children to try to create a menu for a healthful food restaurant. Some restaurants tout the healthfulness of their menus by virtue of vegetarian dishes, low sodium and/or low cholesterol foods. Using their knowledge of the foods they should try to eat each day, ask children to create a menu for breakfast, lunch, or dinner (or all three) for an imaginary restaurant which they can name. Remind them that menus give customers entree choices and that each entree should contain a sentence or two describing its contents and terrific taste to entice the customer to order it. Bring in some take-out menus for the children to look at to familiarize themselves with what should be included in their menu pages.

You might want to use this activity as a jumping off point for incorporation of the math menu activity described in Item 1c of the lesson activities in Chapter 2.

Art and Craft Activities

1. Exploring Me Art

Since this chapter explores how we are made and how we work, children may want to explore part of themselves through an art project. Here are two suggestions for creating portraits or busts.

a. Ask children to use a tear art technique to create self portraits

These should be about 9" x 12" in size and can be displayed with short autobiographies students write.

b. Have children create clay busts of themselves

This can be done with clay you glaze and fire or alternatively with clay which is dried and painted with tempera paint that is mixed with white glue to add strength to the unfired project.

2. Hand Art

The hands provide excellent "source" material for lovely art projects. Since they are parts of our bodies, they are perfect source material for a subject-related art project. Cut out hands can be turned into flowers and trees or used to dramatic effect in an abstract collage. Fingerprints are also a great art source. Consider these two art project ideas:

a. Children can make a dramatic hand collage

Cut 9" x 12" pieces of construction paper in primary and secondary colors. Let children pick four colors. They trace and cut a pair of their hands from each color. When this is done, they glue them to a 12" x 20" piece of black paper in a design of their choice. The results make for a beautiful and varied classroom display. This project can also be used in conjunction with teaching themes of brotherhood and "reaching out" to the people of the world in peace.

b. Making fingerprints is another interesting activity for children

Children can make entire pictures using fingerprints accented with marker in the style of Ed Emberly's fingerprint art books. Fingerprint creatures can be used to make cards and stationary as gifts for parents. You could also use the Fingerprints Activity Sheet at the back of this chapter to help your students learn about fingerprint types.

2. No Junk Food Collage

A week or so in advance of this project, have children start collecting labels and wrappers from food considered junk food. Remember that any foods containing refined sugar can be considered part of this category. Accordingly, children can be encouraged to bring in not only Twinkie® and candy bar wrappers but also labels from bags and boxes of sugar, cake mixes, soda six-packs, and overly sweetened cereals. If an insufficient number of labels is available, children can draw junk food such as ice cream, candy bars, chips, and the like.

With the pictures of junk food, children create collages on pieces of 9" x 12" paper. Children draw and cut out a red or black version of the universal "no" symbol and glue it on top of their collage to send the "no more junk food" message.

2. Art with Food

Many traditional student art and craft projects use food, but it may be useful to enumerate them here to serve as a quick reference for food-related art ideas.

a. Fruit and Vegetable Prints

Entire scenes, repeating linear designs, or abstract pictures can be created using a variety of vegetables, fruits, and tempera paint. Good fruits and vegetables generally are bell peppers, oranges, apples, carrots, potatoes (children can carve additional shapes into these with plastic knives if you choose), broccoli, cauliflower, cucumber, and mushrooms (halved). The broccoli and cauliflower flowerlets make excellent flower designs for a picture.

b. Food Mosaics

Using a variety of dry beans, pastas, coffee grounds, ground walnut shells (available at some pet stores as animal litter), rice, and egg shells, children can create attractive mosaic pictures on any topic you or they choose. Rice and pasta can be colored by taking the dry product and mixing it with food coloring and a tiny amount of water—just enough to distribute the color. Spread the colored rice or pasta out on waxed paper to dry. (Note that while rice can be used for these projects, its small size sometimes makes its use messier and less attractive than larger items such as pasta and beans.)

c. Natural Dyes

Two of the easiest food dyes to make are those from brown onion skins and blueberries. Take the skins from five to seven large brown onions or one cup of blueberries and boil them in two cups water for about five to ten minutes (until the water is deeply colored). Cool and add a tablespoon or two of vinegar to the dyes. Have each child bring in two boiled eggs. Children can dye their eggs in each of the colors. Eggs need to sit in dye for several minutes to absorb enough dye to be showy and pretty. You can leave the berries or skins in the dye even while you use it so children get the idea that early dyes were made from natural materials and sometimes even from things we eat.

Another way to have an egg dyeing project is to have each child bring in two blown-out eggs (in case one breaks) and enough brown onion skins to cover his or her egg. Each child also gets a nine inch square of net. The onion skins are wrapped around the egg and the net wrapped over the skins and secured as tightly as possible with a twist tie. The eggs are placed into boiling or hot water in a large pot and boiled for twenty minutes. Afterwards they are cooled. The next day each child gets an egg (not necessarily his or her own) to untie. The eggs are colored very darkly and have a woodlike look. This is actually a traditional German craft. It can be difficult for some children to cover the eggs with the onion skin and is best undertaken by children working in pairs.

You can enhance this project by using small leaves and vegetable oil. Cover the leaf with vegetable oil and press it onto the side of the egg.

Then follow the directions in the prior paragraph. The finished product then includes a leaf design.

4. Harvest Basket

Each child can make a papier-mâché version of the fruit or vegetable that he or she brought to school for the "Oranges, Oranges Everywhere" writing project earlier in this chapter. Have the child create the shape of his or her fruit or vegetable by crushing newspaper into the desired shape and wrapping the shape with masking tape to hold it in place. Then the child uses thin strips of newspaper to papier mâché´ the surface of the fruit or vegetable. This can be done by dipping the newspaper into starch or a flour/water glue mixture. Place project on waxed paper to dry. Paint with tempera paint and spray with acrylic to give it a shiny finish. You can let children use browns and blacks to make shading designs or repeating small patterns on their produce piece if you or they like. These dark colors should be put on with thin brushes before the item is sprayed with acrylic.

Gather all the produce together and place it in a large basket to decorate the classroom.

6. Book Report

As a twist on the traditional book report project, ask each student to create a food model that illustrates some aspect of his or her book. This model will be presented to the class as part of an oral book report. Food projects can range from produce people (people or objects recreated using garnishing techniques) to recycled sculpture people and structures made from discarded and cleaned food containers.

Some food model examples are: yellow squash for geese, painted boiled eggs in shell make good penguins, potatoes make good faces or heads, and radishes and tomato skins make good flowers.

Food Activities

1. Anatomical Foods

Here are some fun and funny ideas for making healthful food treats that are reminiscent of the human body about which children are learning.

a. Food Face

Have children make healthful snack "faces" using rice crackers as the building base. Children cover rice crackers with peanut butter, cream cheese, or cheese spread and then decorate the treat with healthful foods to make a face—perhaps their own faces in food. Decorator items can be nuts, raisins, apple or orange slices, croutons, olives, cucumber circles, zucchini, cheese chunks, and the like. Hair can be shredded coconut, shredded cheese, olives, alfalfa sprouts, or carrot curls.

b. Nutty Grins

Students can make the traditional apple smiles by taking two slices of apple (each slice spread on one side with peanut butter) and placing mini-marshmallows between the two slices to act as the teeth of this humorous snack.

c. Almond Eyeballs

This food activity is a variation on an hors d'oeuvre food sometimes called cheese coins, cheese rounds, or cheese puffs. To make cheese eyeballs, you will need:

2 cups grated cheddar cheese
1/2 cup butter or margarine, softened
1/4 to 1/2 teaspoon salt
1/2 teaspoon paprika
Dash ground black pepper
1 cup flour
Whole almonds

With a large fork, blend cheese and butter thoroughly. Add flour, salt, paprika and pepper. Mix well. Make your eyeballs by shaping teaspoonfuls of dough into balls. Make sure you have enough balls so each student can have one before you insert the almond "pupils" into the balls. Push the pointed ends of the almonds into the balls leaving the end of the nut exposed. Reshape dough

around the end of the almond so that the appearance of an eye is complete. Bake on an ungreased cookie sheet at 400 degrees until golden brown.

You can make about 30 eyeballs with this recipe. You may want to double the recipe if you want each child to have two to eat.

2. Four-in-One Recipes

These recipes allow children to explore recipes which use three or four food groups in one dish.

a. Pioneer Chicken Stew and Dumplings

This recipe is a meal-in-a-dish dinner. It can be made in an electric soup pot very easily.

1 cup cooked chicken pieces, shredded (you can
*   use canned chicken)*
4 - 5 grated carrots
2 diced onions
Salt and pepper to taste
Water

Dumplings
3 cups flour
1 cup water
1 teaspoon baking powder (optional)

Boil 6-8 cups water in a pot (pot should be about halfway full). Mix flour and water until you make dough. If too dry to work with, add a little more water. If too sticky to work with, add more flour. Give each child a tablespoon of dough to knead, pat flat and cut into one inch strips. Put chicken, onions, and carrots into boiling water. Add dumplings five or six at a time. As they cook in the boiling water, they puff up slightly. When they have plumped, add more until you have enough dumplings to feed the class one or two with stew. Salt and pepper to taste.

Obviously, this simple dumpling recipe results in slightly leaden dumplings but this was probably not uncommon to settlers and cowboys.

Serve stew in hot drink cups and top with grated parmesan cheese so that the four basic food groups are included in the meal.

b. Four Food Group Salad

Combine chopped fruit and nuts of your choice. Children can chop the fruit with plastic knives. Top each serving with granola and yogurt or whipped cream. The completed classroom treat is a four food groups salad—another meal in a dish which is ideal for breakfast or a light lunch.

3. Healthful Snacks

Have children make any one of a number of healthful snacks to have after school or on weekends. Some examples are fruit kabobs, bugs on a branch, and fruit and dairy smoothie.

a. Kabobs

To make kabobs, use wooden barbecue skewers and have children skewer fruit (such as strawberries, chopped apple, pineapple, banana, pear, peaches, grapes, and berries) or vegetables (such as bite-size zucchini, cucumber, mushrooms, bell pepper, celery, and cherry tomatoes). You can use a dip with the kabobs if you like. Good dips for fruit are: 1) honey (a little messy); 2) sour cream mixed with brown sugar to taste and a dash of nutmeg; and 3) instant pudding. Good dips for vegetables are onion or ranch style sour cream dips. Chunks of cheddar or jack cheese can also be used on either type of kabob.

b. Bugs on a Branch

This snack can be made with a nearly infinite variety of bugs and branches. The "branch" is spread with peanut butter, cream cheese, or cheese spread so that the bugs can be affixed to the branch.

Suggestions for bugs are:
   Raisins
   Peanuts
   Almonds
   Pecans pieces
   Olive slices
   Dried fruit pieces

Suggestions for branches are:
   Celery sticks
   Carrot sticks
   Thick stick pretzels
   Italian bread sticks
   Bananas

c. Healthy Shake

Using a blender you can create a healthful smoothie which can be touted as a healthful alternative to a milkshake. To make smoothies, puree bananas and strawberries in a blender. Add a little milk, yogurt or apple juice as necessary to thin. Sweeten with honey if needed. You will need 1/2 to one banana per child depending upon the size of serving you intend.

If you use frozen strawberries and crush them with the blender, you get a frosty drink.

4. Fondue Fun

It seems that fondue began with the Swiss melting Swiss cheese with a little white wine and then dipping chunks of bread, vegetables, and fruit in the warm mixture. Since the early days of fondue, it has expanded into many areas, even dessert, with fruit and cake chunks being dipped into melted chocolate. It remains a relatively healthful treat and can be used as an interesting, tasty, low-meat meal.

a. Cheese Fondue

Melting cheese can be tricky so if you want to try a cheese fondue, have children chop vegetables and chunk bread and dip it into melted processed cheese.

b. Chili Fondue

Melt chunks of an eight ounce package of cream cheese into a 16-ounce can of "beanless" meat chili for a southwestern fondue. You will probably need to triple this recipe to feed a class. Dip vegetables, cheese chunks, and bread chunks.

c. Chocolate Fondue.

Melt 1-1 1/2 pound chocolate chunks or two large bags of chocolate chips with a small amount of canned evaporated milk to make chocolate fondue. Do this over very low heat and stir often. Have children dip fruit chunks, angel food cake or pound cake chunks, or dried fruit slices into this mixture.

Art Masters—Old and New

The two art masters explored here are either relatively recent or current artists who became, at times, media stars. They are explored here because they either used items from the pantry in their art or their style of art lends itself to exploring objects related to food or the kitchen.

Background Information

1. Andy Warhol

Andy Warhol was an American artist who became very famous in the late 1950s and early 1960s as an artist of the Pop Art Movement. He took items from everyday life—often items from the commercial aspects of everyday life—and turned them into wall art and sculpture. Some of his very famous pieces were wall art based on the labels from Campbell's soup cans and sculpture using Brillo pad boxes.

2. Anthony Christo

Christo is a Bulgarian-born artist who has become famous in recent years for making artistic statements in huge expanses of nature. The artwork is temporary and remains in the mind only through photographs but people travel hundreds of miles to pass by or walk under these artistic statements. He has wrapped huge areas of the everglades with pink cloth, hung a vast orange curtain across a valley in Colorado, and placed huge yellow and blue umbrellas in areas of California and Japan, simultaneously. His earlier art, however, involved wrapping small, ordinary objects. This gave them a mystical quality and meaning.

Project Directions

1. Pop Art a la Andy Warhol

Have children create a pop art project in one of two ways. One way is to have children create their own label for a food product on a piece of white paper made from one-quarter of an 11" x 8 1/2" sheet of white paper. The labels are created in black and white only. The teacher then attaches four complete labels to a sheet of paper 11" x 8 1/2" for copying. Eight to ten copies of each sheet are made and the labels cut apart. The child then takes the copies of his labels and places them in some sort of repeating pattern on a sheet of construction paper 12" x 18" in size and glues them in place on the paper. He or she can color or tint the copied labels with crayon or marker if he or she chooses.

In another version of the project, each child brings in a food label from his or her house. These labels are then affixed to a larger sheet of paper for copying. Again, copy eight to ten of each sheet and let each child create a repeating collage design in the manner described above with copies of only the label he or she brought in. Again, children can color or tint the copied labels as they choose.

2. Christo Container Art

This is an art project that can be done in large part at home if you so choose. The project itself is simple. After you introduce Christo the artist and his style of wrapping things and places, ask children to go home and find an empty, unbreakable container from the kitchen. They should find a container (whether can, milk or juice carton, cookie or candy box, etc.) which interests them in shape and size. These containers can either be brought back to school for wrapping in the Christo style or they can be wrapped at home. If they are wrapped at home and then brought to school for an ad hoc Christo art show, the children can enjoy trying to discern the thing within the wrap as viewers of Christo's early sculpture did.

Wrap can be nearly anything. Fabric is a great wrap, but wrap possibilities include newspaper, tissue, garbage bag, foil, and brown bag. While the children may need tape to hold the wrapper in place, string or yarn can also be used to tie the wrapper on to give interesting visual effect. Sometimes Christo's work was painted all one color. This could be completed at school if you like after the sculptural wrapping has been completed at home. Spray painting is one way to paint the items. Tempera will work on some coverings, but probably not very well with plastic or foil wrappings.

If the children and you choose to, share this art show effort with other classes by inviting them to view your Christo art. You might also want to wrap a part of the school for a day if someone can donate fabric for a project like this. Wrapping an object or area draws attention to it. Children can explore whether wrapping a place at school will make an artistic statement about the importance of nature, the need to recycle, or the importance of battling litter. Wrapping a small hedge or tree trunk could have this effect and be used in conjunction with an Earth Day type of celebration or a Keep Our School Beautiful celebration.

Sharing Activities

1. Sharing Healthy Food Traditions Around the World

In many parts of the world, the daily diet contains far fewer refined sugar and wheat products than the daily diet of the average American. Meat is also scarce in some areas so meat is a less prevalent menu item. As a result of these things, many of these traditional meals are more healthful than our daily food habits which all too often include refined foods and high-fat, high-sodium fast foods.

Usually traditional food is served around a major starch from the region such as rice or corn. For example, in most Asian cultures individual dishes are served with rice. In Indian cuisine, the starch may be provided by rice or a flat bread called nan. Rice and flat bread are also basic starches in many Arab countries. In Central and South American cultures, the main starch may be corn (as in tortillas) or rice eaten with beans. In traditional Hawaiian cooking, a mashed root called poi served as the starch. Sometimes the starch is dipped into the other foods and condiments are eaten. Sometimes other foods are served over the starch as in rice, pasta, or dumplings. Sometimes foods are placed inside the starch such as with tortillas and Ethiopian flat bread.

Divide children into learning groups of six to eight. Larger groups are useful for this project as there are many aspects to explore. Working from these groups, children will create a multicultural luncheon event, with each group providing foods from the culture adopted by the group. You might want to assign food cultures generally, such as by a continent. This will give you investigation into Asian, African, South American, and European food cultures at the least.

Children can use cookbooks to do a bulk of their research on characteristics of the chosen culture's food. For example, if you look at Korean, Japanese, and Chinese cookbooks, the recipes often indicate that the meat or vegetable dish should be served with rice. Each child or pair of children in each group will cook a dish at home from the adopted culture. The groups will also be responsible for decorating their tables with cloths, posters and centerpieces that reflect the culture or cultures adopted. You can ask parents to donate paper goods for the event.

By all means invite parents to attend this luncheon. You might want to combine the luncheon with short group presentations about the regions or countries adopted. Students can also talk about healthful or problematic aspects of the cultural cuisine. For example, is it high in fat or sodium?

2. Fitness First Poster Contest

Your class might want to host a fitness poster contest. Students would be encouraged to make posters for display around the school on a health or fitness theme. Teachers or the principal could serve as judges. It would be especially fun to hold such a contest and hang the posters in conjunction with some sort of school-wide fitness event as suggested below.

3. All School Sport or Fitness Event.

Either as a class or with the entire school, hold some sort of fitness-based event. These events can take any number of forms, but in each form they emphasize the need for exercise to have a healthy body and life. Here are some ideas:

a. School Olympics

In this event, children compete first against their classmates in a selection of events. Sample events are 50 yard dash, jumping rope (judged either in terms of length of time without a miss or in terms of creativity and difficulty), basketball free throws, softball distance throw, softball target throw, high jump (child jumps against a wall marked with inches or centimeters and touches the highest spot he or she can), quarter mile run, standing broad jump, and the like. Five or six events are chosen to be the school Olympic events.

The winners (first two or three places depending upon how large a final event you want) in each grade level in each class then compete against the winners of the same grade level in other classes. All participants receive a certificate, and the winners receive special awards or certificates.

b. Sport-A-Thon Sports Fundraiser

Have children participate in a sports/fitness related event as a fundraiser for either school sports equipment or a health organization. The American Heart Association, for example, has an annual Jump-for-Heart program in which children participate in jumping rope, raise money for the American Heart Association, and receive small rewards for money raised.

A walk-a-thon is an event at which children walk a path on school property to raise money for some cause such as school playground equipment. People can donate money based upon flat donation amounts or on a fixed amount per lap or minute walked, depending upon your course. An Olympic type of event such as the one described above can also be structured the same way so that children raise money for the chosen cause based upon the number of events in which the child competes (e.g., $1 per event) or by flat amount.

A different twist on this kind of event is to have a mixed-up sports day in which the events are on the silly side, such as upper graders having tricycle races and lower graders having backwards walking contests or skipping contests.

4. Fitness Assembly

Your class might want to present a fitness assembly for the school. For such an event, students can present several of the class posters they may have created. They can research and present certain health facts. The event can culminate with a speaker from the local community who is a physical education teacher, a high school/college fitness or nutrition teacher/professor, or a local health care or nutrition professional.

Name: _____

Build A Body System

1. **Name of system.** _____

2. **Name the parts of the body that make up the system.** _____

   _____

   _____

   _____

3. **What does the system do?** _____

   _____

   _____

   _____

4. **List interesting facts about the system.** _____

   _____

   _____

   _____

5. **What other systems of the body does this system work with?** _____

   _____

   _____

   _____

6. **Describe how this system works with one other system and how this helps your body work efficiently.**

   _____

   _____

   _____

   _____

Name: _____

Hands-On Activities for Individual Or Paired Student Investigation

1. Nervous System Activity - How the Brain Receives Messages

Get a partner and two toothpicks or dull pencils. On your partner's back, test the message transmitters in the skin. Touch the skin with one toothpick and then two. Can your partner tell if there are two touches or one? When using two toothpicks, can your partners feel two spots when the toothpicks are 6" apart, 5" apart, 3" apart, 1" apart? At some distance, the brain can only translate the message of one touch even though two touches are made. Can you find that distance?

2. Circulatory/Muscle/Respiratory System Activity - How the Heart Responds to Exercise

Working in pairs, check each other's pulse before and after jumping rope for one or two minutes. Check pulse with your fingers on the inner wrist on the thumb side. Do not use your thumb to take a pulse. Count pulse beats for 15 seconds and multiply by four to find beats per minute. Take pulse before jumping, immediately after jumping, and five minutes after jumping.

In this activity, you investigate how your heart (a muscle) responds to exercise. It beats more quickly with exercise because during exercise the other parts of your body have an increased need for oxygen which tissues get from oxygen rich blood. Did you breathe faster after jumping? Can you see how the circulatory, muscle and respiratory systems work together during exercise?

3. Skeletal System Activity - Why We Have Jointed Bones

Work with a partner to tape popsicle sticks to some or all of your fingers. Try to do simple tasks like picking up a pencil or a quarter. Try to write your name. These tasks are much harder, if not impossible, to do without the joints that allow for movement.

4. Digestive System Activity - How Chewing Helps Speed the Digestive Process

Children work in pairs, each with a round hard candy. Both start eating the candy at the same time but one uses teeth and jawbone to bite and chew the candy while the other sucks on the candy. Which one is able to send the entire candy onto the stomach first where digestion will continue? When you do not chew food, saliva only aids in the breaking down of the food in the mouth. When you chew food, saliva, jaw, and teeth work together to break food down. If we did not have teeth, we would have to puree all our food to eat it or eat only soft foods. Chewing and saliva prepare food for digestion at the stomach, the food's next stop.

Name: _____

Name That System

Directions: For each fact stated below, decide which system of the body the fact relates to.

Fact No. 1. Your lungs help you breathe over 3,000 gallons of air each day.

What is the _____ system?

Fact No. 2. A red blood cell lives for about 3 months.

What is the _____ system?

Fact No. 3. Babies have about 270 bones. Some bones fuse together as we grow. Adults have only about 206 bones.

What is the _____ system?

Fact No. 4. During your lifetime, your stomach will help digest food that weighs about as much as six adult elephants (60,000 pounds).

What is the _____ system?

Fact No. 5. The skull is made up of 26 different bones.

What is the _____ system?

Fact No. 6. The intestines are about 25 feet long.

What is the _____ system?

Fact No. 7. The brain is made up of 100 billion cells but it weights less than 3 pounds or 1.5 kilograms.

What is the _____ system?

Fact No. 8. The pituitary gland secretes hormones that help you grow.

What is the _____ system?

Fact No. 9. You have about 650 muscles in your body. They make up 40 to 50% of your body weight.

What is the _____ system?

Fact No. 10. Ductless glands in the body include the adrenal and thyroid glands.

What is the _____ system?

It's Your Check-Up

Name: _____

Age: _____

Height:_____ **Percentile:** _____

Weight: _____ **Percentile:** _____

Resting heart rate: _____
(Take pulse with fingers, not thumb, at wrist or neck for 15 seconds. Multiply by 4 to get beats per minute.)

Blood Pressure: _____
Measures pressure on the artery wall as blood passes through.

Eyes: _____
Doctor checks retinal attachment.

Nose: _____
Doctor checks if passages are clear, whether there is mucus, and whether septum is intact.

Ears: _____
Doctor checks for infection and ear drum punctures.

Throat: _____
Doctor checks tonsils for infection.

Chest and Lower Torso: _____
Doctor checks if lung passages are clear and for swelling or pain in organs.

Reflexes/Balance/Walk: _____
Doctor checks nervous system and coordination and foot bone structure.

Spine/Back bone: _____
Doctor checks spine shape and curvature.

Name: _____

Personal Meal Diary

	Number of Servings	Type of Food
1. Breads/Grains	_____	_____
	_____	_____
	_____	_____
	_____	_____
Total Servings	_____	_____
2. Fruits	_____	_____
	_____	_____
	_____	_____
	_____	_____
Total Servings	_____	_____
3. Vegetables	_____	_____
	_____	_____
	_____	_____
	_____	_____
Total Servings	_____	_____

Name: _____

	Number of Servings	Type of Food
4. Milk/Dairy	_____	_____
	_____	_____
	_____	_____
	_____	_____
Total Servings	_____	_____
5. Meat, Dried Beans, Nuts, Peas, Eggs	_____	_____
	_____	_____
	_____	_____
	_____	_____
Total Servings	_____	_____
6. "Junk Food"	_____	_____
	_____	_____
	_____	_____
	_____	_____
Total Servings	_____	_____

Day of the Week _____   **Date** _____

Name: _____

Nutritional Analysis

Name of Cereal:

1. Look at the front label. What claims does the label make that the cereal is healthy? Does it claim the cereal is

   low in sugar? _____   fat free? _____

   made with real fruit? _____   low in salt/sodium? _____

   high in fiber?_____   no artificial colors or flavors? _____

   provides essential vitamins and minerals? _____

2. Look at the side label titled "Nutritional Information." Look at the column labelled "without milk."

   What is the serving size?_____   How many calories in a serving? _____

   How much of the following are in each serving?

   protein _____   carbohydrates _____   fat _____

   cholesterol _____   sodium _____

3. What percentage of the vitamins that you need each day does one serving provide?

   Percentage

   Vitamin A _____   Vitamin C _____   Calcium _____

   Vitamin D _____   Iron _____

4. Does the cereal contain chemical preservatives? If so, which ones?

   _____

   _____

Name: _____

Exercise Survey

	Monday	Tuesday	Wednesday	Thursday	Friday
Before School					
Beginning of school day (includes morning recess)					
Lunch Hour					
After lunch to end of school day					
After school day to 6 P.M.					
6 P.M. to bedtime					

Name: _____

Sport Day

Sport Event	Distance/Height	Time	Number of Successful Completions
_____	_____	_____	_____
_____	_____	_____	_____
_____	_____	_____	_____
_____	_____	_____	_____
_____	_____	_____	_____
_____	_____	_____	_____
_____	_____	_____	_____
_____	_____	_____	_____
_____	_____	_____	_____
_____	_____	_____	_____

Name: _____

Fitness Day

Resting Heart Rate: _____ **per minute**

Aerobic or Fitness Activity	Score (Minutes/Distance/Time)	Heart Rate (at completion)	Heart Rate (3 min. later)

Name: _____

Pick-A-Part Report

Part of the body: _____

_____

_____

What does it do? _____

_____

_____

Where is it located? _____

_____

_____

What body system does it belong to? _____

_____

_____

What other body system does it work with? _____

_____

_____

Draw a picture of the body part or a diagram of where it is in the body.

Name: _____

Fingerprints

Whorl   **Arch**   **Loop**

There are three basic types of fingerpaints. Each finger can have a different type. While a person's fingerprints will be in one or more of these types, each person's individual prints are different from those of other people. Each person's fingerprints are unique.

My Right Hand Fingerprints

☐	☐	☐	☐	☐
Thumb	**Index**	**Middle**	**Ring**	**Little**

My Left Hand Fingerprints

☐	☐	☐	☐	☐
Thumb	**Index**	**Middle**	**Ring**	**Little**

I have whorl/arch/loop fingerprints. (Circle those you have.)

On the reverse side of this paper, make a picture with your unique fingerprints.

Resources

1. Several book companies have published information and visually interesting book series on the systems and/or parts of the human body and how they work. Some of these which might serve as good classroom resources and be available to you from your local library are:

The Human Body Revised Edition series by Steve Parker published by Franklin Watts (example: *Touch, Taste & Smell*, 1989).

The original *The Human Body* series by Brian Ward published by Franklin Watts.

How Our Bodies Work series published by Silver Burdett Press.

You and Your Body series by Dorothy Baldwin and Claire Lister published by The Bookwright Press.

Two informative and entertaining books on how the body works are:

The Magic School Bus Inside the Human Body by Joanna Cole published by Scholastic, Inc. (1989).

Body Battles by Rita Golden Gelman published by Scholastic, Inc. (1992).

These are especially popular with younger students such as third graders, but can be enjoyed by older children because they provide easy access to research information they might need.

2. Good resources and educational materials on nutrition and food group topics may be available to you from your local arm of the United States Department of Agriculture. The educational Agricultural Extension arm of this federal department is coordinated in some states through the state college system and has education branches for youth such as 4-H and the Common Ground gardening program for low-income children. This program has available free or low-cost educational materials to schools and school teachers.

In addition, state agricultural meat and dairy councils usually provide low- or no-cost educational materials on food groups and nutrition for classroom use.

Finally, a group called the Physicians Committee for Responsible Medicine (P.O. Box 6322, Washington, D.C. 20015, (202)686-2210) provides educational materials and answers questions concerning its nutritional philosophy of the "new" four food groups which eliminate meat and dairy entirely. It may be interesting for your class to ask questions of a group such as this and give thought to whether or not they think milk and meat are necessary foods. Most authorities, of course, do believe milk and meat to be important parts of all people's diets.

3. A number of publishers have developed "sports hero" series for elementary level readers. Other publishers have high-achiever series, some selections of which feature sports stars. These include:

Sports Stars series published by Children's Press (example: *Lee Roy Selmon* by Don Pierson, 1982).

Sports Hero series published by G. P. Putnam's Sons (example: *Reggie Jackson* by Marshall Burchard, 1975).

The Achievers series published by Lerner Publications Company (example: *Florence Griffith Joyner* by Nathan Aaseng, 1989).

A series on baseball greats by Sam and Beryl Epstein published by Garrard Publishing Company

Some suggested biographies on individuals for core reading or class reading aloud are:

Jesse Owens, Champion Athlete by Tony Gentry published by Chelsea House Publishers (1990).

Babe Didrikson Zaharias, Champion Athlete by Elizabeth A. Lynn published by Chelsea House Publishers (1989).

Wilma Rudolph, Champion Athlete by Tom Biracree published by Chelsea House Publishers (1988).

Two books that contain multiple short biographies of interesting sports figures including Olympic greats are:
Great Lives: Sports by George Sullivan published by Charles Scribner's Sons (1988).

After Olympic Glory by Larry Bortstein published by Frederick Warne & Co., Inc. (1978).

4. Some core literature reading ideas which you might be able to use depending upon the reading level of your students are listed below. The books listed here are included either because they have the obtaining of food to survive as a theme, because they involve food in some other way, or because they deal in some way with health or exercise issues. As such, they might be interesting literature books to read along with the activities in this curriculum theme.
How to Eat Fried Worms by Thomas Rockwell published by Dell Publishing Co. (1973).

Julie of the Wolves by Jean Craighead George published by Harper & Row (1972).

Dear Mr. Henshaw by Beverly Cleary published by G. P. Putnam's Sons (1989).

Charlie and the Chocolate Factory by Roald Dahl published by Puffin Books (1964).

Eyeballs for Breakfast by M. M. Ragz published by Simon & Schuster (1990).

Ramona and Her Father by Beverly Clearly published by Dell (1979).

AMERICAN WE — AN EXPLORATION OF THE BILL OF RIGHTS

This chapter is designed to help children focus on and appreciate the constitutional framework that ties us together in American society. People in the United States have come here from countries and cultures around the world. Languages are different. Dress is different. Food is different. What is the same for all who live here and come to live here is a devotion to the principles of freedom and equal opportunity, which are the foundation of this nation's government. That is not to say that it always works perfectly, of course, but children and adults need to be aware of their rights and responsibilities as people of this country for our system to work its best. The purpose of this chapter is to help children understand and to reinforce those rights and responsibilities.

Lesson Activities

The Lesson Activities in this chapter center around a set of discussion guidelines intended to reinforce for children the concepts of rights and responsibilities in our society and the need for laws to assure the protection of individual rights. Some interactive exercises are suggested to reinforce ideas and principles introduced in discussion.

Writing Activities

The Writing Activities section provides students with opportunities to explore colonial life at the time of the writing of the Bill of Rights, to explore in writing the concept of rights, and to find out about leaders who fought for individual rights throughout United States history.

Art and Craft Activities

The Art and Craft section explores traditional colonial types of arts and crafts. These crafts reflect the time period during which the Bill of Rights was formulated. Multicultural crafts in Chapter 4 may also be used with this theme as a way to reinforce the beauty of the cultural diversity within a country based upon principles of individual rights and responsibilities.

Food Activities

The Food Activities section provides ideas for exploring some traditional dishes of the colonial period as well as some dishes from later periods of American history.

Art Masters—Old and New

The Art Masters - Old and New section focuses on the area of portrait art and the many ways in which it can be done. There are many famous American artists who could be explored in conjunction with this chapter, but specific ideas are given here for exploring the portraiture of Gilbert Stuart (famous for his portraits of George Washington). Attention is also paid to Grandma Moses, famous American folk artist.

Sharing Activities

Sharing Events suggested for this chapter provide opportunities to explore events of American history through hosting a colonial crafts art show or staging an assembly on crusaders for liberty and equality.

Lesson Activities

Background Information

The background information here provides the text and, in some cases, brief interpretive information concerning the Declaration of Independence's introductory clauses, the Preamble to the Constitution, the Bill of Rights, and the Thirteenth and Fourteenth Amendments to the Constitution.

Introductory Language to the Declaration of Independence

When in the course of human events, it becomes necessary for one people to dissolve the political bands which have connected them with another, and to assume among the powers of the earth, the separate and equal station to which the laws of Nature and of Nature's God entitle them, a decent respect to the opinions of mankind requires that they should declare the causes which impel them to the separation.

We hold these truths to be self-evident, that all men are created equal, that they are endowed by their Creator with certain unalienable Rights, that among these are Life, Liberty and the pursuit of Happiness.

Preamble to the Constitution of the Untied States

WE THE PEOPLE of the United States, in order to form a more perfect Union, establish justice, insure domestic tranquility, provide for the common defense, promote the general welfare, and secure the blessings of liberty to ourselves and our posterity, do ordain and establish this Constitution for the United States of America.

The Bill of Rights

The following are the first ten amendments to the Constitution. We call them the Bill of Rights. They were adopted in 1791. They mandate the protection of certain personal freedoms and states' rights.

Amendment 1

Congress shall make no law respecting an establishment of religion, or prohibiting the free exercise thereof; or abridging the freedom of speech, or of the press; or the right of the people peaceably to assemble, and to petition the government for a redress of grievances.

Note: This amendment established individual rights to freedom of religion, freedom of the press, freedom of speech, and the right to assemble peaceably. Aside from rights in criminal proceedings and the right to bear arms, most of the rights people commonly think of in the Bill of Rights are encompassed in this first amendment.

Amendment II

A well regulated militia, being necessary to the security of a free State, the right of the people to keep and bear arms shall not be infringed.

Note: The right of the people to keep and bear arms is provided for in this amendment. This is the amendment that becomes controversial when individuals and groups seek to have legislatively enacted gun control laws. Opponents contend this article protects their right to buy and keep firearms and that this right cannot be lawfully infringed. Proponents of gun control contend that this right relates to a state or other governmental entity's right to "buy and keep firearms" to maintain a state militia and similar local government peacekeeping forces.

Amendment III

No soldier shall, in time of peace, be quartered in any house without the consent of the owner; nor in time of war but in a manner to be prescribed by law.

Amendment IV

The right of the people to be secure in their persons, houses, papers, and effects, against unreasonable searches and seizures, shall not be violated, and no warrants shall issue, but upon probable cause, supported by oath or affirmation, and particularly describing the place to be searched, and the persons or things to be seized.

Note: This amendment provides individuals with protection against unreasonable searches and seizures by law enforcement agencies. It further imposes the "probable cause" search warrant requirement—i.e., that warrants may only be issued upon a showing of probable cause to believe that evidence of a crime will be found.

Amendment V

No person shall be held to answer for a capital or otherwise infamous crime, unless on a presentment or indictment of a grand jury, except in cases arising in the land or naval forces, or in the militia, when in actual service in time of war or public danger; nor shall any person be subject for the same offense to be twice put in jeopardy of life or limb; nor shall be compelled in any criminal case to be a witness against himself, nor be deprived of life, liberty, or property, without due process of law; nor shall private property be taken for public use, without just compensation.

Note: The protections of this amendment are twofold. With respect to criminal proceedings, it is this amendment that protects individuals against double jeopardy, that requires a grand jury indictment in capital cases and that protects an individual from having to testify against himself in a criminal trial. When people say that they refuse to answer on the grounds that it may incriminate them or that they "take the fifth," this is the amendment that affords them this right. This amendment also protects an individual's right to own property and provides that the government cannot take the property without providing just compensation. Just compensation is what is determined in governmental eminent domain proceedings.

Amendment VI

In all criminal prosecutions the accused shall enjoy the right to a speedy and public trial, by an impartial jury of the State and district wherein the crime shall have been committed, which district shall have been previously ascertained by law, and to be informed by the nature and cause of the accusation; to be confronted with the witnesses against him; to have compulsory process for obtaining witnesses in his favor, and to have the assistance of counsel for his defense.

Note: This is the amendment that protects individuals with a right to a speedy trial by a jury of their peers. It also provides the right for an accused individual to be able to subpoena witnesses in support of his or her case and to have an attorney appointed by the court if he or she cannot afford to pay for one.

Amendment VII

In suits at common law, where the value in controversy shall exceed twenty dollars, the right of trial by jury shall be preserved, and no fact tried by a jury shall be otherwise reexamined in any court of the United States than according to the rules of the common law.

Note: This is the amendment which provides that in civil suits an individual may request a jury trial.

Amendment VIII

Excessive bail shall not be required, nor excessive fines imposed, nor cruel and unusual punishments inflicted.

Amendment IX

The enumeration in the Constitution of certain rights shall not be construed to deny or disparage others retained by the people.

Note: This amendment makes it clear that just because a right is not specifically enumerated in the Bill of Rights or the Constitution does not mean that there are not additional rights which people retain as citizens of the country.

Amendment X

The powers not delegated to the United States by the Constitution, nor prohibited by it to the States, are reserved to the States respectively, or to the people.

Note: This amendment is the states' rights article that clarifies that the only powers the federal government has are those specifically granted to it or which are specifically restricted from the states and that all other powers and rights are retained by the people and the individual state governments.

Amendment XIII - Constitutional Amendment Abolishing Slavery

Section 1. Neither slavery nor involuntary servitude, except as a punishment for crime whereof the party shall have been duly convicted, shall exist within the United States, or any place subject to their jurisdiction.

Section 2. Congress shall have power to enforce this article by appropriate legislation.

Note: This amendment was ratified on December 6, 1865.

Amendment XIV - Constitutional Amendment concerning deprivation of life, liberty or property without due process of law and providing equal protection under the law.

Section 1. All persons born or naturalized in the United States, and subject to the jurisdiction thereof, are citizens of the United States and of the State wherein they reside. No State shall make or enforce any law which shall abridge the privileges or immunities of citizens of the United States; nor shall any State deprive any person of life, liberty, or property, without due process of law; nor deny to any person within its jurisdiction the equal protection of the laws.

Note: This amendment is known as the Civil Rights Amendment. It was ratified on July 9, 1868. Its provision for equal protection under the law is often invoked by individuals or groups who believe that laws have been unfairly applied to them or that constitutional rights have not been equally applied to them. This is an extremely important amendment for purposes of individual efforts to gain proper protection of individual freedoms such as voting rights.

Project Directions

The lesson activities in this chapter are slightly different in focus than the lesson activities in other chapters of this book. In this chapter, the lessons are primarily taught through classroom discussion. One of the reasons for this is the very nature of the subject matter which focuses on the importance of personal rights and responsibilities and the fact that responsible citizenship in the United States requires participation of the individual citizen in the community. Accordingly, individual participation is the key focus in discussion as well. Children can be advised in advance that they are expected to participate in discussion, that there are few right and wrong answers in the lesson discussions, but that what is important is the exchange of everyone's ideas.

The specific subject area of these discussion guidelines is exploration of the nature of "rules" or laws in our society, the importance of our indi-

vidual rights, and how laws relate to protection of individual rights. The relationship between rights and law is established. Children learn that we each can exercise our own rights only so that they do not infringe upon the rights of others and that government rules and laws help to ensure the free and reasonable exercise of our individual rights. Children learn that to keep their rights they must exercise them responsibly.

The lessons in this section are designed to be taught in 20 to 30 minutes segments. The goal is to relate philosophical principles about our country and form of government through creative thinking and discussion exercises. While the entire text of the Bill of Rights is listed above, all of the criminal protections do not necessarily come up in the discussion materials below. You should feel free to add reference to any constitutional protections that would be of special interest to your students depending upon other curriculum topics you are covering. Discussion guidelines also attempt to use generally applicable social studies subjects to convey ideas.

Part One. Learning About Our Constitutional Rights

1. **Discussion Guideline. Our Rights —What Are They? Why Are They Important?**

What makes living in this country different from living in other countries?

> We have certain basic rights as people. Rights are things that we can have and do so that we can live together peacefully and happily in this country. No one can tell us we cannot have or use our rights unless we use them in a way that deprives others of their rights.

Can you think of anything to which you have a right in this classroom?

> You have a right to have a teacher here to teach you.
>
> You have a right to come to school and not have other children hit or fight with you.
>
> Our country is like this, too. Because we live here and not somewhere else, there are

certain things we can do and nobody can tell us we cannot do them.

Can you think of anything to which you have a right because you live in this country?

Children might answer food, clothes, jobs. This can be confusing to them. Specifically, we do not have constitutional rights to food, clothes, and jobs, but we do have rights to do things that help us get these things.

Now, what kinds of things do we have a right to do?

We have the right to say what we think about things. We can say what we like or don't like about our government, our cities and even our schools.

We have the right to read the books and magazines we want and people have the right to publish the books and magazines they want.

We have the right to decide what church, temple or synagogue we want to go to for worship or if we want to worship at all. No one can tell us whether we should believe in a god or how to worship if we choose to.

We have the right to travel where we want. No one can tell us we have to live in this city or that state.

We have the right to have things and keep them. The government cannot just come and take our things without paying us for them and following a lot of rules.

We have the right to vote. Sometimes we vote about what rules we want. Sometimes we vote for people who then help decide the kinds of laws and rules we will have. We help shape those laws by the people we vote for.

Discussion Follow-Up Lesson Activities
a. Voting Exercise

Have children break into cooperative groups to brainstorm and develop a list of ten classroom or school rules and write them with a marker both on a sheet of paper and on a wall-size strip of butcher paper. Have each group "elect" one student to represent them (as the constituents) at a rules convention. These representatives will then meet to agree on the five most important rules for the class or school. In this meeting, the representative from each group will state his or her group's rules and the representatives will discuss which are the five most important. They will be listed on butcher paper on the wall. Give the convention representatives 15 to 30 minutes to reach agreement on the five most important rules.

While the convention representatives are meeting, have the rest of the class vote directly for the five most important rules. To do this, post all the butcher paper rule listings and read them through with the class, crossing out any duplicates as you go. Each student can vote five times for the five rules he or she thinks is most important. They do this by a show of hands. At this point, list the class's five rules determined by direct voting. The elected representatives then return to the group and present their five rules. Did the elected representatives come up with the same five rules as the class did when they held their vote? There is usually substantial overlap between the convention representatives' list of the five most important rules and the class-voted list. This exercise will show students how elected legislators represent voters when they make laws and rules. Even if the two sets of rules do not substantially overlap, this can also be instructive regarding the democratic process—i.e., sometimes elected representatives get swayed by political pressures and lobbyists to vote in ways inconsistent with their constituents' desires.

b. Rights Writing

Ask students to do a brief essay or paragraph on the subject of rights or laws. Their paragraphs will be inspired at least in part by prior in-class discussion. Topics could be:

Which right that we have in this country do you think is most important and why? How would life be different if we did not have this right?

What is one of the most important laws we have and how do you think that law protects our rights? What right or rights does that law protect?

2. Discussion Guideline. How Does Exercising the Right to Vote Help Us Participate in Making Laws?

What is special about living in this country?
> We have rights.

Can you name some of the rights we have talked about?
> Free speech, free religion, free press, right to travel, right to own property, right to a speedy trial, right to vote

One right is voting. What good is voting? Note: Remind children of their classroom voting experience.
> By exercising our vote, we get to help decide on the rules we live by.

How does voting for a person help us have good laws?
> The person who gets the most votes represents you in legislative voting on laws that protect you and keep you safe.

Let's think about some of the types of laws we have. Can you name some?
> Traffic, criminal, compulsory school attendance, Food & Drug Administration rules and regulations, laws concerning railroad and airplane safety, environmental, pet ownership, business licensing, tax and bicycle safety laws

Would it be possible for everybody to vote on every law we have or would that take all of everybody's time?
> It would take all of your time. In a big country, it helps to have people represent us in making laws.

Do you remember why we need laws and rules?
> So that everyone can get along; so that everyone can be safe

Do we have rules in the classroom?

How do these rules help us?

What are some of these classroom rules?
As children mention rules, ask them why the classroom has that rule. How does it help everyone get along and get work done?

Now, let's think of some specific laws or rules that we have in this country.
> Sample answers: Don't kill
> Don't steal
> Don't hurt people

How does a law against killing help protect our rights?
> If you are dead, it's pretty hard to exercise any of your rights. All your rights have been taken away.

How does a law against hurting people help protect our rights?
> If we are hurt or afraid that someone is going to hurt us, it is hard for us to exercise our rights. For example, if someone on the playground tells you that she or he doesn't want you to talk anymore or to play a particular game or he will hit you, he makes you afraid to talk or play. You might decide to be quiet, not because you want to but because you are afraid. This violates your rights, so we make rules that people cannot hit you just because you want to talk or play. The rule helps protect your rights.

How does a law against stealing help protect our rights?
> We said we have a right to own things. If someone takes your things without asking, then your right to have those things has been taken away from you.

We set up rules so we can all enjoy our rights and live safely together. We talked about not stealing and not hurting people. But everyday you follow other laws all the time. What are those laws?

How do you get to school each day? Do you follow any laws when you come to school?

If you drive, does your bus driver or car driver follow any laws?

What happens when you come to a traffic light?

What happens at a stop sign?

Why do we have these laws? What happens if people don't follow them?
People get hurt.
Things we have get broken.
People can't get where they want to go quickly and safely.

Why are these things bad?
Besides hurting people, they make it hard to exercise our rights.

Example:
We have the right to travel where we want. If people don't follow traffic rules, we cannot exercise our right to travel safely.

Discussion Follow-Up Lesson Activities
a. Dissect the Preamble

Use the Preamble to the Constitution Activity Sheet at the back of this chapter to examine and discuss what it means, phrase by phrase. This is not only a good exercise for understanding the ideas and principles that serve as foundations to our national form of government, it also serves as a good vocabulary lesson. After you have discussed the Preamble phrase by phrase, ask the children to write it in their own words.

b. Intersection Traffic

Take your class outside. Divide your class into four groups. Each student is a car. Place each group of students at one of four places on an imaginary square approximately 10 by 10 (or a foursquare playground configuration). Midway between each of the four groups of students draw three foot squares with chalk. These squares represent the "corners" of your intersection. See the illustration on this page.

Tell the students that these squares are corners with buildings and that they cannot ride on them. Then tell each group of students that they want to drive straight through the intersection. In effect, opposite groups of students will exchange sides with each other. When you give the signal for them to go, they are all to begin walking to their destinations at the same time. Remind them to walk, not run.

Ask students some of these questions:
What happened?

Were they able to get where they needed to go?

Did they end up running into each other or touching each other?

Did they end up walking on the "corners" with their imaginary cars?

What would have happened if each student really had been a car?

Would there have been accidents?

Would someone have been hurt?

Now, line the students up at each starting point again. At each place they line up in a straight line. This time they are waiting at an intersection that has stop sign (or a set of traffic lights, whichever you prefer). Their traveling goal is once again to get to the opposite side. The teacher will direct them as to who has the green light and when it changes to red. If you choose to have your intersection be a stop sign intersection, explain that when a driver reaches a STOP sign, he or she must look both ways before proceeding. If two adjacent drivers arrive at the same time, the one on the right goes first.

After the stop sign/traffic light movement activity, ask the students these questions:

Did they run into each other?

Did they run into the buildings?

Did the stop sign/traffic light rule make it easier and safer to get where they wanted to go?

Ask them how stop signs help us.

Do they think stopping at stop signs is a good law?

Why? How does it help us?
It keeps us safe.

It means things we own like cars don't get broken.

How else does it help us?
It helps us get to where we want to go.

The traffic laws help us exercise one of the rights we have in this country. That right is our right to travel in our city, in our state, and in and through all our states. These laws help us get to school to get an education, to get to our jobs and to move from state to state whether to change residence or merely to vacation.

Following our laws is one way to show our respect for other people's rights.

3. **Discussion Guidelines (Optional). Who's Minding the Store? Who do we depend on to make sure people follow our laws?**
(This is an optional discussion tool that ties into community helpers and community service roles.)

Who helps make sure that people follow laws?
The most important people who make sure the laws are followed are each of us, ourselves. We take care of ourselves and make sure we follow rules so we will be safe and so others will be safe. This is part of being a good citizen.

Does everybody always follow the law?

Can you think of anybody who works in our community who helps people remember to follow the law?
Police
Lawyers
Judges
Nurses/Doctors
Teachers/Principals
Pharmacists

How do policemen help?
They stop fights.

They arrest people who break laws and take them to jail.

They direct traffic.

They participate in school programs and help teach children about the law. Current programs with which children might be familiar focus on teaching children not to use drugs.

How do lawyers help?
They help people find out about laws that protect them.

They help people tell their side of a story to the judge or jury in a court.

How do judges help?
They help make sure that people are treated fairly.

They try very hard to be fair.

How do doctors and nurses help to make sure that laws are followed?
If they see a child who is not being taken care of properly, they tell people who can help the child so that the child is safe.

They help people who have been hurt in car accidents.

Many accidents happen when people aren't following the traffic laws as they should.

What are pharmacists and how do they help to make sure that laws are followed?

There are laws that say many medicines can only be given if a doctor orders them. Pharmacists have these medicines. They make sure that they only give people medicine when the person has a prescription from the doctor. This helps make sure people don't take too much medicine and get sick.

How do teachers and principals help make sure that our laws are followed?

Schools have to follow lots of laws. One law says that children must go to school. Teachers and principals help make sure that this law is followed.

What do you think of this law? Do you think it is a good law? Why should children have to go to school? Why is it important?

Children need to learn to read and write.

School helps prepare you for life as an adult when you will need to have a job and take care of yourself.

Discussion Follow-Up Lesson Activities
a. How Many Laws? What Rights?

This might be a good time to use the Exploring Rights and Rules in Real Life Situations Activity Sheet at the back of this chapter with your class. This activity sheet describes ordinary daily activities in which people both exercise their rights and follow laws. Use this activity sheet to give children an opportunity to solidify the concepts they have gleaned from discussion. Have them complete the activity sheet and then use it as the basis for a short discussion about the laws and rights covered in the stories.

b. Classroom Speaker

Invite a community helper such as a fireman, policeman, lawyer or teacher to speak to your class about his or her job and how it involves the law. Check with your students' parents. Perhaps a parent has a job that he or she can relate to the law for your class. Parents make good speakers.

4. Discussion Guideline. What Were Some of Those Rights Again?

(This discussion guideline helps children and teachers recap some of the basic rights we take for granted everyday.)

Over two hundred years ago, some people sat down to think about how we wanted to live in this country. They decided we should all be free and we should be able to try to be happy. They also knew that it was hard for a government to make sure that everyone had food and clothes. They believed people needed to work for these things. So they thought up a set of "rights" that the government could not take away from anyone that would make our country the kind of place in which people could work and prosper and get the things they needed.

Let's think about what some of these rights might be.

We have the right to travel. How can this help us?

It can help our parents take a job in a new place. We don't have to ask our government if we can move. We can just take the new job and move if we want to.

We have the right to have things of our own. We can own property and the government can't take it away from us without going through special procedures.

How does being able to own things help us?

We can own our clothes.

We can own things we need to do jobs like tools, computers and cars.

What things do you own?

Toys, bikes, furniture

Can the government take them away from you?

Can anyone take them away from you?

Mom and dad can. Mom and dad have an important job and that is to teach you how to become grown-ups who can take care of yourselves and who know how to exercise all the rights you have as citizens in this country. Sometimes to teach you these things, parents have to take things away from you or make decisions not to get you everything you ask for.

Having rights means we also have to know how to respect other people's rights. In this country we all have rights. Let's think about this. Let's say you have the right to own something—a toy. The boy next door has a right to own his toy too. Can you take your neighbor's toy? If you took his toy without asking, what would you be doing?
Stealing.

If you steal, are you respecting your neighbor's right to have his toy?

If you steal his toy, can you expect him not to steal your toy?

Do we have any laws about stealing?

What do those laws do?
They protect our rights to own our own things.

We have many, many laws and most of them help protect us and our rights in some way.

What rights might we have that help us have a voice or a say in the laws we have?
Have you heard of election day?
What do citizens of this country have a right to do on election day?
They can vote.

Sometimes we vote on specific laws or rules.

More often we vote for people. We vote for the people who we think will make the kind of rules we would like.

Part Two. Public Versus Private Law

Use this part of the discussion guidelines to help children begin to understand the different ways laws work in their lives. They learn that there is public law and private law. Being a good citizen means holding up your end of any bargain. As citizens, we must follow the laws that govern traffic, crimes, school attendance and the like. As individuals we must honor private agreements we reach with people as well. These are our personal laws. If we do not keep our word and do what we're committed to, it is hard to get along with one another.

1. **Discussion Guideline. Two Kind of Laws— Laws for Everyone to Follow and Private Laws between People**

   What is a law?
   A law is a rule.

   It tells you what you can and cannot do.

   It is a rule of the government that everyone must follow unless it has clearly stated exceptions.

   Why do we have laws?
   Laws help protect us.

   Laws help guide people as to what they should and should not do.

   How do laws protect us?
   They help keep us safe.

   They protect our rights.

   What are our rights?
   Things that no one can tell us we cannot have or do.
   Can you think of rights which we have because we live in this country?
   Free worship, free speech, free assembly, right to bear arms

   To own property and not have people or police or government take it away from us without following procedures and paying us.

   Where do we get our rights? How do police and government people know what they can and cannot tell us to do?
   Back when our country was formed, some very special people sat down and thought about what people had to have in order to work and live happy lives. They decided people needed certain rights and they wrote those rights down.

Have you heard of the Bill of Rights?
The Bill of Rights lists ten rights. Some of them are very famous.

What are some of these rights?
Free worship

Free speech

What are some other rights you have heard about?
Right to own property

Right to vote

How do our laws protect some of these rights? Think about the right to own property. What kinds of laws protect that right?
Laws against stealing

Laws against arson (setting fires)

Laws against graffiti and other vandalism

Laws protect us. Is there such a thing as a bad law? How would it be possible to get a bad law?
People make laws and sometimes they make mistakes.

How is it that people make laws? Who are these people?
Sample answers are President, Mayor.

The laws are made by people we vote for to act as our voice. We vote for people who we think we will make the kinds of laws we would like. These people are legislators—congressional representatives, senators, assemblypersons, councilpersons, and the like.

What would a good law be?
One that protects our rights.

Does it have to protect everybody or can it just protect a few people?
A good law has to protect everyone's rights equally and fairly.

What would a bad law be?
One that hurts or violates people's rights.

Is it easy to tell the difference?
Sometimes it's difficult. Sometimes two people have two different rights that they want to exercise and a law seems to protect only one of them.

When people fight about whether a law is bad or not, how can they get an answer?
They need to go to court and ask a judge or jury.

Can you think of a law that might be confusing about whether it is good or bad?

Think about a person's right to free speech. How do people speak?
Talking — giving speeches

Doing something (flag burning) — expressing an idea by action

Wearing clothing that has words on it

Writing your ideas so others can read them

To exercise the right to free speech, could someone stand on the street corner where you live at 1 A.M. with a bullhorn and yell for an hour or would this violate your privacy in your home or constitute a disturbance of the peace? Why? Why not?
We have to be responsible when we exercise our rights. Does it seem responsible to yell into a bullhorn on a street corner at 1 A.M.? Why? Why not?

Does it bother other people for this to happen?
We each have to be responsible in the way we exercise our rights. Is there another way, place or time for the person with the bullhorn to make his message heard?

Should there be rules against letting people do this where people live? What about where people work?
When questions like this come up, sometimes the laws about them have to be interpreted. Someone has to decide how the law should work in a particular set of circumstances. This is how questions end up in

court. In court, a judge has to decide if a law against making noise in residential areas in the middle of the night is reasonable or whether it is unfair to the free speech rights of the man with the bullhorn.

Discussion Follow-Up Lesson Activities
a. Good Law or Bad Law? Let's Debate

Divide students into groups of six to eight students. If you have enough class time for more debates, smaller groups (e.g., 3 or 4 students) ensure a higher level of participation by each group member. Assign each group one of the "laws" below. The groups split in half so that each group can debate the good and the bad of the assigned law. The debate focuses on whether the law properly protects our rights, protects the rights of one person more than another or infringes too much on our rights without a good reason. The laws which could be debated are:

- A law against unauthorized graffiti on private property. Questions to be debated include whether graffiti is a protected act under the right to free speech or whether it is a vandalization of a person's or a government's property.
- A law requiring people to wear seat belts. Questions to be debated are whether the government should tell us what we have to do just to keep us safe or whether making us wear seat belts violates our privacy rights.
- A law banning books from school libraries. Questions to be debated are whether such a law infringes the right to free speech, who should have the right to make the determination about what books are banned and whether students and parents should be able to make decisions about what books the school requires/allows students to read. Many famous books and authors have come under attack in recent years by parents or community groups who don't like certain language or who dislike subject matter (often on religious grounds). Whose rights are paramount in these cases? Should a religious group as an exercise of its freedom of religion be able to dictate what other people can read?
- A law requiring helmets for bicycle riders. Questions to be debated are whether everyone, including adults and children, should be required to wear safety helmets when riding their bikes or whether that infringes the person's right to privacy and individual choice. What if a person gets hurt because he or she fails to wear a helmet and the government ends up paying his or her medical bills? Is that fair? Who should pay?
- A law prohibiting people from picketing and passing out political or religious material at shopping centers. Questions to be debated are whether the government or a private property owner should be able to prohibit such activity when the shopping center is used by the public? Does the shopping center owner's private property right get infringed if he or she must allow people to picket and pass out brochures? What if it keeps customers away? Do the picketers have a free speech right to use property to which the public is invited in order to exercise their free speech rights?
- A law prohibiting the sale of obscene musical tapes and records. Questions to be debated are whether such laws violate the artist or musician's free speech rights and whether the government has the right to prevent consumers from exercising their right to buy music of their choice. Should obscenity stickers be required by law?
- A law prohibiting the sale of guns. Questions to be debated are whether people have a right to own and use guns or whether the sale of guns should be restricted to help reduce violent crime.

The student groups each get a law and then half of the group argues for why it is a good law and the other half argues for why it is a bad law. Issues of personal and constitutional rights as well as public safety are raised through such discussions. Fifth and sixth graders are most likely to enjoy the debate process. For younger students, you might want to simply choose a law about which you think they would have strong opinions and discuss it as a class activity.

b. Good Law/Bad Law Essay

Choose one of the laws described above and ask children to write an essay about why it is a good law and protects people's rights or why it is a bad law and infringes on people's rights. Let students make their own decision about whether the law is good or bad.

2. Discussion Guidelines. What's A Private Law? Is It A Contract? What Is That?

Besides the laws that governments make, what other kinds of laws or rules are there?

School rules

Household or family rules

The rules in your family are kind of like a private law. They are very important, but your family directly decides what those rules are, what happens if they get broken and what happens when they are followed.

People make all kinds of private laws. Many times these are called contracts. What is a contract?

It is when you reach an agreement with someone about things you each want to do or have.

Have you ever made an agreement with a friend or sibling? Was it about something you wanted to share or about something you wanted to trade?

How did you reach an agreement? What was the agreement?

Here the idea is that, to reach an agreement, each party has to give up something and get something in return.

Do you ever use contracts in your classroom?

Can you think of a way to talk about your classroom rules as though they were a contract between you and the teacher?

If you follow the rules, do you get something? Is there a special benefit to following the rules? What happens if you don't follow the rules? Do you lose something?

Discussion Follow-Up Lesson Activities
a. Contract Negotiation

The class breaks into groups of three each. In each group one student has a can opener, one has a bag of Oreo® or other favorite cookies and one has a can of soup, a can of applesauce, and a can of juice. The object is for each person in each group to reach an agreement with the other two so that each person in the group can have a full and complete lunch. The premise is that each child is very hungry.

To make the negotiation process more real to the children, ask them to bring in the supplies that each of them "owns" in the negotiation. You can substitute different items if you like. When the members of the group decide how they will share their items so that each can benefit and each has to give up a little, they write down their agreement as a simple contract.

They can use the Write A Contract Activity Sheet at the back of this chapter for this or they can use the "Law Between You and Me" format in Item 8 of the writing activities in this chapter for a group's statement of the individuals' agreements with each other—what each one will do or share so that each member of the group is fed. Children may get creative within their groups. Perhaps the Oreo holder will think it is not enough to get to one half cup of soup for three Oreos but if the other child will give him the soup and sing "Yankee Doodle," the Oreo holder will give him two extra cookies.

Have the groups share their agreements and see how they differ. Talk about how people enforce agreements in this society when one person won't do what he or she promised to do. The lawful resort is to the civil court system.

b. Contract Writing

Ask children to make up contracts individually or in pairs using the writing activity format described in Item 8 of the writing activities of this chapter.

Writing Activities

1. Chapter Vocabulary

Some vocabulary suggestions for this chapter's activities are:

    Bill of Rights
    Citizenship
    Rights
    Responsibilities
    Constitution
    Censorship
    Free speech
    Free press
    Free assembly
    Free religion
    Right to bear arms
    Freedom
    Democracy
    Election
    Segregation
    Integration
    Discrimination
    Suffrage
    Civil rights
    Equality
    Government
    Liberty
    Law
    Court
    Judge
    Jury
    Voting
    President
    Congress
    Legislature
    Abolition
    Underground railroad

2. Student Bill of Rights

Ask children to work in cooperative learning groups to create proposals for a student bill of rights. For each right, the children should identify and write down the corresponding responsibility. Ask children to identify five or ten rights and related responsibilities. The precise number depends upon the students' abilities and the length of time available.

A follow-up activity that is very useful in showing children how the democratic process works is to then have a mock "constitutional convention" at which the individual groups present their rights proposals and the class comes up with a classroom bill of rights. This could be five or ten rights (and responsibilities) upon which the class agrees. These rights can be written on a poster and be posted for the class.

This exercise is similar to the voting activity described in the lesson activities above, but that activity is directed toward the making of rules or laws and this activity is directed toward defining classroom or school rights. This activity helps students relate rights to responsibilities.

3. The Big Right

Ask children to think about which of those rights described in the Bill of Rights they believe to be most important and why. They can then write an essay explaining their conclusions. Ask them to try to relate the right they choose to things they want to be able to do in their own lives.

4. One Law, What Law?

Ask children to think about our system of laws and try to decide upon which law is the most important to the responsible functioning of society. The children can then write a short essay on what this law is and why it is so important to the smooth functioning of our society.

Perhaps the students' essays could be used as the basis for a classroom debate between children or teams of children as to why their law is the most important and why the other group's choice is not. Students can prepare their reasons as a group, prepare arguments and debate in front of the class with the teacher as a moderator. In this way, children experience an aspect of democratic debate that goes on in all levels of government in this country.

5. Protectors of Rights

As a slightly different turn on the typical biography report, ask children to choose a current or past American leader who fought for individual rights in this country and helped or spoke out for a group of people for whom the Bill of Rights and other constitutional rights had not been fairly applied. Children can choose a leader on their own or pick from the list below. You might want to ask that the children talk to their parents about this project and choose such a leader with the input of their parents.

Rights Activists - Past and Present

Martin Luther King, Jr. (African-American civil rights leader and Nobel Peace Prize winner)

Susan B. Anthony (American leader of the women's rights and suffrage movement)

Thomas Paine (American writer and leader who in 1775 wrote an article for the Pennsylvania Magazine proposing rights for women)

Rosa Parks (African-American woman who protested bus segregation in Montgomery, Alabama)

James Meredith (African-American student and leader of African-American voting rights movement)

Franklin D. Roosevelt (American President who by executive order outlawed discrimination in defense industry employment)

Sojourner Truth (first African-American woman orator to speak out against slavery)

Harriet Tubman (African-American woman who helped hundreds of slaves escape to freedom in the underground railroad)

Dolores Huerta (Mexican-American labor organizer and lobbyist for laws to protect farm worker rights)

Lorraine Hansberry (African-American playwright and writer about the civil rights movement)

Paul Robeson (African-American actor, singer, and activist for equality and equal rights for African-Americans)

Susette and Susan LaFlesche (Omaha Native American women lobbyists for Native American rights and laws to protect Native American interests)

Yoshiko Uchida (Japanese American writer of children's books including subjects such as the Japanese internment)

William Still (African-American writer and businessman who was leader of the underground railroad and started YMCA for African-American youth)

Mary McLeod Bethune (African-American educator who fought for quality education for all African-American children)

Lucretia Mott (American women's rights leader who helped organize first women's rights convention in 1848)

Jane Addams (Protector of children's rights and advocate of child labor laws)

John F. Kennedy (American President who proposed the Civil Rights Act)

James Baldwin (African-American writer who also worked for the civil rights movement and whose stories reflected the problems of prejudice in society)

Frederick Douglass (African-American abolitionist, speaker, writer, newspaper publisher, and public servant)

Elizabeth Cady Stanton (American women's rights leader who helped organize first women's rights convention in 1848)

Abraham Lincoln (American President who signed the Emancipation Proclamation)

Amelia Bloomer (American writer and feminist leader who edited a women's rights publication and in 1851 began wearing trousers, then called bloomers)

Robert Kennedy (American senator, presidential candidate, and advocate for poor, underprivileged, and minority rights)

Medger Evers (African-American civil rights leader and field secretary for National Association for the Advancement of Colored People)

Cesar Chavez (Mexican-American farm labor organizer)

Dred Scott (African-American who sued for his freedom when he was taken to a state that outlawed slavery; Scott lost the case in 1857)

Thurgood Marshall (First African-American named to sit on the bench of the United States Supreme Court)

Dick Gregory (African-American comedian and social critic who was a presidential candidate in 1968)

Shirley Chisholm (African-American congresswoman, public servant and presidential candidate)

Eleanor Roosevelt (Crusader for the poor and underprivileged)

Ernest Green (African-American who fought educational segregation and served in presidential administration of Jimmy Carter)

6. Famous American Acrostic

Using the first or last name of an American of the student's choice, the child creates an acrostic about that person and his or her life. To find out facts to incorporate into the acrostic, the children will need to do some library or encyclopedia research. This poetry exercise also allows children to explore aspects of biography.

Examples:

G is for General Washington who led the Continental Army.
E is for everyday life at Mt. Vernon where he lived.
O is for outstanding service to his country as President.
R is for reputation for telling the truth.
G is for giving of himself for the people of the colonies.
E is for eloquent speeches in honor of freedom.

M Moving speeches for racial equality.
A Arguing for peaceful protest.
R Religious and political leadership.
T Tireless efforts for equal rights for African-Americans.
I Interest in the plight of the poor.
N Now is the time for change as it was then.

7. "Right" in the Middle of History

Ask children to choose an event or series of related events from American history or current events. Examples are the Boston Tea Party, the arrival of Pilgrims at Plymouth, the farm worker organization efforts of Cesar Chavez, civil rights march on Washington, D.C., and the like. Ask them to think about the event and to explore in a short report (one page or so) what rights people exercised during the course of the event and whether or not they overstepped their responsibilities. Students can explore whether or not they think it was right or necessary to take the actions which were taken by the people involved in the event.

8. The Law Between You and Me

Contracts are the private laws people make between themselves to get things they need or want. Every time a child buys a pencil at the store, he or she enters into and completes a contractual relationship. It's just that we don't write these things down. Ask children to pair up to write a contract about something they want to decide between the two of them. The issue in the contract can be imaginary such as "I will pay you so much or give you something if you will give me something else." It is more fun for students, however, to reach real agreements about small items parents have agreed to let them exchange.

In any contract, children need to write in complete sentences. They need to identify the parties to the agreement, the date upon which the agreement is made, what each party is giving to the other or doing for the other (i.e. the thing or things about which they are agreeing whether it is doing something or giving something) and when the agreed upon acts are going to be done. They then need to both sign the agreement.

Example:

Contract for Purchase of Silver Pencil

The parties to this agreement are Katie and Maria. We agree to the following:

1. *Katie will give her silver pencil to Maria.*

2. *In exchange for the silver pencil, Maria will give to Katie two scented stickers.*

3. *The parties will exchange these things Friday, September 10.*

The parties agree to do these things and show their agreement by signing this contract.

_____

Katie

_____

Maria

Date: _____

9. Letter Home

Ask children to pretend they have moved to the colonies from Europe. They have brought with them some of their customs from home, but they are in a new place with new foods, new countryside, new people, and new rights such as free religion and free assembly. The children write a letter back home to a friend or relative about their lives in this new country.

10. Yesterday and Today Journal

Keeping a journal or diary is less in fashion these days than it was in years past. This is probably due in large part to the fast pace of living and the availability of electronic media. Have children do a journal entry as they would in a journal today telling what they did that day. Then have children pretend to be children in the American colonies. From the perspective of a colonist youngster, children write another journal entry for the day. It would necessarily be quite different. They might reflect getting up at dawn, feeding cows and other animals the family keeps, helping mother make bread, getting water from a well and doing lessons on a practice board or practicing needlework. Some good resources for children to use to inspire writing ideas for this activity are listed in the resources section of this chapter.

Art and Craft Activities

1. Silversmithing

In colonial times, silversmithing was both a craft and a fine art. Elaborate tea sets, flatware, and serving dishes were crafted from silver and engraved with intricate designs. These designs were often floral patterns. Most towns had a local silversmith who created wares for the townfolk, but the major colonial silversmithing centers were Boston, Philadelphia, and New York City. Silversmiths spent years learning and perfecting their craft. In the early years of the colonies, even though local silversmiths practiced, many thought that the truly fine pieces of silver could still only be created by artists in Europe.

There are two ways for your students to recreate colonial silversmith crafts. In the first way, each child receives four pieces of foil which he or she presses together and folds at the edges. On a piece

of scratch paper, the child sketches a general outline of a teapot, gravy boat, creamer, bowl, or candlestick. The sketched outline is laid on top of the foil and then the outline is pressed onto the foil by using a dull pencil or round toothpick to trace over the outlines of the shape. With the outline complete, the child cuts out the design which seals the edges of the foil together. On this cut design, the child then uses a dull pencil to imprint a colonial floral type silversmith design. The designs of the mid-1700s are called the "Rococo" period. The completed project can then be mounted onto black paper with glue for display.

Another way to do this project is to have children make cotton string or roving yarn pictures on posterboard that are covered with foil. String is glued onto the board in the shape of the silver item to be recreated. Glue and string can be used to make a raised design on the outlined object. When dry, the picture is covered with foil which is pressed tightly over the design and taped down on the back. If desired, rub shoe polish very lightly over the shape and design and rub off any excess. This will highlight the bowl or teapot shape and its design.

2. Quilting

Have the class explore quilting. This was a folk art form as well as practical work. Quilting became a popular form of fabric decoration and design in the 1800s. With little leisure time in daily life, entertainment often took the form of completing practical projects. Women would get together for parties called quilting bees where they would sit around a frame and do the quilting and finish work on a quilt. Quilts were covers (often bedcovers) made from scraps of fabric in many designs. Many different designs were used, often geometric.

To help children explore this tradition, ask them to bring in pieces of old wrapping paper. The wrapping paper will serve as mock fabric scraps. Give each child the Variable Star Quilt Square Activity Sheet at the back of this chapter. (If you can, run off the activity sheet on cardstock to make student tracing work easier.) The activity sheet provides the form with which children create a paper quilt square in the eight pointed variable star pattern. This is one of the oldest quilt patterns, dating back to 1800 or before.

To make the quilt square, the child cuts out the quilt block on the dotted lines. The resulting pieces will be traced onto wrapping paper or construction paper or both and cut out. The quilt square is then reassembled and glued on the remaining quilt square on the other activity sheet. The completed quilt square is then cut off the activity sheet and the individual squares are used to make a classroom paper quilt for display. Let students help with the design of the quilt by deciding on boarders, placement of the quilted squares and any unquilted squares necessary to make a completed paper quilt.

Another way to make a classroom quilt is with quilt squares designed entirely by the children either on the Quilt Square Activity Sheet, or on any 6" to 9" square of graph paper. Children can cut shapes to trace onto construction or wrapping paper. Encourage the children to explore geometric shapes even if they use this free-form version of the project. Pinwheels, flowers and the like can be made using squares and triangles cut from a folded square of graph paper. If a classroom quilt is made from these randomly designed squares, the resulting quilt is called a sampler quilt because it includes samples of many different kinds of quilting designs.

3. Silhouettes and Stencils

In this project, children create individual pictures using the traditional colonial crafts of silhouette-making and stenciling. To create the silhouette, place a 100 watt light lamp without the shade about 10 feet from the wall. Tape butcher paper to the wall, and have the child sit a few inches in front of the paper. Have a partner or preferably a parent trace the child's profile onto the butcher paper. The child then cuts out his or her profile, traces it onto black paper, and cuts it out. The silhouette on black paper is then glued into the middle of a larger sheet of heavy white paper (preferably cut into an oval shape).

Another way to create a silhouette is to have children work in pairs to trace silhouettes. One student lays his head sideways on a sheet of black paper while the partner traces the first child's profile. Each child then cuts out his or her own profile for mounting.

To enhance this project, have children stencil the edge of the white paper before the silhouette is glued on. Stenciling is a traditional form of decoration used on walls, curtains, and pillows. Stencils are usually simple repeating designs such as hearts and stars and flowers. To make a stencil for children to use if you do not have any of the appropriate size, use the flat sides of plastic or cardboard milk cartons or cardboard gift boxes to make your stencil patterns. Trace your stencil shape (using the Stencil Activity Sheet designs at the back of this chapter if you like) with marker, pen, or pencil onto the plastic or cardboard and cut out the stencil design with an exacto knife or similar cutting device. This part of the project should be done by an adult. Perhaps a parent volunteer could help prepare these for you at home.

Children use the stencil pattern to make a design on the top and bottom borders of the white paper that will hold their silhouette. They can do this by sponging in the stencil shapes with tempera or by tracing them and filling them in with colored pencil or marker. If a paint stenciling method is used, the stencil should be cleaned and dried after each use to avoid smudging. These two projects are time-consuming and are best attempted with some adult help in the classroom. They make excellent gifts for parents.

4. With a Capital "P"

Historically, children worked very hard on penmanship skills, and children and adults alike prided themselves on beautiful script writing. This emphasis has been lost in recent years but children can explore the flourish of traditional writing with a quill pen and some food coloring "ink" or India ink if you choose. If children have seen copies of the original Bill of Rights and Constitution, they have seen the very artistic and stylized writing used by colonists—even when writing their names. They can experience both the art of writing and the difficulty of writing with a feather with this project.

Any large feather can be used for a writing quill. Even feathers from inexpensive dime store dusters will work for this project, but not as well as larger feathers. Cut the end of the feather at an angle. For food coloring ink use straight food coloring or dilute it only slightly. On sheets of butcher paper cut to 5" x 5 square or on the blank side of 3" x 5" cards, children use the quill pens dipping them repeatedly in the ink to create dramatic and artistic initials of their first or last names. If you prefer, they can create an entire signature for themselves. They should draft their initial designs or signature designs first, however, with pencil and then recreate them with the quill and ink. When thoroughly dry, mount the initial art on dark construction paper. To give children the idea of fancy writing, they can look at clothing monograms, calligraphy books, and computer font examples.

5. Boat in a Bottle

Building model ships in empty bottles is a hobby that evokes colonial days and later the clipper sailing ships. You can recreate this hobby in several ways. With the first method, each child begins with a bottle shape cut from stiff posterboard or cardboard. Ask children to bring these in precut from home. Trace the cardboard bottle shape onto white or blue paper and cut it out. If students use white paper, they can do a watercolor wash on it or color it with the flat side of a crayon. This bottle shape is glued onto the cardboard shape. Using small pieces of brown and white construction paper, children cut the shape of a boat hull and one or two white sails. In the center of the bottle shape, the boat is glued and assembled. The sails are poked through toothpicks to give a three dimensional effect. Cotton balls can be glued under the sails to keep them from flattening. Plastic wrap is then pulled tightly over the bottle shape and taped on the back side to give the effect of the glass bottle in which the elaborate models were originally built. The complete bottle is then glued onto black paper for display.

Another way to make a boat in a bottle is to use any small plastic peanut butter or other jar in which to display a small boat model made from paper or other materials. The small boat can be made from half walnut shells, folded brown construction paper or other materials of the child's choosing. Using plasticine clay, children can

mount one or more white paper and toothpick sails in their boats. Children put glue, plasticine clay, or gummy adhesive on the bottom of their boats and insert them into their jars. When they do this, the jar is laying on its side and the boat is affixed to the side of the jar. Screw the lids back on. To keep the jar from rolling, put two balls of plasticine clay on the underside of the jar.

Children can get very creative about making boats in a bottle. This is a good project to assign for an at home project to be completed with family help and ingenuity. When all the boats are completed you can hold a show and perhaps even award winners for the cleverest, largest, smallest, and most authentic.

6. The Proverbial Sampler

Needlework was another traditional colonial craft. Cross-stitch samplers are a very familiar needlework tradition. Usually a saying or proverb was recreated on the cloth with floral designs as decoration. Poor Richard's Almanac was a famous colonial publication in the mid-1700s. It was written by Benjamin Franklin and contained advice. poems, weather information. and wise sayings known as proverbs. Such famous words of wisdom as "a penny saved is a penny earned" could be found in the pages of this famous publication.

Have children find a short proverb or wise saying and "stitch" it onto a graph paper sampler using fine-tip markers or colored pencil and the Graph Paper Activity Sheet at the back of this chapter. Each cross-stitch is made by putting an "X" in a box.

Fifth- and sixth-graders can also explore cross-stitch the "real" way—with needle and thread. Purchase simple cross-stitch designs for children to try on real fabric. Cross-stitch fabric, floss, and needles are available in craft and needlework stores. An easy way for children to store their floss supply is to hole punch the edges of a 3" x 5" card and loop a different color in each hole. Each hole should be labeled with the name of that color.

7. Ragdolls

Colonial and other early American children had very simple toys. They were often made from scraps of things adults had left over from projects such as fabric scraps, spools, pieces of wood, buttons, and string. Have children make a rag doll to get the idea for how thrifty early Americans were and how they used what was available to them to create entertainment.

To make a ragdoll, each child begins with 12 strips of assorted cloth, each strip being approximately 2" wide and 24" long. Knot each end of each strip. Tie all twelve strips together tightly just under the knot at one end with string. These knots will be where the head is formed. Take three of the 24" strips, braid them about halfway, and tie with string. Take another three 24" strips, braid them halfway, and tie them tightly with string. These are your arms. Divide the remaining strips into three groups of two strips each and braid down about 3" to make your torso. Then take the remaining strips and divide them into two groups of three each. Braid off these two groups to make legs. Tie the ends of these braids tightly with strings. Look at your doll's arms. Decide how long they should be. Tie them there tightly with string and cut off the excess.

To finish the head, use cotton balls or crushed toilet paper or paper towel to pad the head (the twelve knots you started with), place a 12" x 12" square of cloth over this padded head, squeeze it at the "neck," and tie it off tightly with string. Use marker to create a face on the doll or have children sew on button facial features. Children can cut simple tunic clothing out of other cloth, fold it in half to make a head hole, and slit it over the doll's head. It can be tied at the waist with ribbon or string.

8. Potato Spindles

While spinning wheels were in common use in the colonies and cloth could be purchased, with this craft children can get an idea how labor-intensive American life was for the early settlers. Have students make a portable hand spindle for spinning yarn. To make a spindle punch a dully sharpened pencil through the center of a small raw potato. The pencil should be pushed far enough into the potato so that the sharpened point of the pencil protrudes from the other side of the potato. The potato can be decorated with a construction paper face just for fun, if desired.

Have children try their hand spinning yarn with their spindles. To do this, tie a short piece of yarn (8" to 10") onto the long end of the pencil just where the pencil meets the potato. Then attach

raw fiber to the end of the yarn (even cotton balls pulled apart can be used, but longer fibers such as raw wool fibers are easier to work with), and then set the spindle spinning (as you would a top) as quickly as you can in mid-air to see if you can make the fiber twist tightly enough to become strong like yarn. Demonstrate first; then let the students try.

Hand spinning is very hard work and very difficult. It will not be easy for children at all. The experience reinforces for students how skills of our ancestors took years of practice and training. Children spent a good deal of their youth practicing skills they would need as adults.

Food Activities

The food activities in this chapter are intended to give you a smattering of recipes which can be used to complement discussion of different periods of United States history. Additional recipes from around the world are found in the food activities section of Chapter 4. These recipes are to be incorporated with lessons on immigration to the United States during different periods of American history.

1. Simply Succotash

Succotash is a vegetable dish that was prevalent in early America and made by Native Americans. It was adopted by colonists because corn and beans were often plentiful. It can take many different forms, but is usually a mixture of lima beans, canned or frozen corn, and sometimes chopped tomatoes. To give children a real colonial style cooking experience, have them remove the corn kernels from the cob and boil them for a few minutes with frozen lima beans and chopped tomatoes if desired. Salt to taste.

This dish can also be made by adding frozen, defrosted lima beans to cornmeal pudding. Cornmeal pudding is made by boiling salted water and adding half as much dry cornmeal. It is cooked down over medium heat until you reach the desired consistency.

While this is not the most exciting food, it is a reasonably authentic version of a common early American dish.

2. Baked Apples

Apples were introduced to the colonies when colonists planted apple seeds and trees they brought from England. The seeds and trees flourished and apple dishes became common. One simple but much appreciated dish (that could serve as breakfast or dessert) was baked apples. For classroom cooking, cut apples into quarters. Ask children to use plastic knives to cut out the seeds and core. Place apples face up in a greased baking dish. Add a little water (about 1/8") to the bottom of the baking dish. Dot apples with butter and sprinkle them with brown sugar and cinnamon. Bake covered for 1/2 hour in 375 degree oven. Serve with additional brown sugar and sour cream or whipped cream.

3. Pioneer Stew

A simple recipe for pioneer stew is included in the food activities in Chapter 5. Pioneers traveled lightly and made due with simple resources of root vegetables that traveled well and lasted a long time, flour, and available meat. This recipe calls for scraps of chicken, carrots, and flour-and-water dumplings. Seasoned with only a little salt and pepper, it is quite good and usually a big class hit.

4. Bits and Pieces Pudding

This is a pioneer-style dessert that was made from bits and pieces of whatever was at hand.

1 1/2 cups brown sugar, honey, corn syrup, or molasses (choose one)
1/2 cup walnut pieces
2 cups apple, diced
4 cups boiling water
1/4 cup cornstarch
1/2 cup cold water
Dash of cinnamon (optional)

Mix first four ingredients in saucepan. Cook over medium heat 5 to 10 minutes. Dissolve cornstarch in cold water. Pour slowly into pudding while stirring. Stir over medium heat until thick. If pudding does not thicken quickly, add more cornstarch mixed with water and stir.

5. Chipped Beef on a Bun

During the Depression and war years of World War II, chipped beef prepared in a gravy became a regular family tradition in many American homes. Chipped beef is a dried, thinly sliced beef that can be shredded into a thick gravy and used over toasted bread or a biscuit. Since the meat went far in this meal, it was also inexpensive, which was very important. Sometimes peas were used in such a dish. Another version of this meal is creamed tuna with peas on toast.

Melt 1/2 cup butter or margarine and mix in 1/2 cup flour. Slowly add milk and stir over medium heat. Add shredded beef (or tuna) and thawed frozen peas, if desired. Serve over toast, half a bun, dinner roll, or biscuit.

Biscuit Recipe

2 cups flour
1/2 teaspoon salt
2 teaspoons baking powder
1/8 teaspoon soda
3/4 cup buttermilk
*1/3 cup butter or margarine, cut into small
    chunks*

Mix first three ingredients well in a bowl. Sprinkle in shortening chunks. Using two butter knives, cut the butter into the dry mixture until crumbly and fine. Mix soda into buttermilk and stir. Then add this liquid to the dry ingredients and mix well until dough is formed. Flour your working surface and hands and then knead dough. If the dough is too sticky, add more flour. When easy to handle, press or roll out until 1/4" thick. Cut in squares small enough in size that you have one biscuit for each child in the class. Makes about 22 inch-square biscuits. Bake on cookie sheet at 450 degrees for 10 to 12 minutes or until lightly browned. Shorter baking time is likely if smaller biscuits are made. Serve with chipped beef or tuna gravy.

6. "Social Studies" Salad

Use this easy cooking experience to help show children how we depend upon others for our food and how we benefit from our natural resources (good soil and water). This salad can be made in any number of different ways. It can be a green or vegetable salad or a fruit salad. Since many children respond better to fruit salad, this is recommended. The produce for your salad is simply cut-up (and peeled and seeded as necessary) and mixed. If you make a green salad, a good dressing for children is made with one-part red wine vinegar, one-part sugar, and two-parts vegetable oil.

If you are focusing on state resources, ask children to find out what fruits or vegetables are grown in your state. Use this produce to create your salad. Alternately, you could choose fruits like bananas, apples, oranges, strawberries, cherries, peaches, and cantaloupe. Ask children to research the places where these fruits grow. This is a good task for encyclopedia research. Since nuts and yogurt or whipped whipping cream can be a good addition to any fruit salad, children can also research growing areas for walnuts, pecans, or almonds as well as dairy products.

Have children plot the results of their research on a map to show the places from which the ingredients in their salad might have come.

Discuss the natural resources used to grow food. There is the land upon which the plants grow, the water to nourish them, and assorted energy sources which transport water as well as run farm equipment to care for and harvest the crops. Once crops are harvested, trucking and other transport vehicles use additional energy to get the produce to market.

Discuss the route produce takes from farm to market. This process, which involves something as vital as food, shows children the interdependency of our society as well as the different roles played in the food process by members of the larger community.

The social studies salad is also an opportunity to touch upon nutrition. When you use fruit, nuts, and whipping cream or yogurt, you have a "three-food group salad." Is it more healthful to top off the salad with yogurt or whipping cream? Can a salad supply protein? What food group is not in your salad? How can you solve this to create a balanced meal with grains? Can you top the salad with granola or another crunchy cereal?

Art Masters—Old and New

Background Information

1. Gilbert Stuart

Portraiture is one way in which artists of the past and present have made a living. Styles, of course, have changed over the years. Gilbert Stuart was a portrait painter who became famous for his portrait paintings, especially those of President George Washington. Stuart lived from 1755 to 1828. A version of one of Stuart's famous paintings of Washington graces the one dollar bill.

2. Grandma Moses

Grandma Moses was a famous twentieth century folk artist. She lived from 1860 until 1961. She painted mostly landscapes that captured traditional American scenes of rural life in the 1800s. She did not begin painting until she was in her seventies. She never took any art lessons. Her big scenes of rural landscapes were painted from memories of her young life on the farm. Her pictures have a flattened perspective and were thought by art critics to have a fresh, primitive look.

Project Directions

1. A Stuart-Style Portrait

Use this project to introduce both the artist Gilbert Stuart, and the concept of portraiture. Have students explore pencil or charcoal sketching with this project. If pencil is used, have children use soft, thick-leaded pencils such as those used by students in the primary grades. Using either dollar bills or quarters, students will learn to sketch a portrait of George Washington. (If drawn from a quarter, the portrait will be a profile.)

The student starts with a 9" x 12" sheet of white or off-white construction paper. The student folds the paper into fourths so that the 12" length is divided into four 3" x 9" segments. Using a pencil, the child divides the quarter profile or the dollar portrait into four equal segments as well. The top of the profile or portrait's head will correspond to the top of the student's paper. The next line is at the eyebrow line. The next line is between the

nose and the top of the mouth. The next line is under the chin. The next line is the bottom of the neck and corresponds to the bottom of the student's paper. When the quarter or dollar bill has been divided like this, the child can see the relative proportions of the face and how they should be placed on the paper which has been folded to show four segments.

The pencil or charcoal portrait is sketched in by the child using the monetary portrait as a guide. The dollar bill portrait described above is based on an original Gilbert Stuart portrait of the first president. If children use charcoal, they should probably sketch in the portrait outlines with pencil first and then trace over and shadow with the charcoal.

2. An American Country Scene

Use a very large sheet of construction paper (at least 18" x 24") to create a large primitive folk art rural scene in the style of Grandma Moses. Grandma Moses' country scenes were very expansive. They showed, from a flattened perspective, two or three levels in a country scene. Each level of the scene depicts an area a little further away from the viewer of the picture. The scenes included rolling hills, farmhouses, lots of simple fences and horses, cows, and other animals common to rural American life. Prevalent colors were blue and red farm houses, green hills, and white and brown fences.

For a child to recreate such scenes, have him or her divide the canvas into thirds or fourths horizontally. In the bottom fourth to third of the paper, the first layer of hills is sketched in with pencil. A larger (e.g., 4" x 6") farmhouse might be sketched in as well with a line of simple fence coming out from it. In the second fourth of the paper, another row of hills is sketched in and some fencing as well. These hills are smaller and closer together than those located at the bottom of the picture. In the next section of the picture, a last row of hills smaller than the previous level is sketched in together with ever smaller fencing and farmhouses as desired. The top fourth of the picture will hold the sky, clouds, and perhaps very distant hills, if the child desires. If the child views creation of this huge scene as a series of individual tasks for each quarter of the canvas, the results should be successful. The detail of the picture is then filled in with crayon or paint. Children should feel free to add horses and carts, cows, and people dotting the landscape. To be true to Grandma Moses' vision, any ladies would be wearing long skirts and aprons.

Sharing Activities

1. Colonial Craft Art Show

Use your colonial crafts to form the basis for an art show to which you can invite other classes to share what you have learned. Students might want to demonstrate as part of the show how they created a particular art project, and to explain how the class project related to the actual colonial craft. If you made some potato spindles with your class, some children might want to demonstrate spinning yarn with a spindle if any can get proficient enough with their potato spindles.

2. "Celebrate American Dreamers and Doers" Assembly

Use the following format to provide the basis for an assembly in which children celebrate Americans who have dreamed about justice and the equal application of our rights to all and then gone out and done something about their dreams. If you assigned the "rights activist" biography project, the individual statements in the provided format could be written by the children about the people on whom they wrote their biographies. If you did not assign this project, you will need to have children research some of the individuals listed in Item 5 of the writing activities in this chapter so that they can create one-line statements

about a series of rights activist, each of whom "had a dream."

The framework for the assembly is the phrase "I have a dream" from Martin Luther King, Jr.'s very famous speech. This is used because it is so familiar and because it so aptly describes the spirit of those people throughout American history who have sought to find ways to make our system of rights work for all people. You might want to start and end the assembly with a song or two. Some suggestions are "Everyone is Beautiful," "This Land is Your Land," or the "Hymn to Freedom." American Dreamers and Doers Script ©1994 Pamela A. Marx (used with permission)

Speaker 1: Our country is founded upon basic principles of democracy, justice, and freedom for all.

Speaker 2: But sometimes through our history our Bill of Rights and Constitution have needed help from special people.

Speaker 3: These special people had their eyes on the land. They saw that sometimes people were having trouble exercising their rights. Others were not treated fairly.

Speaker 4: These special people wrote books, made speeches, and talked to government representatives to state their case.

Speaker 5: They told others how our country would be a better place and all of its people happier if everyone were able to exercise their rights and to receive justice.

Speaker 6: Each of these special people had a dream.

Speakers 7 through _____: [Have individual children make brief statements about a number of current or historical rights activists and what these people fought for. Each statement is followed by the group stating, "He [or she] had a dream." An example of an activist statement would be: "Martin Luther King, Jr. led the civil rights movement of the 1960s. He fought for equality and justice for African-Americans and all people."]

Speaker 34: He [she] had a dream.

Speaker 35: All these people had a dream and they helped to make the dream come true. That dream is the American dream.

Speaker 36: The American dream is that our country can be a place where all people are treated with dignity and with respect and where all people can exercise their constitutional rights in harmony with others.

Speaker 37: Many before us have worked for that dream. We will work for that dream every day in the way we treat others and live our lives. We hope you will join us in that effort.

All Speakers: We all have a dream and you can too.

3. American History Presentation

Another performance idea in conjunction with this chapter's exploration of constitutional rights and citizenship issues is one in which our historical heritage is portrayed through songs, dance, poetry and famous writings and speeches.

Ask students to work in cooperative groups to explore different great poets, statesmen, music and musicians, and dance styles relating to particular periods of American history. Each group prepares its presentation with a brief statement of major historical events of the period, poetic readings, speech excerpts and a song or dance performance reminiscent of the period. Each presentation should be no more than 10 minutes in length. Give children between three and five weeks to organize, write, rehearse, and finalize their presentations. If appropriate, invite parents or other classes to view the presentations.

American history can be broken into the following periods or other periods of your choosing:

Colonial/Revolutionary Period

War of 1812/Manifest Destiny/Antebellum Period in the South

Civil War

Late 1880s/Industrialization

World War I/Jazz Age

Depression/World War II

Korean War/Post-WWII Industrial Boom/Beginning of the Space Age

Vietnam War/Civil Rights Movements of the 1960s

Name: _____

Preamble to the Constitution

We the people of the United States in order to form a more perfect Union, establish justice, insure domestic tranquility, provide for the common defense, promote the general welfare, and secure the blessings of liberty to ourselves and our posterity do ordain and establish this Constitution for the United States of America.

Rewrite the Preamble in your own words.

We the people of the United States: _____

_____

in order to form a more perfect Union: _____

_____

_____

establish justice: _____

_____

_____

insure domestic tranquility: _____

_____

_____

provide for the common defense: _____

_____

_____

promote the general welfare: _____

_____

_____

and secure the blessings of liberty to ourselves and posterity: _____

_____

_____

do ordain and establish this Constitution for the United States of America: _____

_____

Name: _____

Write A Contract

Fill in the terms of your contract.

This contract is between the following people: [Name the parties to the agreement.]

_____

_____

_____

We each agree as follow: [State what each party agrees to do and when.]

_____   **will do the following:** _____

_____

_____   **will do the following:** _____

_____

_____   **will do the following:** _____

_____

We sign this contract on _____
                                              (date)

to show our agreement to the terms stated above.

                                    _____

                                    _____

                                    _____

**CHAPTER 6
ACTIVITY SHEET**

Exploring Rights and Rules in Real Life Situations

Story One:

Maria got into the car to go to school. As soon as she was settled in, she buckled her seat belt. Her school was across town. Her mother drove a little way and stopped at a stop sign. There was a small car accident to the side of the road. A policeman who was helping the people in the accident waved Maria's car and others to pass on by. Maria's mother drove down the street and passed through a green light. The school was just down the next street. Her mother turned on her signal to show she was turning. She stopped the car in front of the zone painted green and let Maria out.

The school bus pulled up behind Maria's car. Maria waved to the bus driver as she got out of her car. Maria was excited about school that day because the local librarian was coming to visit. She was also going to have her ears tested by the school nurse. Maria liked school, but her family was planning on moving soon to a new state. Her father had taken a new job, and that meant Maria would start a new school when the family moved.

What laws are referred to in this story?
What rights are exercised in this story?

Story Two:

Jose got into the car with his father. They were going to the market to pick up some groceries. Jose and his father buckled their seat belts. They drove to the end of the street and stopped at the stop sign. His father turned on his signal to show he was turning right. As they drove down the busy street, they heard a siren. Jose's father pulled his car over to the curb and they watched a fire truck rush past on its way to a fire. The paramedic truck followed close behind.

When the street was clear, Jose's father began to drive again. He slowed to a stop to let a pedestrian pass through a crosswalk. They reached the market a few moments later. As they shopped, they discovered that the peanut butter had been moved. The store manager helped them find the peanut butter. Then they took their groceries and the checker rung up their purchases and put them in bags.

What laws are referred to in this story?
What right is explored in this story?
What community helpers are referred to in these stories?

Variable Star Quilt Square

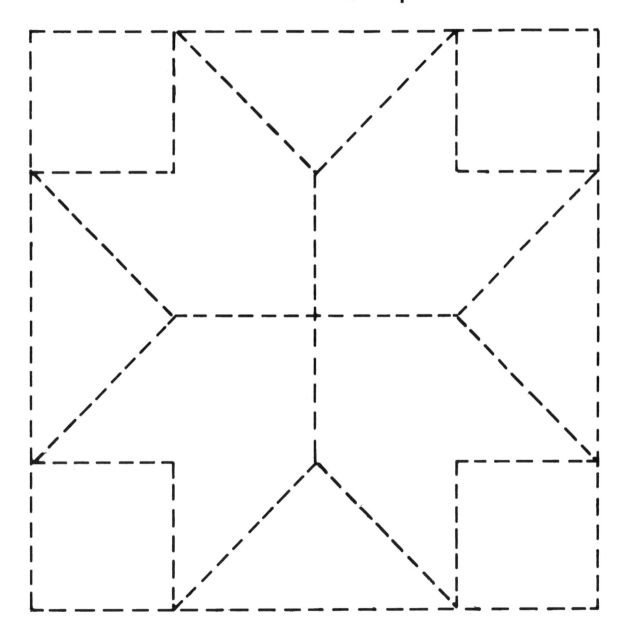

Quilt Square

**CHAPTER 6
ACTIVITY SHEET**

Stencil

Name: _____

CHAPTER 6
ACTIVITY SHEET

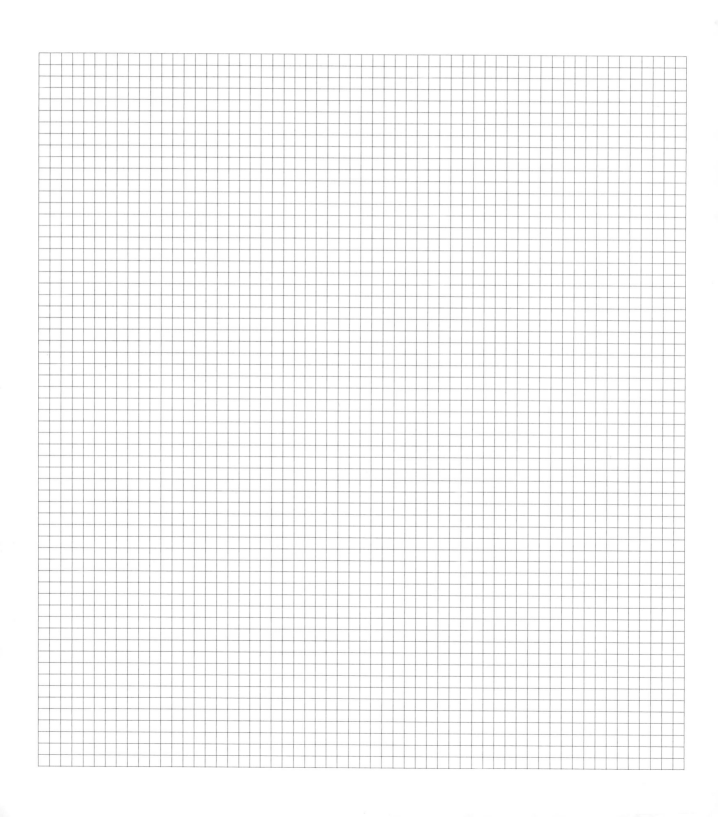

Resources

1. Good books for students to peruse to get an idea of daily Pilgrim and colonial life are:

Sarah Morton's Day by Kate Waters published by Scholastic Inc. (1989).

Samuel Eaton's Day by Kate Waters published by Scholastic Inc. (1993).

Oh, What a Thanksgiving by Steven Kroll published by Scholastic Inc. (1988).

. . . If You Live in Colonial Times by Ann McGovern published by Scholastic Inc. (1964).

If You Sailed on the Mayflower in 1620 by Ann McGovern published by Scholastic Inc. (1969).

Slumps, Grunts and Snickerdoodles: What Colonial Americans Ate and Why by Lila Perl published by Houghton Mifflin Clarion Books (1975).

2. Some class and individual reading resource books which cover issues related to slavery and the effort of the African-Americans to gain freedom and equality of treatment or which deal with the life of Martin Luther King, Jr., renown civil rights leader, are listed below.

Many Thousand Gone: African-Americans from Slavery to Freedom by Virginia Hamilton published by Alfred A. Knopf (1993).

The Day Martin Luther King, Jr. Was Shot by Jim Haskins published by Scholastic Inc. (1992).

Take a Walk in Their Shoes by Glennette Tilley Turner published by Puffin (1989) (stories of 14 African-Americans with skits).

Martin Luther King Jr. Man of Peace by Patricia and Fredrick McKissack published by Enslow Publishing (1991).

Rosa Parks and the Montgomery Bus Boycott by Teresa Celsi published by The Millbrook Press (1991).

Martin Luther King, Jr. and the March Toward Freedom by Rita Hakim published by The Millbrook Press (1991).

Abraham Lincoln and the End of Slavery by Russell Shorto published by The Millbrook Press (1991).

Book series called Black History at an Early Age, an Empack Black History Publication Series edited by Richard Green published by Empak Enterprises. The series includes books on African-Americans as artists, pioneers, and abolitionists among others.

3. A good resource on life in the fifty states which could provide useful classroom information is the *National Geographic Picture Atlas: Our Fifty States* published by the National Geographic society (1991).

4. Some additional literature books which might serve well as literature selections related to this chapter are:

Malcom X by Arnold Adoff published by Thomas V. Crowell (1970).

Martin Luther King: The Peaceful Warrior by Edward Clayton published by Prentice Hall (1964).

Eleanor Roosevelt: First Lady of the World by Doris Faber published by Viking (1985).

Oh, Lizzie! The Life of Elizabeth Cady Stanton by Doris Faber published by Lothrop, Lee & Shepard (1972).

Cesar Chavez by Ruth Franchere published by Thomas Y. Crowell (1970).

Shhh, We're Writing the Constitution by Jean Fritz published by G. P. Putman's Sons (1987).

Franklin D. Roosevelt, Gallant President by Barbara Feinberg published by Lothrop, Lee & Shepard (1981).

Where Was Patrick Henry on the 29th of May? by Jean Fritz published by Coward, McCann & Geoghegan (1975).

Journey to Topaz by Yoshika Uchida published by Scribner's Sons (1971).

Journey Home by Yoshika Uchida published by Atheneum (1978).

Roll of Thunder, Hear My Cry by Mildred Taylor published by Dial Books (1976).

7

NATIVE AMERICAN TRADITIONS OF NORTH AMERICAN

Through the activities suggested in this chapter, children can explore Native American traditions through folk literature, creative writing, and model-making activities. A framework is laid for intensive and thorough exploration of North America's Native American heritage. Sufficient activities and ideas are provided to allow this chapter to be used also to support discussions of Native American ways of life in the context of Thanksgiving and other historical and social studies endeavors.

In addition, information and activities are provided to facilitate study of the early peoples of the Hawaiian Islands. While the Polynesians probably did not arrive in the Hawaiian Islands until 900 or 1000 a.d. and the indigenous peoples of continental North America arrived perhaps more than 20,000 years ago, lifestyles of all these early peoples were affected drastically by the arrival of European and American explorers and settlers.

Lesson Activities

The Lesson Activities provide teachers with a framework for helping children to explore both Native American lifestyles in North America and the peoples and history of Hawaii. The activities include ideas for reports, bulletin boards, and relief maps.

Writing Activities

The Writing Activities suggested complement the written activities suggested in this lesson materials by providing additional ideas for free verse, introduction to simile and metaphor and news writing.

Art and Craft Activities

The Art and Craft Activities provide ideas for recreating traditional Native American crafts from different parts of North America.

Food Activities

The Food Activities section provides many easy ideas for reasonably authentic Native American cooking. Most of the foods can be cooked in an electric soup pot or deep frying pan.

Art Masters—Old and New

Art Masters - Old and New provides art project ideas for exploring Native American artists R. C. Gorman and Harry Fonseca.

Sharing Activities

The Sharing Activities suggested include providing children with opportunities to engage in Native American (or original) legend storytelling with younger students, to investigate or create Native American dances, and to display student recreations of Native American arts and crafts.

Lesson Activities

Background Information

Very brief information is provided here on the general Native American lifestyles in five different regions of continental North America. This information should not be considered definitive in any way inasmuch as, even within regions, Native American groups had and have tremendous diversity in shelter, food, art, and mobility. The information here will serve as a general background resource for use with students as they begin their own research efforts as part of the lesson activities described in this section.

Following the information on Native American groups from the continental United States is a background resource on early peoples of Hawaii.

Background information on Native American groups of the continental United States is adapted from *Classroom Museums: Touchable Tables for Kids* by Pamela Marx (permission granted).

Native Americans of the Southeast

The southeastern groups lived over a wide area of the United States. These areas include the states of Florida, Tennessee, Mississippi, Georgia, Louisiana, Virginia, North and South Carolina, and Alabama. This was an area of lush and diverse plant and animal life. Since this part of the United States is bordered by the Atlantic Ocean and the Caribbean Sea, many groups had access to the food and other resources of the ocean. The groups that lived and live in this area include the Choctaw, Seminole, Chickasaw, Natchez, and Cherokee.

Much of this area has a warm to moderate climate. As a result, common shelter structures were often simple. These included chickees, pole frame structures with bark roofs and woven mat walls, and mud houses with thatched roofs.

Food was plentiful in this area. Many tribes gathered wild fruit, roots and nuts. Some farmed corn, squash, sweet potatoes, and beans. Large and small game was abundant. Native Americans hunted bear, elk, buffalo, and deer, depending upon location. They also fished. Louisiana tribes ate fish, turtles, shrimp, and alligator. Hunting was done with bows and arrows and spears.

Tattooing was a popular art of certain groups. Sometimes it was associated with rights of adulthood. Red, black, and blue were often used as tattooing ink colors. Jewelry and body painting were also used as personal decoration.

Native Americans of the Northeast

Northeastern groups lived in the areas embodied by the states of New York, Delaware, New Jersey, Pennsylvania, Maine, Rhode Island, Massachusetts, and Connecticut. Two great alliances of individual groups made up the Native American nations of the northeast. These were the Iroquois and the Algonquin. The Onondaga, Mohawk, Cayuga, Tuscarora, Oneida, and Seneca were part of the Iroquois nation. The Delaware, Penobscot, Wampanoag, and Narraganset were among the groups of the Algonquin nation.

A common shelter in the northeast was the long house. It was a structure made with logs and covered with bark. Wigwams were another common shelter structure. They were circular in shape and made by covering a structure of strong reeds and branches with bark, mats, or grasses.

In this part of the country, seasonal change affects food availability. During summer, spring and fall, food was available from many sources. Game such as geese, turkey, deer, bear, moose, and even seal was plentiful, depending on how far north the group lived. Fish and shellfish were also available. The Wampanoag who lived by the ocean especially enjoyed these. Wild plants were gathered for food, and corn and other crops were harvested. Meats were dried and stored for the winter. Fruits and berries were sometimes sundried with a little animal fat to make a food called pemmican which could be stored for winter. Maple syrup was available to some groups by tapping maple trees.

Different craft forms were practiced for a variety of purposes among the northeastern groups. Some groups carved wooden masks that were used to help cure sicknesses. Some groups wove baskets. Baskets and masks were even woven from corn husks by some Iroquois groups.

Birch bark canoes provided valuable transportation to groups who lived near inland waterways.

Native Americans of the Plains

The Plains Native Americans include many groups that are well-known to many students. These groups include the Dakota (Sioux), Kiowa, Arapaho, Osage, Blackfeet, Cheyenne, Pawnee, Comanche, Chippewa, Crow, and Mandan. These groups lived in different parts of a vast area of the United States known as the Great Plains. Many of these groups traveled a great deal once the horse was introduced by the Europeans. The states in which these peoples lived and live include Missouri, Kansas, Colorado, Wyoming, Nebraska, North and South Dakota, Minnesota, Oklahoma, Arkansas, and Montana.

Many of these groups were nomadic or semi-nomadic. As such, they needed shelters that were easy to build and moveable. Teepees were common with nomadic groups. Teepees were made with sticks placed in a circular pattern covered with skins. Earth lodges were also made. These structures were kept warm in the summer and cool in the winter by having walls made of sod. Some groups even lived in grass huts.

Food varied depending upon the location and transient nature of the group. Buffalo were an important resource for the Plains groups. Buffalo provided food, clothing, shelter coverings and tools. Many of the Plains groups became skilled horse riders, and followed the buffalo and other game animals of the Plains. While many groups were nomadic, some farmed crops such as corn. They also fished in available rivers and lakes.

Some of the groups decorated shields used in battle or ceremonial dances with symbolic designs. The Plains groups (the Cheyenne and Pawnee, for example) adopted the custom of wearing feather headpieces, ranging from a few feathers to full headdresses.

Native Americans of the Northwest

Native Americans of the Northwest lived in areas that include the states of Alaska, Washington, and Oregon. There were and are many groups or clans in these areas. Some of them are the Haida, Tlingit, Kwatkiutl, Eskimo, and Aleut.

Several well-known shelters were used by northwestern groups. A common shelter was the plank house. A plank house was a large shelter made from cedar logs or planks. Several families could live in one shelter. Another well-known shelter was the igloo built by groups in Alaska. These circular structures were built from blocks of ice.

Those groups who lived near the seacoast fished for much of their food. Salmon was a major fish in the Washington state area. In the northern areas, whales were caught and whale blubber was cooked down into oil for fuel, lamp oil, and preserving foods. Inland groups hunted large and small animals for food.

Woodcarving is a famous art form from the northwestern Native American groups. Huge totem poles were carved. These were large logs carved with animal images and symbols that helped tell about the family carving the log and the family's history. Clans developed distinctive carving styles and also carved boxes, masks and utensils from local woods such as cedar. Some groups carved sea mammal tusks and whale bone into statues, fetishes, and tools.

Native Americans of the Southwest

Many groups of Native Americans inhabited and inhabit the Southwest. In California alone, there were once more than 100 different groups. Some of the most well-known southwestern groups were the Pueblo groups of the area now called Arizona and New Mexico. These groups included the Hopi, Zuni, and Acoma. A latecomer to the area was the Navajo, now one of the largest tribes in the United States.

Depending upon the part of the Southwest, the group might live in a simple grass hut, a hogan or a flat-topped adobe structure. The Puebloans preferred the one and two-story adobe structures called pueblos. Some of the very early groups in the Puebloan areas were called Anasazi (meaning old ones). These groups built elaborate cliff dwellings. Many of them are preserved today in the area called Mesa Verde in Colorado.

Plants and game were plentiful food sources in most parts of the Southwest. Acorns provided a main staple for the diet of many California groups. Other southwestern groups harvested corn for food and cotton for weaving cloth. Those near seashores or rivers fished, often with spears.

Many different art forms flourished among the groups of the Southwest. Many groups were accomplished basket makers, potters, and weavers. The Navajo are especially well-known for their beautifully designed rugs and blankets. Other art forms were part of religious ceremonies. Sand paintings were and are created on the ground and then immediately erased by Navajo people as part of religious ceremonies. Today, permanent sand paintings are made by Native American artists as works of art. The Hopi make Kachina dolls to represent helping spirits of their religion and to help teach Hopi culture to the people.

Early Peoples of Hawaii

The Hawaiian Islands comprise our 50th state. Located in the middle of the Pacific Ocean, they are unique among the states in that they are the only island state. The eight southern islands of this archipelago are the islands that form the state. The islands are called Hawaii, Oahu, Kauai, Maui, Lanai, Molokai, Kahoolawe, and Niihau. It is the only state once ruled by a monarchy.

Just as no one knows precisely when North America first became inhabited, no one knows exactly when people first arrived on the Hawaiian Islands. What we do know is that the first people were ocean travelers from parts of Polynesia such as Tahiti. In perhaps a.d. 900 to a.d. 1000, the first of these seagoing people reached the Hawaiian Islands. These early peoples relied on the fruits of the sea as their primary food source.

As the number of people on the islands grew, they formed clans and lived in villages. They lived in bamboo or wooden huts with roofs made from large-leafed tropical plants and trees. The climate was hospitable, so little clothing was needed. Clothing that was used was made from grass, pressed bark cloth called tapa cloth, and fish skin. Women wore flower necklaces called leis. Men wore elaborate headgear for battle. Leaders and royalty wore headdresses and robes of feathers, shells and leaves—often decorated in the royal colors of red and yellow.

The people used the resources available to meet their daily needs for tools and furnishings. Wood, coconuts, gourds, and large leaves (which could be braided) provided many simple tools, bowls, and other household items.

Over the years, wars between tribes became common. In the early 1780s, a leader called Kamehameha gained control of the island of Hawaii, and by the mid-1790s he and his armies controlled the major islands.

Hawaii was first visited by Europeans in 1778 when English Captain James Cook arrived for a short visit. Later, the Americans of North America arrived, primarily as missionaries intent on converting the native peoples.

Project Directions

1. Native Americans of North America

The lesson activity ideas for this chapter center on having children work through a series of activities, some written and some not, through which they will learn about the culture, traditions, and life of a chosen Native American group. Divide the class into cooperative learning groups to complete some or all of these lesson explorations.

a. Explore a folk legend

A wide variety of Native American legends are now available in beautifully illustrated picture books. (Literature suggestions by region are provided in the resources section of this chapter.) Either check a number of these out at the library or ask each of your cooperative learning groups to take responsibility for getting to the library, agreeing upon a folktale that the group wants to explore, and checking it out. Remind them that the stories they are reading are adapted from oral storytelling traditions of the Native American group from which the folktale is taken. This information is usually provided on the face of the book. Alternatively, some groups might want to investigate whether or not local Native American legends exist, and focus their efforts on a local tale.

The folktale chosen will determine the Native American group "adopted" by the cooperative learning group. Each group will explore its folktale by: 1) reading it aloud together; 2) determining daily activities of the Native American group to which the folktale relates by examining the facts and pictures provided in the folktale book (this information to be recorded on the Facts in the

Folktale Activity Sheet located at the back of Chapter 4); and 3) creating a storytelling or skit version of the legend to be orally presented to the class.

In analyzing the folktale to determine daily activities of the Native American group, some folktales will be more productive than others in this regard. The point of this exercise is to have children think analytically about information provided in the story. Some stories will not give children information for every blank space on the activity sheet. Help children to view this exercise as a sort of "treasure hunt" for facts within the fictional tale.

To create a performance version of the folktale, each group can either retell the story orally with props and gestures, or the students may choose to make a "play" presentation with simple costumes and props.

b. Research and Write a Group Native American Report

The cooperative learning group (concurrently with the activities described above) explores the Native American group from which its legend derives by doing an investigative report on the lifestyle and history of the particular Native American group. The information completed on the group's activity sheets will be useful information with which to begin research.

Each group divides up the reporting responsibilities so that each student has to research only two or three subject areas. These individual page reports are then included in the group's overall report along with at least one picture by each student depicting some aspect of the Native American group's daily life. Suggested research areas are:

> Food
> Clothing
> Geography and location of group
> Shelter
> Art forms
> Ceremonies
> Sports
> Tools
> Local plants/animals and use thereof

c. Create a Model Village

Have students in their groups create models of a shelter or village scene relating to the Native American group the students have chosen to study. These can be made in a variety of ways and serve as good "spare time" projects for the classroom. Models can be created simply from paper or by using more diverse materials such as popsicle sticks to make hogans, twigs and cloth to make teepees, papier-mâché, glue, and grass clippings to make grass huts, toy logs to make plank houses, cookie or salt dough to make adobe pueblos, and sugar cubes to make igloos. The models should be placed on sheets of plywood or particle board or three layers of corrugated cardboard taped together.

d. Fold-A-Book Animal Legends

After students have completed their investigations, ask them individually to identify an animal (or a plant) that figures in the culture of the Native American group they chose. Using the fold-a-book pattern below, have children create and write a short legend of their own for their mini-book about the animal (or plant) they choose. Half of each page is a small pencil or colored pencil illustration; the other half contains two or three short sentences telling the story.

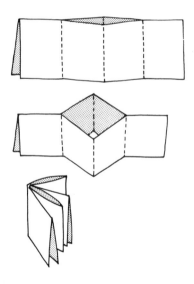

As part of this project and to help them identify features of the animal about which to focus a legend, you might also ask children to write a short, one paragraph or five-point report about the animal. The animal report can include information such as habitat, reproduction, food, life span, and family/living patterns, daylight/nocturnal hunting patterns, and color and size.

e. Native American Shelters Bulletin Board

Devote one bulletin board in your classroom to an exploration of types of shelter used by Native American groups in the different regions of the country. Place a large United States map or an outline of the United States on the bulletin board. Encourage children to fill it with small pictures of the types of shelter that Native Americans would have used in different parts of the country. Members of the cooperative learning groups can place a picture or two on the map which depicts the shelter from their "adopted" Native American group. Individual students should also be encouraged to add to the board as they discover shelters from different parts of the country that they would like to draw and place on the board. Remind children to staple or glue their pictures to the map in the appropriate location in which it was used.

2. Early Peoples of Hawaii

Explore the history of Hawaii with these project ideas.

a. Mapping the Hawaiian Language

The Hawaiian language is related to the other languages of Polynesia which were spoken in Samoa, Tahiti, and the Marquesas Islands, among others. The alphabet has only 12 letters. The vowels are A, E, I, O and U. The consonants are H, K, L, M, N, P, and W. The vowels are pronounced in a manner similar to the pronunciation of vowels in Spanish. All Hawaiian words end in vowels.

Divide students into cooperative learning groups to explore the different islands through each group's creation of a relief map of one of the eight major islands. Using plywood bases, have children make simple flour and water relief maps which they can paint with tempera paint when dry. Ask students to label the different geographic formations such as mountains, rivers, and the like with the Hawaiian word for that formation.

A short glossary of relevant Hawaiian words is provided here:

Hill - pali, pu'u
Mountain - kuahiwi, mauna
Ocean - moana, kai
Island - mokupuni, aina
Lake - loko wai
River - kahawi, wai
Valley - awaawa
Water - wai
Bay - kuono
Volcano - lua pele

b. Short Island History

Ask children to choose one of the eight Hawaiian Islands upon which to do a short report. The report can talk about uses of the island and people on the island today, but should also include any history of before and during European and American exploration and settlement. The more populated islands will have more available history and you may want to encourage children to report on the islands of Hawaii, Oahu, Maui, Kauai, or Molokai. A history report will show the students how life changed for the early Hawaiians with the arrival of European and American explorers and settlers. For example, Molokai was a leper colony at one point and now has a growing tourist trade.

c. Hawaiian Legend

Religion was an important part of islander life. Pele was goddess of fire. Kane was the god of life. Ku was a war god. Ask students to research legends related to these and other Hawaiian mythic figures. Have them report the legends by writing them up in their own words, and sharing them orally with the class. Perhaps students would like to work together to create short skits on some of the legends.

d. Traditional Foods

Various fish have been staple Hawaiian foods for a long time. Polynesians brought chickens and pigs from the other Pacific Islands. Poi, a gooey starch made from mashed taro root, was a traditional food. Poi came to be eaten with kahlua pig—whole pig roasted underground. With the coming of new settlers, the Hawaiian islands became home to plantations that grew sugar cane and pineapple.

Have students explore the history of the islands by making the fruit kabobs suggested in the food activities in this chapter. As part of the process of making the kabobs, ask children to think about what part of the fruit snack early Hawaiians might have eaten, and which part became prevalent only with later settlement. Encyclopedia research on the fruits used might be helpful.

Writing Activities

Note: This section suggests written activities related to the chapter theme. Many of the lesson activities in this chapter have a writing component as well. You might decide that some of the writing exercises suggested below meet your students' needs better than the writing activities suggested in the lesson activities. Or you might assign one or two of these writing projects as a complement to those assigned as part of the directed lesson activities.

1. Chapter Vocabulary

Vocabulary suggestions for this chapter are:

Native American
Legend
Long house
Igloo
Plank house
Teepee
Pueblo
Adobe
Chickee
Hogan
Wigwam
Ceremony
Ritual
Tattoo
Nomadic
Potlatch
Totem pole
Sand painting
Kachina
Pemmican
Pottery
Pinch pot
Mortar
Pestle
Anasazi
Patchwork
Rebus
Weaving
Warp
Woof/weft
Tapa
Lei

2. Create a Local Legend

Have children think about their community and identify natural geologic features, plants, and animals. Ask them to pretend that they are Native Americans of their community long before settlers came. What legends might they tell about why a flower is a certain color or why an animal hunts at night? Ask each child to write a legend about a local creature in the wild, a place, or a local natural phenomenon. Have them illustrate their legends. You might choose to have children make mini-books of their legends using the fold-a-book concept in Item 1d of the lesson activities in this chapter.

3. Notching Stick Story

The Papago of the Southwest and probably other groups as well carved notches and designs on sticks to keep track of time and record events. Other groups probably did similar things to track time on hunting trips or chart crop growing seasons. Ask each child to bring in a twig approximately 12" long and 1/4" to 1/2" in diameter. Ask them to create a notching design on the stick with markers. Tell them to think about what they are keeping track of with their notches. Are they notching each sunrise? Are they notching the full moons? Ask them to imagine they are on a hunting trip or traveling to a new location to live. Their notches keep track of time on the trip. Ask them to write a first-person story about their adventures on the hunting trip or their travels to a new home.

Alternatively, if you do some clay art as described in the arts and crafts section below, you might have each student write a story about an adventure the student had with his or her creation. Examples using a pinch pot might include going to the spring to collect water, cooking mush in it, or gathering plants to cook in it.

4. Explore Nature Through Free Verse

Native Americans have traditionally lived close to the land and had a deep respect for it. Many

Native American religious and ceremonial activities center around their natural surroundings and natural forces. Prayers and songs were often homages to the earth. Ask children to write five to ten lines of unrhymed free verse to celebrate the earth.

Examples:

I honor you, Earth.
You are my home.
I get my life from you.
You are why I live.
You are my purpose.
You send me all my hope.
I would not leave if I had the choice.
You will always be my treasured voice.
I respect you with all my heart.

In the world there are the creatures.
That stay in their homes
Because danger might appear.
Sometimes the world can be dangerous.
And sometimes the world is peaceful
And no danger is around.

5. Try Simile and Metaphor

Ask children to give themselves Native American names. They should think of names that describe themselves—that are, indeed, metaphors for who and what they are. For example, if a child sees him- or herself as small and quick, he or she might want the name "Little Rabbit." If a child sees him- or herself as tall and gentle, he or she might want the name "Tall Deer."

Once students have chosen their names, ask them to write a trait poem using simile as the method for conveying information. In this poem, they describe what they are like using similes from nature. It is an unrhymed poem. The poet can describe anything about him- or herself so long as the trait is described using a simile, preferably a simile from nature. Traits can be based on artistic, musical, or dance ability, physical attributes such as appetite, sleep patterns, or athletic ability.

Example:

Tall Deer sees as clearly as the eagle.
She grows as straight as the cedar tree.
She dances as happily as a wildflower in the breeze.
She sleeps as deeply as a bear in winter.
She dreams as high as the sun sits in the sky.

6. Coming of Age Report

Older children might find it interesting to do a short five-point report on a coming of age tradition for boys or girls in a native peoples clan or group of the child's choice. There are ceremonies that occur at certain crucial ages in many cultures, including Native American. A common basis for ceremonial rites is celebration of the transition to adulthood. These celebrations might include tests of skill, ritual dances, body or face painting, or tasks to be completed. A "coming of age" book based on Apache culture that might interest students is *The Gift of Changing Woman* by Tryntje Van Ness Seymour published by Henry Holt and Company (1993).

7. Write a Turnabout Newspaper

In the 1800s, as settlers moved west in greater numbers, there were years of Native American conflict with the settlers. Native Americans saw the settlers take their best lands and kill the animals they needed to survive. Most of the information printed about the struggles was from the settlers' perspective. By the early 1800s, however, the Cherokee under the leadership of Chief Sequoyah did have a newspaper.

Have children choose one or more major historical event involving the conflicts that occurred during the settlement of the West, and create a newspaper from the Native American perspective as though they were writing for Chief Sequoyah's newspaper.

Students can report on a variety of events or they can write an entire newspaper dedicated to different aspects of one issue. A good issue is the decimation of the buffalo after the railroad came through the Great Plains. Buffalo were slaughtered for sport and left to rot, something the Native Americans would never have done because of their deep reverence for nature, the land, and its gifts. Students could write news articles, advertisements, editorials, letters to the editor, and the like.

If you choose to, you could even divide the class into two groups. One would write a newspaper from the perspective of the settler, and one would write a newspaper from the perspective of the Native American. Each newspaper would cover the same event or series of events, but from an obviously different perspective.

8. Native American Rebus Story

Using the Native American symbols on the Native American Rebus Story Activity Sheet at the back of this chapter or symbols of their own creation, have children create a rebus story. A rebus story uses words and symbols to tell a story. Children should provide a key to any symbols they create or use for their stories that are not shown on the activity sheet.

9. News from the Front

Before European exploration and then American domination, the clans of Hawaii fought many wars and had many great leaders. Have children research some of these leaders or the history of battles during a particular period and write a newspaper article telling who, what, where, why, when and how about a particular leader's rise, or about a particular battle or series of battles. King Kamehameha is credited with bringing the islands under common leadership, but other leaders include Kalaniopuu, Kawalao, and Liholiho.

10. Volcano Legends

Pele is the traditional Hawaiian goddess of fire. Since the volcanoes on the Hawaiian Islands were active (as they are to this day), she was an important goddess to appease. Ask children to write a legend of their own about Pele, goddess of fire and volcanoes. The legend should be set on one of the Hawaiian Islands and reflect the landscape and vegetation of Hawaii.

Art and Craft Activities

1. Seminole Patchwork Wall Hanging

Much Seminole traditional clothing is brightly colored with linear designs. Bands of linear patchwork designs are sewn together to make skirts and other clothing. Some designs were repeating horizontal designs that were made more interesting by being cut apart and stitched back together at an angle.

Give each child a 9" x 12" sheet of white construction paper. The child folds it in half the long way, and cuts on the fold line to make two 4 1/2" x 12" sheets of paper. With markers or crayons, ask children to make horizontal linear Native American designs of their choosing across the length of one of the sheets. To be most effective, each linear design should not be more than 1" to 1 1/2" wide. The designs can be colored with crayon, pastels, or marker, and then displayed with no further work, if desired.

You can make a more intricate patchwork activity by having children make their designs by gluing on pieces and strips of different colored and designed fabric. Through this project, the children explore the linear patchwork traditions used to make much of this regional clothing.

If you want students to make a slightly more complicated but very attractive patchwork, have them follow these additional directions. Children measure across the completed, designed, and colored 12" strip, and mark it on the top and bottom at 3" intervals. They then draw lines to divide the sheet into four equal segments and cut the

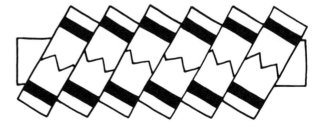

segments apart. (This can also be done by folding the 12" sheet in half, in half again, and cutting on the fold lines.)

Once the four pieces are cut apart, the remaining half sheet of unmarked construction paper is trimmed so that it is 3" x 12". The four previously cut pieces of designed paper are glued onto the second sheet of white paper at an angle so that the top right corner and the bottom left corner of each designed piece touch the top and bottom edges, respectively, of the second sheet. The child should glue the first piece on so that the top right corner touches the middle of the second strip of paper. The remaining pieces are glued on next to the previously glued pieces. The Seminole-style design is complete. Once each child has finished his or her piece, each patchwork strip is glued to a large black sheet of paper to create a Seminole patchwork wall hanging. (Note: The patchwork designs can be cut into 6 pieces as shown on the illustration.)

2. Navajo Sand Painting

Using paper plates, colored chalk, and salt, have children work in groups to make the different colors of salt "sand" that they will use for this project. Colors most commonly used in actual sand paintings are earth tones (yellow, orange, black, brown), blue, and white.

To make the colored salt, children rub the sides of sticks of colored chalk into table salt until they get the color desired. (You can also color salt by mixing it with powdered tempera paint.) Put colored "sand" into different bowls and consider each bowl a different painting station. Each child creates his or her sand picture in stages on a piece of construction paper or posterboard. Have children design their pictures to utilize traditional Native American designs and symbols for people, animals and plants. To help children create their designs, you might want to photocopy for them the Native American Rebus Story Activity Sheet at the back of this chapter which includes some sample designs.

Before children begin gluing the sand on, ask them to sketch their pictures in pencil and to decide which parts will be painted which colors. Then they place the glue on the paper for all those parts of the picture they intend to color a particular color, go to that station, and "paint" the glue

with the color. This is done using a spoon to drizzle the sand over the glue until all the glue is covered and then shaking the excess off. Students then squeeze glue over all the areas to be colored the next color, and repeat the process until all the sketched parts of the picture are colored with the salt "paint."

3. Shields from the Great Plains

Round shields (9" to 12" in diameter) can be cut from corrugated cardboard or tan or brown posterboard. (Some paper plates have brown undersides and are also suitable for this project.) To complete the shield, hole punch six holes at intervals around the edges of the shield. Sisal or other string or leather strips are tied through the holes to attach the strings to the shield. Beads, shells, bones, feathers, or pods of seeds are tied or hot glued onto the strings for decoration.

The center of the shield is filled with a Native American design of the child's choosing. The child might decorate the center of the shield with a stylized animal or person. Do the decoration in earth colors such as browns, blacks, white, gold, and reds or rusts. Paint them with small brushes or use oil pastels. You might want children to outline the artwork in black to help highlight their designs. Sample designs can be found in resource books on Native American lifestyles, or children can use the symbols on the Native American Rebus Story Activity Sheet for inspiration.

4. Corn Husk Masks

The Iroquois made baskets and masks from corn husk material. Using stiff paper plates, have children recreate corn husk masks with pieces of corn husk, feathers, shells, popcorn kernels, and glue. First have children draw two eye openings and a mouth opening on the domed side of the plate. These can be cut out if you like, but need not be. Then children use strips and pieces of corn husk cut in about 1" to 2" squares to cover the domed face of the plate in a pattern of their choosing. Small shells, small chicken bones ,and feathers can be used to decorate the masks if the children so choose. The entire face of the plate should be covered so that the finished mask gives the appearance of being completely woven from corn husks. One package of corn husks is usually sufficient for the class project.

5. Pinch a Pot Pottery

Some of the southwestern Native American groups were skilled potters. There are three basic types of clay construction which students can explore: the pinch pot, the coil pot, and slab construction. If children have not had much clay experience, the most successful method is probably the pinch pot. Use a terra cotta-colored clay, if possible.

To make a pinch pot, the child starts with a fist-size ball of clay. The child inserts a thumb into the center of the clay to begin the formation of a small bowl or pot. He or she shapes the bowl with the palm of the other hand. When the desired shape is obtained, the child can etch or carve Native American designs into the sides of the pot with a toothpick. Let completed pots dry. Once dry, they can be glazed and fired or, if no kiln is available, they can be painted with tempera paint mixed with white glue. This "glue paint" helps strengthen unfired pieces which, unfortunately, are quite fragile. There are some new oven-fired, terra-cotta clays which are now available through teacher supply stores. They are, however, much more expensive for classroom projects than regular clay, but you can have a relatively durable finished product without a kiln or the cost of firing up the kiln.

6. Navajo or Sioux Dreamcatcher

A simple legend goes with the craft of the dreamcatcher. It is said that if you hang the dreamcatcher where you sleep at night, bad dreams will become tangled in the webbing and only good dreams will find their way to the center of the web, there to slide down the feather and into your head as you sleep.

To make a dreamcatcher, you need flexible vines or stems, string or yarn, a feather, and a bead. Take the stems and vines and twist them into a 5" diameter circle. Tie the circle in place with string, twist ties, or wire. You might ask that children complete this part of the project at home where they will collect their vines and stems; this way the stems are still pliable when the wreath shape is made. (Your wreath can also be made by cutting the inner circle from a plastic margarine or whipped topping lid to make a ring.) Once this wreath shape is made, loop (as you would a string sales tag over a button) seven 24" pieces of yarn and one 30" piece of yarn over the edges of the wreath at evenly spaced intervals. Pull loops tight.

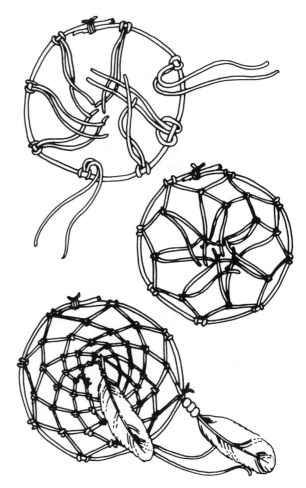

Begin to create a web or net by taking one strand of the looped yarn from one spot on the wreath and tying it to one strand of the yarn from the spot next to it. This process is completed for each spot on the wreath and then a second set of knots is made. When you have knotted the strings three or four times, you will be at the center of your circle. Use a separate string to tie your webbing strings together tightly at the middle of the circle so that the netting will not unravel. Cut off the shorter strings near the knot, leaving one or two long yarns on which a bead and feather can be tied. Feathers can be attached to the edge of the wreath and beads can occasionally be tied into the webbing of the dreamcatcher to make it more decorative.

7. Weave on the Warp

Southwestern Native American groups, especially the Navajo are renowned for their beautifully woven and designed rugs and blankets. Use yarn, a pencil or popsicle stick, and a shoe box lid to create a woven hanging. Seven to nine slits are cut on the two short ends of the shoe box lid about 3/8" to 1/2" apart and about 3/8" to 1/2" deep. To create the warp, weave a long string of yarn up and down the lid (the long way) from slit to slit. Leave about 4" of yarn hanging out of the lid at the beginning and end of the looping. Tie knots on the outside of the lid at each end to help hold the yarn in place.

Then make your woof/weft (or weaving) yarn and shuttle with a length of yarn tied onto a popsicle stick or pencil. This will be your shuttle when you start to weave over and under the warp strings. Tie the loose end of the yarn onto an end warp yarn and begin the over/under, back/forth weaving process. You can change colors by tying a new piece of yarn onto the pencil. Use a pencil or comb to push the woof threads up tight on the warp threads. To complete the weaving, fill in the length of the shoe box. Tie off the ends and remove carefully from the loom. Children can work on this project in their spare time during class. The project can take several weeks to complete. It can be hung on a dowel or mounted on posterboard.

8. Carving - Bone Sculpture and Petroglyph Art

Often northern groups, especially those in Alaska, carved sculptures from whale and other large animal bones. Other Native Americans carved or etched picture stories on rocks and cave walls.

Have children create bone sculptures using plastic knives, toothpicks, nails, and bars of white bathing soap such as Ivory®. Children should try to sculpt things the Native Americans would have been familiar with such as fish, simple dugout boats, plants, and sea mammals.

An alternative carving project would be to have children think of their bars of soap as stone such as a stone or rock on which a Native American might have etched a petroglyph picture or story. If this project is chosen, children can use the Native American Rebus Story Activity Sheet at the back of this chapter to get ideas for symbols to use or can use other general resource books which contain symbol samples. Children can get rid of any brand imprint in the soap by running a serrated plastic knife back and forth over the imprint until it is gone. If the surface is rougher than desired

after this process, children can smooth it by running a damp washcloth or sponge over the surface until the soap is smooth.

Students then etch their chosen designs into the soap with round toothpicks (they are stronger than the flat ones) or small nails. Once their designs are complete, have children paint over them with soy sauce, brown shoe polish, or wood stain so that the coloring agent gets into the carved crevices. Remove the excess by rubbing very lightly with a paper towel. This will help highlight the carved designs.

9. Vests, Belts, and Headbands

Children can make mock articles of clothing such as vests and belts. Using crayons and markers, they can decorate them with Native American symbol art, perhaps to represent aspects of their Native American name (if they did the "Try Simile and Metaphor" writing activity in this chapter). Belts can be cut from heavy paper such as a brown paper bag about 4" to 5" wide. Vests can be made from brown paper grocery bags as well. Remind children that these paper materials are recreations of clothing that would have been made from animal skins.

Headbands can be made inexpensively from 1 1/2" to 2" strips of cloth 36" long. Marker can be used to decorate them with Native American symbols.

10. Totem Pole Construction

This project can be organized in a couple of ways depending upon your available room and time. If you plan a little ahead, you can ask a local ice cream store to keep its five gallon containers so that each of five or six cooperative groups can make one segment of a class totem pole. This results in a large floor-to-ceiling style of pole. Alternatively, each group can make its own totem pole using empty oatmeal containers or one-pound coffee cans.

Whichever pole you decide to have the students make, the method of design and construction are roughly the same. On the outside of the container, the children build up the design of their totem pole segment using crushed and/or rolled newspaper and tape. To make the design, the students must first decide what animal they are recreating on the pole and how they want to stylize its features on the pole. It is always useful to have some reference books with pictures available during this part of the process. Once the raised designs are taped on, they are papier-mâchéd over with strips of newspaper dipped in starch or equal parts glue and water or thick flour and water paste. (If you are making a class totem pole with larger containers, each group makes one segment and works on it together. If each group is making its own pole with smaller containers, each child makes his or her own segment and joins it with the rest.)

When the papier-mâché is dry, the project can be painted several ways. The children can simply use tempera paints to paint the totem pole in colors of their choice or they can attempt to recreate a wood look on their pole over which they can highlight certain features with colored paint. To create a wood-like look, first paint the pole white or light beige. Then with large 3" house-painting brushes, children brush a thin coat of thinned dark brown paint over the white paint leaving noticeable brush strokes to simulate wood grain.

If papier-mâché is not suitable, children can decorate totem pole segments by covering them with construction paper and adding three-dimensional features with folded and glued construction paper decorations—in other words, paper sculpture.

11. "One with the Earth" Pictures

In conjunction with discussions about how Native Americans revere the earth and view humans as one with all the other creatures of the earth, ask children to make a "one with the earth" picture. To do this, children need to work in pairs for part of the project. The picture is created by the child placing his or her profile onto a 12" x 24" sheet of construction paper, and then placing other symbols or representations of the natural world on the sheet in juxtaposition to the profile.

To make the profiles, children work in pairs. One child lays his or her head on a piece of scratch paper. A second child traces the outline of the child's profile onto the paper. The first child cuts out this traced profile, traces it (with any modifications to its shape that he or she chooses) onto another piece of construction paper in the color is his or her choice, and then cuts its out. The first child in turn traces his or her partner's

profile. The remainder of the art depictions on the project are of the child's choosing but should represent the child's relation to the natural world.

12. Hide Painting

Have children make their own hide by dipping a brown paper grocery bag in water and then wringing it out. A wash of brown watercolor or thinned tempera paint can then be lightly applied. Once dry, children can use black marker to recreate a Native American story on the "hide." The symbolic art on the Native American Rebus Story Activity Sheet at the back of this chapter can be used for ideas or children can make up their own symbols.

13. Storyteller Sculptures

Helen Cordero, a Native American of the Conchiti Pueblo in New Mexico, is credited with inspiring the current popularity of contemporary storyteller clay art. She began making her ceramic storytellers in the early 1960s. Storytellers as a folk art form were inspired by the Native American storytelling traditions. Storytelling has traditionally been a way for people from many parts of the world to keep their culture and traditions alive. The Puebloans of New Mexico also followed this long tradition with stories being passed from mother to child, grandfather to grandchild. Storyteller sculptures are usually structured as a large human or animal figure with mouth open as if telling a story. The lap, back, and arms of this large figure are full of small children listening. These sculptures can be as short as two inches or as tall as two feet.

The storyteller craft will be a class project. Each child will create a figure of a listening child to be attached to the storyteller. Have children decide whether the storyteller will be human or animal. Sample animals which have been used are owls, turtles, and bears. The storyteller itself can be a group project, with students taking turns working on it. The individual listening children will be small and can be affixed to the storyteller with hot glue.

To make your storyteller structure, crush and tape newspaper into appropriate shapes. The overall head and torso structure will be 20" to 24" high. Roll and tape newspaper with masking tape to create arms and legs for the storyteller. Tape these onto the torso. Students will papier-mâché the storyteller with strips of newspaper dipped in starch or equal parts glue and water. Once dry, students can take turns painting the storyteller. Traditional colors are off-white or tan as the base color with detail in black, brown, rusts, and earth tones. The individual listening children can be created simply be taking clothes pins, wrapping them in newspaper, taping them to form a soft-edged oval shape, and covering them with papier-mâché. Once dry, the object is painted white. When the white paint has dried, the outline of the child with arms, legs, head, and body can be painted in the traditional colors onto the figure, and hot glued to the storyteller.

14. Make a Tapa Cloth Design

Refer to directions in Item 2c of the art and craft activities of Chapter 4 for suggestions for the recreation of classroom tapa cloth. In addition to the white, brown, rust, and black designs often seen today, some sources report the Hawaiians used blue, red, and yellow in dying their bark cloth. Royal Hawaiian colors were red and yellow. Students might like to incorporate these colors into their tapa cloth designs.

15. Poi Balls

Poi balls are a Maori dance accessory, often seen today in Hawaiian dance revues that reflect the dances and influences of all Polynesia. Directions for making these are found in Item 3a of the lesson activities of Chapter 4.

Food Activities

The food activities in this chapter are adapted for the classroom from traditional Native American recipes from around the United States.

1. Northeastern Fish Stew

This stew has a unique taste and can be an interesting experience for children. Ask children to bring in canned fish such as shrimp, crabmeat, clams, and oysters (in juice). Filleted white fish is a great addition if you can assure proper refrigeration. The stew is made by boiling the fish in six to eight cups of water and adding cornmeal (1/4 cup at a time) while stirring until the stew reaches the desired thickness or consistency. You can also add lima beans, onions, or mushrooms, if desired.

Make sure no students have an allergy to shellfish before you plan this project. Students with allergies can make and eat plain cornmeal mush. Cornmeal mush is made by adding dry cornmeal to boiling water, and stirring constantly until you get the desired consistency.

2. Native American Fry Bread

Fry bread was and is made by a number of different Native American groups. Recipes are found among the southwestern Navajos, the Plains Osage, and others. Fry bread is a favorite with students. This is one recipe you can use.

2 cups flour
1/2 teaspoon salt
4 teaspoons baking powder
2/3 water
Oil for frying

Mix ingredients. If it is too sticky to work with, add a little flour. If the dough is too dry, add a little water. Have children flour the working area and their hands and then take pieces of dough to knead. Once a dough-like, stretchy consistency is obtained, have children press or pound dough flat on the floured working area. They can cut it into 1" x 3" strips with plastic knives. Fry strips in hot oil at least 1" deep until light brown. Turn at least once. Remove from oil and drain on paper towels.

Sprinkle with granulated sugar or powdered sugar or drizzle with honey. Eat while still warm.

3. Native American Pumpkin Bread

2 cup corn meal
2/3 cup water to moisten
1 cup cooked pumpkin
Oil

Mix cornmeal and water. Add pumpkin and form into patties using tablespoons of dough. Flatten patties and fry in hot oil until golden brown.

4. Blueberry Pudding

Wherever berries were available, Native Americans made puddings or stews with them. The basic recipe is always fruit and water with a little flour to thicken it.

Blueberries grow in the northern parts of the United States. To make blueberry pudding, dredge 4 cups fresh berries in flour, and place in large saucepan with about six cups water. Cook over medium heat. Bring to a boil. Simmer over medium to low heat until thick. If desired, thicken pudding even more by lightly sifting a little flour over the mixture. Sweetening the pudding with honey is optional. This dish is good with Native American fry bread.

To thicken the pudding when using frozen or canned berries, first bring berry and water mixture to a boil. Then mix hot water with two to three tablespoons cornstarch and add slowly to hot berry and water mixture, stirring constantly.

5. Corn Meal Wasna Candy

Some version of this corn treat is probably found among most tribes who grew corn. This recipe is similar to wasna recipes from the Plains area.

4 cups cornmeal
2 cups raisins or tidbits of other dried fruit
1 cup sugar (preferably brown)
2 cups butter
1 cup water

Toast cornmeal in a dry pan or in the oven before starting and let cool. This can be done at home ahead of time and brought by a student to school.

Melt butter and add sugar. Next, add cornmeal and raisins or fruit. Add water a little at a time until candy dough is a consistency that you can handle. Roll into small balls to serve.

6. Mock Acorn Mush

Acorns were a staple food for the California Native Americans. Ground acorn meal looks like uncooked Cream of Wheat®. Cooked acorn mush looks and tastes like cooked Cream of Wheat®. Make mock acorn mush by cooking Cream of Wheat® according to box directions leaving out salt and butter. You can boil small chunks of beef-steak with it if you like or add black walnuts which may have been available to some California peoples. Or combine this food treat with another cooking activity to give the children an idea of a real Native American meal among early California peoples. In recent years, local markets in some areas have begun to stock unique vegetables such as yucca root and nopales (cactus leaves). Perhaps these can be sliced and boiled to serve with the mock acorn mush.

7. Black Walnut Corn

This recipe comes from early peoples in the Northeast and something similar to it may have been eaten by the Mohawk group. To make this dish you need:

3 16- to 17-ounce cans whole kernel corn
Black Walnuts or other available walnuts
1/2 cup butter, cup into chunks

Have children shell walnuts. (You can use preshelled walnuts, but this is not as much fun for students or as instructive as doing the work involved in utilizing walnuts as food.) Place corn, walnuts, and butter in a saucepan. Heat over medium heat until butter is melted and corn is heated through. Serve warm.

8. Plains Corn Chowder

This type of soup would have been made by Native American groups who grew sweet corn and is specifically identified with the Plains groups who farmed corn. To make it you will need:

3 cans kernel corn, drained
3 17-ounce cans of creamed corn
2 cups chicken broth
4 tablespoons of butter
1 1/2 to 2 cups diced onion (frozen diced onion
    can be used or 1/4 cup dry minced onion)
2 12-ounce cans evaporated milk
Salt
Pepper (preferably white pepper)

Melt butter in soup pan. Add onions and sauté over medium or medium-high heat until translucent. Add corn kernels and sauté until fully heated and cooked. Turn off heat and mash with a potato masher to break down kernels and onion. Add creamed corn, chicken broth, and milk. Mix, heat (do not boil), and simmer. Add salt and pepper to taste and serve hot.

9. Northwestern Salmon Soup

1 can salmon (remove bones)
6 peeled and diced potatoes
1 bunch diced green onions
1 cup fresh watercress, chopped
6-8 cups water
1/2 teaspoon dill seed or 1 tablespoon dill weed
1-2 cups milk
Salt and pepper, to taste

Bring water to boil. Add salmon, potatoes, and onions. Cook until potatoes are tender. Add dill seed and cool. Mash potatoes slightly. Add salt and pepper to taste. Add milk and watercress to cooled mixture while reheating over medium heat. Serve warm.

10. Herbal Tea

Native Americans brewed tea from available plants for medicinal and food purposes. Mint tea is one example. It can be made by taking 10 or 12 stalks of fresh mint and heating it with 12 cups of water. Bring to a boil slowly and then turn off heat and let it steep for a few minutes. Serve warm or cold. Perhaps your students would like to investigate with community experts such as park rangers and museum docents local plants that might have been used to make teas. Or students could research Native American herbal teas from other parts of the country at the local library. Tea is an easy treat to make and can be served with wasna, fry bread, or any dish of your choosing.

11. Dried Meat Stew

Many Native American groups dried meats so that they could be stored and used during winter or times when food was short. Jerky is dried meat. Usually it was seasoned in some way and then smoked or dried. When it is dried or dehydrated in this way, it lasts for a long time. This stew recipe lets children see one way in which dried meats could be used. In a stew or soup the meat is rehydrated by cooking and eaten with other stew ingredients.

1 cup wild rice, cooked (or other rice if wild rice is not available)
2 cups yellow squash (you can substitute another squash or vegetable)
4-5 pieces of 6"-8" beef jerky, cut or torn into small pieces
6 cups beef bouillon
1/2 cup diced onion (or use minced frozen or 1 tablespoon dry minced)
1/2 teaspoon garlic powder
4 fresh minced sage leaves or 1/2 teaspoon crushed dry sage
Salt and pepper to taste
Oil for sauté

Have children bring in rice that has already been cooked at home. If children cannot bring in precooked wild rice, use a quick rice to make your soup. Add more water to soup as necessary to let the rice expand and cook before serving.

If using fresh onions, sauté in a little oil over medium-high heat until browned. Add sage, meat, and garlic powder and cook for 2 to 3 minutes. Add cooked rice, squash, and bouillon (and onions if using dry onions). Bring to boil and simmer, uncovered, for 10 to 15 minutes or until all ingredients are tender. Add salt and pepper to taste. As soup is cooking, add water as necessary or to serve as an extender if you will need to stretch soup to make enough servings. Serve hot.

12. Southwestern Fruit Pies

Use this fruity treat as a method for discussing food rehydration. One food preservation method used by Native Americans was dehydration. To make these fruit pies, you will need:

2 packages prepared crusts
3 cups dried fruit, diced
5 cups water
1 cup sugar or 3/4 cup honey (you can add more sweetener to taste)
1 teaspoon cinnamon

Bring water to boil. Heat fruit bits in water until they plump up and get soft. Add sweetener and cinnamon. Cook down until juice is thick or drain off excess juice. You can also mix a bit of hot water with a teaspoon of cornstarch and add that to fruit mixture to thicken it.

Let fruit mixture cool while you cut pie crusts into the appropriate number of small (4") squares so that each class member and teacher can have a pie. Fill crusts with a tablespoon full of fruit. Seal shut using egg white or water and pressing edges with a fork. Bake according to crust directions.

13. Northwestern Buckskin Bread

4 cups wheat flour
2 teaspoons baking powder
2 teaspoons salt
2 cups water

Mix ingredients. Add flour as necessary to eliminate stickiness. Shape dough into biscuits. Drop onto cookie sheet. Bake at 400 degrees for 15 minutes. Option: Break dough into two pieces and bake in two separate pie tins. Bake at 400 degrees for 30 minutes. Serve with butter.

14. Plains Pemmican

1 cube butter, melted
4-5 pieces jerky, shredded into tiny pieces
3 cups dried cherries (chokecherries were common on the Plains), diced

Mix butter, jerky, and cherries together. Work a spoonful of mixture together with fingers so that it sticks together. These pemmican patties can be eaten like this or you can bake them on a cookie sheet in a slow oven (250-300 degrees) for about an hour. Pemmican was stored for winter. Sometimes the fruit patties were made with animal fat and berries, and then dried on a stone in the sun. They could be eaten later plain or used in hot water to make a soup base.

15. Southwestern Sweetened Oranges

Local Native Americans found ways to use the sour orange fruit that grew on wild orange trees in the southeastern coastal areas. Anyone who has tasted sour oranges knows they can taste more sour than lemons. Here's a way to approximate this dish.

10 oranges, peeled, sliced, or sectioned and slightly mashed
10-12 tablespoons honey
Juice of two small to medium lemons to help give modern oranges the tangier taste of wild oranges

Mix all ingredients and mash somewhat. You can add honey as necessary to make the treat palatable to children, but to approximate the Native American dish it should be served somewhat tart.

This type of sweetened fruit dish was found around North America. In the northwest, for example, wild raspberries were sweetened with honey and served cold. The blueberry pudding described above is a hot version of sweetened fruit.

16. Hawaiian Fruit Kabobs

Pineapple and papaya are found around the islands of Hawaii. Coconut is a traditional Hawaiian food. To combine the taste of these three delicious fruits, skewer canned pineapple chunks and chunks of papaya onto small wooden barbecue skewers. One or two papaya will be enough to give an entire class a taste. Dip the kabobs in orange juice and roll them in flaked coconut to serve. Try other tropical fruits that are available in your local markets. Examples might be kiwi fruit, mango, or passion fruit.

17. Pineapple Chicken

Polynesian settlers probably brought chicken to Hawaii along with other domesticated animals. Pineapple was brought to Hawaii later but grew well. Remind children that food combinations now associated with Hawaii reflect a long history of change from the early days of Hawaii's first Polynesian settlers.

Pineapple chicken can be simple to make. You need:

Chicken strips (or canned chicken)
Diced sweet bell pepper
Pineapple chunks
One part soy sauce to one part sugar (teriyaki sauce)
Garlic powder

Place chicken strips in a baking dish. Sprinkle with peppers and pineapple chunks. Pour soy and sugar mixture over meat, fruits, and vegetables. Sprinkle lightly with garlic powder. Bake at 350 degrees until meat is done—about 45 minutes. Stir once during cooking. Serve with white rice. Instant or one-minute rice works well in the classroom setting to "sop up" the sauce.

18. Coconut Cake

The introduction of missionary and settler practices into Hawaii led to traditional coconut cake. This is simply white cake with white frosting topped with coconut. This treat should be palatable to most of the students in any class.

Art Masters—Old and New

1. R. C. Gorman

Gorman's art is well-known throughout the world. Born in 1932, his early years were spent on a Navajo reservation. He is perhaps best known for a special line or design in his drawings and paintings. Often his subjects are women covered by a blanket, shawl, or draping loose garment. The suggestion is of a full body with feet, hands, or face peering out from the fabric. Gorman lives in Taos, New Mexico, but his paintings and drawings can be viewed the world over.

2. Harry Fonseca

Fonseca is a Native American artist with a strong colorful style. Many of his works focus on the coyote as a character in modern life. The coyote is a central animal in many Native American legends. Fonseca's coyote images are brightly colored, often dressed in modern clothing, and sometimes embellished with glittering effects. His works have been exhibited in many galleries and natural history museums.

Project Directions

1. In the Style of Gorman

To create a sketch in the style of Gorman, the child will draw three large, overlapping oval or egg shapes on the paper. The resulting figure shape should be large on the bottom, representing the hips and lower torso. Erase lines that show where the three shapes overlapped. This shape will be the blanket-covered body of the person in the picture. Children should then decide where the person's head, hands, and feet will be. The child need not draw a face but can indicate the head by showing hair. The picture can be filled in with colored chalks, pale pastels, or watercolors.

2. A Modern Coyote

Have children try their hand at coyote art a la Fonseca. In Fonseca's paintings, the coyote's head is often turned sideways and the coyote is standing upright, clothed in modern day apparel such as jeans and a leather jacket. The perspective is flattened and simple. Bright pinks, blues, oranges, and the like are used to complete the images, and sometimes glitter or other sparkling substances dot the painted canvas. Have children use a large sheet of construction paper to draw and color a coyote inspired by Fonseca. Children should draw the coyote first and then clothe it. They can choose to draw the head only or the entire body. Acrylics and oil pastels make good media for completing this project.

Sharing Activities

1. Native American Game Day

Native Americans played a wide variety of games using available natural resources. Students can recreate some of these types of games with natural or modern equivalents, learn the games, and then invite another class or classes to learn them. Some possible games are:

a. Stick and Hoop

This game helped youngsters build the skills needed for hunting, namely using a spear and hitting a target. A large hoop is rolled on the ground and the child runs by the hoop and tries to throw a stick through it. This game can be recreated using Hula-Hoops® and 24" long, 1/2" wide dowels.

b. Bone Toss

This game has many modern equivalents and has been played from Mexico to the Northwest. Traditionally, a stick or bone awl was used with a leather strap attached to one end of the stick. At the other end of the strap, one or more hollowed-out bones was attached. The player would try to catch the hollowed-out bone on the end of the stick. Several straps might be attached to the stick in more complicated versions of the game. This game can be recreated by using dowels, pencils, or rolled and taped posterboard dowels, string, and 2" to 3" diameter circles cut from posterboard, plastic six-pack tops, or 1" slices of toilet paper roll cylinders for the rings. These could be made by invitees to your game-day presentation. In this way, visiting students would have a souvenir to take home with them to remember what they learned.

c. Hand Toss and Catch

This game required only a few simple resources and some practice. Games like it have been played by children in many places. To play, each child is given or collects three to six sticks about 3" to 5" in length. The sticks should be about 1/8" to 1/4" in diameter. The child lays them on top of the back of his or her hand, throws them into the air and catches them on the palm of the same hand.

As skill is developed, children toss sticks, spin around once, and catch them on the palm of the hand. Beginners may need to cup their hands to catch the sticks. This game can also be played with popsicle sticks or small pebbles.

d. Target Tossing Game

Corn cobs, pine cones, large seed pods, and other natural items were used in playing target games by different Native American groups. Such games developed accurate throwing skills.

If pine cones were available, for example, Native American children found ways to use them in tossing and accuracy games. Pine cones are relatively sturdy, and could be used over and over again. One such game might use hoops made out of flexible branches or strong stems. Hoop size varied and could be 12", 24", and 36" in diameter. The hoops were laid on the ground, and the children tried to toss the cones into them.

Have children devise a scoring system which provides for a certain number of points for cones that bounce in and then out and a higher number of points for cones that stay in the hoops. Set the hoop(s) on the ground 10 to 15 feet away from the throwing line and give each child three pine cones. Hoops can also be hung from branches and playground equipment to serve as targets. Other items such as corn cobs, seed pods, and bones might be used in target games.

e. Animal Races

Different Native American groups devised races based on imitating the running styles of local animals. Crabs, bears, and rabbits are easy animals to use in racing and relay games. A bear walk is a lumbering, wide-legged gait. A crab walk is done on all fours and sideways with heads facing up or down as you decide. A rabbit run can be a hopping or jumping race.

f. Pebble Toss

This game is similar to jacks but harder because the player does not get the benefit of a bounce. The player has five small stones or pebbles. Four are left on the ground, and one is held in the hand. The one in the hand is tossed in the air, one pebble on the ground is picked up (with the throwing hand), and then the pebble in the air is caught. The pebble is tossed again, and a second stone picked up. This is repeated until all four stones are picked up. In the next round, the child tries to pick up two stones at a time, and so on.

g. Pit or Pebble Game

Use six peach or plum pits or six similarly sized small pebbles to create this game. Children think of three different local creatures, such as beetles, spiders, lizards, birds, snakes, coyotes, and turtles, that Native Americans were probably familiar with. Children give the three animals a different number of points. For example, if the chosen animals are turtle, bird, and snake, the point system could be turtle = 3, bird = 4, and snake = 5. On one side of each of the stones or pits, with permanent marker each animal is drawn. Each animal appears on two different stones or pits. Turn all the stones or pits over. On three of the reverse sides (three are left blank) each of the three animals is drawn again with permanent marker. The stones or pits painted on two sides should not necessarily have the same animal on each side.

To play the game, the pits are put into a basket and tossed slightly in the air so that they all land in the basket. (Only those that land in the basket get counted.) After each toss, the player counts the number of points he or she gets for the animals shown face up on the pits. No points are scored for blank sides up. At the end of a round or two, the player with the most points wins. This game can be played so that when a player tosses and all pits show an animal, he or she automatically wins. This, however, is optional and you do not have to use this permutation of the game.

h. Make Up Your Own

Students may want to make up their own game to play at a game day. To do this, they need to think about the resources the Native Americans had available to them. They also need to remember that games were often designed to develop particular skills such as target accuracy.

2. Native American Storytelling on the Road

Children can share their exploration of Native American folktales and legends by taking their reenactments and retellings on the road to other classes. Encourage students to wear costumes and use props in the telling of their stories or in their skits. Children can also create an assembly presentation with their storytellings and intersperse the legends with "show and tell" about the background of some of the arts and crafts they have made or the Native American games they might have learned.

A simple Native American costume can be made by using fabric to create a tunic. The child wears tan pants and a plain white t-shirt over which the tunic is worn. To make a tunic, cut a 4-foot length of beige cloth in half lengthwise. The cut fabric will be about 18" to 22" wide and 4 feet long. Fold this fabric in half widthwise. Cut a head hole and slit so that the tunic can be slipped on easily. Have children fringe the bottom of the tunic and use markers to decorate it with Native American signs and symbols. Belt the tunic with yarn or a 2" wide length of the fabric you used to make the tunic. Headbands can also be made.

If you choose to do an assembly presentation, you might want to close the performance by having children dance a Native American friendship dance. The drum beat for such a dance is: one hard beat, one soft beat, repeat sequence. The dance is done by dancers forming a winding line in the staging area. The step to the drum beat is step right with the right foot, step right with the left foot or step, together, step, together. As the dancers dance, they call up or go get participants from the audience to join in the dance as the line snakes around the staging area. When the drum beat stops, the dance is over.

3. Recreate a Powwow for Parents

Perhaps your class would like to share what they have learned by inviting parents to a powwow. A powwow is one name for a community tribal meeting at which business and social time mix. Your powwow could include cooking and sharing some Native American dishes with parents, telling and reenacting legends, displaying arts and crafts, and performing the friendship dance described immediately above.

4. Host a Hawaiian Luau

Children love a luau. So do their parents. Explore the old and new of Hawaii by hosting a Hawaiian luncheon luau. Decorate with large brightly colored tissue flowers and crepe paper streamers in red and yellow (traditional Hawaiian royal colors). Have students greet guests with greetings of "aloha" and thank them for coming by saying "mahalo." Perhaps students would want to make string, straw, and paper flower leis for guests.

Have students bring potluck foods that contain lots of tropical fruit such as pineapple, papaya, mango, and coconut. Pineapple chicken and white rice make a good main dish/side dish combination. You might have children present skits or readings of Hawaiian legends they have researched or written. Some could present a Maori poi ball dance. (See directions in Item 3a of the lesson activities in Chapter 4.) Still others could sing a song like the "Hawaiian Wedding Song" in Hawaiian. If your event is scheduled for December, the Hawaiian Christmas song, "Mele Kahilikimake," could be sung.

Name: _____

CHAPTER 7
ACTIVITY SHEET

Native American Rebus Story

Write a story using words and symbols. If you make up your own symbols, list them in the Symbol Key.

Plant

Bird

People

Insects/Worms

Lizard

Water

Fish Net

Horned Mammal

Hunter

Symbol Key: _____

Resources

1. General resource books of factual information about a variety of Native American groups can be found in:

Series of First books published by Franklin Watts on different Native American groups (examples: *The Seminoles* by Martin Lee and *The Sioux* by Elaine Landau).

A New True Book series on Native American groups published by Childrens Press (example: *Aztec Indians* by Patricia McKissack (1985).

A series called *Indians of North America* published by Chelsea House Publishers (example: *The Huron* by Nancy Bonvillain (1989).

Native Dwellings: the Far North (Houses of Skin) by Bonnie Shemie published by Tundra Books (1989).

Native Dwellings: the Far North (Houses of Bark) by Bonnie Shemie published by Tundra Books (1990).

From Abenaki to Zuni: A Dictionary of Native American Tribes by Evelyn Wolfson published by Walker and Company (1988).

Handbook of American Indian Games by Allan and Paulette Macfarlan published by Dover Publications Inc. (1985).

The Village of Blue Stone by Stephen Trimble published by Macmillan Publishing Co. (1990). (Recreates one year in the life of an Anasazi community.)

The Earliest Americans by Helen Roney Sattler published by Clarion Books (1993).

The People Shall Continue by Simon Ortiz published by Childrens Book Press (1977) (revised 1988).

Series by Karen Liptak published by Franklin Watts regarding different aspects of Native American life: *Indian Ceremonies* (1992), *Indian Survival Skills* (1990), *Indian Sign Language* (1990), *Indian Tribal Chiefs* (1992).

Gifts of the Season: Life Among the Northwest Indians by Carol Batdorf published by Hancock House (1990).

2. The following cookbook is an excellent resource for Native American dishes that can be adapted quite easily for classroom cooking. The book is also filled with interesting facts about Native American foods, culture, and history, and contains a good bibliography.
Spirit of the Harvest-North American Indian Cooking by Beverly Cox and Marten Jacobs published by Stewart, Tabori and Chang, Inc. (1991).

3. These two books deal with modern Native American life and the creation of recognized art forms:
Pueblo Storyteller by Diane Hoyt-Goldsmith published by Holiday House, Inc. (1991).

Totem Pole by Diane Hoyt-Goldsmith published by Holiday House, Inc. (1990).

4. Here is a sample listing of some of the many wonderfully told and illustrated Native American tales which have been published in recent years.

Southeastern
Dancing Drum, A Cherokee Legend by Terri Cohlene published by Watermill Press (1990).

The First Strawberries, A Cherokee Story by Joseph Bruchac published by Dial Books for Young Readers (1993).

Northwestern
Grandmother Stories: Northwestern Indian Tales by Nashone published by Sierra Oaks (1987).

Raven: A Trickster Tale from the Pacific Northwest by Gerald McDermott published by Harcourt Brace Jovanovich (1993).

Ah Mo: Indian Legends from Washington State edited by Arthur E. Griffin published by Bainbridge (1989).

Plains
Where the Buffaloes Begin by Olaf Baker published by Puffin Books (1981).

The Legend of the Indian Paintbrush by Tomie DePaola published by G. P. Putnam's Sons (1988).

Quillworker, A Cheyenne Legend by Terri Cohlene published by Watermill Press (1990).

Iktomi and The Berries, A Plains Indian Story edited by Richard Jackson published by Franklin Watts (1989).

Northeastern
How the Seasons Came, an Algonquin Tale by Joanna Troughton published by Blackie Children's Books (1992).

Great Rabbit and the Long-Tailed Wildcat by Andy Gregg published by Albert Whitman & Company (1993).

The Rough-Face Girl by Rafe Martin published by Scholastic Inc. (1992) (a Cinderella-type story).

Southwestern
The Mouse Couple, A Hopi Tale by Ekkehart Malotki published by Northland Publishing (1988).

The Goat in the Rug as told to Charles L. Blood & Martin Link by Geraldine published by Macmillan Publishing Company (1990).

Arrow to the Sun, a Pueblo Indian Tale by Gerald McDermott published by Puffin Books (1974).

Monster Slayer: A Navajo Folktale retold by Vee Brown published by Northland Publishing Company (1991).

Compilations of North American Folktales from all over North America
Keepers of the Earth by Michael J. Caduto and Joseph Bruchac published by Fulcrum, Inc. (1988).

Keepers of the Animals by Michael J. Caduto and Joseph Bruchac published by Fulcrum, Inc. (1991).

North American Indian Stories: Star Tales by Gretchen Will Mayo published by Walker & Company (1987).

North American Indian Tales: Earthmaker's Tales by Gretchen Will Mayo published by Walker & Company (1989).

They Dance in the Sky: Native American Star Myths by Jean Guard Monroe and Ray A. Williamson published by Houghton Mifflin Company (1987).

Why the Possum's Tail Is Bare and Other Native American Indian Nature Tales collected by James E. Connolly published by Stemmer House (1985).

5. In addition to the classic *Island of the Blue Dolphins* by Scott O'Dell published by Dell Publishing Company (1960), here are three additional suggested novels with Native American themes:
Anpao by Jamake Highwater published by Harper Trophy (1992).

Julie of the Wolves by Jean Craighead George published by Harper & Row (1972).

The Listening Silence by Phyllis Root published by HarperCollins Publishing (1992).

6. Locate one of the following Hawaiian language resources to help you in exploring Hawaiian words and names:
The Pocket Hawaiian Dictionary by Mary Pukui, Samuel Elbert, and Esther Mookini published by the University of Hawaii Press (1975).

Let's Learn a Little Hawaiian by Ray Helbig published by Hawaiian Service, Inc. (1990) (contains translated boy and girl names).

In addition, *Hawaiian Legends of Tricksters and Riddlers* by Vivian L. Thompson published by Holiday House (1969) and *Spooky Stuffs-Hawaiian Ghost Stories* by Eric Knudsen published by Island Heritage Publishing (1974) provide selections of stories and legends from Hawaiian folk traditions.

THE OCEANS OF THE WORLD — OUR LAST FRONTIER

Through the study of the ocean as a theme, students can explore life science aspects of the ocean, geography of oceans and continents, the properties of water, and scientific exploration techniques.

CHAPTER AT A GLANCE

Lesson Activities

The Lesson Activities of this chapter provide children the opportunity to explore the different types of life that inhabit the ocean at different depths, and how animals adapt to their unique environments. The activities also provide ideas for exploring the issues of under - sea geography and how it relates to above-sea geography, vehicles for exploring the ocean, and the properties of water itself.

Writing Activities

The Writing Activities provide suggestions for both fanciful creative writing opportunities as well as research-based poetry and report projects.

Art and Craft Activities

The Art and Craft Activities provide ways for children to explore both fish and the action of the ocean through art.

Food Activities

The Food Activities provide ways in which children can explore cooking seafood as well as foods that use resources from the sea such as kelp to maintain their consistency and flavor.

Art Masters—Old and New

Art Masters - Old and New gives children an opportunity to explore the artistic works of the fauvist art movement of the early 1900s, a movement in which Henri Matisse and André Derain were leaders.

Sharing Activities

The Sharing Activities suggested for this chapter include ideas for assembly-style presentations and for meal events.

Lesson Activities

Background Information

1. Ocean Life Forms

The background information in this section provides general information about ocean habitats and life forms, the tide pool as a specific ocean habitat, and some of the ocean's scarier or odd-looking creatures.

a. Habitat Zones of Ocean Life

An amazing number of plants and animals inhabit the oceans of our Earth. Some sources suggest that more than 200,000 species of life inhabit the ocean waters of the world. The depth of the ocean waters as well as temperature, water pressure, currents, nutrient supply, and light affect the animals that live there.

The ocean is divided into both horizontal and vertical habitat zones in which the animals and plants of the ocean live. Several of these zones are divided again into sub-zones depending upon ocean depth, light, and life forms. Detailed background information about zones can be obtained from most encyclopedias and from ocean resource books. The information provided here is very basic. It will provide only general guidance for informing students about ocean habitats and helping them to undertake the lesson activities suggested in this chapter.

Horizontally, it can be said that the ocean is divided into the photic zone and the aphotic zone. The photic zone is that part of the ocean waters into which sunlight from the surface can penetrate. The depth of this zone depends upon the clarity or murkiness of particular ocean waters. It can go from the surface of the water to depths of 160 to 330 feet (50 to 100 meters). Plants can only grow in the photic zone where there is sunlight to nourish them.

The aphotic zone is the dark zone of the ocean into which no sunlight penetrates. It begins where the photic zone ends and continues to the ocean floor.

Two other basic zones of ocean life exist, and these can overlap with the photic and aphotic zones. These are the pelagic zone (open ocean water zone) and the benthic zone (ocean floor zone). The photic and benthic zones overlap in coastal areas such as tide pools. However, vast areas of the ocean are in the aphotic benthic zone (dark ocean floors) and we know little about life in these remote parts of the ocean floor.

Different ocean zones support different animal life forms. In the pelagic area, sharks, squid, eels, and jellyfish are found. In the deep benthic areas, luminous sharks and large-eyed or self-lighting creatures can be found. Nutrients are more limited at the aphotic ocean floor.

b. Tide Pool Life

Tide pools host a wide variety of ocean animal and plant life. Ocean plants can be green, red-brown, or brown in color. They can be delicate such as sea grass or large such as kelp. They have no roots, but holdfasts that anchor them to the ocean floor. They absorb nutrients from the water through stem and leaf. They often have air bladders that help them stay erect in the ocean current.

Most tide pool animals are invertebrates. The few small swimming fish are among the only vertebrates. Larger vertebrates such as ocean mammals (seals, porpoises, whales) can sometimes be seen from shore. Very basic background information is provided here on the animal groups commonly found in tide pools.

- **Invertebrates**

  Coelenterates. Coral and sea anemones are well-known coelenterates. In certain warm parts of the world coral may grow in tide pools. Coral are tiny animals that live in colonies and excrete the strong outer covering that we commonly think of as coral. Really this outer covering is like the skeletal remains of the once living coral colony. The animal itself looks like a very tiny sea anemone. Sea anemones are sometimes called the "flowers of the sea," but they are really animals. They settle in a location on a rock or hard place and live their whole lives there. They use their tentacles to sting small fish floating by which they then eat with a central mouth cavity.

Mollusks. The mollusks you think of first are those that grow one or two shells of their own in which to live. Those with one shell such as snails, tritons, and abalone are called univalves. Those with two shells such as clams, scallops, oysters, and mussels are called bivalves. The squid and the octopus are also mollusks, but they have no shells. They are called cephalopods and have soft bodies and brains located in the head area.

Echinoderms. Some well-known echinoderms are starfish, sea urchins, and sand dollars. Echinoderms are characterized by having a limy outer covering and being structured in a radiating pattern. Starfish arms radiate from the mouth cavity. Sea urchin spines radiate from the central cavity. The round sand dollar exoskeleton has a radiating star-like pattern on it.

Crustaceans. Crustaceans are very popular seafood with many people and include such delicacies as shrimp, crab, and lobster. They are related to the arthropod family on land and have complex nerve and muscle systems. Their outer coverings are made from a lightweight but strong substance called chitin. Most are scavengers and feed on dead or decaying animals. Barnacles are a very common crustacean and grow on ship bottoms, rocks, shells, crabs, and whales.

• **Vertebrates**
Fish. Fish have fins, scaly coverings, and internal skeletons. They are cold-blooded. Although many people think of tide pool fish as synonymous with colorful tropical fish, most tide pool fish are dull in coloring and small in size. Their dull coloring helps to camouflage them from predators such as sea birds and coastal sea mammals.

There are two basic types of fish: bony fish and cartilaginous. Bony fish have bone skeletons. Cartilaginous fish have skeletal structures made from cartilage, not bone. A shark is this type of fish.

c. "Monsters" of the Deep
Certain marine creatures have been the subject of legend over the years. Fish that were seldom seen, had poisonous qualities, or were just plain weird-looking were prime candidates for the creation of fantastic and exciting folk legends about their behavior. Many were and are harmless to humans. Background information is given here on some of these creatures. Students should be encouraged to find their own strange creature of the deep or to do additional research on an animal described here.

• **Poisonous Fish**
These fish are usually found in shallow water, most often in the tropics. Most are slow swimmers who live in reef or rocky areas so that they are protected, and some spend much time buried in the sand.

Stingrays. There are a number of different kinds of stingrays. They are usually flat with a tail that acts as the striking organ. They spend time buried in the sand, and when they strike, it is often because a human has stepped on them. The stinging tail has spines that also cut the victim's flesh.

Ratfish. The ratfish has a pointed spine in front of its top fin. The spine can inflict a painful wound, and certain parts of the body such as the reproductive organ seem to be poisonous when eaten.

Stonefish. This fish gives off poison through its spines. It is thought to be the deadliest of all fish. Its poison can kill a human in only a few minutes.

Sculpin. The sculpin is a type of scorpion fish, the body of which is covered with sharp spines. These appear in the fins, head, and gill coverings.

Filefish. This fish can grow to three feet long. Its flesh is poisonous when eaten.

Rockfish. These fish have spines in their fins which contain venom.

Pufferfish. The flesh of this fish is poisonous when eaten.

Lionfish. This fish has fins that look like bird feathers. They are very sharp and have a poisonous sting.

• **Ocean Animals with Odd Looks**
Oar fish. These long fish are seen in deeper waters, and may have looked like sea serpents to early sailors.

Squid. The squid is an unusual mollusk because it does not have a shell. It has a large head/body area and ten tentacles which it uses for mobility. As a defense, it can spray an inky substance into the water to hide and then escape from a predator.

Porcupine fish. This fish has spines and puffs up to protect itself.

Octopus. The octopus is also a mollusk without a shell. It is a shy but intelligent animal. Because of its strange looks with a large soft head and eight free-floating legs, it has been described in fiction as a dangerous animal that will wrap its tentacles around a victim and squeeze. This animal can also spray ink into the water to help distract an attacker while it escapes.

Hammerhead shark. This shark has a large, flat, hammer-like head with eyes protruding from the sides of it. Although it is a relatively docile shark, its looks have inspired fear and legends.

Sunfish. This giant fish can grow to 13 feet in length and weigh 1,000 pounds. It is found in tropical waters and often floats on its side on the water's surface. It is not a good swimmer.

Whale shark. This fish is perhaps the world's largest. It can weigh up to two times as much as an African elephant. Despite their size, whale sharks are harmless plankton eaters.

Swallower. These fish can swallow other fish twice their size because of their hinged jaws. The whole fish is then digested slowly.

Angler fish. This is a deep sea fish that has a lure in front of its head to attract prey.

Great white shark. This huge white shark has been described as a man-killer and has on occasion attacked swimmers. Its tremendous size and huge jaws, together with reports of actual attack incidents, give rise to stories of its attack abilities.

Electric eels. Eels are long slender fish that look like snakes. The electric eel has the ability to sting a victim with an electric-type shock.

2. Under-Sea Level Geography

The oceans of the world are not really separate bodies of water. Oceans cover over 70 percent of the earth's surface, and the oceans of the earth connect with one another around the continents.

If you could drain the oceans, what would the ocean floor look like? It would look surprisingly like land on the continents. You would see valleys, mountain peaks, plateaus, and plains. These surfaces are lower on the earth's crust because the rock that formed them was heavier than the rock that formed the continents that sit above sea level. This heaviness helped the rock form deep depressions in the earth's surface.

Where do our continents end? We commonly think of continents as ending at the seashore, but scientists who study oceans (oceanographers) do not agree. These experts consider the end of a continent to be the end of a gentle slope of submerged land that continues downward from the continent's coastline to a depth of about 600 feet. There are mountains, valleys, hills, and plains on this area which is called the continental shelf.

After the continents end, there are many more geologic structures similar to those found above sea level. There are huge mountain ranges called ridges. In the middle of most oceans between continents is a mid-ocean ridge which is like a massive range of underwater mountains. There are also individual underwater peaks called seamounts. If a seamount is tall enough, it may form islands in the middle of the ocean. Underwater flat-topped mountains are called guyots.

Lower parts of the ocean floor are called basins and abyssal plains. Huge trenches also dive to incredible depths in the ocean floor. All of these geologic formations—mountains, plains, and trenches—have names just as mountain ranges and canyons do on the continents.

The surface of the continents continues to change because of erosion and volcanic eruption. Similarly, volcanoes beneath the ocean's surface continue to change the shape of the ocean floor. The Hawaiian Islands were created over millions of years by volcanic activity beneath the sea. To this day, the islands continue to be changed and shaped by active volcanoes.

3. Ocean-Going Vehicles and Exploration of the "Seven Seas"

Here is a short history in bullet format of exploration of the oceans. The changes in ocean-going vessels are apparent when the information below is read together with the background information in Chapter 3 which describes timelines for water vehicles.

600 b.c. - Egyptian pharaoh Necho circumnavigates Africa.

112 b.c. - Greek explorer Eudoxus sails to India and western Africa.

100 b.c. - Poseidonius measures ocean to depth of 6,000 feet.

a.d. 20 - King Juba of Morocco explores Canary Islands.

a.d. 150 - Ptolemy makes a map of the world that shows oceans and a sphere-shaped Earth.

a.d. 950 - Maori sailors discover New Zealand.

a.d. 1000 - Vikings explore Atlantic coast of North America.

1492 - Christopher Columbus explores the West Indies.

1502 - Vespucci concludes that South America is not India, but a separate continent.

1521 - Ferdinand Magellan dies on an expedition that resulted in the first circumnavigation of the earth. He attempted deep sea experiments.

1606 - Portuguese Luis Valdez de Torres sails between New Guinea and Australia.

1607 - Englishman John Smith reaches Virginia.

1620 - Pilgrims reach North America.

1642 - Abel Tasman sails around Australia.

1723 - Russian explorer Fedorov explores northwestern coast of North America.

Late 1700s - James Cook sails around New Zealand and Antarctica.

1840 - French explorer Dumont d'Urville discovers Antarctic Islands.

1853 - American Elisha Kane leads expedition to the Arctic.

1854 - U.S. Commodore Matthew Perry travels to Japan.

1892 - Scottish oceanographer William Bruce explores Antarctica.

1943 - Jacques Cousteau and Emile Gagnan invent scuba apparatus.

1947 - Thor Heyerdahl of Norway sails a balsa raft called the Kon Tiki from Peru to Polynesia.

1958 - American explorer Anderson crosses the North Pole in submarine.

1960 - Submerged Triton submarine circumnavigates the earth.

early 1960s - Navy's SEALAB I does underwater sea investigation.

1985 - Robot submarine Argo discovers sunken Titanic.

4. Properties of Water

Nearly three-quarters of the earth is covered with water. Some of it is fresh water in lakes, streams, and rivers. The vast majority, however, is the salt water of our oceans. Over millennia, as water rushes over rocks and geologic formations on dry land, it picks up salt which is then deposited in the sea. Over time, the collected salts have resulted in the oceans becoming salty. There are about thirty pounds of salt in every 1,000 pounds of ocean water. Salt water is about 3 1/2 percent heavier than the same amount of fresh water.

Water can be found around the earth in three forms. It is in liquid form in rain, rivers, oceans, and unfrozen lakes and ponds. It is in solid form in glaciers, snow, hail, ice, and frozen lakes and ponds in winter. It is vapor in clouds and steam.

Water is made from molecules. All molecules are made from atoms. Each molecule of water is made from two atoms of hydrogen and one atom of oxygen. The atoms stick together to make each molecule of water. The oxygen atom provides most of the weight of the water molecule. When lots of water molecules are together as they are in the ocean, they can create great pressure. At a mile under the surface of the ocean, water pressure is about 2,300 pounds per square inch. Just as people cannot survive in outer space without protective equipment and clothing, people can not survive in deep sea waters without protective pressurized vehicles.

Water molecules on the surface of a body of water, even a body of water as small as that contained in a glass, have a tendency to want to stick together. Below the surface of the water, the molecules pull at each other from all sides, but on the surface of the water nothing pulls at the molecules from the top. As the molecules pull toward each other and downward from the surface, they form an invisible skin that is called "surface tension." A number of different insects take advantage of surface tension to stride on top of pond and lake water.

5. Conservation and Pollution of Water

Water is a precious resource on our Earth. We need fresh water to live. The ocean is a vast resource. It participates with forces in our atmosphere to create weather conditions. It is perhaps foremost an incredible source of foods and useful plant and animal by-products. For the waters of our Earth to remain healthy for us to use and for important marine animals and plants to inhabit, they must not be polluted. While the oceans are vast and can absorb some pollutants, they and their inhabitants are not unaffected by human actions.

Our oceans become polluted by human carelessness such as litter, dumping of wastes and sewage by cities and manufacturers, and accidents such as oil spills and hazardous waste disposal leaks.

Sometimes entire habitats can be polluted and harmed by a major oil spill such as the one by the *Exxon Valdez*. Scientists have developed some ways to clean up oil spills, but great damage is still done. Some of the clean-up methods include using polyurethane chips to absorb oil, skimming of the oil, using detergents and dispersants to clean up the spill, and simply burning the oil off.

A major source of continuing pollution is regular, deliberate dumping of human sewage and industrial waste. While most sewage is treated before being dumped, it can still pose health and contamination problems to off-shore waters and fish. Industrial wastes can include dangerous chemicals and animal and plant matter. Electric energy plants that utilize ocean water for cooling and then discharge warmed water into adjacent waters can also harm marine habitats.

Litter is very damaging to ocean waters. Plastics are especially bad because they do not break down in the environment. Six-pack tops and hard plastics trap animals. Soft plastic bags and mylars can look like floating jellyfish to predators who try to eat them and then choke or suffocate. A reduction in simple human carelessness could help markedly reduce marine animal deaths.

Another way to help our world's water is to conserve it. Simple acts each day can waste or save water. A typical five minute shower can use 20 to 30 gallons of water. A bathtub of water uses the same. Can we use low-flow shower devices? Can we take shorter showers? Can we bathe in less tub water? There are many ways to conserve in our every day practices. The average person uses as much as 50 gallons of water each day.

For more information on water pollution and conservation, please refer to the background information in Chapter 1.

Project Directions

1. Ocean Life Forms

The following projects offer some ideas for different ways of exploring the different types of animal life supported by the ocean environment.

a. Ocean Zones Wall Mural

Create a dramatic over-sized wall mural that depicts the different life forms found at different ocean depths. If you have the room, have each zone be 12" to 30" high and 5 to 6 feet long, as you decide. Animals in the various ocean habitat zones look different from one another in some ways and have different survival adaptations. For example, below the photic zone, there is no light at all, save for that generated by the animals themselves. You might want to dramatize this habitat change by using darker and darker background paper or paint for each deeper ocean zone. Children will see in the completed project the different types of animals that inhabit each zone as well as the diminution of plant life which, of course, cannot grow without some sunlight.

One way to create the watery background of these ocean depths is to use strips of colored butcher paper that has a shiny side so that the water part of the scene can be fingered painted onto the strip. Again, the colors used to finger paint would be progressively darker as you descend to the ocean depths. Finger painting seems to be exclusively an activity for younger children, but older children enjoy the process just as much.

A fun way to recreate some of the ocean plants of the surface zone of the ocean is to glue green cellophane Easter grass to the mural. It is glued at the top to suggest that it is floating on the ocean's surface, and then drifts down in a random fashion from there.

Fish can be created by first coloring, painting, or pastel drawing the individual fish on white paper. Then cut the fish out and glue it into the proper zone. If children research this mural from the "Ocean" research heading in an encyclopedia, they should be able to find information about the different animals at the different depths or zones. Many encyclopedias even contain ocean depth charts with animal life visually depicted.

Remind children to label both the different zones, and the animals and plants they add to them.

b. Create a Tide Pool Environment

If you live near an ocean, you may be able to visit a tide pool or marine museum with a tide pool exhibit. Even without this experience though, you can create your own tide pool in the classroom. Use either an old aquarium, a discarded children's small summer splash pool, or a large sheet of blue paper (3 x 6 feet) on the floor in a corner of the classroom.

To fill your tide pool, ask children to bring any shells, starfish, sand dollars, crab shells, and the like that they may have at home. Put some sand or sand-colored aquarium gravel at the bottom and some rocks and coral. Tide pools are rocky areas with many places for fish to hide. Have children make some tide pool animals to put in the display. Perhaps they can work in groups to make different tide pool animals, write group reports on those animals, and make labels for the tide pool display.

Here are some ideas for how to make models of some tide pool fish children might want to include in the exhibit:

- **Sea Urchin**
  Use a ball of soft clay or half of a Styrofoam ball to create the exoskeleton of a sea urchin. Paint this part purple. Dye toothpicks purple in food coloring or paint them. When dry, insert them around the body of the sea urchin. Dry spaghetti "spines" can be stuck in a soft clay exoskeleton.
- **Starfish**
  Make a starfish from a structure of crunched and taped newspaper. Papier-mâché over this structure with thin strips of newspaper and starch. Students might want to add to the surface texture by inserting rows of round-end push pins into the surface of the starfish papier-mâché. When dry, paint it in the golden-orange color of a starfish. A child might want to decorate the surface by painting additional small designs on it with a darker color and a fine point brush.
- **Vertebrate Fish**
  Small, dull-colored fish often inhabit tide pools. These can also be made from papier-mâché, and hidden among the rocks and shells of your tide pool. These types of dull-colored fish are often a dark gray color which helps them to remain camouflaged in the midst of their environment. Small fish can also be made by stuffing two-sided paper fish with cotton for a three-dimensional effect. They can be made to stay upright by affixing them to wooden skewers or chopsticks and standing them in small balls of plasticine clay.

- **Other Tide Pool Animals**
  You can use papier-mâché or clay to recreate other sea creatures such as sea cucumbers,

limpets, and chitons. Unfired clay objects can be painted with tempera paint mixed with glue to make the finished product stronger and glossier.

c. Ocean Food Chain

Have children recreate an ocean food chain or ecosystem by using a sheet of white paper and three paper clips. The child folds the paper in quarters and cuts out the four rectangles. Each rectangle is hole punched at top and bottom. Each of the four pieces of paper shows one animal of an ocean food chain. Children can research a particular food chain or they can use a big fish/little fish/plankton approach. Some sample food chains are:

Sharks eat pollock who eat herring who eat plankton.

People eat cod who eat whiting who eat herring.

Birds eat starfish who eat mollusks who eat plankton.

One animal is drawn on each piece of paper. They are then assembled in food-chain order using the paper clips to attach one to another. They can be hung on bulletin boards or from the ceiling like mobiles. Food chains can also be made using strips of white paper which are then assembled like a paper chain.

d. Fish as Food Report and Geography Display

As a report concept for the study of ocean life, consider having children explore a fish (or an invertebrate) as a food resource used by humans. To do a report on life in the sea with this twist will help reinforce the sea as a major resource and geography concepts since different ocean life forms are harvested from different parts of the world. It also reinforces environmental issues as related to the sea, both as a friend and a resource to humans.

To choose a fish to report on, children can first look in an encyclopedia under the name of a fish of their choice, under the research caption "Fishing Industries," or under the "Industry" heading of a seacoast or island nation of their choice.

The report on the fish or invertebrate can include:

-Whether the creature is vertebrate or invertebrate
-Bony or cartilage skeleton
-Life habits such as food, reproduction, habitat, solitary or schooling, life span, etc.
-What countries harvest the fish
-Any endangerment or pollution problems faced

To complement this report, ask children to make small paper version of their fish (labeled as to species) to pin onto a class bulletin board that displays a map of the world. The fish (or several copies of it) is placed on the location(s) of the world in which it is found and harvested.

e. "Sea Serpent" Report

In legend, stories of sea serpents abound. They probably derive from sightings of strange looking fish, fish that attacked humans or fish with poisonous attributes, along with, of course, a generous helping of human imagination. Ask children to do a short research report on a "monster" of the deep. Some ideas for fish subjects for such a report are included in the background information above, but each child should feel free to research strange ocean creatures and come up with a research subject of his or her choice.

The report should include information about the marine animal's classification (fish, mollusk, etc.), food and hunting habits, adaptations (camouflage coloring, defense mechanisms such as spines, ink spray, speed, poison), reproduction, ocean habitat zone, endangerment, and a statement as to why the student believes this animal and its habits might have led to legends about terrifying sea monsters.

2. Under Sea Geography

Use sea-related geography map-making exercises to relay general principles of geography while reinforcing lessons about our oceans and the roles they play in our lives. This can be done in several ways.

a. Undersea Relief Map

Divide children into cooperative learning groups and have each group be responsible for creating a relief map of one of the world's ocean areas. Each group needs a plywood board (approximately 24" to 30" square) to begin the project. Using undersea relief maps which can be found in ocean reference books as well as encyclopedias, children draw the general area of ridges, basins, and trenches. They then recreate these in as accurate a manner as possible with papier-mâché. Different levels are achieved by crushing newspaper and taping it to appropriate parts of the map. Once height levels are in place this way, thin strips of newspaper dipped in starch are used to papier-mâché over the surface of the map. When it is dry, the map is painted according to levels and depths, a key is made, and major ridges, basins, plains, and trenches are labeled.

This activity reinforces the concept that geographic formations on the earth exists both above and below ocean levels.

b. United States Relief Map

Another way to explore this issue but with a twist is to make a class relief map of your state or your region of the United States. The relief map is made in the same way as the maps described in the preceding section. Once the map is completed, children will imagine that the sea level rises in the area covered by the relief map. This is consistent with history in vast parts of the United States. At times during the evolution of the earth to the state of the continents and oceans as they exist today, different sections of the North American continent were underwater. Many today claim that with the threat of global warming, thawing glaciers will result in future changes in coastal areas and the submersion of some currently dry lands.

The idea with this activity is to help the children explore how different their state or region would look if the ocean level rose substantially, and to draw the parallels with existing undersea geography. It can also help children appreciate why ocean fossils are present in local mountain and foothill areas—that indeed these areas really were underwater at some point millions of years ago.

To show how their relief map would change if part of the area covered were submerged under the ocean water, students decide what the new sea level on their map will be. They will locate on a sheet of blue or blue-painted posterboard (which is the same size as the plywood base) those areas of their maps that are higher than their designated "new sea level." Once these areas are located on the posterboard, they are cut out. An exacto knife works well for this project. Adult help may be necessary with this part of the project.

When the cut-out board is placed over the relief map, only the areas higher than the new sea level protrude from the holes in the second board. As a result, the students can see that their state or region would be a series of islands if the sea level rose. The features that sit under the new sea level are the same kinds of geographic features that exist under the ocean waters today.

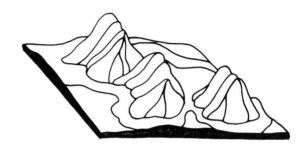

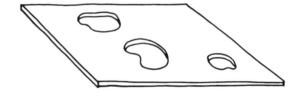

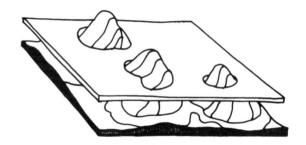

c. Active Islands

Another way to explore these geography issues is by focusing the activities described above on the formation of Hawaii, the group of islands that make up our fiftieth state. Volcanic activity continues today both above and below the water's surface in this island area. Consider having your students explore ocean geography by:

- Creating a relief map of the ocean floor around the Hawaiian Islands in the manner described above.
- Once the relief map is completed, have the children cut a second piece of cardboard or

posterboard so that the islands of Hawaii come through the holes, thereby allowing the children to see the ocean floor and to better visualize how subsurface ocean features relate to above-sea geography.

- Use this as an opportunity for children to build their own volcanoes. Here are two possible volcano activities:

i) Children can make individual volcanoes by using a plastic cup glued to a piece of cardboard, strips of newspaper, and thinned plaster. The newspaper strips are dipped into the thinned plaster, and draped from the inside of the cup to the outside cardboard so that the cup forms the center of a small volcano. When the entire circumference of the cup is finished, let it dry. Then put baking soda into the cup; add a few drops of red food coloring. Pour white vinegar into the cup and watch your eruption happen!

ii) Another activity is making an underwater volcano. In a clear pitcher of cold water, submerge a small cup of boiling water colored with red food color. To securely submerge the cup, push it into the pitcher with clothespins that you have attached to each side of the cup. As the cup is submerged, the hot red water will erupt out of the small cup into the cold water. Have children discuss what happens to underwater eruptions of molten rock as the rock cools. It often creates what are referred to as lava pillows.

3. Ocean Vehicles and Exploration of the "Seven Seas"

The history of human exploration of the continents, space, and the ocean is a history of human curiosity about the unknown, a history of trial and error, and a history of educated scientific method and exploration technique. All these things contribute to human success in finding out about the unknown. The ocean is considered by many to be a last frontier, although there is obviously still much to be learned about outer space.

Help children develop an appreciation of the history of ocean and ocean-going exploration by making a timeline of major developments in the sea-going vessel, as well as major ocean explorations. The timeline can be two-tiered. The top tier shows the changes in vessels from the dugouts of early peoples to the first sailboats in Egypt, from the clipper ship to the submarine. The bottom tier could mark major scientific explorations, expeditions, or discoveries that utilized travel on the seas or travel under the seas. Each child could adopt a vessel or event, and illustrate it on a 3" x 5" card with a sentence or two about its significance to display on the timeline.

4. Properties of Water Explorations

You can use ocean studies to explore basic physical science issues related to water and its properties. Surface tension and liquid densities are areas easily covered in detail. Here are some ideas for inexpensive and easy class experiments that students enjoy. As you and your students do the experiments, make sure to have students use the scientific method by recording the steps, hypotheses, and results on the Scientific Method Activity Sheet or by using the Scientific Hypothesis and Results Activity Sheet, both of which are at the back of Chapter 9.

a. Density and Buoyancy

Here are several ways to explore the relative density of liquids such as water and oil, discover the differences in density between fresh and salt water, and look at the buoyancy of objects in salt and fresh water.

- **Liquid Layers**
Have children begin to explore the concept of different densities both in liquids and in other things such as wood, plastic, and metals. Have dark corn syrup or molasses, water, and vegetable oil on hand. In a clear cup, carefully and slowly pour in molasses or corn syrup until you have a layer 1 1/2" deep. The second layer is water which should be poured gently down the side of the cup until it is also about 1" to 1 1/2" deep. Again, very gently, pour the oil down the side of the cup to form a third layer on top of the water. With the liquid layers, children can see that liquids have different densities from one another, and, as a result, one layer will float on top of the other. This experiment can be used to draw parallels between the behavior of oil in the cup and the behavior of oil spills on the ocean.

Once you have created your liquid layers, ask children what they think will happen when other items such as small erasers, paper, Styrofoam, paper clips, rocks, toothpicks, and leaves are dropped in. As you and the students experiment, you will discover that different things stop sinking at different levels. When you have completed the initial drop into the layers, try dropping a cotton ball in to let the children see what will happen over time.

As a holiday twist on this experiment, you can do an investigation into the density of liquids using slightly different liquids, and coloring them for the holiday of your choice. Use water, baby oil, rubbing alcohol, and clear plastic cups for each child to create the liquid layers.

To make a holiday liquid layer, color the water and the alcohol with different food coloring depending on the holiday. For example, if you do this project near the Fourth of July or Presidents' Day, you can color the water red and the alcohol blue. If you do the project near Cinco de Mayo, you can color the water red and the alcohol green. The clear baby oil remains uncolored. Water is the bottom layer. Oil comes second. Alcohol is the last, carefully dribbled down the side of the cup.

An interesting related activity is to weigh equal amounts of the different liquids. Alcohol weighs less than water, but you will need a fairly sensitive scale to show this in a class setting.

• Egg in Water Experiment

Can the density of water be changed? What are the differences between less dense and more dense water? Use this progression of activities to help students answer these questions. Have children use the Scientific Hypothesis and Results Activity Sheet at the back of Chapter 9 to record their thoughts as the demonstration proceeds.

First, place a clear cup of tap water on the table. Mark the water line on the cup with marker or tape. Then drop a fresh, unboiled egg into the cup. Have the students predict whether or not it will float or sink. The egg will sink.

Next, have children change the density of the water by adding salt one tablespoon at a time. They should stir between each spoonful. Does the water level change? How much salt

can they get into the water before the water level starts to change? The water absorbs the salt to become more dense.

Lastly, the students drop the egg into the water again. Does it sink or float? It will float. Now the water is heavier than the egg.

Questions for teachers to use on the Scientific Hypothesis and Results Activity Sheet at the back of Chapter 9 for children to consider during the experiments are:

Will the egg float in fresh water?
Will the water go over the water level marker if we add salt to it—e.g., 1/4 cup salt?
Will the egg float in salt water?

• Boat Building

Children can explore buoyancy and water displacement by engaging in some simple boat building. Give children the dimensions for the boats they are to build (no longer than 6" to 7" inches, no wider than 3" inches). Mark the water level on the side of the container with marker or tape. Then have a cargo contest. Which boat can carry the most cargo? As a boat is filled, it displaces more water in the container in which it sits, and the water level will rise depending on the respective sizes of both boat and container. For more information about holding a boat float contest, see the lesson activities in Chapter 3.

b. How Strong is Surface Tension?

With this group of activities, children explore the makeup of the water molecule and surface tension in many ways. Water molecules try to stick together, and the process of these molecules trying to stick together and forming what some refer to as an invisible skin creates what is called "surface tension."

Before further exploring the properties of water, have children recreate a water molecule using toothpicks and marshmallows. To do this, have children bring in bags of colored marshmallows and toothpicks. Each child picks two marshmallows of one color (for the hydrogen atoms) and one marshmallow of another color (for the oxygen atom). Since the oxygen atom is heavier than the hydrogen atom, you may want children to use a big marshmallow for the oxygen and two little ones for the hydrogen. With three toothpicks, the children put their marshmallows together in a triangular way to reinforce the structure of the water molecule.

Some ways to explore the surface tension of water are described below:

• **Wax and Water**

On a sheet of waxed paper, drop a few droplets of water. Have children try to move the water within the drops with a toothpick. The water tries to stay contained in the droplet shape. If you rub the toothpick across a bar of soap and then try the same exercise, the drops begin to break down because soap destroys the surface tension of water. Put a few drops of liquid soap in a glass of water, and ask the children what they think will happen when they try to move the soapy drops on waxed paper with a toothpick. Put a few soapy droplets on the waxed paper. How do they act differently from the non-soapy drops?

• **Pepper in a Pie Plate**

Pour 1/2" of water into a pie plate. Shake some pepper onto the water. Rub your finger on a bar of soap, and put your finger into the pie plate. What does the pepper do? It races away from your finger. Why? Because the soap particles rush into the water dispersing surface tension.

Or you can float a needle on the water, and then break the surface tension by dripping a couple of drops of soap into the water which will cause the needle to sink.

• **Fill it to the Brim**

Fill a glass of water to the brim. Can you put anything else into this glass? Have children see if surface tension will help them if they try to put pennies or paper clips one at a time and gently into the glass of water. How many pennies or clips can they fit into the glass before the surface tension breaks?

• **Drops on a Penny**

Using an eye dropper, water, and a penny, have children investigate surface tension in another way. First, children guess how many drops of water they think the penny will hold. Then they add water drops to the top of the penny, one at a time. Drops must be added gently and close to the surface of the penny. Have them try the same experiment on the reverse side of the penny. Are the results different? Why might they be different? How are the sides different from one another? Does the engraving change the amount of drops the penny will hold? Next, try the same experiment, but this time use water with a few drops of soap in it. What happens? Is there any surface tension?

c. Characteristics of Water Poster

Reinforce concepts about water by letting each child use half sheets of posterboard or construction paper 12" by 24" in size to make a poster about some water concept covered in class or which the child has researched. Many poster ideas can be gleaned from looking at resource books on water or encyclopedia articles on water. Some ideas are:

-Fresh water sources - ground water, rivers, lakes, glaciers
-The three physical states of water
-Temperatures at which water boils and freezes (and changes caused by altitude)
-Water conservation - ways to conserve water
-Water pollution - ways water gets polluted
-Water delivery systems such as canals, aqueducts, screw wells
-Water treatment
-Water cycle
-Salt water versus fresh water
-Water molecule
-How water gets to the ocean
-Surface tension
-Buoyancy and water displacement

5. Conservation and Pollution of Water

For activities in which students explore how water becomes polluted and how to conserve water as a resource, see the activities in the lesson activities section of Chapter 1. Another good resource is the experiment in this chapter on liquid layers that provides a parallel for oil spills on the ocean's surface.

Writing Activities

1. Chapter Vocabulary

Vocabulary words and phrases for this chapter's theme can include:

Oceanography
Continent
Geography
Topology
Elevation
Seamount
Abyssal plain
Bay
Sea
Ocean
Gulf
Invertebrate
Vertebrate
Coelenterate
Echinoderm
Mollusk
Crustacean
Tide pools
Photic zone
Benthic zone
Habitat
Bivalve
Univalve
Bony fish
Shark
Continental shelf
Island
Volcano
Fishing industry
Fisheries
Harvest
Fossil

2. Marine Careers Report

Ask children to talk with their parents and others about different jobs and careers that involve exploration of the ocean, ocean or water safety, or jobs that must be performed in or near ocean waters. Ask children to write a short five-point report on the career. Students can do library and encyclopedia research to obtain information for the report. If appropriate to your geographic locale, they can interview people they know who might have water-related jobs or people who work at marine environments or facilities such as Coast Guard offices or marine museums. Some sample careers to give children ideas are:

U.S. Navy crew and officers
U.S. Coast Guard careers
Off-shore oil riggers
Fishermen
Oceanographer (biological, geological, and others)
Marine biologist
Fisheries manager
Divers
Cargo ship crew or workers
Cruise ship crew or workers
Yacht racers
Pier construction workers
Ocean reclamation workers
Merchant marines
Lifeguards
Environmental engineers (oil spill clean-up)

3. If I Were . . .

After you have begun your classroom exploration of the ocean frontier, ask children to pretend that they are marine researchers. What would they investigate? What kind of underwater vehicle would they travel in to explore ocean depths? Would they want to explore how the ocean and weather relate? Would they want to investigate tide pool life? Would they want to explore ocean ecology and how to clean up oil spills? Have the children write a short essay stating what they would like to learn more about or what question they want answered, and why their chosen investigation interests them or is important to them and the world.

4. Marine Acrostic

Combine an art project with an acrostic writing project by having children pick a marine animal and write an acrostic about it using the animal's name. Any ocean animal can be chosen and the writing project can be fanciful about the creature and its characteristics or it can be factual based upon a short research effort.

Example:

A is for always using its tentacles to capture prey.
N is for not moving around from place to place.
E is for eating small fish that it stings.
M is for making people think it is an ocean flower.
O is for often closing up when danger is near.
N is for never having a skeleton or a hard outer covering.
E is for eating with a central mouth cavity.

The completed acrostic can be written out and mounted on or adjacent to the child's artistic version of the sea creature. This can simply be drawn on paper, painted, or cut out of construction paper.

5. Fish Riddles

Children enjoy coming up with riddles about any subject. Ocean creatures are good fodder for such creative writing activities.

Examples:

Q. I have small tooth-like scales, a cartilage skeleton and as many teeth as I need through my life. Who am I?

A. A shark.

Q. I have five arms, thousands of tube feet and one mouth. Who am I?

A. A starfish.

6. Plan a Voyage

Have students work in cooperative learning groups to plan an ocean exploration voyage and write a joint report. Each child works on one element of the report and writes his or her paragraph upon a sheet that is bound with the others in the final report folder. Children can illustrate the report if they want.

The voyage planned can be of the Columbus variety, the Pilgrim variety, the Darwin type, World War II submarine type, or a modern sea exploration. Resource books abound for the supplies and materials carried on board during the ocean explorations of the 15th through 20th centuries. Areas to be explored in the report are:

-Food to be taken, both live animals and stored food
-Purpose of the trip - what is to be explored, investigated, or discovered
-Type of sea vessel used to make the trip, including a basic description of its physcal features
-Route of the trip and time it will take in the vessel chosen
-Other supplies and materials such as navigational devices, ropes, etc.
-Staffing that will be necessary such as captain, navigator, first mate, boatswain, cook, sailors

7. Captain, We're Sighted A Sea Serpent

Ask each child to create a fanciful sea serpent. Tell children to let their imaginations run wild about how the creature looks, what it eats, where it spends most of its time, and its adaptations to live in the sea environment (for breathing, moving, etc.). You can structure the project as a descriptive project only or ask that children think of a sea creature and write a story about it from its point of view. Perhaps some children will want to focus on what the sea creature thinks of the humans and their sea-going vessels.

8. Fish Tales

Have children take a traditional fairy tale and rewrite it in a short story with fish as the main characters and a watery habitat as the locale. Examples might be "Goldiscales Goldfish and the Three Bass," "Little Redfish Riding Hood and the Wolffish," "Amberjack Fish and the Seaweed Stalk," and "Three Little Pompanos and the Big Bad Shark."

Art and Craft Activities

1. Ride the Wave Monoprint

Children create wave monoprints using 12" x 18" white construction paper, blue tempera paint, brushes, and a felt marker. First, children use a squirt of blue paint on a washable table surface or flat linoleum board to create a simple wave design. This can be done with one finger or with a brush. When the wave design is complete, the child presses the white construction paper firmly and evenly on the design so that the design is transferred to the paper. The paper is then pulled off the paint and set out to dry. Once dry, the children can highlight the wave design with a thick black marker. Caution students to use the black highlighting in only two or three places on the wave design; otherwise the marker can overtake the wave design and undermine the overall look of the monoprint.

2. Try Gyotaku

Gyotaku is Japanese fish printing. It can be done on t-shirts, fabric, and, yes, paper. To make a fish print, ask a local fish market or fresh fish section of the grocery store if you can have two or three fish to use for the project. (Oriental fish markets can be great source of inexpensive whole fresh fish.) Fish must have prominent scales in order to make a good print. For example, red snapper and flounder work well. Trout do not. Ask your fish seller to donate fish that are too old to sell. They smell a little bit, but work very well. Once you begin painting with them, the smell seems to dissipate.

Before you start the art part of the project, let children explore the fish by touching its scales, eyes, fins and gills. Once all the children have had a chance to look at the fish, begin the fish printing process. For printing on paper, the child paints completely one side of the fish with slightly thinned tempera paint. Dark colors like black, green, or blue look very good. A very thin coat of paint works best. Then a sheet of white construction or art paper is placed on the fish, and pressed firmly over all parts of the body so that the paint

is transferred to the paper. The paper is gently pulled off the fish, revealing a dramatic fish print. For printing on fabric or clothing, fabric or acrylic paint must be used. Also, the process is reversed in that the painted fish is picked up, pressed carefully onto the fabric, and then removed. Remember to use a thin coat of paint if you want your scales to show up clearly on the print.

3. Life in a Fishbowl

Have children create their own "art" versions of a fish tank habitat with this project. Using a white paper plate as the background for the tank or fishbowl, children finger paint the plate blue or use marker or the side of a blue crayon to color it. They glue sand and small shells onto the bottom of the plate, and then cut out small fish from construction paper to glue onto the "water." Sequins, glitter, or salt can be added for a shimmery, scaly look. Once the project is complete and dry, cover it with a sheet of clear or blue plastic wrap for a fishbowl effect. The plastic wrap is simply taped in place on the reverse side of the plate.

4. Tide Pool Tear Art

There are a couple of ways children can create a tide pool scene using tear art.

The first method is to have children create a finger paint background from blue finger paint. For finger paint, use liquid starch and a spurt of blue paint or a teaspoon of dry blue tempera powder. As children finish their finger painting, have them think about the final designs they want to leave on the paper. With their fingers, they can create layers of turbulent sea designs. If the children want their tide pool to be calm, they create layers of rolling designs. If they want a more stormy, wave-crashing look, they finger paint rows of twisting designs. Some children really reject the idea of leaving the page with rows of "sea" designs so feel free to let them complete their papers with any abstract design.

Once dry, children tear pieces of gray, black, and brown construction paper into rock shapes for the tide pool area and glue them to the bottom of the paper. At the top of the paper, children can indicate floating kelp and plant life by gluing on a few shreds of green cellophane Easter grass. Another way to create plant life is to use thin, 1/4" to 1/2" strips of green tissue paper that are glued vertically onto the picture at 2" intervals. Fish for the tide pool can be torn or cut out of construction paper or cut out of magazines or wrapping paper and glued in and around the rocks.

A second way to create the tear art tide pool is to simply start with a blue sheet of construction paper and create the tear art picture on top of it in the same way described above.

5. Fish Mobile

Consider using a Hula-Hoop®, stiff florist wire, and paper fish to create one or more educational fish mobiles. One kind of mobile is a schooling fish mobile. Some types of small fish swim in a tight pattern. They swim close together and follow one another closely. They do this to help protect themselves from predators.

To create this mobile, pick a simple shape for the fish, and reproduce that shape so that each child has two copies. To make each fish, cut out the fish shapes and have children paint or decorate them. Remind children that a real fish is symmetrical—that is, each side is the same. When the fish shapes are dry, the sides are stapled together, leaving an opening to be filled with crushed tissue, toilet paper, paper towel, or cotton balls. Then the fish are stapled shut. A hole is punched in the top of the fish, and one end of the stiff florist wire is inserted. The other end of the wire is wrapped around the hoop and taped in place if necessary to assure that the wire remains in position and all the fish "school" in the same direction. Tie three or four evenly-spaced pieces of string onto the hoop. This will insure that the hoop hangs flat and the fish can "swim" in mid-air.

Another kind of mobile is a food chain mobile. This is a class project too. Using the food chain ideas provided in the lesson activities in this chapter or a food chain of your class's choice, have groups work on creation of different parts of the food chain. Some groups will be creating many small, two-sided stuffed fish while another group may be creating one large fish or shark. The assembly is the same as for the schooling fish

mobile except that larger fish may need to be wired to the hanging structure in more than one place.

If you decide on a shark as your biggest predator, one group (separate from the shark-making group) could be assigned to be responsible for making small remora to affix to the shark. These small fish live as parasites on the bodies of some sharks and clean their scales.

6. Crayon Resist Ocean Scene

Use the crayon resist technique to create attractive underwater scenes. First, have children recreate rocks, fish, and plant life using different colors of crayons and pressing very hard on a white sheet of paper. Once this step is complete, a thin wash of blue paint is painted over the crayon picture. Since the crayon repels the paint, the ocean scene shows through the paint. Children might prefer to create a "deep-sea" scene using black paint. The crayon fish have the luminous look of many deep-sea creatures. Finalize the picture if you like by having children create an underwater exploration vehicle out of construction paper and crayon or marker to glue into an open space on the underwater scene.

You might choose to have this art project relate to the sea serpent creative writing project described in the writing activities section of this chapter. In this case, the child's sea scene could illustrate the story.

7. Carp Windsock

Refer to the art and craft activities section of Chapter 4 for instructions on how to make a carp windsock for class decoration. This is an Asian craft.

8. Fun Fish

Here are just a few of the ways you can decorate fish to use in your classroom in conjunction with this theme. Some of these appeal to younger children more than older children (such as the cereal "scale" decoration), but most can be used with children of any age. The fish is cut out of construction paper or tagboard and then decorated with:

-Small pieces of torn or cut colored tissue which are affixed with starch
-Scales that are printed with the ends of toilet paper rolls dipped into tempera paint or wine corks pressed onto ink pads

-Scales made from sequins or buttons
-Sponge painting and a plastic wiggly eye
-Painted glue onto which paper hole punches or confetti is dropped
-Crushed eggshell colored with food coloring
-Small macaroni shells or other pasta that give a scale-like effect
-Cereal such as toasted oat "o" shaped brands (good also for squid and octopus tentacles)
-Finger paint scales made from dipping a single finger into a stamp pad or paint and repeating until scale design is complete
-Mylar confetti

If children want to make fish puppets for use in a puppet show, have them make two-sided fish that are glued together and stuffed as described for the fish in the mobile in this section. The puppet can then be glued onto a chopstick, pencil, or rolled paper dowel to create a stick puppet. Sealed envelopes can also be used to make fish puppets, especially for predator fish such as sharks and piranha. One end of the sealed envelope is cut off entirely. This is where the child inserts his or her hand. The other end of the envelope is cut out in a mouth shape. Teeth, eyes, fins, and scales are then drawn onto the rest of the envelope to finish giving this simple puppet a fish effect. Old socks can also be decorated to make fish puppets.

9. Ocean in a Bottle

Children can make small (baby food jar size) or large (liter bottle size) ocean bottles using blue-colored water and salad or baby oil. About equal parts of each liquid are placed in the bottle and it is sealed shut. When tipped and turned, waves form. If you have small, inexpensive plastic fish toys available, place one in each bottle. To do this project cheaply, have children bring in the necessary oil. This project also allows children another way to explore the different properties of oil and water.

Food Activities

1. Fishy Desserts

Stabilizers in many foods are created from that very abundant and useful ocean plant, kelp. Pudding and ice cream are two desserts that often use kelp by-products as stabilizers. Plan a dessert day when you provide ice cream (perhaps cones or sundaes) or pudding with toppings as a way to reinforce the many ways each day that we rely on the ocean as a major resource for products we use. Shampoos, skin lotions, and other products also use kelp by-products.

2. There's a Fish in the Dip

Fish is a very healthful food. In recent years, it has gained in popularity as people have become more health conscious. Have children bring different fish shaped crackers to class for a tuna dip day. You could either use the recipe below to have the class make a single kind of healthful tuna dip or you could have children work in groups to create their own healthy tuna dip recipes. In the latter case, children from each group are responsible for bringing the ingredients for their group's dip and for recording their recipe for others to enjoy.

Some ideas for foods to add to tuna (in addition to your choice of dressing such as salsa, sour cream, Italian dressing, or mayonnaise) are green onions, celery, bell peppers, zucchini, pickle relish, boiled egg, parsley, diced carrot, and corn kernels. You could invite the principal to judge the dips for taste and healthfulness and offer a small prize to the winning group. This could be something simple such as rights to be first at some project or some class activity or no-homework coupons.

Tuna Dip Recipe

1 large can tuna
2 tablespoons mayonnaise or salad dressing
2 tablespoons diced green onion
2 tablespoons sweet pickle relish
4 tablespoons diced celery
Drain tuna and mash with fork. Add remaining ingredients and mix well. If too dry, add more dressing one teaspoonful at a time.

3. Native American Fish Stew

See the food activities section of Chapter 7 for a Native American fish soup.

4. Easy Clam Chowder

Directions for this easy Boston clam chowder are listed below. This soup makes a great meal in itself.

1 cup butter
1 1/4 cups flour
9 6-ounce cans chopped clams
8 carrots, diced finely or grated
5 medium potatoes, peeled and diced finely
2 medium onions, diced small or 1 cup frozen
    diced onions (or 1/2 cup dry minced onions)
3 celery stalks, diced finely
5 cups half and half
1 teaspoon salt
1 teaspoon parsley flakes (optional)
Pepper

Melt butter in soup pan and mix in flour to make roux (gravy base). Remove roux and save. Put vegetables into soup pan and pour clam juice from clams and enough water to cover vegetables into pan. Heat to boiling over high heat, covered, until vegetables are tender. Mash slightly with potato masher. Lower heat. Mix a little of the hot vegetable broth with roux to heat and remelt cooled roux. Add this slowly to soup while stirring soup. Add half and half slowly while stirring over medium heat (do not boil) and add in clams and remaining seasonings. Serve hot.

5. Italian Fish Soup (Cioppino)

This soup is an easy version of Italian cioppino. Any fish can be used in it. Canned fish is suggested here for ease of preparation.

2 jars Italian seasoned spaghetti sauce
2 small cans chopped clams with juice
1 can shrimp
    Any other fish of choice including imitation
    crab meat, shredded
1/4 cup minced green or brown onion (dry minced
    onions are fine)
4 cups water
1 teaspoon minced garlic (or 1 teaspoon garlic
    powder)
1/2 teaspoon oregano
1/2 teaspoon salt
Dash pepper
1/2 teaspoon any other Italian herb(s) of your
    choice

Heat all ingredients until just under a boil. Reduce heat and simmer for 10 minutes.

Since shellfish is used in this recipe, make sure students have no allergies to shellfish before you serve.

6. Salmon in White Sauce

Melt 3/4 cup butter in a saucepan. Mix butter with 1 cup flour over medium heat until melted and smooth. Add 1/2 teaspoon salt, 1/4 teaspoon pepper, 1 tablespoon minced onion, and 2 tablespoons parsley flakes and mix. Over medium heat, slowly add 5 cups milk to make thick white sauce. (Evaporated milk can be used.) Add 1 14-3/4 oz can drained salmon, flaked into sauce. (Be sure you remove any bones.) If lumpy, stir briskly with a whisk. Make four cups of quick rice according to package directions. Pour some salmon sauce over rice and serve.

Canned tuna can easily be substituted for the salmon.

7. Fish-Shaped Cookies

These cookies are decorated with egg yolk paint which when cooked gives a very scaly appearance. It is also a good decoration for reptile or dinosaur cookies.

Cookie Dough Recipe

2 cups soft butter or margarine
4 cups sugar
2 teaspoons soda
1 teaspoon salt
1 tablespoon vanilla
6 eggs
7 1/4 to 7 1/2 cups flour mixed with 4 teaspoons
*   baking powder*

Mix first five ingredients until smooth. Add eggs and beat until smooth. Slowly add flour mixed with baking powder. Chill briefly. Flour hands, rolling pin, and rolling area. Have each child roll out about 1/2 cup of dough. Cut out with fish shaped cutters. In the alternative, give each child a heaping tablespoonful of dough and ask that the child mold a cookie on waxed paper into a fish shape no more than 1/4" thick.

Mix egg yolk with 1 tablespoon water and 2 to 3 drops food coloring. Paint onto fish with thin water color brushes. Place on greased cookie sheet or non-stick baking sheet. Bake at 450 degrees until light golden brown—about 7 to 10 minutes.

For one cookie per child, half of this recipe is sufficient. For two or three cookies each, use the recipe as written.

Art Masters—Old and New

1. André Derain

Derain was born in 1880. He became a leader of an artistic movement called Fauvism. "Fauve" means "wild beast" in French. Fauve artists painted scenes with bold short strokes and used intense colors, especially reds, blues, and oranges. These works were generally flat in perspective. Fauvism as a style only flourished for a short time—from approximately 1903 to 1907. Derain was also known for his book illustrations, costumes, and set designs for theatrical productions.

2. Henri Matisse

Matisse was born in 1869. He was one of the most influential painters of the early 1900s. His own artistic efforts were influenced by the works of Paul Cézanne and the Cubist movement. He created large, boldly-colored canvases. His works feature interesting designs and patterns from a painted subject such as wall paper and table coverings. He was also a talented sculptor and a leader in the Fauvist movement. In his later years, he did a well-known series of cut-paper designs.

Project Directions

This project helps children explore the Fauvist art of Derain and Matisse. If you emphasize using a seascape (e.g. a coastline or marina with a simple sailboat as the central feature) or a still life which includes a fish, you can also incorporate this chapter's ocean theme.

To do the Fauvist art project, each child starts with a white sheet of paper on which he or she sketches a very simple outline of either a seascape or a still life. If doing a still life, set up a model for children to use. It could include a cloth on which a bowl, fish, and loaf of bread have been placed. The Fauvist version of this scene or any other was to see it in bold, almost fluorescent color. Using oil pastels and making strong use of red, blue, and orange, the outlines of the child's drawing are filled in using short, strong, quick strokes of color. The entire paper or canvas should be filled in when the child is done for the effect to be complete. As an example of the vivid Fauve colors, the loaf of bread might be largely orange, but highlighted with strong lines of red, and even an occasional blue stroke for effect.

Sharing Activities

1. Playground Painting

A challenging, educational, and fun activity is to take part of the playground blacktop, and devote it to a life-size outline of a large whale. Perhaps you can enlist the aid of a local artist or high school or college student to help children plan the outline and painting.

Outline the whale on the pavement. Place wide masking tape on both sides of the outline. This way, the line can be easily painted straight and neat. Check with a local paint store as to the appropriate type of paint to use, and whether the store can donate some paint and brushes for the project.

2. Fish Tales on the Road

If children did the "fish tales" writing activity in this chapter, they could use fish puppets as props to tell their stories to other classes. These stories would be of immense interest to children in younger grades.

3. Ocean Ecology Poster Contest

Invite other classes to participate in a poster contest that encourages children to reflect ways that we can all help protect the ocean environment. Hang the posters around the school, and have a local official or community person come to judge them.

4. Seafood Fare

Plan a meal event with another class where each student is encouraged to bring some sort of seafood or fish related dish. Ideas for "seafood" include tuna and oyster dips, fish and oyster crackers, fish casseroles and stews, gelatin salads and desserts molded into fish or shell shapes as well as ice cream, puddings, and other foods which contain kelp by-products. You might want to display other products that contain kelp by-products such as hand lotions and shampoos. This activity helps reinforce student awareness of the ocean as a valuable resource and the importance of keeping it clean and healthy.

5. The Living Aquarium Assembly

Children can also put on an educational assembly for other classes using the format provided below. As props, children can create larger than life (e.g., 2 by 3 feet) papier-mâché replicas or posters of the animals referred to in the text of the assembly performance. Divers can be dressed in black clothing such as pants, leggings, turtlenecks and so forth. Air tanks can be recreated by covering plastic soda bottles with tin foil, and strapping them onto the child's back with string. The pollution actors should wear black with litter pinned to them. They can also wear pipe cleaner armbands with black crepe paper streamers hanging from them.

The performance can be rounded out with some statements of fact about ocean ecology and environmental issues, and a challenge to all in attendance to do their part for the ocean, one of our last frontiers. Songs such as "Don't Go Near the Water" by the Beach Boys, other environmental songs, or perhaps even old sailor songs could be sung as part of the assembly.

Text for Assembly Script reprinted here by permission of author, copyright for script by Pamela Marx, 1994.

Assembly Text for "The Living Aquarium:"

Divers are on stage at the beginning of production. They move around stage during performance with swimming motions. Sea animal and pollution actors enter and exit (or sit back down after their speeches) in conjunction with indications in the script text. Whenever the divers ask about the polluting mass (the "grunge" or "goo"), the pollution actors should enter from the sides, and then retreat as appropriate to text.

Diver 1: We want to welcome you to the Talking Sea.
On our dive today, many animals you'll see.

Diver 2: You know them, I'm sure, by their common names.

Though they have fancy names, too,
they're still the same.

Diver 3: It's time to see this underwater show.
Come on, it's time. Come on, let's go.

Divers swim around on stage to some appropriate underwater music such as from the soundtrack of "Jaws" or another well known ocean film.

Diver 4: Oh, here we come now to one of our
friends.
It's the simple sponge who sits without
end.

Enter sponge actor(s).

Diver 5: It's real name is porifera but you know
it best
As plain old sponge and that's the real
test.

Diver 6: Sponge, can you tell us, what's happening today?
What's to eat? What do you have to
say?

Sponge part can be divided among several actors if desired.

Sponge: I'm a simple sponge and I just sit.
I let the water flow out and in.
I eat what I like right out of the flow.
As I sit and eat, I grow and grow.

Diver 7: But look there, sponge, what is that
grunge?

Sponge: That grunge is waste from a people
machine.
To put it in our water seems awfully
mean.

Diver 8: You're right, it's awful, but what can
we do?
Let's swim away now or we'll be
drenched with goo.

Divers swim to chosen underwater music for a few seconds. During this time the anemone actor(s) enters.

Diver 4: Oh, here we come now to another
friend.
See the anemone's tentacles turn and
bend.

Diver 5: Anemone is in the family of the coelenterate.
Let's ask some questions and see what
answers we get.

Diver 6: Anemone, can you tell us, what's happening today?
You look like a flower but you're not,
they say.

Anemone: I'm not a flower. I'm an animal too.
But, once I plop, I don't move.
Except to reach my tentacles out
To sting some food. That's what I'm
about.

Diver 7: But look there, anemone, what do you
see?

Anemone: That's oil and litter from people
above.
I wish they would think about the
ocean we love.

Diver 8: You're right, they should think and not
make waste
But that goo will get us if we don't
make haste.

Divers use swimming motions while anemone actors exit and clams enter.

Diver 4: Oh, here we come now to another
friend.
It's a bivalve clam sitting on its end.

Diver 9: A clam is a mollusk. What a name!
A mussel is another whose family is
the same.

Diver 6: Clam, can you tell us, what's happening today?
What's going on? What do you have to say?

Clam: I'm a mollusk who has two hard shells.
I also have a foot to travel well.
I open up when the water comes in
But close down tight when it's air I'm in.

Diver 7: But look there, clam, what do you see?

Clam: That murky muck can make us sick
But whining about it won't do the trick.

Diver 8: Let's swim away fast before that muck
Swallows us up and gets us stuck.

Divers use swimming motions while clam actors exit and starfish enter.

Diver 4: Oh, here we come now to another friend.
Watch the starfish and his legs that bend.

Diver 10: The starfish is in the family of echinoderms.
I don't know where they get these funny terms.

Diver 6: Starfish, can you tell us what's happening today?
You're like a star, but underwater you stay.

Starfish: To find mussels to eat, I'll go far.
Walking on my tube feet. I'm a strange kind of star.
When I find a mussel or I find a clam
I pull on its shells, then I eat it—Wham!

Diver 11: That's hard work to eat a clam
But, starfish, look at that murky jam.

Starfish: That's no jam. That's people stuff.
They drop their garbage all over us.

Diver 12: That's too bad but we can't stay
From that murky jam we must—away!

Divers use swimming motion as starfish actors exit and crab actors enter.

Diver 4: Oh, here we come now to another friend.
To that crab in the tide our greetings we send.

Diver 13: A crab's a crustacean. Did you know
That a shrimp and a lobster are his cousins below?

Diver 6: Crab, can you tell us, what's happening today?
You look kind of hungry. Has it been a hard day?

Crab: I'm a crabby crustacean. I scavenge the shore.
I look for leftovers to eat and more.
I can always live off what others leave behind.
There's always something left for me to find.

Diver 14: But look there, crab, look out to sea.
There's a dark, floating mass. It's so ugly.

Crab: That's waste and muck and people stuff.
They throw and drop and heave their junk.

Diver 15: Too bad, too bad, but we can't stay
Or we'll get stuck in its awful way.

Divers use swimming motions while crab actors exit and fish actors enter.

Diver 4: Here we come to some familiar friends.
A school of fish is around the bend.

Diver 5: A fish is a fish and a vertebrate, too.
It has scales and fins and a skeleton—true!

Diver 6: Fish, can you tell us, what's happening
to you?
You look kind of tired . . . a long day at
school?

Fish: We little fish must always be
In school or we get in trouble you see.
Being in school helps hide us away
From other big fish who see us as prey.

Diver 8: But look there, fish, there's a gloomy
mass!
Ready to float by you to pass.

Fish: Yes, big fish are not the only trouble we
face.
People are making a mess of this place.

Diver 9: Well, we are sorry but we can't wait.
We've got to leave or it'll be too late.

All Sea Animals Enter Stage: It's easy for all you
divers to leave
But this is our home and we must retrieve
What does remain so that we'll be safe.
We have no choice, no other place.
The mess is spreading from here to there.
If you do nothing, it'll be everywhere.
Divers, here it comes. Please don't hesitate.
Tell the people above it's nearly too late.

*Enter to center stage the polluting mass which has
been threatening from the side of the stage every
time a diver has pointed out the gloomy, littered
mess.*

Goo: Our brooding toxic messy goo
Is made by people like you and you.

Each person on land can do a part
In being careful. Well, it's a start.

Recycle the bottles and paper you can.
But carefully. Make it part of your plan.

Shun chemical products that you find
Then less that's bad will be left behind.

Try hard for every little step you take
Is important when the sea and the earth are at
stake.

So, divers, teachers, students and friends
Make this moment a start not an end.

*All actors join on stage to sing the song "Don't Go
Near The Water," or another environmental song of
your choosing.*

Resources

1. Children of all ages enjoy reading and listening to Greek myths as literature selections. They fit well into a theme on ocean issues because so many of the myths involve ocean crossings and journeys or mythical gods who rule the oceans. The following are a couple examples of books either about or which include stories involving the sea and adventure on the sea.

D'Aulaires' Book of Greek Myths by Ingri and Edgar Parin D'Aulaires published by Doubleday (1962).

Theseus and the Minotaur by Warwick Hutton published by Margaret K. McElderry Books (1989).

2. Other fish or ocean-related stories suitable for elementary students depending upon their reading levels are:

Time of Wonder by Robert McCloskey published by Viking/Penguin (1989).

Kermit the Hermit by Bill Peet published by Houghton Mifflin Company (1965).

The Fisherman and His Wife by Margot Zemach published by W. W. Norton and Company (1966).

Island of the Blue Dolphins by Scott O'Dell published by Dell (1987).

The Cay by Theodore Taylor published by Avon Books (1969).

Shark Beneath the Reef by Jean Craighead George published by HarperTrophy (1989).

You might also consider reading passages from a classic such as Jules Verne's *20,000 Leagues Under the Sea*. Scenes involving the giant squid might be useful in sparking student imagination for creative writing projects such as those suggested in the writing activities section of this chapter.

3. Some interesting factual books which children will learn from and enjoy, depending upon their reading level are:

Houses from the Sea by Alice Goudey published by Scribner's Sons (1959).

The Magic School Bus on the Ocean Floor by Joanna Cole published by Scholastic Inc. (1992).

Amazing Creatures from the Sea by The National Wildlife Federation, published by same (1987).

Seashore, An Eyewitness Book by Steve Parker published by Alfred A. Knopf (1989).

Seashores, A Nature Club Book by Joyce Pope published by Troll Associates (1990).

The Ocean World Encyclopedia by Donald G. Groves and Lee M. Hunt published by McGraw-Hill Book Company (1980).

The following are biographical books about real people who are involved in ocean research or with marine animals:

Shark Lady: True Adventures of Eugenie Clark by Ann McGovern published by Macmillan (1978).

Sevengill: The Shark and Me, A Sierra Club Book by Don C. Reed published by Scholastic Inc. (1986).

CHAPTER

9

BE-A-SCIENTIST

In this chapter, children will be given opportunities to explore the scientific method. The experiment process and development of scientific thinking skills will be the focus of the chapter with related activities celebrating the importance of science in our world and the important position scientists hold in improving our health, safety, and future.

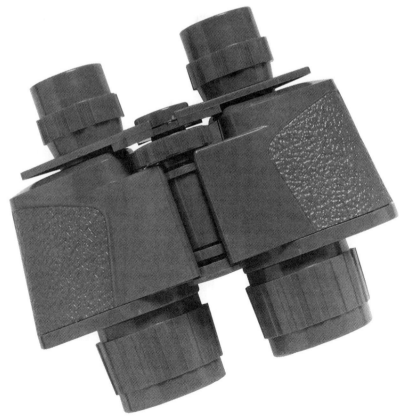

Lesson Activities

The Lesson Activities of this chapter provide children with a multitude of exploration opportunities. Ordinary substances such as bubble solution and cornstarch and water "goo" will be explored with an eye to having children think about these substances creatively and scientifically.

Writing Activities

The Writing Activities provide opportunities for children to focus on historical scientific contributions to society and to examine the role of science in our lives today.

Art and Craft Activities

The Art and Craft Activities provide children with opportunities to make things that have a science experiment component to them. When undertaken together with the chapter activity sheets, an art and craft activity becomes yet another opportunity to explore ordinary objects and materials from a scientific perspective.

Food Activities

Food Activities will focus on activities with food that demonstrate a scientific principle. When the students do these food activities or observe them as classroom demonstrations with the chapter activity sheets, they allow children to explore ordinary kitchen foods and materials yet again from a scientific point of view.

Art Masters—Old and New

Art Masters - Old and New lessons will explore art forms in which artists have examined the mystery of everyday things. Scientists, like artists, are fascinated by things that most of us take for granted or simply fail to observe.

Sharing Activities

Sharing Activities will suggest ways that the teacher and class can share interest in science and scientific method with others in the school community.

Lesson Activities

The lesson activities in this chapter are exploratory in nature and, while exposing the children in a very real way to principles of scientific analysis, are deemed by most children to be great fun. It seems the best of both worlds to have children engaged in active scientific exploration at the same time that they are having a great time.

The three suggested materials to be used for the scientific explorations are bubbles, cornstarch-and-water goo, and plastic putty. An additional investigative activity is suggested using materials the children can bring from home. All basic materials to be explored are homemade and inexpensive. Before beginning any substance investigation, however, introduce or reintroduce the concept of the scientific method to your students. To do this, you may want to use the short discussion guideline below.

1. Hypothesis - What Is It?

Most children are familiar (at least in principle) with the idea of the scientific method by the time they reach third grade. However, they don't always identify it as such. To the extent that the activities in this chapter help the children come away from the day's activities saying "I'm a scientist," they have been a success. The child feels like a scientist, and indeed is one, when he or she has questioned and investigated a subject or substance.

To help focus these investigations, introduce or reintroduce the concepts of hypothesis and scientific method and the subject of what scientists do. To do this, consider using part or all of these discussion guidelines:

What is a scientist?

What do scientists do?
They do experiments.

How do scientists decide what they want to find out about?
Sometimes they are employed by a corporation and the corporation management tells the scientists what to find out about.

Sometimes they are employed by a university and the university lets them investigate whatever they are interested in.

Sometimes scientists work on their own as a hobby and learn about things that interest them.

Do scientists ever find anything out by accident?
Many scientific breakthroughs have occurred by accident. For example, recently physicians in India were looking for new ways to treat burn victims. Someone noticed that skin tissue looked a lot like potato skin. This led to experimentation with using potato skins as burn dressing. This treatment method turned out to be not only highly effective but very inexpensive compared to the synthetic skins used in the United States for the same purpose.

How do scientists go about doing experiments?
First, scientists figure out what hypothesis they are going to test.

What is a hypothesis?
A hypothesis is the scientist's educated guess about what will happen in the experiment. For example, if you wanted to do an experiment to find out which plant would grow better—a plant in sunlight or a plant in a closet—your hypothesis would likely be that you think the plant in sunlight would grow best because you know that plants need light to grow. Remind children, however, that hypotheses are not always right. If they were always right, that would mean that scientists weren't finding out anything new.

You may want to incorporate this discussion activity with a follow up activity from the writing activities section of this chapter. One pertinent writing activity is found in Item 2 of that section, "If I Were . . ."

Anytime you do a class experiment or demonstration, you can formulate questions for it and students can use the Scientific Hypothesis and Results Activity Sheet at the end of this chapter.

2. The Bubbles are Coming, The Bubbles are Coming

The first substance to be explored in this chapter is bubble solution. Bubble solution is an excellent vehicle for many kinds of explorations. And, perhaps most importantly, the children will be so interested in the bubbles that they will think of their own investigations to undertake.

If you decide to undertake this investigation, it is probably best to devote the better part of a school day to it. You might want to start in the second half of the morning and finish up in the afternoon. The bubble activities here are designed to be completed at separate work stations around a room, each station to host at any given time a group of 4 to 6 children. Have plenty of newspaper handy to quickly blot up spills, a few terry cloth towels, and rolls of paper toweling (at least one roll for each station). Tell children they must wear rubber-soled shoes on the day of the event to help make the day go as slip-free as possible. Also, of course, there can be no running in the classroom and it is ideal if you can have a minimum of one adult volunteer for each station or every two stations.

The activities described here work best inside, as bubbles break too quickly outdoors. Bubble activities also work best on days when there is some moisture in the air. Finally, make up your bubble solution at least two days ahead of time (and as many as four days), as aged solution seems to work a little better than fresh solution.

An activity sheet is provided at the back of this chapter for each station. To ensure that children remain on task, require that children record their findings on the activity sheet for each station. It is this writing activity that focuses and reinforces the scientific thinking process.

One good bubble recipe is: 1 part Dawn® or Joy® dish detergent, 10 parts water, 1/4 part glycerin. Mix ingredients slowly and well and let sit. You will need one dishpan of bubble solution for each station in addition to the other materials required for that station's activities.

a. The All-Class Bubble Blow-Out

Start the day's activities by taking all children outside to get some of the excitement and playfulness out of their systems, and to simply make bubbles before your begin. Have children bring in all kinds of bubble blowers or objects from home that they think they can blow bubbles through and let them experiment with these objects outdoors. Strainers and colanders, for example, make fun blowers for this activity.

But before you head outside for this fun activity, let children know that the first thing they will do on their return to the classroom is list five or ten characteristics of bubbles, i.e., things they know about bubbles or found our about bubbles during their "blow-out" activities. As such, while they are having fun outside, they are also required to use and build their observation skills. Examples of observations they should be able to make after the outdoor activity are:

Small single bubbles in the air are round.

Bubble come in different sizes.

You can see colors in bubbles.

Bubbles pop in the air.

Bubbles stick together.

Bubbles can fly.

Bubbles can fall.

Students can use the Bubble Observation Activity Sheet for this. When the class returns to the classroom, children make a listing of all the bubble characteristics they can think of. They put this list aside. If you do use this sheet, you might choose to have children return to the sheet at the end of their bubble experiences to record new observations about bubbles they can then write down as a result of all of their bubble station experiences.

Before students begin work station activities, the teacher should explain to students what they will be doing at each station. Groups should spend approximately 20 minutes at each station. It is useful to give children their own plastic straw to carry with them and use at each station for which straw-blowing activities might be appropriate.

b. Are All Bubbles Round?

At this station, you need only your dishpan of bubble solution, an extra roll of paper towels, and the children's hands. Children explore what kinds of bubbles they can make only with their hands. Have children see what shape the bubbles are and see whether they can make bubbles on the table. They can also analyze how bubble shapes change when bubbles touch each other. Use the Are All Bubbles Round? Activity Sheet for this station.

c. Electro-Bubbles

Children can work in pairs at this station to see if they can use static electricity to affect the movement of bubbles in the air. Make sure you have a roll of paper towels available at this station to keep it dry. Otherwise, it won't work very well. Have several pieces of wool, several plastic combs, small containers of bubble solution, and blowers. One child rubs a comb vigorously on the wool and the other child blows bubbles in the air. Once the comb is charged, the child puts it near a bubble in the air. The bubbles should move in response to the charged comb. This activity probably works best on days when the air is not too moist. The activity can also be done using plastic spoons as the plastic item to be charged. Use the Electro-Bubbles Activity Sheet at this station.

Since children can have trouble generating static electricity when the air in a room is moist, this station can be deleted if the other stations suggested here are sufficient to meet the needs of your class.

d. Bubble Inventor

Have children experiment at this station with a variety of simple objects and materials to create their own creative bubble makers. Some materials and tools to include are: aluminum foil, string, scissors, straws, rubber bands, pieces of plastic netting from produce bags, tape, plastic strawberry boxes, plastic spoons, disposable cups and plates, squares of fabric netting or tulle, paper clips, toothpicks, and the like. Bubble-makers can be as simple as a molded circle of foil or more complicated such as the straw and string bubble-making window described below. To give the children ideas at this station, you might want to have other ordinary household objects available from which they can get bubble maker ideas. These objects include things like funnels, colanders, and hand strainers. Use the Bubble Inventor Activity Sheet at this station.

e. How Big a Bubble?

Rulers, strings, and scissors are needed at this station. For the bubble-blowing activity, children can blow bubbles with their hands directly onto the table surface. A wet ruler can be inserted from the top of the bubble to the table so that children can measure the height of the half-circle dome. They then pop the bubble and use pieces of string to measure the circumference of the circle which remains on the table once the bubble pops. They can then measure the string against a ruler to find out the circumference of the circle in both or either inches and centimeters. This station exercises math measurement skills as well as concepts such as radius, diameter and circumference. Use the Measure Your Bubble Activity Sheet with this station's activities.

f. Foam Up the Suds

For this station, you need magnifying glasses, strainers, an egg beater, and straws. For best results, you will want two dishpans of soap, one to be used with the egg beater. Have children experiment at this station with blowing multiple bubbles and seeing how this changes bubble shape. On a table, they can insert a wet straw into a table bubble and blow more bubbles inside the larger bubble. They can use strainers and blowers with small holes to make suds or foam which they can analyze with a magnifying glass. Have children try to make a single layer of foam on the table to press under a magnifying glass or a small clear acrylic board. An egg beater can be used to foam up the suds for this station.

The Foam Up The Suds Activity Sheet for this station asks children where they might have seen bubble shapes in nature. Some of the more obvious answers are in the hexagonal bee hive construction (honeycomb). Similar shapes are also seen in the "skeletal" structures of some leaves.

g. Candlelight and Bubbles

With close adult supervision at this station, have children blow a few bubbles at a time to see how bubbles respond to the heat of a candle flame. Do not let children light the candles. This job should be undertaken exclusively by a parent or other adult volunteer.

At this bubble station, children have to watch carefully to discriminate between bubble responses to the lit versus unlit candles. Note that bubbles do tend to veer away from the candlelight and the candle-heated air, but these responses are sometimes too subtle to be easily observed in a busy classroom setting. Use the Bubbles by Candlelight Activity Sheet with this station's activities.

h. Bubble Windows

For this station you need six bubble windows. These are made by using two plastic straws and threading a 36" piece of cotton string through the two straws and tying a knot to form a square. Two opposing sides of the square are the straws and the remaining two opposing sides are string. Children will explore the surface tension of the bubble window at this station and use the Bubble Windows Activity Sheet.

The surface tension of the bubble window or any bubble holds the walls of the bubble in place. It is created by the effort made by the bubble solution molecules to stay together. Children can explore the strength of that surface tension at this station. Additional exercises and experiments on surface tension are described in the lesson activities in Chapter 8.

In a single-day bubble event, children can move from bubble station to bubble station in small groups. If you prefer to use the bubble investigation as a center idea or a one-activity-a-day idea,

this can be done as well. In either case, however, an important part of the activity is for children to either record their findings and observations in a journal or on the individual activity sheet included in this chapter. This helps assure that this fun scientific investigation remains scientific and does not become an excuse for horsing around.

3. Animal, Vegetable, or Mineral?

Divide children once again into cooperative learning groups to analyze the characteristics of the substance you will place before them. This substance is a cornstarch and water mixture. Before you give them the substance to analyze, ask students to pretend they are scientists who have been brought together from universities around the world to analyze the strange new substance called C-Substance found deep in a previously undiscovered rain forest or mountain top cave.

Children will need to decide in a creative writing project at the end of the exploration activities if the substance is animal, vegetable or mineral. They will need to analyze its characteristics. This substance particularly challenges students to determine if it is liquid or solid. Actually, it is a colloid, a solid suspended in a liquid.

The recipe for C-Substance is approximately 4 parts cornstarch to 3 parts water. To test the substance for proper consistency, drag one finger through it. Your finger should leave a clean trail that closes over a few seconds after your finger has passed. If the trail is not created, add a little more cornstarch. If the trail is difficult to make, add a little more water. The C-Substance should be made up in the morning before class begins and divided into pie tins. Cover the tins with plastic wrap or foil until ready to use. Two boxes of cornstarch should be enough to provide an entire class with C-Substance.

Students will investigate C-Substance in 8" pie tins in their individual groups. Their investigations can be guided by using the C-Substance Activity Sheets at the back of this chapter. Each student records his or her own interpretation of the investigation activities on his or her individual sheet.

After allowing the students 30 to 40 minutes to analyze the substance, ask them to reach agreement within their groups as to five characteristics of C-Substance upon which they all agree. They will record these five characteristics on poster size posterboard or butcher paper. These posters will then be hung in visible locations around the classroom so that all students can see all the posters. At this point, the final investigative activity begins.

The final C-Substance activity is a classroom discussion in which children hone their investigative and language skills by reaching a classwide agreement on five to ten precise characteristics of C-Substance. The discussion should begin with one group presenting its set of characteristics. Other students are encouraged to challenge characteristics with which they don't agree. The object of such challenges is to better define a given characteristic so that all or a majority of the class can agree that the stated attribute is indeed a true characteristic of C-Substance. Children can demonstrate the C-Substance attribute to which they ascribe using the cornstarch mixture itself to demonstrate a point to the class.

Five to ten "rules" about how C-Substance works should be the end result of the classroom discussion. For a rule to be accepted, at least two-thirds of the students should agree with it. When you get students who disagree with a characteristic as stated, they should explain why they disagree, demonstrate their point with the cornstarch mixture and then the class should work to better define the characteristic to meet those concerns.

As a closing to the activity, children can decide if the substance acts more like an animal, vegetable, or mineral, and explain their conclusion in a short essay. Ask children to include in their essay a practical use to which they as scientists would like to put C-Substance. What kind of product would it make? What common problem might it be used to help solve? You might also want to use the C-Substance experience for additional creative writing opportunities. One possibility is for children to describe themselves adrift in a sea of C-Substance.

When the classroom exploration activities are complete, leave the C-Substance out (some covered and some uncovered) so children can see evaporation at work. This process changes the C-Substance into a solid, albeit a powdered one. Also, the covered container will begin to ferment in a day or two, creating a gas reaction strong enough to push a cover off the container.

4. Plastic Putty

This exploration uses a plastic polymer such as Silly Putty® or the putty made by the recipe below as the substance to be analyzed. Different putties have different qualities, and you may want to have some children work with Silly Putty® while others work with one or more of the homemade putties.

Children can analyze the substance's properties to determine whether the substance is liquid or solid. Have children work in pairs with a ball of the putty about the size of a walnut. Give each child a straw as well to help in the analysis.

Plastic Polymer

1 cup Elmer's®, Dapp®, or other white glue
1 cup water with 1 teaspoon Boraxo®, 20 Mule Team Borax® or Borateem® mixed into it

Pour glue in a bowl and slowly add the borax and water mixture as you stir constantly. Strings of "plastic" will begin to form quickly. Mix until all parts of glue have been plasticized by the water mixture. Pour off extra water. Place on table. Dot dry with paper towels and knead until the putty is consistent. This entire process takes only a few minutes. You may want to make three batches if the entire class will be working on the activity at one time or make several batches with different glue each time so that each group analyzes a slightly different substance.

Note that different glues do result in different qualities in the putty. Elmer's® glue usually results in a more elastic putty (closer in characteristics to liquid) while generic brands may result in a more brittle, less elastic putty (closer in characteristics to solid). Boraxo® and Elmer's® glue used together in the recipe result in a very elastic, almost sticky putty.

Children can use the Plastic Putty Polymer Activity Sheet in this chapter to help guide their substance investigations. After children have investigated the substances working in pairs, you might want to hold a classroom discussion in which groups that worked with the same type of putty present their findings about its particular characteristics and their suggestions for how the putty might be used.

The final activity could be a creative writing activity similar to one of those suggested for C-Substance in the preceding section.

5. What Will Make It Shine?

In this activity, ask children to pretend they are scientists for a company that wants to discover a new substance to market as a penny (or copper) cleaner. Ask each child to bring in a household liquid (not a cleaner, solvent, or caustic) to test as a penny cleaner. Liquids should be those used in cooking and harmless hand soaps and lotions. Sample liquids are vinegar, soy sauce, Worcestershire sauce, baking soda in water, salt water, catsup, milk, soda pop (specifically to include a cola), vegetable oil, orange or lemon juice, and the like. Ask each child to bring in five to ten tarnished pennies as well.

Once the liquids and pennies are collected, divide children into cooperative groups to test a variety of liquids for their penny-cleaning qualities. Have plasticized disposable cups or small plates for children to use to soak the pennies in the different liquids. They can record their results on the Penny Cleaner Research Scientist - What Will Make It Shine? Activity Sheet in this chapter. (This classroom experience can lead to a discussion of acids and bases and litmus paper experiments since many kitchen substances work well in such analyses.) If several liquids seem to have good cleaning qualities, can children hypothesize about their similar properties or common ingredients?

Writing Activities

1. Chapter Vocabulary

The suggested vocabulary words for this chapter are somewhat diverse in nature. Some are designed to introduce children to basic scientific concepts and disciplines. Others are suggested based upon the principles covered by individual activities contained in this chapter. Use only those words out of these suggested words that relate to concepts relevant to your students' activities.

Science
Scientist
Experiment
Hypothesis
Scientific method
Chemistry
Biology
Botany
Geology
Physics
Chemical
Research
Theory
Pointillism
Chemical change
Physical change
Liquid
Solid
Static electricity
Attract
Repel
Circumference
Diameter
Radius
Surface tension
Color spectrum

2. If I Were . . .

For this writing exercise, ask children to think of themselves as scientists and then write about what they would research and the problem or question to which they might want to find an answer. Before they begin this activity, brainstorm with them some great scientific discoveries through history so they have a sense of the kinds of research and discoveries scientists can make.

To help you with this discussion, the following is a brief list of scientific developments and discoveries listed chronologically.

1543 - Copernicus publishes the theory that the sun is the center of the solar system.

1604 - Galileo makes the discovery about speed and distance of falling bodies.

1607 - Galileo develops the thermometer to measure air temperature.

1668 - Sir Isaac Newton invents the reflecting telescope.

1687 - Sir Isaac Newton publishes his three laws of motion and his universal gravitation theory.

1704 - Sir Isaac Newton publishes his finding that white light is made up of the colors of the spectrum.

1745 - Leyden jar is used to collect and hold an electrical charge.

1752 - Benjamin Franklin uses a kite to show that lightening is electricity and he describes electrical charges as positive and negative.

1775 - Alessandro Volta invents a device that makes and stores static electricity.

1783 - English chemist Henry Cavendish and French chemist Antoine Lavoisier learn that water is made of oxygen and hydrogen.

1783 - Hot air balloon is invented. Eventually it is used by scientists to study the atmosphere.

1791 - Researchers use fossils to find the age of rocks and rock structures.

1840 - Ocean researchers begin using underwater diving gear.

mid-1800s - Gregor Mendel researches and identifies the basic laws of heredity.

mid-1800s - Louis Pasteur learns that microorganisms cause disease.

1850 - Jean Foucault calculates the speed of light.

1855 - German chemist Robert Bunsen popularizes the Bunsen burner.

1859 - Charles Darwin espouses theories of evolution.

1871 - The concept of the chemical chain reaction is developed.

1884 - The first man-made fiber is developed, a type of rayon.

1885 - George Eastman creates coated photographic paper.

1895 - Wilhelm Roentgen discovers x-rays.

1897 - J. J. Thomson discovers the electron.

1898 - Pierre and Marie Curie discover radioactive radium.

1902 - Layers in Earth's atmosphere are discovered.

1905 - Albert Einstein proposes the theory of relativity.

1905 - Scientists discover the chemical structure of chlorophyll.

1906 - Richard Oldham demonstrates that the Earth has a core.

1928 - Alexander Fleming discovers penicillin, the first antibiotic.

1931 - Synthetic rubber is made.

1935 - Charles Richter invents the Richter scale to measure earthquakes.

1938 - Teflon is discovered by Du Pont Corporation scientists.

1952 - H-bomb is built by Edward Teller and his scientific team.

1953 - Jonas Salk discovers a polio vaccine.

1956 - Sub-atomic neutrino is discovered.

1957 - Soviet Union launches the first artificial satellite.

1961 - Sub-atomic quark theory discussed.

1968 - Theory of plate tectonics is developed.

1985 - Scientists discover a hole in the ozone layer.

3. My Science Experiment

Ask children to sign up for science experiment presentations over a several week period. Have no more than three presentations a day. For the presentation, the child presents an experiment that he or she did. For older children, you may want to require them to submit a written report of one to two pages that contains the following information:

- **Nature of the experiment**
  The child describes what the experiment is about and what subject is investigated in the experiment.
- **Hypothesis**
  The child writes what he or she thought would happen when he or she did the experiment.
- **Directions for the Experiment**
  Have the child describe the experiment process step-by-step, including materials needed to conduct the experiment.
- **Observations and Results**
  The child describes the observations made during the course of the experiment. The child explains the results of the experiment and whether or not his or her hypothesis was correct.

If you prefer, the children can provide the foregoing information using the activity sheet in this chapter. If you have children report on their science experiments using a standard form such as the My Science Experiment Activity Sheet in this chapter, you might want to make a class book of experiments. Then each child could take a copy of a book of experiments home so that students could do some of the other students' experiments at home.

4. Scientific Biography

Ask children to explore writing a biography by researching a scientist of their choice. The Science Biography Activity Sheet in this chapter can provide the basis for the biography and help structure the research and writing effort.

Here is a list of some well-known scientists. You might want to provide guidance by allowing students to choose a scientist from this list:

Galileo Galileo, Italian astronomer and physicist

Nicolaus Copernicus, Polish astronomer

Robert Boyle, British scientist

Sir Isaac Newton, British mathematician and physicist

Albert Einstein, German physicist

Tsung-dao Lee, Chinese physicist

Chen Ning Yang, Chinese physicist

Werner Heisenberg, German physicist

Marie Curie, French chemist

Hideki Yukawa, Japanese physicist

Benjamin Franklin, American physicist and philosopher

Niels Bohr, Danish physicist

Robert Bunsen, German chemist

Jons Jacob Berzelius, Swedish chemist known as father of modern chemistry

Linus Pauling, American chemist and scientist

Edmund Halley, British astronomer

Charles Darwin, British naturalist

Charles Richter, scientist

Alfred Wegener, German geologist

Rachel Carson, American marine biologist

Leonardo Da Vinci, Italian scientist and artist

George Washington Carver, American botanist

Luther Burbank, American botanist

Jane Goodall, British ethologist (famed for African chimpanzee research)

Jonas Salk, American scientist

Alexander Fleming, British bacteriologist

Gregor Mendel, Austrian scientist

Louis Pasteur, French biologist

Michael Faraday, British physicist

5. Inventormania

Some of the writing activities in Chapter 3 on technology issues could also be used to advantage with the explorations in this chapter. Technological advances are possible only through the research and investigation efforts of scientists and engineers, whether professional or educated hobbyists.

6. Scientific Timeline

Each child will "adopt" a scientific discovery and prepare it for use on a timeline of important scientific developments. One way to create the timeline project is:

- Each child decides on the scientific discovery he or she will investigate. To do this, he or she can use the list in Item 2 of this section for ideas, solicit input from parents or research a scientist of interest to find a major discovery made by that person (see resource information under Item 4 above for suggested scientists). Once the child chooses his or her scientific discovery, he or she researches the date of its occurrence and some basic information about who made the discovery and how it was used to further scientific thinking, inventions, medicines, or other technological changes. This information is written neatly on an index card.
- Each child is then given a banner to complete. Each banners will be one part of the class' continuing scientific timeline. On the banner (which can be simply cut from 12" x 18" construction paper or similarly-sized butcher paper), the child prints the year of discovery boldly at the top followed by a short title and description of the discovery. Next the child draws a picture or symbol that graphically depicts the discovery. Under the picture, the child glues his or her index card report. The banners are hung around the room in chronological order to create a classroom timeline.

7. Discovery Staircase Poems

This writing exercise suggests another written way for students to explore a scientist and his or her discoveries. Using a stair step framework, this unrhymed poem allows children to explore a scientist and coincidentally reinforce parts of speech. The poem is structured as follows:

Summary of how discovery helped the world or changed the world

Three adjectives describing the discovery
(**adjectives**)

What the scientist discovered or invented
(**verb/noun**)

Name of Scientist
(**noun**)

Example:

Children and adults could be safe from polio.

Helpful, Preventive, Safe

Discovered polio vaccine

Jonas Salk

8. Four Senses Science Poem

This unrhymed poem is a creative writing opportunity for children to explore with their senses substances described in the lesson activities—bubble solution, C-Substance or plastic putty—or any other substance of your choosing or theirs. The poem's structure is four lines with each of the four senses of sight, hearing, touch, and smell being used to explore the substance.
Examples:

Plastic putty feels like squishy rubber.
It looks like a glob of dried paint.
It sounds like a bouncing ball.
It smells like a school art project.

Bubbles smell like doing dishes.
They look like rainbows in flight.
They sound like a tinkling bell you cannot quite hear.
They feel like a soft tickle.

 Art and Craft Activities

The scientific themes of this chapter are not on any particular scientific subject. Rather, the chapter activities are designed to focus children on creative scientific thinking and the scientific process. Accordingly, the "art and craft" activities in this section really combine science experiments and investigations with the creation of tangible items which the students can enjoy and take home. Use these classroom craft activities to engage the students in once again exploring the scientific thinking process by having them use the Scientific Method Activity Sheet in this chapter as part of each craft endeavor.

1. Take a Spin with the Color Spectrum

Sir Isaac Newton was an early researcher and writer about the color spectrum. With the activities in this section, children can explore how colors combine as well as the relatively advanced idea that all colors together make white insofar as light is concerned. Of course, with paints, when children combine all colors, they create a brownish-black shade.

a. Spin a Colored Top

Give each student a 4" diameter circle of white posterboard and a pointed pencil stub or 4" long dowel with a pointed end. The child colors on the circle using the primary and secondary colors. The colors can be applied in a random artistic fashion or by dividing the circle into sixths and applying a different color to each sixth.

When complete, the pencil is pushed through the center of the circle so that the colored side of the circle is up and it is about 1" to 1 1/2" from the pointed end of the pencil. With the pointed end of the pencil down, the resulting object is spun like a top. As it spins and the colors of the spectrum blend, the only color seen is a grayish white.

The primary colors of light are different from the primary colors we use for mixing paint. The primary colors of light are red, blue and green. These are the colors our eyes can see best. To make for a more interesting scientific investiga-

tion in the top-making activity, ask some children to divide their circles into sections and use only the colors red, blue, and green. Ask still another group to make their circles using only two of these three primary colors of light. Do the different color combinations change the colors visible when the disks are spinning?

b. Fly a Space Spinner

This same principle is applied to make a different toy, the space spinner, with which the color spectrum can be analyzed. This is a paper version of the old-fashioned button-and-thread spinning toy. A caveat here is that sometimes these kinds of spinners seem to go together quite easily and work very well, and other times they seem impossible to spin. Try this project in advance to see how it works for you. Remember that learning to do the "space spin" does take a little practice. Once you get the hang of it, though, this toy is a lot more fun than spinning the colored top.

Use a 3" diameter circle of lightweight white posterboard for this project. After you have colored the circle in the manner described for the tops above, pierce two holes in the center of the circle about 1/4" to 3/8" apart. Using a 30" piece of cotton string or heavy thread, loop the thread through the two holes and tie a knot to hold the thread or string together. Pull the posterboard circle so that it is in the middle of the string and so that the knot is at one end. Hold the looped ends of the string one in each hand and "wind" up the spinner by swinging the circle toward you over and over again. Then, with a sharp pull of the strings apart/hands together/hands apart, the spinner will begin to spin back and forth so quickly that, again, the individual colors seem to melt into a grayish white.

c. Other Color Explorations

You can use the following techniques to help children explore the ways in which primary colors blend to make shades of secondary colors. These simple techniques are:

• Play Dough Day

Either make play dough as a classroom cooking project or ask several mothers to bring in two or three batches of prepared play dough. The total play dough is divided into three parts. Each is colored with a different primary color—red, yellow, or blue. Each child is given a small piece of each primary color, and the children can then mix the colors as desired to get the colors they would like. They can then mold a sculpture of their choice to take home.

A good play dough recipe is:

2 cups white flour
1/2 cup salt
3 to 4 tablespoons cream of tartar
2 cups water
2 tablespoons vegetable oil
Food coloring

Combine all ingredients except food coloring in a large saucepan over medium heat. Stir constantly. In about four to five minutes, just when you think it will never get done, a large play dough mass pulls away from the side of the pan. Remove from heat and let cool completely. Work in food coloring by hand until you get the desired color. Keep covered in a plastic container.

Make your colors strong and bold. To do this, you will need to use quite a bit of food coloring. As a teacher, you might want to have extra flour and food coloring on hand to assure easy workability of dough and bright colors.

• Cookie Caper

Using refrigerated sugar cookie dough or three batches of sugar cookie dough made from the recipe below, have children make colored cookies. Divide the dough in thirds. Precolor the pieces of dough red, blue and yellow with food coloring. Have extra flour on hand for children to dust their hands with before they start working with the dough.

Give children one teaspoon/tablespoon of each color of dough. Let them blend the colors to make new colors, finally forming one large cookie to bake from the dough. If you bake the cookies on a layer of waxed paper or greased foil, you can write each child's name by his or her cookie.

Easy Sugar Cookies
1 cup butter, softened
2 cups granulated sugar
1/2 teaspoon soda
1/2 teaspoon salt
1 teaspoon vanilla
3 eggs, slightly beaten
3 3/4 cups flour
2 teaspoons baking powder

Mix first five ingredients together until creamy. Add eggs and stir briskly until well mixed. Add last two ingredients and mix well. If dough is too soft to work with, chill in the refrigerator for 20 minutes or add more flour, a little at a time. Bake on a greased or non-stick cookie sheet for about 8 to 10 minutes at 450 degrees.

This "cookie caper" activity can be adapted well to different holidays during the school year. Red and yellow dough can be given to children for Halloween to make orange pumpkin cookies. Blue and yellow dough can be given to children for St. Patrick's Day to make green shamrock shape cookies. (These are made by rolling the green dough into three small balls which are placed near each other in a triangle design; when pressed, their sides meet and a shamrock is formed.) Blue and red dough can be given to children for spring or Easter cookies to make a lavender flower cookies.

2. Exploring Crystal Gardens

Children can use these scientific craft activities to grow a variety of crystals.

• Colorful Crystals

Directions for creation of a colorful crystal garden are as follows:

> *6 tablespoons water*
> *6 tablespoons laundry bluing*
> *6 tablespoons salt*
> *2 tablespoons ammonia*
> *4 to 6 charcoal briquets*
> *Red, blue, yellow, and green liquid food*
> * coloring*
> *Aluminum or glass pie pan*
> *Empty coffee can*

Pour the first four ingredients into an empty coffee can or similar container. Stir the ingredients until well mixed. Place the briquets in the pie tin and squeeze drops of different food coloring on the briquets. This can be done randomly or the children can squeeze a different color each of four briquets, all the colors on the fifth briquet and no color on the sixth briquet. Pour the liquid mixture evenly over the six briquets and place the pie tin in a warm place in the classroom. Mix another batch of the liquid solution each day and pour it over the briquets to "feed" the crystal garden and make the crystals grow. Squeeze additional food coloring onto the crystals every two days to keep color strong.

If you can purchase bluing cheaply in the grocery store, you might want to have each child or pairs of children grow gardens, but if you are buying your bluing at a science supply store the costs can add up. In this case, have the children work in cooperative learning groups to create and feed their gardens. Groups of six are workable for this project.

As each day passes, have the children keep a journal record of the changes and development of crystals in the garden. They should try to observe the changes (or lack thereof) carefully and record them in detail as a scientist would with any experiment he or she undertook. If crystals grow at different rates, have children speculate as to why this is and what differences might exist between the gardens or between briquets within gardens.

• Sparkling Salt Crystals

For children to make salt crystal gardens of their own, they each need one 10 ounce clear plastic cup, a popsicle stick, a 9-inch string, paper clip, water and salt. Mix 1/2 cup water with 1/2 cup salt in the plastic cup. Tie one end of the string to the middle of the popsicle stick and the other end to the paper clip. The paper clip is submerged in the salt mixture and the popsicle stick is laid across the lip of the cup so the string is straight.

Salt crystals will begin to form on the string and "grow" up the string. Have salt and sugar crystals available for children to observe with a magnifying glass and microscope.

Food Activities

The food activities described here are designed to give children additional opportunities to exercise their scientific thinking skills since the development of such thinking skills is the focus of this chapter. As such, the food activities touch on scientific areas as varied as crystal structure and the color spectrum.

Food activities can help explore chemical and physical changes. Bring this out as part of the class discussion as you do these cooking activities. A chemical change occurs when the two substances or chemicals are mixed together and cannot again be separated or changed back to their original nature. A physical change occurs when two substances or chemicals are mixed together, but will eventually return to their original states such as in the evaporation of water from a salt water mixture.

1. Sugar Crystals, Sugar Syrup

Have children do some crystal investigation by looking at and heating sugar crystals.

Before you begin any cooking activity, have children look at sugar and salt crystals under magnifying glasses and microscopes. Have them explore rock crystals as well as quartz and amethyst or any other available crystal formations such as their own crystal gardens, if you made them.

The crystal food activities focus on heating sugar crystals, changing them to liquid, cooling them, and returning them to a hard state. In the "nut" recipe, it is particularly easy for children to see a physical as opposed to chemical change take place in the sugar. The sugar starts out as white crystals, melts to a clear liquid, and returns to a hard white candy coating as it cools around the nuts.

a. Candied Walnuts (or Pecans)

1 1/2 cup sugar
1/2 cup orange juice (or milk flavored with 1/2 teaspoon mint or cinnamon)
1 teaspoon light corn syrup
1/4 teaspoon salt
2 1/2 cups nuts

Combine all ingredients except nuts in a 2 quart saucepan. Heat over medium heat until the mixture reaches 238 degrees. Measure this with a candy thermometer attached to the side of the pan. This should take about five minutes. Turn off the heat and immediately add nuts. Stir until dry. This will take several minutes of constant stirring with a large wooden spoon. As you stir, the mixture changes from clear to opaque. It then dries onto the nuts.

b. Sugar Lollipops

2 cups granulated sugar
1/2 cup water
2/3 cup corn syrup
2 tablespoons orange, lemon or lime extract or other flavoring of your choice.

Combine all ingredients (except flavoring) in a 2 quart saucepan over low heat, stirring until sugar dissolves. Increase heat to a medium heat and continue cooking, without stirring, until a drop of the mixture hardens in a glass of cold water (hard ball stage). Remove from heat and stir in flavoring. Drop a tablespoon of hot syrup onto a generously greased cookie sheet. Immediately press a sucker stick or popsicle stick into the syrup. Cool. When cool and hard, gently lift lollipops from cookie sheet with a pancake turner.

2. From Primary to Secondary - Colors, That Is

The cookie caper activity described in the preceding section is a food activity through which children can explore how primary colors blend to make secondary colors.

Art Masters—Old and New

Background Information

1. Georges Seurat

Seurat was born in Paris in 1859. When he was 20, he entered the French Academy for Art. He was interested in the Impressionist art movement. He wanted to learn more about the Impressionists' ideas on light and color in painting. He wanted to learn about color so that he could create a set of rules that would allow him to use a more scientific approach to painting. The technique he developed is now called pointillism. He devised this technique after much experimentation, some of it with his artist friend Paul Signac. The technique was to apply small dots or points of primary color (red, yellow, and blue) to a canvas to achieve different shades without losing the brightness of the primary colors.

2. Leonardo Da Vinci

Leonardo was born near Florence, Italy in 1452. When he was fifteen, he worked in the studio of Verrocchio, a famous sculptor and painter of the period. In 1481 he moved to Milan, where his scientific and engineering expertise was put to good use. There he designed canals and fortifications for the city's defense and planned buildings as well as painting famous works such as the Last Supper fresco in a local convent. Later he returned to Florence, where he designed a major bridge, completed the Mona Lisa, and wrote a scientific treatise on water. Leonardo was truly a Renaissance man. He was a gifted artist, a talented scientist, and a creative inventor. During his life, he produced many sketches of his inventions, scientific designs, and anatomically accurate drawings of the human body as well as his more famous painted works.

Project Directions

1. Pointillist Painting

Using tempera or acrylic paints in the three primary colors, have children paint a picture using only dots. The basic outlines of the picture should be placed on the blank sheet with light pencil.

Then the child uses a thin brush or cotton swab to place colored dots on the picture. If a brush is used, remind the child not to stroke with the brush or push down hard. The tip of the brush is dipped in paint and dabbed lightly on the blank sheet to put the color on the picture.

2. Leonardo Inventor Sketch

Using charcoal or soft, thick-lead pencils, have children recreate a picture in the style of Leonardo's sketches. Visit your local library before you begin this project to locate examples of Leonardo's sketches to show your class.

Thousands of Da Vinci sketches are on view in museums around the world. He sketched many subjects for many reasons. Some sketches examined the mathematical proportions of human and animal anatomy. Others laid the groundwork for architectural designs and proposals. Still others were studies of a single subject from a variety of perspectives or in a variety of positions. Subjects might be animals such as cats, or parts of the human anatomy such as hands or heads. These studies show the keen observational skills of Da Vinci, the scientist and artist.

Have students do a Da Vinci-like study of an object that has moveable parts so that the child can sketch it in several different positions on a single sheet of paper. Children can bring items from home to serve as their models. Such studies help the artist-scientist understand how the model is put together and how it works.

A sketch study of some part of the human anatomy is also interesting for children. Practically speaking, however, the only "model" that each child would have available and that could be stationary while sketched is the foot. If you choose, each child can do a sketch study of his or her own foot from two views, if possible. To learn from this exercise, children need to look closely and seriously at the model and sketch exactly what they see so that the final sketches reveal the proportion, bone structure, etc., of the foot sketched.

Sharing Activities

1. Junior Science Fair

Invite other classes to participate with your class in a science fair. Experiments, models, displays, and posters on scientific issues can be encouraged. Have children organize the displays by discipline such as Earth sciences (rocks, volcanoes), chemistry, life sciences, and physical sciences. Class projects and individual projects should be encouraged and accepted.

Make every effort to have students utilize scientific method in their experiments. Their displays or posters should reflect how they used scientific method. The activity sheet in this chapter might be a good way for students to show science fair visitors and judges how they used scientific method in the experiment process.

You can have the class decide whether there should be prizes for the most innovative or challenging scientific experiment or investigation. Awards or prizes can simply be certificates of achievement or can be ribbons or trophies. Perhaps a committee of community representatives or the principal and a teacher or two could serve as judges.

2. Science is Important Because . . .

Hold a school-wide bookmark competition in which students design bookmarks that explain or show why science is important in our everyday lives. A 2" x 8 1/2" strip of paper is a basic book mark size and can be easily reproduced for children.

You might want to have some of the best bookmarks printed up on lightweight cardstock and given to the local library or the school library to use to encourage reading of science-related books. If you decide to do this, tell children that their bookmark designs must be in black ink or black felt marker.

3. Experiments to Go

If the children have performed individual science experiments, have them practice demonstrating their experiments in front of the class or a small group of peers. Then send these students on a traveling tour of some of the other classrooms. Have students tour in groups of three. Each student's presentation is likely to take only about five to seven minutes. Accordingly, a three-student presentation will be well under 30 minutes.

The benefits of a program like this are many. First, the presenters gain experience and poise from their presentation activities and necessary preparation. They learn in detail the particulars of their experiments. Also, other students benefit from seeing experiments performed and from seeing peers or older students excited about science. Lastly, such a program can have a positive affect on science activities undertaken by other teachers. Unfortunately, even today with the myriad of books available on easy science experiments, too few teachers have their students engage in interactive science experiments and activities in the classroom. Your students' traveling show could well serve as a reminder of easy, inexpensive science experiments teachers might have forgotten about.

4. Scientists Among Us

Have your children plan a careers-in-science assembly for the school or a group of classes. To do this, they will put to real-world use a wide variety of classroom skills. They will need to think of potential speakers. They will need to write letters to ask the speakers to come. They might make follow up telephone calls.

There are many scientists in many communities, and we forget about all the jobs that have this component. Here are some ideas to get you started on your speaker list:

- Water filtration plant lab technicians and analysts
- Biology, botany, chemistry, physical and Earth science university or college professors, graduate student teaching assistants
- Utility and defense company engineers
- Engineering firm professionals
- Health care lab technicians and pathologists

Name: _____

The Bubbles Are Coming
Bubble Observations

For the Post-Bubble Station Observations, list things you learned about or observed during your bubble station activities. Try to list at least six observations.

**Bubble Blow-out
Observations**

1. _____

_____

2. _____

_____

3. _____

_____

4. _____

_____

5. _____

_____

6. _____

_____

7. _____

_____

8. _____

_____

9. _____

_____

10. _____

_____

**Post-Bubble Station
Observations**

1. _____

_____

2. _____

_____

3. _____

_____

4. _____

_____

5. _____

_____

6. _____

_____

7. _____

_____

8. _____

_____

9. _____

_____

10. _____

_____

Name: _____

The Bubbles Are Coming
Are All Bubbles Round?

1. Can you blow a bubble in the air with your hands? Describe its shape, size and appearance.

_____

_____

2. Can you blow a bubble on the table? Describe its shape, size, and appearance.

_____

_____

3. Is there a difference in what happens to a bubble when it lands on a wet surface rather than a dry surface? What difference did you observe if any?

_____

_____

4. Can you put a straw through the surface of your table bubble? Does it make a difference if the straw is wet or dry? Describe the difference.

_____

_____

5. Can you make a table bubble move by blowing at it with or without a straw? Describe any difference in movement that you observe.

_____

_____

6. Blow several bubbles on the table so that their sides touch. How does this change the shape of the bubble?

_____

_____

Name: _____

The Bubbles Are Coming
Electro-Bubbles

You can make static electricity yourself. Everything is made up of tiny particles called atoms. Inside these tiny atoms are tinier particles called electrons, neutrons and protons. Static electricity is created by the electrons in an atom. If an atom gains or loses electrons, it becomes electrically charged.

1. Make some electricity. You can create static electricity by rubbing a plastic comb quickly back and forth over a piece of wool. Put the charged comb next to a friend's hair. Describe what happens.

_____

_____

2. Will a comb charged with static electricity attract or repel airborne bubbles? "Attract" means the bubbles will move toward the charged comb. "Repel" means the bubbles will move away from the charged comb.

   My hypothesis: _____

_____

   What I did: _____

_____

   What happened: _____

_____

   Conclusion: _____

_____

Try your static electricity experiment at least twice to verify the accuracy of your results.

3. Why do you think the bubbles reacted the way they did? _____

_____

_____

_____

Name: _____

The Bubbles Are Coming
Bubble Inventor

1. What are the characteristics of a bubble blower? Try to think of general characteristics.

_____

_____

_____

2. Make your own bubble blower. What materials did you use to make your bubble blower?

_____

_____

_____

3. What shape is your bubble blower? What shape bubbles does it make? What size bubbles does it make?

_____

_____

_____

4. What works well about your bubble blower? _____

_____

_____

_____

5. What could be improved about your bubble blower? _____

_____

_____

_____

_____

Name: _____

Measure Your Bubbles

Bubble 1

1. Height of your bubble   _____

2. Diameter of your bubble   _____

3. Radius of your bubble   _____

4. Circumference of your bubble   _____

Bubble 2

1. Height of your bubble   _____

2. Diameter of your bubble   _____

3. Radius of your bubble   _____

4. Circumference of your bubble   _____

Bubble 3

1. Height of your bubble   _____

2. Diameter of your bubble   _____

3. Radius of your bubble   _____

4. Circumference of your bubble   _____

Name: _____

The Bubbles Are Coming
Foam Up the Suds

1. Describe the shape of a single airborne bubble. _____

_____

_____

2. Describe the shape of a single bubble sitting on a table. _____

_____

_____

3. How does the wall of a bubble change when another bubble attaches to it?

_____

_____

Make some foam.

4. How are foam bubbles different from most airborne bubbles?

a. _____

b. _____

c. _____

d. _____

e. _____

f. _____

5. Draw a picture of connected bubbles. Are the connecting walls round or flat?

Where have you seen these shapes in nature? _____

Name: _____

The Bubbles Are Coming
Bubbles by Candlelight

1. What happens when a bubble floats near the candleflame? Why?

_____

_____

_____

2. Is there any difference between the way big bubbles and small bubbles respond to the flame?

_____

_____

What happens when small bubbles near the flame? _____

_____

_____

_____

What happens when a big bubble nears the flame? _____

_____

_____

_____

3. If you hold a bubble on a blower and bring the bubble near the candle flame, what happens? Why?

_____

_____

_____

Name: _____

The Bubbles Are Coming
Bubble Windows

1. What happens when you blow on a bubble window? Does it make a difference if you blow hard or soft? Describe the difference.

_____

_____

_____

_____

_____

2. What happens if you wave your bubble window in the air? Can you make an air-borne bubble with it? How big a bubble can you make?

_____

_____

_____

_____

_____

3. Can you pass an object such as a straw through your bubble window? Does it make a difference whether the object is wet or dry? Describe the difference.

_____

_____

_____

_____

_____

Name: _____

C-Substance Investigation (pg. 1)
C-Substance Analysis Notes

Let's find out when C-Substance acts like a liquid and when it acts like a solid.

1. What happens to C-Substance when you drag your finger slowly through it?

_____

_____

_____

_____

What happens if you move your finger more quickly?

_____

_____

_____

_____

Describe the ways in which C-Substance acts like a liquid and the ways in which it acts like a solid.

Liquid	Solid
_____	_____
_____	_____
_____	_____
_____	_____
_____	_____
_____	_____
_____	_____

Name: _____

C-Substance Investigation (p. 2)
C-Substance Analysis Notes

2. What happens when you strike C-Substance slowly with your fist?

_____

_____

_____

_____

What happens when you strike C-Substance quickly with your fist?

_____

_____

_____

_____

Describe the ways in which C-Substance acts like a liquid and the ways in which it acts like a solid.

<u>Liquid</u>	<u>Solid</u>
_____	_____
_____	_____
_____	_____
_____	_____
_____	_____
_____	_____
_____	_____
_____	_____

Name: _____

CHAPTER 9
ACTIVITY SHEET

C-Substance Investigation (p. 3)
C-Substance Analysis Notes

3. What happens when you let a small piece of C-Substance drop from between your fingers? Describe the ways in which it acts like a liquid and the ways in which it acts like a solid.

<u>Liquid</u>   <u>Solid</u>

_____   _____

_____   _____

_____   _____

4. Make a ball out of C-Substance. Describe how it looks and what happens to it.

_____

_____

5. Drop a teaspoonful of C-Substance into water. Does it float or sink?

_____

_____

Does it change appearance? _____

_____

_____

What happens when you stir the water? _____

_____

_____

6. Describe some of your own investigations with C-Substance and the results on the reverse side of this paper.

_____

_____

Name: _____

Plastic Putty Polymer

1. What happens when you try to stretch the putty slowly into a rope horizontally?

Does it stretch? _____

How thin does the putty get? _____

How long a rope can you make? _____

Does the rope break? Where does the rope break? _____

_____

2. What happens when you stretch the putty slowly into a rope vertically?

Does it stretch? _____

How thin does the putty get? _____

How long a rope can you make? _____

Does the rope break? Where does the rope break? _____

_____

3. What happens when you pull the putty with a quick jerk?

Does it stretch? How far? _____

Does it break? _____

If so, how does it look when it breaks? _____

How is this different from the way it looks when you stretch it slowly?

_____

4. Can you blow a bubble with the putty using a straw? _____

_____

_____

**CHAPTER 9
ACTIVITY SHEET**

Penny Cleaner Research Scientist (p. 1)
What will make it shine?

You are a scientist in the research department of a small company. You and a team of colleagues have been asked by the company president to find a new copper cleaner to market to consumers. The president wants the new cleaner to be so safe even a child can use it.

You will test several different substances. Record your test results below.

1. Substance _____

Did the substance remove tarnish after soaking

10 minutes? _____

20 minutes? _____

60 minutes? _____

With rubbing, was tarnish removed? _____

_____

Substance 2 _____

Did the substance remove tarnish after soaking

10 minutes? _____

20 minutes? _____

60 minutes? _____

With rubbing, was tarnish removed? _____

_____

**CHAPTER 9
ACTIVITY SHEET**

Penny Cleaner Research Scientist (pg. 2)
What will make it shine?

Substance 3 _____

Did the substance remove tarnish after soaking

10 minutes? _____

20 minutes? _____

60 minutes? _____

With rubbing, was tarnish removed? _____

_____

_____

[Testing of additional substances can be listed on the reverse side of this sheet.]

2. Which substance(s) worked best? _____

_____

What ingredients are in these substances? _____

_____

3. If more than one substance worked, what ingredient(s) did the substances share?

_____

_____

_____

_____

_____

_____

Name: _____

My Science Experiment

Please write information in complete sentences.

1. Description of Experiment. Describe what the experiment is about and the scientific subject or area investigated by the experiment.

_____

_____

2. Hypothesis. Before you conduct your experiment, explain what you think the experiment will show or prove.

_____

_____

3. Directions for the Experiment. Describe the materials needed to conduct the experiment and the steps you take to do the experiment.

_____

_____

_____

_____

_____

4. Experiment Results. What happened in the experiment?

_____

_____

5. Analysis of Hypothesis. If right, why was your hypothesis right? If wrong, what did you learn from the experiment that you did not know before?

_____

_____

_____

Name: _____

Science Biography

Please write information in complete sentences.

Name of scientist: _____

Date of birth: _____

Date of death: _____

Interesting childhood facts: _____

_____

_____

_____

Education and training: _____

_____

_____

_____

Scientific jobs and discoveries: _____

_____

_____

_____

How the scientist's work changed the world: _____

_____

_____

_____

Do you think this was a good change or a bad change? Why or why not?

_____

_____

Name: _____

Scientific Method

Title of Experiment _____

1. Describe the experiment. _____

_____

_____

2. Hypothesis _____

_____

_____

_____

3. Materials needed _____

_____

_____

_____

4. Directions for the experiment _____

_____

_____

_____

5. Experiment results (Was my hypothesis right or wrong?) _____

_____

_____

_____

6. What I learned. _____

_____

_____

_____

Name: _____

CHAPTER 9
ACTIVITY SHEET

Scientific Hypothesis and Results

Question 1. _____

_____

Yes   **No**   **What happened?**

_____

_____

_____

_____

Question 2. _____

_____

Yes   **No**   **What happened?**

_____

_____

_____

_____

Question 3. _____

_____

Yes   **No**   **What happened?**

_____

_____

_____

_____

Resources

1. Some general resource books that provide useful information and timelines on scientists and scientific developments are:

The Timetable of History by Bernard Grun published by Simon & Schuster, Inc. (1982 Touchstone Edition). This book is laid out as a yearly timeline of developments through world history with a section for each year that covers scientific, technological, and other developments for the given year.

Asimov's Biographical Encyclopedia of Science & Technology by Isaac Asimov published by Doubleday & Company, Inc. (1982). This book provides short biographies of over 1500 scientists of history. Biographies are presented alphabetically.

Best Books for Children by John T. Gillespie and Corinne J. Naden published by R. R.. Bowker. This book provides reading ideas for children by subject and can provide suggestions for classroom, book report, or extracurricular reading for students on scientific figures from history. It suggests books appropriate for children up to sixth grade.

2. There are a number of series of books on science experiments for children that are useful classroom resources or good books to which to refer children for finding experiments to do. Some of these are:

a. Vicki Cobb has authored many good science experiment books. The set on edible science experiments may be of particular interest.

Science Experiments You Can Eat by Vicki Cobb published by Lippincott (1972).

More Science Experiments You Can Eat by Vicki Cobb published by Lippincott (1979).

b. Janice VanCleave has written a variety of books on science topics. An excellent series that is under expansion is the *Science for Every Kid* series. Some of these titles are:

Earth Science for Every Kid by Janice VanCleave published by John Wiley & Sons, Inc.

Biology for Every Kid by Janice VanCleave published by John Wiley & Sons, Inc.

Chemistry for Every Kid by Janice VanCleave published by John Wiley & Sons, Inc.

Astronomy for Every Kid by Janice VanCleave published by John Wiley & Sons, Inc.

Physics for Every Kid by Janice VanCleave published by John Wiley & Sons, Inc.

c. Rose Wyler's Science Fun series provides interesting and easy to do projects for elementary school children. Some titles from this series are:

Science Fun with a Homemade Chemistry Set by Rose Wyler published by Julian Messner (1987).

Science Fun with Mud and Dirt by Rose Wyler published by Julian Messner (1986).

Science Fun with Peanuts and Popcorn by Rose Wyler published by Julian Messner (1986).

Science Fun with Drums, Bells, and Whistles by Rose Wyler published by Julian Messner (1987).

d. Don Herbert of Mr. Wizard television fame has written for children as well. A recommended title is:

Mr. Wizard's Supermarket Science by Don Herbert published by Random House (1980).

3. A book from the Magic School Bus series by Joanna Cole may be an interesting literature selection to enhance children's scientific awareness and to reinforce the "coolness" of science as a subject to be investigated. Some titles from this series are:

The Magic School Bus at the Waterworks by Joanna Cole published by Scholastic, Inc. (1988).

The Magic School Bus Inside the Human Body by Joanna Cole published by Scholastic, Inc. (1989).

The Magic School Bus Inside the Earth by Joanna Cole published by Scholastic, Inc. (1988).

4. Student reading of biographies on scientific figures from history is appropriate to reinforce the scientific issues raised by this chapter's activities. Some suggestions are:
The Many Lives of Benjamin Franklin by Aliki published by Prentice Hall (1988).

A Weed is a Flower: The Life of George Washington Carver by Aliki published by Prentice Hall (1988).

Rachel Louise Carson by Philip Sterling published by T. Y. Crowell (1970).

Great Lives: Invention and Technology by Milton Lomask published by Charles Scribner's Sons (1991).

5. A book that combines kitchen activities with scientific learning in an interesting and fun way is *Cooking Wizardry for Kids* by Margaret Kenda and Phyllis S. Williams published by Barron's Educational Services, Inc. (1990). This book could be a useful reference for a variety of classroom activities.

6. An interesting resource on Leonardo Da Vinci is Ernest Raboff's *Leonardo Da Vinci* published by HarperTrophy (1978).

Chapter 2

How Many—Estimate, Guess-timate
Red is the mode.

Fraction Fun
1. 2; 4; 2.
2. 4; 2; 6.
3. 8; 1/4; 4/8.
4. 3; 2; 3/6
5. 6; 4; 3.
6. 12; 8; 9.

Counting Musical Notes
1. Whole; four
2. half; two
3. quarter; one
4. eighth; one-half

Chinese Tangram Puzzle
1. Triangle, parallelogram, square
2. Use the three smallest triangles as follows:

3. Use these pieces to make the tall house:

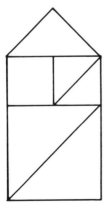

4. Use these pieces to make two different 5-piece rectangles:

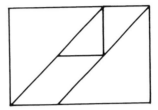

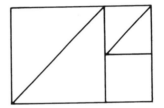

Chinese Tangram Puzzle

1. Nesting Bird

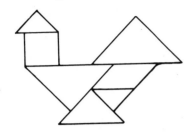

2. Anteater

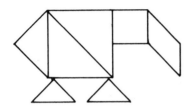

3. Tent

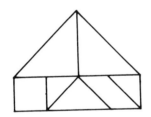

4. a flying squirrel

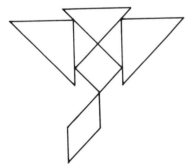

5. Fish

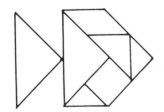

6. Submarine

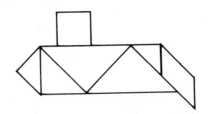

7. Ship

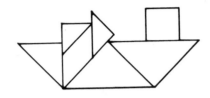

Chapter 5

Name that System

1. Respiratory
2. Circulatory
3. Skeletal
4. Digestive
5. Skeletal
6. Digestive
7. Nervous
8. Endocrine
9. Muscle
10. Endocrine

Chapter 6

Exploring Rights and Rules in Real Life Situations

Story One:

    Maria got into the car to go to school. As soon as she was settled in, *she buckled her seat belt.* Her school was across town. Her mother drove a little way and *stopped at a stop sign.* There was a small car accident to the side of the road. A policeman who was helping the people in the accident waved Maria's car and others to pass on by. Maria's mother drove down the street and *passed through a green light.* The school was just down the next street. Her mother *turned on her signal to show she was turning.* She stopped the car in front *of the zone painted green* and let Maria out.

    The school bus pull up behind Maria's car. Maria waved to the bus driver as she got out of her car. Maria was excited about school that day because the local librarian was coming to visit. She was also going to have her ears tested by the school nurse. Maria liked school, but her family was planning on moving soon to a new state. Her father had taken a new job and that meant Maria would start a new school when the family moved.

    The laws in the story are traffic laws.
    What rights are exercised in this story? (Right to travel; right to own property [car]; freedom of press [i.e. librarian brings books to read]).

Story Two:

    Jose got into the car with his father. They were going to the market to pick up some groceries. Jose and his father *buckled their seat belts.* They drove to the end of the street and *stopped at the stop sign.* His father *turned on his signal* to show he was turning right. As they drove down the busy street, they heard a siren. Jose's father *pulled his car over* to the curb and they watched a fire truck rush past on its way to a fire. The paramedic truck followed close behind.

    When the street was clear, Jose's father began to drive again. He *slowed to a stop to let a pedestrian pass through a crosswalk.* They reached the market a few moments later. As they shopped, they discovered that the peanut butter had been moved. The store manager helped them find the peanut butter. Then they took their groceries and *the checker rung up their purchases* and put them in bags.

    The laws in the story are traffic laws and laws against theft (e.g. store purchase).
    What right is explored in this story? (Right to own private property)
    The community helpers referred to are: Story One) policemen, bus driver, librarian, school nurse; and Story Two) firemen, paramedics, store manager, checker.